My
Heavenly
Year In

Jerusalem

ירושלים

Cheryl Zehr

Olive Press
צהר זית
Messianic & Christian Publisher
Rochester, NY 14609
Port Leyden, NY 13433

My Heavenly Year in Jerusalem

Published by
Olive Press צהר זית
Messianic and Christian Publisher
P.O. Box 567
Port Leyden, NY 13433
www.olivepresspublisher.org

We at Olive Press pray that we may help make the Word of Adonai fully known, ... and spread rapidly and be glorified everywhere. May our books help open people's eyes so they will turn from darkness to Light and from the power of the adversary to God and ... trust in ישוע Yeshua (Jesus).
(From II Thess. 3:1, Col. 1:25, Acts 26:18,15 NRSV and CJB, the Complete Jewish Bible)
    May this book in particular inspire people to intercede for Israel.

Dedicated to Annie

Who, at age one, had to sacrifice a year without Grandma, while this book was happening

The walk on the Wall around the Old City

Contents

Door to the courtyard of the Church of the Holy Sepulchre

Introduction

I have always loved Israel. My father, who was also my pastor, taught me to have a special love for the Jewish people because the Bible says they are God's chosen people. In 1967, I remember my father being very excited that Biblical prophecies were being fulfilled in Israel. He enthusiastically told us children about all the miracles God was doing to protect Israel against its enemies—as when enemy tanks were stopped by someone in the road who looked like Moses.

So in the fall of 2005 when my husband, Glenn, said, "Let's go to Israel for Christmas!" I exclaimed, "Yes, let's!"

It was a wonderful trip. Taking two of our grown daughters with us, we rented a car and visited all the normal Biblical spots: Joppa, Caesarea, the Galilee, etc. We loved it except we were a little disappointed that so many of the places—even the feeding of the five thousand hill, had big churches built on top of them. (We later learned to be thankful that those churches have reserved those sights for us.)

The Sea of Galilea

We ate in restaurants a few times, but spent many meals in our hotel rooms eating scrumptious falafel's or dipping circle bread in delicious Israeli hummus, all of which we bought from street vendors or tiny local shops.

At the Tel Aviv University, we watched a history film at the Museum of the Diaspora, which showed how much the Jewish people suffered in every European country, over the centuries, after being banished from Jerusalem by the Romans in 70 AD. The persecution in each country would eventually become so great that they would be forced to move on to a different country. The worst places for them were first in Spain and later in Russia until the Holocaust which is by far the worst suffering the Jews have ever experienced in history. The film was very educational. I wish I could have taken notes.

We picked up a hitch-hiker on the way from Galilee to Jerusalem. She was a very cute, Israeli 18-year-old. We wondered why a young girl would even think of going hitch-hiking. (We had seen several doing so at other places around Tiberias.) She said they hitch-hike because the bus fares are very expensive. Apparently it is a safe thing to do here, which seemed unbelievable to us.

She told us, with her heavily accented English, that everyone here has to serve in the military as soon as they graduate from high school—boys for three years, girls two. She somehow got an extension and has a few months before she has to enter. She was going to Jerusalem to meet with relatives.

She also told us about the Ultra Orthodox Jewish families where the fathers spend all their time studying the Torah and the mothers are left to do all the work. I didn't know whether to believe her or to take it as from an ill-informed, naïve, young teenager's mind.

Our Tour Guide
from my journal notes

In Jerusalem, we hired an inexpensive Arab Christian tour guide who drove us to the Dead Sea, Bethlehem, Bethel, and also the Holocaust museum and walked us to the Wailing Wall, which were each overwhelmingly wonderful experiences. He also took us through Harod's palace where he gave us an extensive review of Israeli history.

His parents were born in France, so he knows four languages: Arabic, French, Hebrew, and English. He was raised as an Armenian Christian, but was only a nominal in his faith. Then at Bethlehem Bible University, he met Christians whose faith had great meaning in their lives. At a special meeting he accepted Christ and his life changed dramatically.

He got married a couple years ago after he finished building a new house north of Jerusalem. Now a wall is being planned and his house is currently on the Palestinian side. He has to go through a lot of check points to get to his work in the hotel. He has a three-month-old son. After his son was born, he decided he must move because they want to be able to get to the clinic quickly. So his house is empty right now. He can't sell it until the wall decision is settled. If his neighborhood does end up on the Palestinian side then a Muslim family might just take it over without paying him or asking him. He won't be able to sell it or go there to keep an eye on it or anything. He will just have to trust God.

We told him stories of how God blessed us and told him we will pray for him.

He also needs prayer that he can get a license to be a guide in the Palestinian area. Then he will be one of a very few who has both an Israeli and a Palestinian guide license. However, this will be very difficult to get, especially since he is a Christian. Getting his Israeli one was also hard for the same reason, and because of the economy. He finished school in 2000, but at that time tourism had died down due to terrorist uprisings and violence. Just this year he took a refresher course and finally could take the exam and get his license.

Here is what we learned from him.

About Jerusalem

Before the 19th century no one lived outside the city walls because it wasn't safe. People were afraid to be outside the walls after dark. But then Yemen Moshe, a Dutch man, built some shops or something outside the wall. At first people would go outside during the day only, and would come back at night. Gradually that changed. Now most of the city is outside, and the place just outside the city wall where that man first started building is the most coveted and most expensive neighborhood in Jerusalem.

The history of Jerusalem starts 5000 years ago. It has been conquered and destroyed eighteen times, our guide said.

David conquered Jerusalem from the Jebusites. It was hard to conquer because it is on a hill with deep valleys around it, which is why Joshua was unable to conquer it. David chose this spot for the capital city for that reason and because it didn't belong to any tribe. It was between the Benjamin and Judah tribal lands.

About the Gilo neighborhood

On the way to Bethlehem we could see the Jewish neighborhood in southern Jerusalem called Gilo. It's the biggest neighborhood in Jerusalem. It is on the top and side of a hill. Across the valley from it is the small Christian neighborhood of Bethlehem called Bejala. (Christians make up less than 2% of the Israeli population.) A few years ago, Palestinian Muslim terrorists forced their way into these Arab Christian homes and began shooting at the Jews in Gilo. The Jewish military shot back and then came full force into Bethlehem to quell the uprising. These poor Arab Christians suffered from both armies.

In Bethlehem, we ran into a little difficult traffic after going a very long way around Bethlehem to avoid the check point at the new wall. In talking about the new walls being put up to bring peace, our guide gave us this Jewish saying: If a lady is named Ha Zuee (Luck) she may not have luck. If another is name Ha Yafa (the beautiful) she may not be beautiful. ☺

About the Byzantines and Christmas

Constantine (the Byzantine ruler around 300 AD) was pagan and at first tried to squelch Christianity, but then he became a Christian himself. His mother, Queen Helena, after they conquered Israel, came to find important Christian sites. She interviewed local people to find out exactly where things happened. She built the Church of the Nativity, The Sepulcher, and the church in Nazareth.

To placate their pagan citizens, the Byzantines chose December 25 as the Christmas holiday since December 24 was the holiday of the Sun, and Jesus brought light into the world. However, our guide says Jesus was most likely born in the spring when shepherds are out with their flocks.

About the Dead Sea

Ezekiel 47:9-10 says the Dead Sea will become alive again. Today Jordan is talking to Israel, making plans to bring water through a canal from the Mediterranean Sea to the Dead Sea and then on to the Red Sea. Thus the Dead Sea water will become more useful!!

About Rebuilding the Temple

Plans are being made for the Third Temple at the Third Temple Institute. They have all kind of things ready. (We went there and saw special Temple vessels and priestly clothing, etc.) Our guide told us that the Jews had found a red heifer they could use for the special sacrifice and the cleansing ashes needed for the new Temple, but then they found a white hair on her tail, so she can't be used. Now she is at a kibbutz near Jerusalem.

Our guide believes that the Third Temple WILL be built. He says that when they make their first sacrifice expecting God to send fire from heaven as He did for Solomon, they will find that God will not respond to them. They will be doing everything exactly as God commanded so they will ask Him why He's not listening to them. Then He will open their blind eyes to realize that Jesus is their Messiah!!

[He told us that the really strict sect of Jews (that our hitch hiker told us about) is called Hassadim].

The Dome of the Rock is on actual rock, but the platform on which the other mosque is built is on pillars, not on rock. If there was an earthquake, it would crumble. This happened once in the Muslim era in the 1500's. Our guide said many Jews believe that might be what will happen to put the Temple Mount back into Jewish hands.

About King Harod

According to our guide, Harod the Great came from a group of people who had been forced by Israel to become Jewish, so they weren't really Jewish in heart or blood. The Romans chose him to rule the Jews because of this Jewish connection. Harod was very intelligent in politics, warfare, and in architecture and building. He knew the Jews disliked him. To placate them, he rebuilt them an elaborate Temple. They were pleased, but hated the huge Roman tower he built over and above the Temple in order to have political control over all activities in the Temple. This felt like oppression to them. They didn't like being watched while they prayed and worshipped!

Harod lived a life of paranoia. He was always paranoid that there would be a Jewish insurrection against him. He even feared opposition by his own family, and thus killed some of his own sons. He even killed the wife he loved the most. Afterwards he missed her so much that he had her body preserved in a jar. Yuck!!

This paranoia is what caused him to fear a baby born to be king and why he subsequently killed all the boys 2 years old and under in Bethlehem. Our guide took us to a place most tourists don't get to see. He asked for a key from one of the caretakers, took us down a narrow street around behind the Church of the Nativity into a gate and door both of which he unlocked with the key. Then we went down some stairs and slopes into a dark, cave-like area where he shined a flashlight onto piles of tiny bones that they say are the bones of the babies Harod killed. There were a few larger bones among them. They think these are bones of mothers who tried to use their bodies to protect their babies. It was a heart-wrenching sight.

About Gethsemane

Our guide showed us an olive press in Bethany. He told us that the Garden of Gethsemane, being in a huge olive grove on the Mount of Olives, would have had an olive press. He said that the olive trees there are most likely from the same roots that were there in Jesus' day. He told us that the olives in that day went through two pressing processes. First the olives are crushed, then baskets of them are put under very heavy weights for a couple days to press out the oil. This produces clean oil that is used for food, for fragrances, and for anointing oils. Then the olives are placed in a huge round wooden vat and pounded to a pulp with a massive wooden pestle to get out every remaining drop of oil. This produces a cruder oil that is used for lighting lamps. Our guide pointed out that in the Garden of Gethsemane Jesus was being crushed and pressed to the point of sweating drops of blood. Soon afterwards he received the further excruciating pounding in order to become the Light of the world.

This touched me very much.

Later we visited Gethsemane on our own. As I stood, gazing through the fence at the ancient, gnarled trees, I thought about the crushing and pounding Jesus went through, and I couldn't stop the tears from flowing. I was so overwhelmed with a sense of worship that I couldn't tear myself away to follow the others into the adjacent ancient church building.

The Via Dolorosa

The last few days we spent just exploring Old City Jerusalem on our own, mostly getting lost, but finding some interesting shops in the Jewish section, and eventually figuring out where to go to walk the Via Dolorosa in the Muslim and Christian sections.

I was so disappointed that the Via Dolorosa route took us down shop-lined streets packed with eager shoppers and noisy, aggressive shopkeepers trying to persuade people to buy from them. I couldn't get into a reverent, worshipful mode at all. Then we

Singing "Lest I Forget Gethsemane"

came upon a group of Asian Christians singing the hymn, "Lest I forget Gethsemane" in Chinese while walking along this path of Jesus. I was extremely touched and blessed. I sang that song the rest of the way. Whenever we got stuck in a standstill pedestrian traffic jam, I closed my eyes in reverence and continued singing. Several times I heard a store hawker's voice badgering me, getting louder the closer they got. "Excuse me, Ma'am. I'm talking to you, Ma'am." When they got so close that I could feel their forceful breath hitting my hair, they would suddenly get quiet, finally noticing I was a worshipper, not a shopper. Thus, I was able, in the midst of the chaos, to keep my thoughts focused on our Savior's sacrificial suffering.

✳   ✳   ✳

We came back from Israel with a strong desire to return to Jerusalem for long term service and began praying for the opportunity. We joined a small group that met bi-weekly for the sole purpose of praying for Israel. Then God led us to a Messianic Jewish synagogue. ("Messianic" means Jewish Christians who continue to live as Jews.)

In the fall of 2006, God miraculously opened a door for us. Glenn had grown a beard for our trip to Israel which he had never shaved off. People teased him about looking Jewish. So, when his Bible college dean saw him at the beginning of the semester, he said, "Hello, Rabbi!" Then he added, "We just heard that they need an English Teacher in Israel."

I don't think the dean knew we were looking for such an opportunity, or that I was qualified for such a position, but Glenn came running home to tell me. We checked it out and on October 1st, I came home at 3 am from my hospital nursing job to find this note on the door, "Pack your bags. You're going to Israel!" They needed someone right away. Glenn didn't want us to lose this amazing opportunity, so he sent me on ahead even though he couldn't come until after he finished his classes.

Moving to JERUSALEM!

Oct 5, 2006

Dear Friends and Relatives,

Glenn and I visited Israel last Christmas, and God grabbed our hearts. Since then we have been attending a Messianic synagogue on Saturday mornings and a Judaism class taught by our beloved Rabbi Jim on Tuesday evenings. In April we went to New York City to a seminar on reaching Jewish people for Jesus and practiced what we learned on the streets of Brooklyn. In July we were at the 2006 Messianic Conference in Pennsylvania. Jewish believers from all over the world gathered there. It was such a blessing. We also just started taking Hebrew lessons.

Our plan was to serve God in Israel next spring after Glenn graduates. But God opened an earlier door—a teaching position starting this fall semester (Oct. 22 for them).

My plane leaves Oct. 20 at noon. I will be teaching English to graduate students—pastors and ministry workers from all over the world—at a Christian graduate university. Many of them are Chinese-speaking people. This just shows how awesome God is. He is bringing my heart for Israel and for China together in one place!

I will also be teaching some English lessons to the general public at the YMCA in Jerusalem. So I will be meeting Arabs, Palestinians, and Jews from all walks of life.

In exchange for forty hours a week, they will provide all my room and board. This is such an answer to our prayers. The only support I will need is for extra things (toiletries, bus tickets, etc.) and for plane tickets home for renewing my visa every three months.

Glenn will be moving out of our apartment and staying with friends, commuting to Bible college, and doing some work with his brother. He will join me in December. We pray God will work it out for Glenn to finish his school in Israel.

Thank you for all your prayers for us that helped make this happen. Please keep on praying. I will keep you updated on how God answers your prayers via e-mail.

✳   ✳   ✳

[This book is the compilation of those newsy e-mails and of some of my Israel journal entries.]

I wrote another e-mail to my friends before I left for Israel:

A Messianic event

Oct 5, 2005

I wanted to tell you about an exciting Jewish event I was privileged to be a part of. (Glenn couldn't go because he had class.) On September 20 (before I knew for sure that I was going to Israel) I went on a bus with a large group of Christians to join a rally in support of Israel in New York City. We started out at 3 am!

It was a historic event because it was the very first time Christians stood together publicly along side Jews in support of Israel. It was a rally specifically in protest of the president of Iran speaking at the UN and of everything he says against Israel. The event was organized by the top Jewish organizations in NYC and they invited Christian groups to join them. That is a first!

All of us Christians held up big blue and white signs declaring our support in the huge plaza outside the UN. I'd say it is as big as three football fields, and it was packed full of people squeezed shoulder to shoulder! It was amazing! They kept telling us to move in closer so more people could join us, when we already seemed squished as tight as we could be! Yet somehow we moved in tighter. They are saying now that there were 50 thousand people there! And our blue and white signs peppered the whole crowd. The Jewish people were amazed and pleased, especially when they heard how far we had come. (Some Christians came all the way from Chicago!)

There were many news cameras there while the famous people were speaking. John Bolton spoke (US ambassador to the UN), Pataki, the Governor of NY State spoke, a lady from the Israeli Knesset (their senate) spoke, a mother of one of the kidnapped soldiers and a brother of another spoke, along with many top leaders of Jewish organizations. John Hagee's wife also spoke. This was a very significant and very huge event, yet you saw it nowhere in any news, did you?!

Well, I was there, and I tell you it really did happen. However, sad to say, I didn't take my camera because I was afraid I would drop it or lose it in the crowd. Oh how I regret it now! (Others in our group did take photos.)

[They held another rally in 2008 when the Iranian leader spoke at the UN the second time!]

A street in the Old City

1.

FINDING MY
WAY AROUND

Safely in Jerusalem

Sat, Oct 21, 2006 at 6:34 PM

Thank you for all your prayers. I arrived here safely. On the first plane I sat next to a Chinese businessman who spoke almost no English so I got to use my limited Chinese. I found out he lives 5 miles south of Shanghai. He has a 16-year-old daughter who knows English pretty well. He invited me to come to his hometown to teach English and talk with his daughter. (That was after I told him I am a Christian.) I found it very funny that on my way to Israel I got to practice Chinese! Life with Jesus is very interesting and humorous.

[Later note: I lived in an Israeli cement apartment that was shared with other staff. It had a classroom and a university office in it. I had my own cute little private bedroom with a red curtain and red bedspread. A little night stand and a wardrobe were the only pieces of furniture. Later they added a small desk and bookshelf.]

There is a small olive grove behind our building where a shepherd sometimes brings his sheep and goats. (One day they watched three baby goats being born.) Behind that grove there is the highway to Bethlehem. They said there used to be tons of foot traffic of Palestinians coming from Bethlehem every morning for the purpose of going to work or to the doctor, etc. They came through a tunnel under the highway to avoid the checkpoint. But now since the wall is being built the tunnel is closed off. Most of those people were coming illegally, and now they can't come at all. Now they have no work and cannot get good health care. Many of those workers, especially construction workers are being replaced by Chinese being brought in from China.

A lot of history is happening here. They tell me things are changing all the time. I will keep you informed on everything I find out about, if you are interested.

Blessings,
Cheryl

Journal Oct. 22 7:30 am
    I got here in Jerusalem at
8:30 am their time yesterday. I woke
up this morning at 4:30am their time.
The Islamic prayer chants started soon
afterward—coming in my window from
Bethlehem. I began to pray that they will
be silenced, that prayers to Jesus will be
heard instead.
    I spent a lot of time with the
Lord. I read about the beast who will
blaspheme against God (Rev. 13:5) speaking noisily and arrogantly (Dan. 7:11). It
makes me think of the president of Iran.
He was on the news at the airports over
and over.

Sun, Oct 22, 2006 at 8:13 AM
Hey Glenn you called at 4 am!! I was lying
in bed awake actually. I heard the phone, but I
couldn't answer it because I didn't even know
where the phone was yet! It's not out in the
main rooms anywhere. Now I know. I found
one upstairs where my bedroom is. So if you
call again, I'm ready, but try to pay attention
to the time so you don't wake everyone up!
We are 6 hours ahead of you.
    I want to tell you dates: The break
between semesters here in Israel is Feb.
4 to 23 or so. We only get two days off
for Christmas because it is not an official
holiday here.
Got to go and do some work.

With all my Love,
Cheryl

To My Husband and Children:
    I thought you all might be interested in this. The chef here is an Australian Jewish
man. He's gray haired, thin with the deep grooves of a long, hard life in his cheeks. He
has that wonderful Australian accent. I already heard him use the word "bloke" in his
casual conversation.
    He was so surprised that my son-in-law went to college in Australia.
    He has had a miraculous conversion. I guess it was a powerful encounter with God.
He says he has to pinch himself sometimes to see if it really happened. He has a deep
burden for the Jewish people here. He is a Jew, but was not raised as a practicing one.
He's taking a break from street ministry in Australia to get his master's degree here. He
says then God has told him to go to China for awhile.
    I've only been here one day and already I've met such interesting people.
See ya, Mates!

YAY!
Mom,
    Wow! An olive grove in the back yard with a goat shepherd
sauntering through! How much better can it get! I will definitely be
praying for you, as I have been so much. We prayed for you at my
Bible study Thursday night, and I told the nurses at my work about you. He is SO
with you! I prayed for who you would sit next to on the airplane ride. So that was partly
my prayer ☺ Did you exchange information with him and you'll really go to his house in
Jerusalem to teach him English? The place you live sounds comfy and nice. Keep me up-
to-date! Especially on all the world news that we might not hear. That's so cool that you

met an Australian, Jewish, Christian man who wants to go to CHINA! Interesting! Will he be a contact in China for you (or me?) also? Find out where he lives! Man, I can't wait to go.

I love you! Keep e-mailing!
In all of Christ's love,
Sabrina

You're on line now??? Can we try this e-mail chat thing??? --me (Sabrina)

Reply: Sorry, I wasn't online long. They had work for me to do today. Sunday is a workday here in Israel.

P.S. Did you know that it feels weird for me to sign my name 'Sabrina' in letters to you. Because it sounds impersonal, like I have to let you know who I am, by title. That's why I sometimes write 'Brina' or Your daughter. I think it is because I am so close to you that I feel like you know me so much better than my name tells about me. anyhoo, I love yooo! :o)
~your little girl,
Sabrina   (that's better)

Muslim Loudspeakers

Oct 22

Hi Brina, My Daughter, Whom I Know so Well, ☺

The Australian lives here. He is our chef! He won't go to China until next year or so. The Chinese guy lives in China five hours south of Shanghai. Yes, he gave me his phone number and everything. I hope I don't lose it before I get to China. Thank you so much for praying. Prayers are so powerful! Yours too, especially!

This morning I woke up at 2:30 am. Soon the Muslim prayers started over the loudspeaker. I could hear them from across the valley in Bethlehem. (Bethlehem is run by the Palestinian Muslims.) Later I was reading the Bible and praying while those Muslim prayer-chants were still in the background. Since I couldn't ignore them, I began to think about them. Then it hit me that these prayers—to a god that is not God—are being sounded loudly all over Israel every morning. The "god" is satan and he has people crying out to him loudly and faithfully all over God's land! And all over many other lands! This is just not right! It is no wonder evil prevails, when prayers to evil gods are always being prayed. Just think what would happen if it was prayers to our Holy God sounding faithfully all over the world over loudspeakers every morning!

In thinking those thoughts, I suddenly decided to begin my own solitary prayer campaign to pray that these wrong loudspeaker prayers be silenced. I began praying so right away. Then suddenly I realized the loudspeakers had stopped! It was 5 am.

I know they probably were going to stop anyway (although I thought they usually start at 5 am, not stop then) but it still meant something to me—as if God was saying to keep on praying and all those wrong prayers WILL be stopped!

I have to go. They need me to do some work for them.

Love,
Your blessed Mom

Editing

Oct 23

I get to begin editing two books by the president here (whom I have yet to meet). One is about the special people God used to communicate His way up until Jesus' day. It shows that God has always had one special person on earth during that time period. It is written for the general public and is to go with an archeological museum display.

I forget the other book, but it is also for the general public. They already have publishers who want these books. I just have to get them ready.

I am so excited. I can't wait to start reading and editing.

The book I Edited in the U.S.

As you know I was working for a small publishing company since January 2006. I learned to edit. The first book for which I was the main editor is now in print. You can see it at this website.

destinyofdiscipleship.com

It is a good book for new and not-so-new young adult Christians. If you buy it you will be supporting the author, Eric Foster, who is a missionary for the new discipleship and church planting department of Campus Crusade for Christ. He works in India and Africa to create follow-up materials with which to disciple people who received Christ through watching The JESUS Film.

When you are reading it, remember it is the very first book I ever edited. When I look at it now I see all kinds of places where I could have done a better job. But I guess in this line of work it is hard to ever feel like you are finished, because everything can always still be improved.

So, buy the book, look it over, then give it to a young adult who could benefit from it. Help the author's work to not be in vain.

Eric's website is

ericandallison.org   (Allison is his wife's name.)

Go there to see his latest projects. Last summer he met with leaders and church planters from all over Africa. He is a nice guy doing a lot for the Lord. I feel extremely privileged to have had a part in getting his book published.

Happy reading,
Cheryl

Brina,

I can't send you pictures because I haven't taken any yet. I haven't been out yet, really. I may go out in a minute or two. This computer is a Mac. So I will have to figure out how to send photos. It is also a very slow computer, thus the double I above. Sometimes it's so terribly slow that I type several words and have to wait for them to show up on the screen.

Class went very well, last night. Praise the LLord. (Ugh! I'be got to quit. It is too frustratingly slwo today.)

lvoe,
Mom

The Gilo Neighborhood

I never e-mailed this or told this to anyone back home because I didn't want them to worry too much.

The university people picked me up from the airport and started telling me about Gilo, where I was going to live. "Gilo?!!" I asked. "Isn't that the neighborhood where they were shooting into from Bethlehem?!!" I was remembering the story our Arab tour guide had told us.

They said yes it was that neighborhood, but they assured me that not many houses were hit, and that there hadn't been much shooting at all since then. To further reassure me, they drove me around the neighborhood to show me the places that were hit the worst and to point out that they were a few blocks away from our apartment.

I felt a little reassured until later when I was looking out the big sliding doors and they were pointing out Bethlehem right across the fields and highway. A couple days later another volunteer, who knew nothing of my earlier questioning, showed me a bullet hole in the window right beside the glass door! It was from those Bethlehem shootings!! Both that window and the glass door have metal blinds on the outside that can be pulled down for a little protection from bullets! Oh my!

The window in my bedroom was very tiny and high above my head, so there wasn't much worry about bullets hitting me in there.

Later, I started noticing that one of the downstairs bedrooms had a very heavy metal door and its window had a heavy metal shutter that completely closed and locked. When I asked about it, I was told this was the "safe room," that every house has at least one. In other words, it is a bomb shelter! Ooh hoo!

Thank the Lord that I had learned years before to trust Him, otherwise I might have been terrified! But I wasn't. I knew He had called me to Israel. He had provided miraculously to get me here. And He would protect me while I was here, no matter what happened. I felt a special, miraculous peace from Jesus in my heart. I even slept well, after I got over jet lag. The Lord is good.

From left to right: my bedroom window, the view out the sliding door, and the window beside it.

Journal Oct. 23 "Beasts" Against Jews, North Korea

✎ I've been awake since 4 am because the prayers on the loudspeakers of Bethlehem have been sounding. I prayed for them to be silenced. They were for awhile from 4:50 am to 5:30 am. Then they started again.

Dan. 7:27 The kingship and dominion and the greatness of the kingdoms under the whole heaven shall be given to the people of the holy ones of the Most High; Their kingdom shall be an everlasting kingdom ... and all dominions shall serve and obey them.

Dan. 12:11-12 From the time that the regular burnt offering is taken away and the abomination that desolates is set up, there shall be one thousand two hundred ninety days. Happy are those who persevere and attain the thousand three hundred thirty five days.

(The Dome of the Rock was built in 691. It's 2006 now. That is 1315 years!)

Dan. 12:6-7 One of them said to the man clothed in linen, who was upstream, "How long shall it be until the end of these wonders?" The man clothed in linen ... raised his right hand and his left hand toward heaven. And I heard him swear by the One who lives forever that it would be for a time, two times, and half a time, and that when the shattering of the power of the holy people comes to an end, all these things would be accomplished.

O Lord Jesus, let the shattering of the power of the holy people come to an end. Let the kingship be given to the holy ones of the Most High. Let Your people attain the 1335 days and be happy and blessed.

O Yeshua, help me to intercede. Give me victory in intercession here in Israel. Guide me by Your Holy Spirit. Help me take the authority You gave over all the power of the enemy (Lk. 10:19). Shorten the time, Yeshua (Matt. 24:22). Bring it to completion. Annihilate all the beasts.

Let me list some "beasts" that have been against Jewish people, and/or blaspheming God
  Greek's abomination (set up the Temple to Zeus, sacrificed a pig)
  Rome: destroyed the Temple. Banished Jewish people from Jerusalem
  Catholicism's Replacement Theology started around 300 AD (terribly against Jews)
  Islam 700 AD set up the Dome of the Rock
  Communism
  Naziism and the Holocaust
  Hollywood (mocks Christians and God many times)
  Socialism, Humanism, Secularism, Liberalism... (mostly anti-God)
  Islamic Terrorism

So many beasts. O Yeshua, help me to understand. Make me wise so I understand it clearly (Dan. 12:10).

❧   ❧

Oh, Derek says his advanced Korean students told him that the capitol of North Korea was once called the "Jerusalem of the East" because of a great outpouring of the Holy Spirit and revival that happened there about one hundred years ago. Now it is the site of extreme persecution and is ruled by a totalitarian dictator.

(The university is having Derek teaching for me for awhile to give me time to read the material and prepare my lessons.)

Journal Oct. 25, 3:30 pm Cave Dream

I'm starting to learn about the Dead Sea Scrolls and the book project.

I walked to where the university office is with my upstairs-mate. I'm making supper tonight and she took me to the corner store, where they speak very little English, to buy onions and celery.

I ate ripe olives picked off olive trees. (See e_mail p. 27)

5:00 pm *(Supper's in the oven)*

Joel 1:1 (CJB version) Hear this, you leaders!

> Listen all who live in the land!
> Has anything like this ever happened in your days or in your ancestors' days?
> Tell your children about it, and have them tell it to theirs,
> and have them tell the next generation.
> Wake up, drunkards and weep! Wail, all you who drink

Joel 2:13 Tear your heart not your garments; and turn to ADONAI, your God.

> For He is merciful and compassionate,
> Slow to anger, rich in grace,
> and willing to change His mind about disaster.
>   / / / / / /
> Who knows? He may turn, change His mind
> And leave a blessing behind Him   .
>   / / /

O yes, what was my dream last night? It was so vivid! We were so close to the ANSWER! *It was about to be revealed!*

We were in a cave. There were several people. The leader or guide was about to tell us the answer through an interpreter—about to unveil something. It was here in Jerusalem underground somewhere, maybe under the Old City.

I went to bed at 11 pm and woke up at 1 am from this dream that seemed sooo real!

I just now had opened my Bible to 1 Sam. 27. I read until I got to 28:6 But when he consulted ADONAI, ADONAI didn't answer him—not by dreams, not by urim and not by prophets. *I thought, 'O that's how God spoke then.' Then suddenly I remembered my dream.*

I was reading in Daniel the other morning. At one point I asked God to reveal the meaning and to reveal where we are in the End Times. And in the dream that was part of what was about to be revealed!!

Now I just earlier opened to Joel 1 (see above) Listen, you who live in the Land (I live in the land now!!!) Has anything like this ever happened...(before)? I really do have a sense that something spectacular is about to happen!

God is willing to change His mind about disaster (Joel 2:13 above) **IF** *we are wail-*

ing and weeping and tearing our hearts (Joel 2:12-13)! So perhaps if we cry and weep and beg enough, God will change His mind about the disasters of that last horrible battle in Jerusalem (Ezekiel 38-39). Perhaps He will shorten the time so He can come much sooner—so He can come now!!

Come, Lord Jesus. Come to the Mount of Olives! (Zech. 14:4 and Acts 1:11-12)

Journal Oct. 27 Prayer House. Lecture on Counseling

Dan. 6: 26-27

For He is the living God,
enduring forever.
His kingdom shall never be destroyed,
and His dominion has no end.
He delivers and rescues,
He works signs and wonders
in heaven and on earth....

Dan. 2:20

Blessed be the Name of God
from age to age,
for wisdom and power are His.
He changes times and seasons,
deposes kings and sets up kings;
He gives wisdom to the wise
and knowledge to those who have understanding.
He reveals deep and hidden thing;
He knows what is in the darkness,   *(He knows what is in the darkness!!)*
and light dwells with Him.

I give thanks and praise, for You ... have now revealed to me what we asked of you. (!!) (Wow!) So, is Jesus saying He has revealed to me what I've asked? I don't feel like I know—know. But I do know that God "rescues and delivers"!!

I got to go to the 24/7 Jerusalem House of Prayer last night! It was kind of by accident. I was supposed to meet a friend, visiting from America, there. Her daughter is a prayer volunteer who plays piano and leads worship, but they weren't there. Janet and I sat down and worshipped and prayed awhile anyway! It is in this huge, beautiful room with exquisite hardwood floors. It has big windows facing, I think, the Old City. (It was dark, so I couldn't see what was outside the window.) To get to the outside door of the room from the street, you have to walk down wonderful quaint, winding stone steps. It has had 24/7 prayer for two years now.

❧   ❧

I was listening to the lecture on Biblical Counseling today in the lecture room here at Gilo. It was the first lecture of the semester. Here are a couple interesting notes.

Philosophy was a rebellion to religion.
Science was a rebellion to philosophy.
Psychology is a combination of philosophy and science.
Before that psychology was a cult and was persecuted.

Journal Oct. 27 Wedding Dream About End Times

My dream the night before last was about a wedding. In the dream, I had been in a small group who had been praying regularly for the couple—especially the bride. We were at the reception. (It seems like we were all talking about how miraculous and wonderful it was that they had finally gotten together and were able to have this wedding.) I was telling someone that I was so glad that I had been praying for her because otherwise I would be sitting there feeling guilty right now and would be crying from the guilt. Then I was telling them how much I loved the bride when she came and hugged me. I was so overwhelmed with love for her that as I told her I loved her, I cried.

That was my second very vivid dream here. (I hardly ever have dreams this vivid.)

Then yesterday while I was working, suddenly I knew that the dream was about Jesus and His Bride and their wedding. And I was reminded that I have been praying earnestly about Jesus' Bride and the wedding!

So

Both dreams are declaring that the End Times are very near. The wedding is very, very near!

Oh!! I must tell you. I walked to the church at the kibbutz. It is on a hill. While I was coming home it was raining lightly off and on. Then we saw a rainbow. The tip of it was right on the Old City!! Right smack on it!!! That carried a lot of meaning for me. At one point it was a two-ring rainbow!

It has two meanings to me. 1. That Glenn and I will get to live there. (I just sense that it means that. I hope it really does!) 2. (The most important.) That Jesus is coming soon to the Old City to the Temple Mount!!!!

Acclimating to Israel

Sat, Oct 28, 2006 at 5:23 PM

Hello Family and Friends—all praying for me,

I started teaching ESL levels one and two. And guess what? I came all the way to Israel to teach someone from Mexico!! For a minute I was wondering if I was back in Virginia; or if my class from Virginia came with me to Jerusalem. The last class I taught at the university in the U.S. was full of guys from Mexico, and Central and South America. I fly half way around the world to a Jewish nation and I have a student from Mexico, one from Ecuador, and another from Spain! I thought I'd be hearing my students speak Hebrew and would be learning about the culture here. But instead I'm hearing Spanish!

I think the Lord is soooo funny! He makes me laugh all the time!

Actually, I mostly hear Korean. Most of my students are devout Christians from South Korea. They want to study the Bible in the Holy Land, but they need to learn English first. One of my students wrote in her journal assignment that her main reason for being here is to pray. The registrar told me that many of them pay 500 dollars a month for the privilege of living here, doing volunteer work and praying. They get up at 5:30 am to pray. She also told me, they are mostly from Yonggi Cho's church and that his church has sent missionaries all over the world. She met a South Korean family in Austria once whose two teenage daughters' first language was German.

Oh, got to go catch a bus for a Messianic evening service.
So much to tell you.
Keep praying,

Shabboth Meal, Honor Killings, and Hands of Mercy

Sat, Oct 28, 2006 at 12:18 midnight

Dear Glenn

I don't get much time on the computer anymore. Now that school has started, I'm not allowed to use this computer during the day. Sometimes I borrow my upstairs-mate's laptop, but I don't feel good infringing on her too much.

My upstairs-mate (the girl who has the other bedroom upstairs with me) is another volunteer. She is a very sweet, cheerful, friendly, talkative girl. She loves the Lord. She is quite conservative in her dress and in her Christian beliefs. She is very intelligent and brave. She has been here in Israel off and on for a couple years already. She and I get along great! She has been taking classes here at the University. She comes from a large family.

Tonight I was invited to two Shabbat dinners! One here with the president's family and staff; the other in the home of a darling, cute, older couple. I chose the latter. The older couple and all the guests are Americans now serving in Israel (except for a visiting mom). So that was nice.

Then Janet (The only volunteer who has a car!) who drove me there, stopped at another apartment where several men were having a Shabbat meal. They, too, are all Americans now serving in Israel. One of them runs an organization, Hands of Mercy, whose sole purpose is to visit terrorist victims and wounded soldiers to give them comfort and compassion. While I was there Janet was passing around an article from the newspaper about a 25-year-old girl who was found almost dead in a pool of her own blood, the victim of an honor killing. (An honor killing is when a Muslim kills a family member who has brought shame on the family. You've heard of these killings, I'm sure.) The police arrested her brother who admitted he tried to kill her. He was only sorry that she didn't die. She was dating someone that the family didn't approve of. He had attempted to decapitate her but the knife got stuck on her back bone. The cut was on the back of her neck. Bystanders found her and called the ambulance. The amazing thing is that doctors were able to save her life. These "Hands of Mercy" people want to go visit her. She is recovering in the hospital without any family by her side, the paper said

The paper says there have been 4 such honor killings in the last year. The brothers of one girl in her twenties choked her to death. She didn't quite die the first time. She screamed for them to spare her life, but they choked her again. The brothers acted out the whole killing for the police. The report says the honor killers readily confess to the crime because they are proud of it. The American men sharing the Shabbat meal said this all shows that the fanatic Islam religion is growing here in Israel. I think it's just so horribly awful!!!

Remember the musical Jewish family we listened to at the Messianic conference? Well, that family is coming here for three months to play music at hospitals for these kinds of victims and children with cancer. Isn't that awesome for their family to do that? I'm so amazed. I feel like such a midget among all these giant-charactered people here! I would love to be more like them!! To have brought our whole family to the mission field to serve like that. How awesome!!

Anyway, my heart was tugged the whole time the guy was telling me about his organization. He said it takes a special kind of person who can really feel people's pain, and express that feeling back to the person, and can just listen with an ear of compassion. Well! That's the part about nursing that I loooooove!! But I don't know Hebrew.

Well, it is late. I must go to bed.

I love you and miss you so much. I wish we could explore Jerusalem together.

Keep me next to your pillow tonight.
Hugs and kisses,
Cheryl

Journal Oct. 29 City of Truth, Seed of Truth

Sunday morning.

Well, I prayed and asked the Lord to wake me up if He wanted me to go on the Botanical Garden field trip to which the university kindly invited me. And I'm awake—wide awake at 7 am, even though I went to bed near 1 am last night. I had to take a cold shower. Brrrrr!

It's cold and rainy today. I wonder if they will still go on the field trip.

I opened my Strategic Prayer book to the "Nations" section (p. 107) and it looks like those verses are coming true!! The Messianic service last night was Charismatic! The preacher/leader/church planter is a Jewish man from the Philadelphia area who was formerly a hippie and art major, then a bank president, I'm told. Then he became a believer and God told him to come to Israel to start a church. His whole family is here (adult children).

Well, at his church there are people of all nations! I sat in the middle of a row of S. Koreans! I met people from Norway, Kenya, etc. (See e-mail p. 43) People were standing in line to be prayed for by this minister. And his sermon was absolutely POWERFUL!!!

It seems to be fulfilling Zech. 8::23 Ten men from nations of every language shall take hold of a Jew ... saying "Let us go with you, for we have heard that God is with you." And Zech. 8:3 I will return to Zion and dwell in Jerusalem. Then Jerusalem will be called the city of Truth (NIV).

May it be true, Jesus.

It is coming true. Praise the Lord.

(It's too muddy. The field trip is called off so I will continue my devotions.)
Then He will give you rain for the seed
you use to sow your land;
and the food that comes from the ground
will be rich and abundant (Isaiah 30:23 CJB).

O Jesus, Your seed of Truth is being sown here in Jerusalem! There are several churches and Messianic congregations that are preaching and teaching Your Truth! ("Messianic" means Jewish people who have come to believe in Jesus as the Messiah, and continue to celebrate Jewish holidays, etc.) Even a couple colleges and universities are Christian!

O Jesus, let more of Your Truth be sown!

I have so much to tell people

I Have So Much to Tell You

Hello Friends and Prayer Warriors,

I finally have time to finish telling you all that I have been learning.

Columbus a Jew?

To continue on about my Spanish students, I'm learning that many people in South and Central America are actually Jews. Some can trace their roots all the way back to Spain at the time of the Inquisition when the Queen of Spain expelled all Jews from her country. Jews had to leave or convert to Christianity which meant they had to quit doing all Jewish things, like eating a Sabbath meal, lighting Sabbath candles, praying their prayers, celebrating any of their feasts, including Passover, etc. If they refused to convert they were either killed or expelled. Thousands upon thousands fled. Thousands more were executed. This was at the time of Christopher Columbus. The names of the men on his ships are mostly Jewish names. So it is clear that many Jews fled on his ships. I even read an article pointing out many things that show that Columbus himself could have been Jewish. The main proofs are from what he wrote in his journals. Even his wording of things is very Jewish.

So, when I get a chance I want to find out if my students are Jewish. Jews really have been dispersed throughout the world. My lady student from Ecuador is a grandmother whose daughter and grandchildren emigrated from there to Israel. One grandson is going to have cleft palate surgery and she came to help. Her grandchildren only know Hebrew and English so she needs to learn one or the other. She tried Hebrew. Now she is trying English. She looks the picture of an "old world" grandmother.

One of my student's is Ali. He is Israeli, most likely Arab. He smiles a lot, and joins in the English practice with enthusiasm. Another is Edna, also Israeli. She didn't come the second day. Pray for these two that if they don't know the Lord, they will come to know Him.

Don't Eat Fresh Olives

On my first outing on foot, I picked some ripe olives right off the trees and ate a couple. I wanted to see what they taste like. Well... the first one tasted awfully bitter—yuck! The second one was blacker and softer than the first. The juice of it looked purple—made me think of a grape. It tasted a teensy bit like a black olive, but still a terrible bitter after taste. And it left my teeth feeling a weird un-slippery feeling—made me think of chalk scraping on a chalkboard. I have since found that olives have to go through a three step process that takes maybe a month long to get them to the palatable stage. They have to be soaked in salt water first for a week or more. It's kind of like pickling but they assure me that pickling is not what it is.

One guy said he and his daughters were given a bunch of olives with the instructions of how to process them, so they tried. But the procedure took so long, and the olives looked so scrumptious that they kept snitching them. When it was finally time for the olives to be ready, there weren't any left!

It Hardly Feels Like I'm in a Foreign Country

I've come all the way to Jerusalem to be fed by an Australian chef who loves to cook gourmet Italian and French food! (And boy, is it ever delicious, too, with sauces made with butter and cream! I'm asking God to help me not get fat!) I hadn't had any Israeli food at all until I was taken to the grocery store and picked out some hummus for us.

All the signs here in Jerusalem have English under the Hebrew. Almost all the food packages have some English on the back. Every shopkeeper can speak English. I'm living with Americans in a kitchen stocked with American food. I was invited to a Shabboth meal. Exciting! But it was in an American home. They served lasagna and salad. Only the Shabboth bread looked Hebrew.

Archeology Stories

On Shabboth morning (Saturday) I walked to church with my darling upstairs-mate (Charity) and an archeologist's family. (No buses run on Saturdays here because it is the Sabbath.) It was threatening rain which is much needed in Israel. (This is the beginning of the rainy season. They tell me it hasn't rained since April.) I had my rain poncho along. There was also a chilly wind, so I wore my winter coat and scarf. We walked twenty minutes on the sidewalk along the highway between Bethlehem and Jerusalem. Then we climbed a steep hill another fifteen minutes on a dirt path (past excavation sites of all kinds of ancient ruins) to a kibbutz on top of the hill. The church rents space from the kibbutz. By the time we got there, I was a little sweaty and my hair was a mess. I didn't feel very church-ready. ☺

I sang "Lord I lift Your Name on High" in Hebrew with them. The sermon was spoken in English first, then translated in Hebrew. Finally I feel more like I am in Israel

I walked home from church with the archeologist and his wife. (His girls hurried on ahead. with Charity.) He is from America. He lived all over America as a child. His father's job moved them around. For a couple years he lived in Indianapolis. He was delighted because he loved the Indy 500. He was 10. He would read about the famous race car drivers in the magazines and then go meet them. He would sneak into the pit to look at the race cars up close and talk to the drivers. Interesting.

He came to Israel many years ago. He's been working for the Israeli government as a head archeologist. So, on our leisure walk home I had the awesome privilege of getting an extensive archeology education, FOR FREE! It was fascinating! I not only learned about archeology digs and discoveries, but I learned about the behind-the-scene Israeli politics of it! This is far beyond anything I ever imagined!!!! We walked past a huge pile of broken pottery pieces. He said it is a mixture of pieces from all periods of history going back to the Stone Age. They were all dug up by his team this past summer, and then by university teams that took over this fall. (That happened after the universities sued the government team and the government lost! Imagine that!) He said the teams have gone carefully through all those pottery shards and have already taken the ones they consider valuable. The rest they are discarding. I picked up a few pieces with handle parts on them. Two, he told me, were from Old Testament times, one was from the Stone Age, and one from Jesus' time. Can you believe it? These kinds of things are found in such huge numbers here that they lose their value. I have the pieces on my desk right now.

Last summer he and his daughter were digging at that site. His daughter wanted so badly to find something significant. She came upon something she thought was important. She kept carefully digging around it trying to see what it was. They worked late into the night because the next day they had to give the site over to the university team. Finally, they had to stop because he had to clean it up and straighten up the sides, etc., to get it ready for the next team. The next day the other team finished digging around what she had found. It was a whole jug, all intact—a wonderful find! How sad for her!

I'd love to tell you everything I learned about archeology, but though it is all fascinating it might be boring to you. So I will tell you only a few things.

We walked past some awesome things on the hillside away from the official excavation site, totally unprotected: a wine press with a mosaic tile floor that people are stealing from and vandalizing; and a shepherd's well with indentions in the stone around it where they would have put water for the animals to drink. Some shepherds still use the well today. There was a rope tied to a grate with an attached bucket down in the well in the water. There were olive trees around it. Even a crocus was blooming nearby. (They tell me that crocuses bloom as soon as it gets cold here. They don't wait until late winter like they do in America.)

If those things were found in America they would have fences built around them and you would have to pay buckoos of money to get close enough to see them. These were ancient, ancient ruins—back to Jacob's time even!

James Brother of Jesus Bone Box

Remember when that was in the news? Well, they are still debating the authenticity of the inscribed words, "Brother of Jesus." (Everything else is true about it.) In fact, there is a court case coming up soon with the government's archeology team against the antique dealer.

A Real-Life Israeli "Crying Wolf" Story

There was an antique dealer who was always hoping to find a real treasure that would make him rich. It wasn't happening, so in his desperation, he began to make forgeries and try to sell them for a fortune. He became known all over Israel and Europe for his forgeries. But one day his dream really came true. Among some things he bought cheaply, he found an intact scroll that was from many centuries ago. He was so delighted. Finally his day had arrived. Finally he would be a rich man!

He immediately took it to the government archeology department to sell it. But because of his bad reputation the government wouldn't believe that it was real. They were sure it was just another of his scams. He tried over and over to convince them. They examined it but still didn't believe him. They didn't believe it could be possible at all for a scroll to survive intact for that long, since scrolls are made of bio-degradable material, leather, cloth, etc., as apposed to pottery which is not biodegradable. Finally he gave up and committed suicide.

Decades later when the Dead Sea Scrolls were discovered they realized that his scroll could have actually been authentic! They have searched frantically since for his scroll but haven't found it!

So, there is an intact Dead Sea Scroll still at large! Isn't that intriguing? What a story! And I heard it for free!

(Lord, I pray it will be found and will reveal even more to the world that Your Word is really true! I pray it has something in it about you being here on this earth, Jesus!)

Archeology here is important to reaching the world for Jesus!

May God's Blessings Abound to you,

Churches and Messianic Congregations.
Sun, Oct 29, 2006 at 11:00 PM

Churches and Messianic congregations here need American Christians' prayers. (Again, "Messianic" means Jewish Christians who continue to live as Jews.) There are several alive and growing congregations here in Jerusalem. The one I visited Saturday morning had a discussion at the end of the service about the building they are thinking of purchasing. They are renting now and are "bursting the walls" of the space they have. The auditorium is huge, yet there weren't enough seats for everyone. People had to wait until the children were dismissed and then maybe they could sit down!! Their Sabbath school (Sunday school) was held in the lobby. The nursery was just layers of blankets on the cement floor in the same lobby! Immediately after the service everyone began stacking the sanctuary chairs, while the lobby was turned into a serving place for drinks and deserts. The church has tons of college-age kids and always has tourists visiting. Thus their lobby was packed with people waiting to get the refreshments.

Here are the hoops they have had to jump through to buy property. They have had the money to buy for quite awhile and have attempted to purchase several places here in Jerusalem, but each time the government has denied them—claiming zoning rules, etc. Finally they talked to a government official "unofficially" asking him where they could buy. He told them the government will NEVER let them buy any Israeli land; that they will only allow them to buy land already owned by a Christian organization.

So they spent several months checking with all the monasteries, etc. in the city. They found one lead, but it didn't pan out. Then they found land owned by an Arab outside the city, but he wanted to sell it for $2 million with no building on it. That was too much money. He had an ancient, but nice building from generations ago on another part of the property. They offered to buy that, but his relatives weren't ready to let it go.

So, they were back at square one, looking in the city for Israeli property again. They have now found a building that the city government is finally letting them buy, but will give them only a five-year lease. After five years, the government may take away their rights to it and make them leave! They are bringing this before the congregation, to pray and see if they can believe God to take them through a potential court battle with the government in five years!

The speaker told me afterwards that another church bought under similar circumstances. The property cost $2 million. (I'm talking American dollars here!) The government did take them to court after the short lease was up. The court case cost them $5 million!!! But they won.

So, pray for churches and Messianic congregations here! Pray that God will do a work in the Israeli government and give churches favor with them.

Things to Pray for Glenn and I

Glenn received some bad news from his Bible College. They have changed a couple courses in their curriculum which will not be offered next spring as planned, but in the fall of 2007 and the spring of 2008!. Glenn needs these courses to graduate and was planning to take them next semester.

Last spring the registrar and Glenn went over his courses together and got things all worked out so he could graduate this spring. He took two summer courses and two independent courses to help make that happen. Now it can't be so. She says they cannot allow him to do either of these rescheduled courses independently. Glenn also asked if he could do all of next semester's courses on line or independently so he could stay in Israel. He was refused.

Glenn has gone to the dean about this, but hasn't gotten any different answer.

This is very frustrating to Glenn and I. He has waited ten years to finish his degree. I have felt guilty that I let him quit last time. He was quitting to stay home and take care of me and the family when I had a stroke and they thought I wasn't going to live. If I were a noble woman I would have insisted he get his degree. But I was selfish. I liked having him focused on me. I have since repented to God about this, but it doesn't change the fact that he quit.

So I have been encouraging him in his desire to finally finish—to finally have his dream. And now this.

So please pray. Please stand with us against the enemy trying again to foil Glenn's goal. And pray that God will reveal to Glenn what to do. Glenn desires to serve the Lord, full time!! Just pray for direction. And pray for Glenn to not give up and to not respond incorrectly to the college.

Pray for our finances, so Glenn can buy a ticket to come in December. Also pray that I can always afford to pay for bus tickets to my English classes, to attend Saturday evening services in Jerusalem, and go to the House of Prayer in Jerusalem. (All of these are an hour and a half walk away from where I live.)

Also, please pray for a computer or laptop for me. I need one pretty badly here. If I had one I could have been writing to you every day, and you would have gotten these updates as they were happening and in smaller pieces. And you would get a picture or two now and then. I could use the computer for teaching my classes, too, and for doing the editing work they will soon give me. This computer is used by other people doing other important work here during the day. (I am writing at 10 and 11 pm in the evenings now.)

Thank you so much for your prayers!

I still have more to tell you—important stuff!

Journal Oct. 30 Possessions, Covenants, etc.

Monday

I had to take a cold shower yesterday. Today I had a warm sponge bath instead, using water heated up on the stove.

Possessions

Matt. 19   The disciples were shocked at two things

1. That it is wrong to get divorced. "Then it is better not to marry!" I wonder, if Peter was saying that too? Was he unhappily married?

2. That it is hard for a rich man to be saved. "Who then can be saved?" And it is hard. Look at rich America. It is becoming less and less saved. Why was it hard for the rich man? It was because he was told to sell all his possessions and give to the poor.

We in America have a lot of possessions. We like to hang on to them, too—at least I do. In each stage of my down-sizing in my preparation to become a missionary, I hesitated over each possession—each book, each piece of furniture, especially over the piano and other very sentimental things. It was hard for me to give them up.

The older couple who hosted the Shabboth meal have a teeny, tiny apartment. Their whole great room—kitchen, living room, and dining room—was only the size of most American people's living room. Her kitchen is just a corner of the room. Her stove is out in the open. It had a shield attached to the back of it so things won't splatter onto their bedroom door. Her washing machine was built into the end of her cupboards like a dishwasher. I didn't see any dryer. There was no dishwasher, of course. There wasn't any space for one! Their computer was on a tiny desk in the living room. There was very little space to walk between the furniture. This couple was pretty well off when they were in America. They gave up a lot to come here.

We are not only supposed to give up our possessions and give to the poor. We can't stop there. Jesus told the rich man to then, "Come and follow Me."

So, Jesus, I must follow You. Please help me to follow You every day. It is not enough to give up everything and come here. I must follow You while I'm here. Please guide me. What do you want me to do today? The university hasn't given me any work to do today yet.

The Dead Sea Scrolls and the Essenes

I'm reading, The Complete Dead Sea Scrolls in English by Geza Vermes because I'm going to be working on a book about them. I'm reading only the Introduction which is 92 pages long!

I had my long-time question answered. The Roman's did worship in the destroyed Temple, in other words, they did set up an 'abomination that desolates—for a moment anyway. Here's a quote from Josephus from p. 60.

"The Romans, now that the rebels had fled to the city, and the sanctuary (Temple) itself and all around it were in flames, carried their standards into the Temple court, setting them up opposite the eastern gate, there sacrificed to them."

Here's information from page 61 about the priests of that time. The priest referred to as the "wicked priest" in the Dead Sea Scrolls is Jonathan Maccabeus. He was not entitled to be the High Priest or any priest at all, nor to wear the priestly vestments. The Zadokites were the true priests and High Priests by blood. One of them fled to Egypt and set up Temple worship there.

So, the Essenes (who are the people who lived at Qumran where the Dead Sea Scrolls were found) were governed by the true High Priests. The Essenes considered themselves the final remnant. They were trying to obey the Law of Moses to the letter so that God would let Israel and the rightful priests return to power in the Land.

For some reason Jesus has me here studying all this. I learned from professors here that Zechariah, John the Baptist's father, may have been a member of the Essenes, and John also, and that was why Jesus was baptized by John—because he was from the line of the true Priests, not the priests concurrently in Jerusalem. (I'm told there was a short window of time when the Greek ruler allowed the true priests to return to Jerusalem which was why Zechariah was serving in the Temple when the angel appeared to him.)

The Essenes were most likely tortured by the Romans in 68 AD in order to get them to "blaspheme their Law-giver or to eat forbidden food." The Romans then killed them, wiping them out (p. 66).

Covenants

The heading on page 67 is "Understanding Jewish Theology." Jewish Theology is a series of covenants.

1. God with Noah: God will never again destroy mankind by a flood. Man must not shed human blood or eat animal blood
2. God with Abraham: God will bless Abraham and his offspring, will make them into a nation, and give them the land of Canaan. Abraham and his descendants must circumcise all males.
3. God with Moses: God will make Israel a "kingdom of priests and a holy nation." Israel must obey the whole Torah.
4. God renewed the Mosaic covenant with Joshua
5. New covenant between God and Israel: God will write the covenant (of Moses) on the people's hearts (Jer. 31:33-34).

Gilo Shopping Center and Lookout

I went to the Gilo shopping center. It is really just some teeny shops carved out of the ground floor of several huge stone buildings all on the same side of the highway. They are spread out from each other quite a bit. I was looking for the ATM machine. I followed the directions given me, but after ending up in a couple very wrong places, like a gym-type place, and not being able to communicate with the Hebrew-speaking people to find out where I should go, I began to wonder, but I did find it. Then I headed on farther up the hill and found a wonderful lookout that gives a marvelous view of

Jerusalem. It has the scene sketched on a huge plaque in front of you with the buildings labeled so you know what you are looking at. Far in the background, I could see the Mount of Olives and the Old City. What a wonderful place to pray over Israel!

I went to a wonderful prayer meeting for Israel. (See e-mail on p. 48.)

Journal Oct. 31 Tues. *Flood Dream, Esther and Hezekiah*

I dreamed last night about a flood. It was blue water, crystal clear—like water from a picture or ornaments—like the water with those dolphin figurines—beautiful, fantasy water. We were scared and taken by surprise, but instead of drowning us, the flood carried us (me and the little boy I was raising) to our house and lifted us to the upstairs.

Then our Australian chef read from a Wigglesworth devotional about the Lord Jesus coming like a flood to us—like rivers of living waters!!

O yes, Saturday night at church I met the son of the pastor who is a lawyer educated here in Israel. I told him my daughter is in law school. He told me that Jesus is a lawyer. He's our advocate before the Father. That word 'advocate' is the same Greek work for 'lawyer.'

That really blessed me. No wonder our daughter felt drawn to become a lawyer!

Deut. 31:10-13 Every seventh year, the Law was to be read during Sukkoth!! Every seventh year, ... during the festival of booths, ... Assemble the people—men, women, and children as well as the aliens residing in your towns—so they may hear and learn to fear the Lord your God and to observe diligently all the words of this Law. Next year, 2007 is the seventh year, someone told me!

II Sam. 7:25-29   And now, O Lord, as for the Word that you have spoken ... confirm it forever; do as You promised. ... For You, O Lord of hosts, the God of Israel, have made this revelation to Your servant, ... therefore Your servant has found courage to pray this prayer to You. ... And now, O Lord God, You are God, and Your Words are true, and You have promised this thing.... ...Now ... may it please You to bless ... Your servant ... for You, O Lord God, have spoken....

What an awesome prayer!

At the prayer meeting they read from Esther and pointed out that she was also gaining access to pray about Iran (Persia) to save them from a Persian leader who wanted to destroy Israel. She had to prepare herself for 12 months. Six months of myrrh—a bitter herb that points to the cross. (For us it is six months of repenting and mourning for our sins, being cleansed of our sins and of dying to self.) Then she had six months of spices and perfumes (sweet smelling fragrance!). And finally, she took nothing with her in obedience to the one in charge.

II Kings 19:32 (The Lord answering Hezekiah about King Sennacherib) "Therefore thus says the Lord concerning the King of Assyria: He shall not come into this city, shoot an arrow there, come before it with a shield, or cast up a siege ramp against it. By the way that he came, by the same he shall return; he shall not come into this city, says the Lord. For I will defend this city to save it, for My own sake and for the sake of My servant David."

Prayer

So, Yeshua, please keep this Word of Yours. Please keep this promise of Yours. Please keep on protecting the city of Jerusalem. Please do not let the President of Iran enter this city. Do not let his arrows (missiles) reach this city. Do not let him come near Jerusalem. And do not let the Hizbullah come near or shoot arrows (missiles) here. And do not let Syria come near or aim any missiles here either.

And, Lord, do not let the gay pride people come near here. Do not let them gain access to march or celebrate here. Do not let them defile this city—Your Holy City, according to Your promise to protect it, I pray. Confirm Your promise. Do as You have spoken. Protect Jerusalem. Protect Israel.

II Kings 19:16 Incline Your ear, O Lord, and hear; open Your eyes, O Lord, and see; hear the words of (Ahmadinejad, President of Iran,) which he speaks to mock You the Living God and to mock Your people Israel.

Journal Nov. 1 / Shrivel Up the Enemy in Jesus Name

I opened my Bible to Hosea 6:7 about anger smoldering all night that "blazes like a flaming fire" in the morning. "None of them calls upon Me."

Hosea 6:3 Let us press in to know the Lord;
His appearing is as sure as the dawn.

I'm also reading in Matthew in the Complete Jewish Bible along with its commentary. I'm in chapter 21 today.

Jesus withered a fig tree. (They tell me here that a fig tree in leaf should have ripe fruit because the unripe fruit shows up before the leaves.)

Jesus is telling us we can do the same with faith—wilt fig trees and tell mountains to be cast into the sea. Both are destructive. He didn't tell the fig tree to have fruit. Nor did He tell us to call a mountain into existence.

Rom. 4:17-18 It is God, not Abraham, who gives life to the dead and calls into existence the things that do not exist.

Rom. 4:20 Abraham grew strong in his faith as he gave glory to God, being fully convinced that God was able to do what He had promised.

Matt. 21:21-22 "Truly I tell you, if you have faith and do not doubt, not only will you do what has been done to the fig tree, but even if you say to this mountain, 'Be lifted up and thrown into the sea,' it will be done. Whatever you ask for in prayer with faith, you will receive."

So, is Jesus telling us that by faith we should wither and remove fruitless, mountainous things? (According to Isaiah mountainous things can be prideful things.)

Luke 10:19 See, I have given you authority to tread on snakes and scorpions, and over all the power of the enemy

So, shrivel and remove all enemy things!? So, we can speak to the Muslim prayers and religion to be wilted and to the Iranian President to be removed and to the gay pride organization to be shriveled up to nothing?

So, maybe the only times we can call into existence things that are not is when God has spoken thus! Then we can believe, as Abraham, and pray Gods Words to come to pass.

John 15:1 He (the Father) removes every branch in Me that bears no fruit. Matt. 7:1 Judge not that ye be not judged (KJV) So, we must be VERY careful in all this!

Journal Nov. 3 Jesus' Words Absolute, Final Authority

I'm beginning to not like to hear or read believing Jewish people's comparison of Jesus' Words with Rabbis' sayings from the Talmud and the Mishna, etc., putting them on equal level. Sometimes it seems to take the life right out of the Scriptures for me. (I'm sure they don't mean for that to happen, but for me it does.) They are refer- ring to the very Words of YESHUA/JESUS!! His Words are sacred! They are full of AWE and POWER and LIFE. We should reverence them, not equate them to another rabbi's words, like pointing out that Jesus said almost the same things as another rabbi, so therefore Jesus must be right—as if that other rabbi's words are higher and more authoritative than Yeshua's/Jesus' Words!!! NO WAY!! Jesus' Words are higher than anyone's words on this earth! His are as high as the heavens are above the earth!! His Words are the absolute, final authority on everything!!

Journal Nov. 4 Essenes Preparing the Way

I am learning that the Essenes (the group of people who wrote the Dead Sea Scrolls) were trying to fulfill Isaiah's command to "prepare the way for the Lord in the wilderness." And they did! They formed their society just a few hundred years before Jesus came and were still in existence at the time of Jesus and until 68 AD. And one of the things they taught was how to recognize the Messiah when He comes. This prepared the way for people of that day to recognize Jesus as the Messiah.

My ideas: perhaps Jesus was near them when He went into the wilderness to be tempted! The Spirit drove Him there! Perhaps He fed the 4000 near there. (There was no grass, so it was in the wilderness, according to Women's Bible Study Fellowship.) Of course, the desert is huge, so I could be wrong. But it is exciting to think about.

The Weather

Sat, Nov 4, 2006 at 2:54 PM

(To Shawn and Jane who were coming to Israel)

The weather was quite chilly last weekend. I needed my winter coat to be walking outside because the wind made it cold. But then when we started walking up a hill, I warmed up too much and had to take my coat off.

This weekend it is nice and warm. When I stand still, I need long sleeves, but when I'm walking I want only short sleeves. I have been wearing long leggings under my skirts almost every day. This weekend I haven't really needed them.

So the best thing is to wear layers that you can easily put on and remove. And carry a warm jacket, just in case, especially if you are going to be outside for very long. Also bring rain gear. This is the rainy season, after all. It rained last weekend.

Jerusalem is at a higher elevation. So it is colder than the rest of Israel.

One also needs sunglasses, sun screen, and hats to live in Israel. The sun shines very bright here. Sometimes even when it is raining, the sun is still shining brightly!

All the religious women here wear skirts, and there are a lot of religious women in Jerusalem—maybe half or more of the population. (They also wear sleeves that cover their elbows.) But the rest of the women dress the same as in America, except they cover more of themselves it seems. I've only seen young teen girls revealing their bellies. And I haven't even seen many doing that. They look odd in the conservative, well-covered crowd.

Of course, I know you weren't planning on showing your belly. : 0 ahaha.

May God direct your packing!
Heavenly Blessings,
Cheryl

To Sabrina

Thu, Nov 2, 2006 at 11:01 PM

Wow, Brina, that is soooooo awesome about you and the Holy Spirit telling Emily where all to read in the Bible. How wonderful!! Praise the Lord!!!

I just got back from class a half-hour ago. I ate supper and now I'm writing to you. It's late and I'm kind of tired. But I do want to tell you about my students and all the things you asked. I love it when people are interested enough in my life to ask me lots of questions. So thank you!!

I will tell you this, because it is so neat. My student from Mexico is studying to be a Fransiscan priest!!! I'm flabbergasted and in awe!! I feel so honored to have him as a student. He is really, really nice. He looks like the typical Mexican guy. But he doesn't flirt with you like most of them do. Now I know why!! ...

Several people have come up to me on the street or at the bus stop to ask me questions. They just start rattling off in Hebrew. I must look like I belong here or something. I hope I'll be able to start studying Hebrew soon.

Anyway, I'd better get to bed. Everyone gets up pretty early around here.

I love you until Israeli's stop speaking Hebrew,
Mom

Israel Happenings

Sat, Nov 04, 2006 at 5:56 PM

Dear Praying Friends Who Want to Know,

Here are some things that have been happening:

We had a week with no hot water. "Again!" the others tell me. So I guess it happens often.

I rode the bus by myself to teach English and actually got off at the correct stop! But I cheated. I asked the lady beside me. She spoke no English, but she finally figured out that I meant the Great Synagogue. When she said it in Hebrew, I remembered that is how they say it, "Knesset Hadag." I have to walk from there to the YMCA.

Olive Picking

I watched an Arab family pick olives in the grove behind out house. I asked if I could take pictures. At first the stern father said no. So I put my camera down. Later the scarf covered mother sitting on the tarp on the ground collecting the olives that her daughter was scraping off the branches said, "Take picture. It's okay." The little daughter started posing like a model. The father said, "No, pictures!" The grandfather up at the top of the tree on the ladder leaning against the branches kept silent and did not look at me. I just stood behind the fence and kept smiling and watching them with interest. The little boy peeked from behind a tree. Finally the father said, "You want take pictures? It's okay. Take how many you like. Go ahead." So, I took pictures.

I walked to church again today. It took an hour. It is warm today, so I only needed a sweater which I took off as soon as I started uphill.

Advice for Walking in Israel

1. Don't jay walk. You can get a ticket for that, I've been told.

2. Remember there are two lights for cross walks. One for each half of the street. If you look at only the farthest one, you WILL get hit—no maybe about it. And it is best to wait until both walk signs are green before you walk. Otherwise you end up on the tiny raised area in the center of the street with big trucks and buses passing precariously close on both sides of you! You can get behind the light post, but that only protects you from one direction of the traffic!

3. As a woman, if you wear long skirts, long sleeves, and your hair up, like I've been doing, people seem to think you're a Jewish woman. They come up to you while you're sitting at the bus stop or even while you're walking and start chattering away in Hebrew!

About My Students

The kind man from Mexico is here studying to be a Fransiscan priest! And Thursday

I had a new student. She is a nun from Poland, dressed in the old-fashioned full garb! I was so surprised. I thought I'd be teaching Orthodox Jews, but again God is being humorous with me. He's throwing me a curve. Life with Jesus is never dull!

One student is Arab. He has been coming late ever since the first class. I think he wants to avoid the prayer. I open class with prayer, because I need help teaching. I could never do any of this without the constant help of Jesus. The praying Koreans join wholeheartedly with their amens at the end. I could get in trouble with my boss for praying. What do you think? Should I stop praying openly so as not to offend my student and to stay out of trouble?

All the students seem to be enjoying the class. They smile a lot and often we laugh together. They all join in trying to use this new language. I frequently divide them up in pairs to practice speaking and they all participate well. The other day I divided the level one class into two teams and they had to write on the board in competition. They really got into that. It was fun to watch them.

I really love teaching. I spend hours preparing though, because I want to pack every minute with helpful activities. I want their time in my class to be productive.

Oh, I must tell you about a prayer group I've joined. They pray earnestly about current events here. I love it. Most of them are Scandinavian!! We prayed about the Iran situation. Also we prayed that the gay pride parade won't happen here in Jerusalem. It is scheduled for two weeks from now. The one last summer planned for Tel Aviv got cancelled by the war. We are praying this one will also get cancelled in some spectacular way so the people will know it is God! The Orthodox Jews are vehemently against it. I'm not sure what they will do, but they are saying they will do something to stop it.

I've got to go to the evening church meeting!

Next time I have to describe the interesting Scandinavian home where we met for prayer.

Keep praying!
Blessings

Re: Israel Happenings Sun, Nov 5, 2006 at 6:01 PM

Dear Ellen,

Thank you again for writing to me. It cheers me up.

At the church I went to Saturday night. The preacher was visiting from the U.S. and he prayed for the elections in America. That was a reminder to me from God not to forget to pray for my own country.

As to your mention of using Scripture, etc. in my teaching, I am keeping that in mind. I used Scripture when I taught in America. I want to do that here, too, soon.

My boss is very much a Christian, but if I try to evangelize while teaching, it could cause us to lose the opportunity to teach at the Y. I think my boss is hoping that the friendships that develop between the Christian students and the community students will grow into evangelistic opportunities. I'm hoping and praying for that, too, of course.

So, pray that I do the right thing.

A Must-Hear Sermon
(And a must-review sermon for me!)

Sun, Nov 5 at 10:08 PM

Hi Spiritually Tall, Praying Friends,

I heard this most awesome sermon last night that I feel compelled to re-tell to you. It was preached by a Jewish pastor who grew up in America and became a hippie in the 70's. When someone told him about Jesus, he says he thought it was the most foolish thing he'd ever heard, and "besides," he told the person, "Jesus is only for the Gentiles, not the Jews."

Well, later he came across the verse, I Cor. 1:22 that says the Gospel is a stumbling block to the Jews and foolishness to the Greeks. He saw the truth it proclaimed, that to him being a Jew, Jesus was a stumbling block, and being just enough of a "Greek," the message was also foolishness. That got him!

So he became a Christian and later a banker. Then God told him to sell everything and move his family to Israel to start a congregation. So that is what he did 20 years ago. He made "aliyah" which means he immigrated to Israel and became an Israeli citizen. (Aliyah is a privilege extended only to Jews.) All his now grown children (4 or 5 of them) and their spouses serve with him in the congregation. His home church in America has supported him from the beginning. His congregation is growing. The overflow section they opened for the first time last night is already overflowing!!

He's a thin, dark, shaved-bald, good-looking, smiling man with round wire glasses. He has a strong voice, and a friendly, humorous yet commanding personality. When he starts preaching you know he is going to get you clearly to the point.

He started out telling about coming home last week from a trip to America and finding what he thought was a huge, curled up, dead spider in a corner of his suitcase, that turned out to be a very much alive poisonous yellow scorpion! He tried to kill it but it got away and scurried under the dresser. He ran out to get a broom, which was a mistake because when he got back he couldn't find the scorpion!! He said there was no way he was going to be able to sleep with a poisonous scorpion loose in their bedroom!

He said he felt that God was using this scorpion and the current political situation here in Israel to teach him a spiritual lesson. For example: Israel gave land over to its enemy and then last summer had thousands of Hizbullah missiles pointed at them, being launched to destroy them. And now they are being shot with rockets from Gaza. He said there is a lesson here about not giving place to the enemy or bringing the enemy into your house, as he did the scorpion.

By the way, he did get the poisonous critter and says it doesn't look like a scorpion anymore.

The Sermon

Here's the sermon, abbreviated. [The words inside the brackets are mine.]

Eph. 4:26-27 *Do not let the sun go down on your anger. Do not give place to the devil.*

This verse reveals two points:

1) That going to bed with the wrong attitude only one night opens the door to the enemy!! —which shows that the devil and his demons are in a HURRY!

2) That God gives us the authority to decide whether the devil can come into our lives or not.

We're going to talk about two things, tonight. First we're going to talk about what the devil and his demons are like. Then we are going to talk about us.

The devil and his demons are displaced and desperate. Isaiah 14:13-14 *You said in your heart, "I will ... ascend to the tops of the clouds, and I will make myself like the Most High."*

That was a mistake to say that!

Jesus said He saw him fall like lightning. CRASH! The devil FELL! Revelations 12:12 says the devil knows his time is short. (That's why he is in a hurry.) I Peter 5:8 says he walks about like a roaring lion. He is only LIKE a lion. There is only one True, spiritual roaring Lion!!

Matt. 12:43 (the demon) *wanders through dry places seeking rest and finds none.*

The devil and his demons are unclean, thirsty, tired, and homeless! They wander in dry, dirty, dusty—awful, disgusting—places, and find no rest. They are not at peace. They can't relax. They are in chaos. They are agitated.

Luke 8:31-32 (About the legion of demons in one man.) Demons hate wandering around. They'd rather go into filthy pigs. They begged Jesus not to be sent back to the abyss—the filthy place.

But demons are so powerless that a thousand of them could not keep that man from falling in worship at the feet of Jesus!! (Luke 8:28) [Makes you think, doesn't it?]

The presence of Jesus tormented demons. Jesus is in us, so wherever we go demons should also feel tormented.

Even pigs had enough sense that they each said, "If these disgusting demons are going to live inside of me, I might as well jump in a lake." [That made me laugh.]

That's the devil and demons. Now, let's talk about us.

Jesus has ALL power for ALL time for ALL eternity. Job says this in Job 42:2. But it took Job 42 chapters to learn it. [I laughed again.] Genesis 1:28 God gave man dominion over every living thing that moves upon the earth. "Dominion" means: to tread down, prevail over, rule, and reign over. The devil is a living thing, and he and his demons are moving on the earth. So God gave man authority over the devil, too!!!

But Adam and Eve gave "place to the devil." Eph 4:26 *Do not give place to the devil.* God's authority never changed. But man lost his authority.

Satan had to ask permission from God to touch Job. In Job 1:9-10 we see that God had made a hedge around Job, his household, land, and all he had on every side.

Man had no defense against the enemy—no authority or dominion anymore. When God took the hedge away, there was nothing Job could do. [This really shed light for me!! A new lesson from Job!!]

But then God came to earth as a man and stripped the devil of his authority over man. John 12:31 *Now the ruler of this world is cast out.* Hebrews 2:14 tells us that through death He destroyed the power over death—the devil.

Jesus took the keys to death and hell. So the devil doesn't even have the keys to his own house!!!

Matt. 28:18 *All authority in heaven and earth is given to me.* God already had all authority, but here Jesus was speaking as a man. Luke 10:19 *See, I have given you authority to tread on snakes and scorpions* (Remember, scorpions is how we got started on this.) and over all the power of the enemy.

You have authority!! DON'T GIVE PLACE TO the devil!!! Here are ways we give place. I'm giving this is as a warning. Paul warned the Ephesians in tears for three years. So I don't feel bad about giving a warning.

1. Believing a lie

The devil had no authority over Eve unless he could get her to believe a lie. "You're gonna be like God." Did him a lot of good [trying to be like God]! He can't get it out of his system!

2. Believing a bad report

You can sometimes get these bad reports from doctors or psychologists who display on their walls their degrees in bad reports. Numbers 13:31-33. If you open your life to a bad report, fear comes in. The Israelites were in fear.

3. Negligence or laziness

In Matt. 12:43-45, God comes in our hearts, kicks out the devil, cleans us up, and puts the Holy Spirit in us. Then the devil goes wandering in circles and comes back to see if we will let him back in again. Jesus fought the devil with the Word. We are responsible to learn the Word of God.

4. Violating our conscious

Romans 14:23 *Whatever is not from faith is sin.* If you feel like something is not approved by God—DON'T DO IT! IT'S SIN!! The Holy Spirit is convicting some of you right now.

5. Unconfessed sin.

It says IF we confess our sins. [He said a lot more here. It was very convicting.] But know this: Rev. 12:10 says the devil accuses the brethren day and night. The devil never stops accusing you! You can read the Bible 23 hours and 59 minutes and the devil will say it's not enough. Don't believe his accusations.

6. Unbelief

Resist the devil. Stand against him and oppose him. Fight the good fight of FAITH. Put on the whole armor. Take up the shield of faith which will quench ALL the fiery darts of the enemy.

There's not one dart that can get through the shield of faith.

You might say you are non violent and you want to just live in peace. But if you don't fight you're gonna lose the battle. You might be angry with me for saying that. But you would be better off getting angry at the devil!

7. Being angry

Don't let the anger last. Remember, the demons are desperate and in a hurry. It takes only one night! Don't give place to the devil!

"Deliver me from evil." There should be no evil in your life—only suffering for Jesus.

John 14:30 *"The ruler of this world is coming and he has nothing in me."* Wow. He had nothing in Jesus. NOTHING.

Let's get to that place to where the devil has nothing in us, too.

That's the sermon.

I wish I could have written this right after I heard it. I've forgotten some of the stuff that I didn't get into my notes. But it was 11 pm by the time we got back and I was just too tired. I hope I remembered enough of it to bless you. I was blessed writing it up for you. It's still pretty powerful! I can't wait to hear him preach again.

I would send you to their website, but they don't have one! They are working on it. I can hardly believe that such a big congregation with such talented musicians, lively worship, and eloquent preachers doesn't have a website yet. But it's true. As soon as they get it I will give it to you so you can be inspired to pray for them.

A week ago they prayed for one of their members who was witnessing to a heroin addict. Last night they gave the praise report that the addict was set free and has accepted the Messiah.

One of their members is a former Orthodox Jew who still wears his zit-zit (tassels). He is on fire for God.

These congregations here are a gathering place for the nations. You meet people from all over the world. Last week I sat in the middle of a row of South Koreans. (As I said in the 10/29 Journal p. 26.) In front of me there was an older guy who looked very Mexican. I met a man and wife and darling baby girl from Norway. They had a friend from Kenya whom the husband met while both men were witnessing on the streets of Jerusalem. Both of them come several times a year to do that. Last night I met a girl from Holland and a retired lady from Canada. And I sat beside a native Israeli. They all come to hear the truth from a Jewish man. Scripture is being fulfilled. Zech. 8:3 in the NIV says Jerusalem *"shall be called the city of Truth."* Many preachers are preaching the Truth here in Jerusalem. The number of congregations and the numbers in the congregations are growing. Praise the Lord!

Well, may God have a special blessing for you for reading through this whole thing!

I feel overwhelmed about the book I'm working on for them here. I need your prayers to be able to accomplish the task. It could have enormous influence in reaching the Jews for Yeshua (Jesus)!

Please pray!
Blessings,
Cheryl

Journal Nov. 5 Deep Meaning of Hebrew Words

It's Shabbath again!

I'm studying Hebrew this morning. The depth of meaning of the words is so profound! (From a book I bought in America: *Hebrew Word Pictures* by Dr. Frank T. Seekins, 2003. It doesn't teach conversation, but it is very interesting.)

Redeem is "gaal" גאל which means "to lift up God." (Jesus said, "And I, if I be lifted up...." He was doing a play on words to show us that He is our Redeemer and He will redeem us by being lifted up on a cross!! Amazing! He was explaining the Hebrew word redeem—giving it its full meaning!) (In Exodus 6:6 "I will redeem with outstretched arm," God told how He would redeem right from the beginning!!)

Fear is "amah" אימה which means "where there is no mother." (!!!) (I know someone who had no mother during some of her formative years and she is afraid of so many things!!)

Peace Shalom שלום "destroy the authority that establishes chaos." (That's what Jesus did!!!)

Repent shoov שוב "destroy the house." —like burning bridges behind you.

Egypt meets ra eem מזרים "trouble" in the midst of "water" —Egypt was the place of water. They worshipped the Nile. (So, perhaps the Nile drying up in Isaiah 19:5 means their religion will dry up!)

Love is "ahav" אהב which has "window" in the middle of "av" which means "father." So, love is seeing the heart (middle) of the Father. (Isn't it awesome?!!)

Hatred is "oyev." איב It has the letter yood (a closed hand) in the middle of father. So, when the hand is closed inside the father—when there is no fathering—there is hatred.

Moody sar סר "the propped man." (!!!) (Isn't that exactly what a moody person is? You have to keep propping them up—keep trying to make them happy!)

Trouble tsar צר "the hooked man." (!)

Unite eeched אחד "to lock the door." No one can run from the problem. They must stay and fix it!

Bitter mar מר "the chaos man" or "full of chaos inside and out"

Rebellion marah מרה "what comes from the bitter"

God El אל "the first strength"

No lo לא (the same two letters but arranged the opposite of "God") "to control strongly"

Yes ken כן "open your hand to life or activity"

Priest Cohen כהן "window" or "behold" in the middle of "yes" "Reveals the heart of yes." (Or to have yes in your heart toward God!!)

Journal Nov. 5 (cont.) Beggar lady

There are two verses the Lord lifted out to me during the sermons yesterday. (I go to two different meetings on Saturdays, one in the morning at the kibbutz and another in the evening in Jerusalem.)

> Heb. 13:5 Keep your lives free from the love of money,
> and be content with what you have; for He has said,
> "I will never leave you or forsake you."
> So we can say with confidence,
> "The Lord is my helper;
> I will not be afraid.
> What can anyone do to me?"

This is God comforting me and declaring that I do not need to worry. I haven't been worrying. I've resisted the temptation by saying, "The Lord will provide," but the temptation has been strong!

The other day on my way to teaching, I saw an older lady begging near a street corner. Many people were walking by, but no one was giving her anything. I don't know if she was a pretender or not. It seems like she could go to the synagogue right in the next block—the Jews are commanded to take care of the widows and fatherless—and there are Catholic charities here in Jerusalem, too. But seeing the shocking view of someone just sitting on the sidewalk in clothes that looked like they hadn't been washed in awhile, the thought hit me that it could be me! We have no home and very little money. (We used up our savings to pay Glenn's Bible college tuition.) I'm only earning my room and board, no extra and Glenn is barely making anything! But I rebuked the thought before it could make me afraid.

After I passed her, I stopped and searched my purse for something to give her, but I had nothing except big American bills. I didn't feel God wanted me to give her those. Those are all I have for buying my monthly bus passes.

(Added on 3/17/07: The next week when I went that way again, I gave her an American twenty dollar bill. I had felt convicted by the Lord for not giving it to her before. She seemed overwhelmed with relief and thanked me profusely. And I haven't seen her begging there since.)

Opportunity to Return

The other verse was Hebrews 11:15 If they had been thinking of the land that they had left behind, they would have had opportunity to return.

Just the day before I was wondering how I can ever do what they are asking of me here—interior book layout in color! So, I was thinking I'd rather just go back to America and live in a woods all alone and do my own thing.

So, I believe God is telling me through this Scripture that if I keep thinking that way I will have an opportunity to return, but the inference in Hebrews 11 is that I would miss out on the awesome miraculous things God has for me.

The sermon last night on the parable of the talents was about Jesus being the "man who has the goods." He has left the goods behind Him with us because they are not needed in the "far country," the place where He is headed.

So, Jesus, I need "the goods." I need you to equip me to do this layout. Please help me. Please instill these professional skills into me in a miraculous way. It has to be by miraculous means because I am NOT trained for this at all!! You are the God of impossibilities! Praise Your Name. You have the goods. You heal, You raise the dead, and redeem, as he preached last night. You also create. So please create through me. PLEASE!

I rebuke pride in me. Help me not to be doing this to impress people. How can I be proud when I am around such intelligent, highly educated, extremely talented people! Who am I? Nothing! But I'm here! Jesus brought me here. So, here am I, Lord. Use me. Do Your work through me.

I wait before You. Inspire me. Pour out Your thoughts to me. Pour Your ideas into my minds eye. Please give me the picture of what the pages should look like. Please. I wait as an open, ready, useful vessel of honor. Purify me until I am a vessel of honor. The importance of this job overwhelms me, Jesus. Help me not to be afraid. (I spent time on my face.)

O Lord, I think of the Hassidim men—both old and young—last night on the Ben Yehuda Street outdoor mall, singing and dancing wildly, their sideburn curls and tzit-tzit flying—all for the wrong Messiah. They need You, Yeshua, their "Salvation."

My heart cries out for Your people, Yeshua. May they soon say, "Blessed is He who comes in the Name of the Lord!" Thank you for the Jews who are already saying that: for the Messianic pastors and leaders; for the young Jewish man (the former orthodox who became a drug dealer!) dancing during worship with his tzit-tzit trailing joyfully!

O Yeshua Adonai, may the Jews all soon accept You as their Cornerstone instead of their stumbling block! O Yeshua HaMashiach (the Messiah), You have spoken! You spoke the Words, "You won't see me until...." O Lord, let Your Word, "until" come to pass! Bring it to pass NOW!!

And create this book. Use it to help that happen, if that is part of Your plan!

Journal Nov. 10

Well, the killing of 20 people in Gaza (which the IDF says was a mechanical error in the aiming equipment) has caused the "gay pride" march to be cancelled. The news of 20 deaths is very, very sad. God be with those families!! Twenty people!!

But praise the Lord about the march being cancelled. However, they are still having a rally at Hebrew University and going down one side street, I guess.

So, God answered our prayers for that, but not for the US congress and senate elections. Why?

I just had a thought. This "gay pride" thing could be another abomination that desolates!! It sure fits the description of something desolating! (But it is in the city, not the Temple, so I guess not.)

I heard a helicopter go overhead this morning which is very unusual here. No planes or anything are ever in the skies here. It was because of the potential danger of the parade. No one wants them here. The Ultra Orthodox Jews have threatened violence. Plus there is a heightened terror threat due to the killings in Gaza.

I looked up the Scriptures about the abomination:

Dan. 9:27 For half of the week he shall make sacrifice and offering cease; and in their place shall be an abomination that desolates, until the decreed end is poured out upon the desolator.

Dan. 11:31 Forces sent by him shall occupy and profane the temple and fortress. They shall abolish the regular burnt offering and set up the abomination that makes desolate.

Matt. 24:15 So when you see the desolating sacrilege standing in the Holy Place, as was spoken of by the prophet Daniel (let the reader understand), then those in Judea must flee to the mountains.

This is so clear to me, (although more knowledgeable people than me disagree). Rome caused sacrifices and offerings to cease when they burnt the Temple and banished Jews from Jerusalem in 70 AD. The 'abomination that desolates' 'in their place' and the 'desolating sacrilege standing in the Holy Place' to me has to be the Dome of the Rock! It is supposedly built right where the Holy Place once stood!

Isaiah 25:6 American Standard Bible (Charity's Dad's old Bible given to her as a gift.) And He will destroy (swallow up) in this mountain the face of the covering that covereth all peoples and the veil that is spread over all nations.

Jesus said, "It is finished" when the veil was torn!
It <u>is</u> finished! Now we have to pray this further fulfillment into existence.

1905-1908 Prayer Team

We volunteers had a long Shabboth meal and evening together. Derek shared about his visions and we prayed. Then Charity showed us the pictures she has from 100 years ago from 1905-1908 of the Holy Land When her ancestors and some people from her Bible College came here to pray. Two of the young men took the daunting, risky and very long journey to pray all around the Bible times border of the Holy Land. This was back when there was no Israel border—when the Turks controlled the Land!!!

(!!!!!) God used a tiny group of people to travel the border to pray for the Holy Land. These faithful people helped pray the Nation of Israel into existence!!

Freedom

I just read the Israel news again. It is Israeli citizens, too, who want to do the gay march, not just outsiders. Some Israelis who say they aren't gay, say they just want to support freedom and people's rights.

So, the devil has taken freedom and defiled it, too.

Freedom used to be a noble thing. Now it is about freedom to do disgusting and shameful things.

Watch Out Here Comes Another Long (Probably), Not Boring (I Hope) E-mail From Cheryl

Sat, Nov 11 2006 at 2:25 PM

Dearest, Most Wonderful Friends and Prayer Supporters,

A big thanks to all of you for being there for me. It means so much to me to have people back home listening to and interested in my excitement. May God's blessings pour upon you abundantly.

And special blessings to my two sisters whom God has laid on your hearts to begin supporting me monthly. I am so awed and delighted. The timing of this with how the devil was tempting me to worry, and what God was saying to help me overcome the temptation is so amazing! God is so marvelously good. He shows His goodness in such a personal way. I'm astounded every time.

Small, Prayer Group

I must tell you about the prayer group I plan to attend as faithfully as the Lord will allow. A wonderful, young Charity took me to the neighborhood outside Jaffa gate (of the Old City). (Yes, Glenn, it is the neighborhood our guide said was the most coveted, and most expensive neighborhood in Jerusalem.) She took me through the parking lot, down several flights of stone steps, along stone walkways to a door, one of many other front doors that open right onto the stone paths—no porches or front yards or anything like that.

We rang a couple times and waited quite awhile. Then a very tall, broad-shouldered, blond-haired guy, who looked the picture of a Scandinavian youth, opened the door and heartily welcomed us in. He and another young guy sent us on to the prayer room. We walked through a dining room full of elaborate, expensive-looking furniture, including glass door cupboards full of ornate china, etc. I could see part of a large living room beyond the dining room. Charity led me down some very narrow steps whose walls were lined with fabulous artifacts—ancient Chinese art, glass display things full of tiny stone carved figurines on the little shelves. A couple of them held collections of the most brightly colored moths and butterflies you've ever seen. I stepped very carefully in the center of the steps so as not to knock any of this off the wall.

Then I found myself in a sitting room that looked like it belonged in a museum! It seemed like there should be a rope keeping me from touching anything. All the furniture looked like ancient antiques! The room was chock full of more ancient artifacts from all over the world—huge wall hangings, more big glass cabinets full of fascinating things, and some fully blooming big orchids and vining plants in the deep set, low window ledge. (The house is on a hillside.) I followed Charity, stepping between the valuable Queen Anne stuffed chairs and the majestic coffee table, and gingerly joined her on the afghan and pillow-ladened, overstuffed such and such period parlor-sofa (I'm trying to sound like a museum curator, but I don't know the proper words. ☺ Hahahaheehee.)

It was there in that dimly lit room where three Scandinavians, us two Americans, and an Israeli immigrant doctor sang soft hymns and choruses along with a young American guy's guitar, and then prayed for Israel, as the Spirit led.

The group is led by an older, Jewish man who travels all over the world, thus the museum-like, international items all through his house. The two young guys live there and take care of it while he is gone. They were redoing the kitchen. (That is why we had to wait for them to answer the door and why they sent us downstairs ahead of them. They apologized over and over for not being ready.) I'm told Mr. Chad is from Italy, but was based in England for many years. I haven't met him yet. He is out on a speaking tour.

The group seems to be run mostly by Scandinavians who met him when he spoke there. One is a very cute, short, little elderly lady with a very long, thick, gray braid hanging over her shoulder and into her lap. Her dress and scarf have the look of 1800's Scandinavia. She smiles sweetly, is quite talkative, and not shy at all. She prayed earnestly for Israel and all the current events, including the gay pride march coming up.

About the Gay Parade

God answered all our prayers. Due to the many terror threats, and heightened terror alert (because of the twenty deaths in Gaza), the gay group decided not to march, but to hold a private, indoor rally at the Hebrew University instead. Only 3000 attended. Some people did try to march in a park. Those people were arrested. Many roads in Jerusalem were blocked by police to prevent suicide car bombs, etc.

So God prevented them again from defiling the Holy City. We are praying here for a revival among them. I don't understand why they have to march in this city. They have all the cities in the world to choose from and to march freely. Why do they have to choose the city that stands for God's Holiness? It has to be the devil within them. Otherwise why would they care if they march here or not? Why should it mean anything to them? The really sad thing is some of the marchers are actually Israeli—Jews.

We are also praying for the whole Gaza situation. May God's light shine into people's hearts there.

Journal Nov. 11 Notes of Interest

I'm learning some interesting things here.

The Essenes believed the Scriptures that say God blesses the Land ("Land" capitalized means the Land of Israel) when the people are faithful. The people hadn't been faithful, so the Essenes left the defiled Land and went to Damascus to purify themselves. Later they moved back into the wilderness of the Land to Qumran, but still far from Jerusalem.

John the Baptist's teaching of confessing sin and then being baptized was a new thing to the Jews. Immersion wasn't new, but confessing sin beforehand was.

John ate a kosher insect. Locusts are kosher!

Kingdom of God: The Essenes thought it was a Kingdom you enter. The Pharisees saw it as something you take on your shoulders. Jesus said, "The Kingdom of Heaven is upon you."

Nathaniel: "In whom there is no guile." Jesus was comparing him to Jacob in whom there was guile!

Notes of Interest (cont.)

Transfiguration: Moses told the people there would come a prophet like him. "Listen to Him." So the Jews have been looking for the Messiah who would be like Moses. Jesus is that prophet. The transfiguration is one of the many things that proves He is not only like Moses, but better. Moses' face glowed. Jesus' whole body radiated.

Jesus said, "You have heard it said, 'Love your friends, hate your enemies.'" I was told by a professor today that this is not in the Old Testament, but it was taught by the Essenes. So, Jesus could have been teaching against an Essene teaching!

Eunuchs could not enter the Temple because their bodies were not whole (Lev. 21:17-23). So the Eunuch from the Queen of Sheba came all the way to Jerusalem from Ethiopia even though he couldn't enter the Temple.

I felt led by God to read this....

Matt 22:29 (CJB) The reason you go astray is you are ignorant both of the Tanakh (OT) and of the power of God.

(Re-worded) The reason you go astray is
because you are ignorant of the Old Testament
and ignorant of the POWER of GOD.

Jesus said that!

Derek told us last night about his vision of Lebanon, Jordan, Syria, and Egypt having the light shining on them and becoming a buffer zone around Israel. We all told him it is like Isaiah 19:18-25! He was surprised!

So, I must be here to help pray that Isaiah prophecy into existence.

Matt. 22:7 (CJB) The king was furious and sent his soldiers, who killed those murderers and burned down their city. (The Romans burnt Jerusalem! Jesus was prophesying through His parable!)

[From Matt. 23:8-10 (CJB) D] Do not let yourselves be called "Rabbi"; because you have one Rabbi, and you are all each other's brothers. Nor Father. You have one Father and He is in heaven. Nor be called leader. You have one leader——the Messiah.

(It doesn't say, "Don't call yourself rabbi, father, leader. It says not to let others call you that!)

Whoever promotes himself will be humbled....

So, we shouldn't think we have so much better revelation and are special—raised above others—as my flesh so badly longs for. But praise the Lord, He's delivering me from this tendency. Coming here and seeing the Koreans who pray early in the morning; seeing Charity's school that came here to pray 100 years ago; seeing Derek whose mind is always on spiritual things; and Janet who helps everybody (!); and the professors who have such deep insights into Scripture—all this is making me see that I am just one among many and a lowly one at that—one who got here by some fluke stroke of events—some glitch in the computer ☺ —only by the awesome MERCY of Jesus.

Happenings in the Early 20th Century:

1900 Boxer Rebellion in China when missionaries who had come in the mid 1800s had to flee. But later more missionaries came back as soon as things were settled.

Early 1900's A great revival in North Korea by natives (not missionaries!) who had read the Bible in Korean which had been translated by the Chinese and possibly some Americans.

1906-1908 Azuza street outpouring of the Holy Spirit

1905-1908 Charity's college came to Israel to pray

Journal Nov 12 Proof to Them

The inscriptions inside the Dome of the Rock, according to our Messianic Rabbi Jim, basically are saying that it was built to prove that their Islamic god is God and not our God.

It's been there for 1300 plus years! So to a Muslim that would be proof! It would be to me if I were Muslim. So, it's no wonder they believe their god is God! They have proof that has stood for more than 1000 years, that's a THOUSAND YEARS!!!

Why, Lord Jesus? Why have You allowed it for more than a thousand years? Why, why, why? How can they come to You, Yeshua, when they have such rock solid proof—in their eyes? How, how, how?

So, besides praying that their prayers be silenced—that their loudspeakers malfunction and/or their voices become hoarse, should I be praying all the more earnestly that their Dome fall?

I pray, Lord, bring the earthquake You promised—the earthquake where all the fish and birds and people tremble—the earthquake that will split the Mount of Olives.

Lord Jesus, give them a chance. Show them that their god is NOT God; that You, Jesus, Yeshua, are GOD, that Your Father is GOD ALMIGHTY. Let them see. Prove it to them and give them a chance to accept You and believe in You!!

Please do it, Jesus. Do it now, Jesus. Why wait? It's been one thousand three hundred years!!!

Where is there a prophecy to be used to pray about this?

These verses are about the Israelites, but...

Jer. 16:17 For My eyes are on all their ways; they are not hidden from My presence, nor is their iniquity concealed from My sight. And I will doubly repay their iniquity and their sin, because they have polluted My land with the carcasses of their detestable idols, and have filled my inheritance with their abominations.

Jer. 16:21 "Therefore I am surely going to teach them, this time I am going to teach them My power and My might, and they shall know that My Name is LORD."

Yes, Lord, please teach the Muslims Your Power and Your Name.

Prodigal Son Teaching

Jesus told a parable about law-breaking sinners and law-keeping sinners, otherwise called, "The Prodigal Son." I want so badly to tell you the wonderful different angle of this parable I heard at a graduate lecture here by a man who lived among Bedouin villages which is the setting of the parable. You would be amazed. But all I have time for is a quick summary:

The law-breaking son does many shameful things against his father: asking for the inheritance, leaving, spending it on riotous living, and causing the father to have to run to get to him. The father, who would've been the village elder, had to run to reach the son first, to protect the son from the villagers who were angry at him for shaming their venerated leader.

The older brother was a law-keeping sinner. He also did many things that brought shame on his father: He refused to go to the banquet. Rather than going in to ask his father, he asked his questions of a younger boy who was outside with other boys waiting their turn to eat. He chose to have a public disagreement with the father. The father had to leave the banquet of which he was the host, to talk to the older brother. He addressed the father without a title, breaking respect. He talked about 'serving' as if he were a slave—working out of aversion—instead of a son—working out of love.

Whee as - son   Tech nos - my beloved son. The Father uses 'Tech nos.'

Inside Jaffa Gate!!!

Tue, Nov 14, 2006 at 10:39 PM

To Glenn

Hi, My Darling,

I walked around town today. I went inside Jaffa gate!!! I went into the hotel lobby. I didn't see our guide, only his twin. I felt too shy to talk to him.

So now I know it doesn't take long to walk to the old city from the Y where I teach. So I might go there more often. I might go there and pray before I teach.

I miss you sooooooo much.

Everything is breaking down here. We had no hot water again for several days; the washing machine quit working; and water leaked under the kitchen sink. The plumber came and fixed the water heater for the 4th time now since I have been here. He worked on the washer, but said he did not have some parts. He said he fixed the sink, but it leaked right after he left. The guy in charge here called the plumber's cell phone immediately. He could not have been farther than around the corner, but he said he could not come back until Friday! They called the landlord and complained vehemently. But I think to no avail.

That is Israel for you, they tell me.

I love you!!!

Cheryl

Nov 14, 2006

Hello, My Beloved Daughter,

That is sooooo awesome about your friend accepting Jesus.

Praise the Lord, HALLELUJAH!!!!

... Yes, I feel safe here. They say that things are still bad in Gaza which is only a couple hours away, but you can't tell by anything that is happening here. It is so safe here that young girls walk alone on the street at night. Crime is very low. And suicide bombings haven't happened for more than a year here in Jerusalem.

I've got to tell you a funny story, but I can't now. I have a very sore throat. I guess I got too cold yesterday working on the computer. Today they brought in an electric heater, but at first that caused a whole ruckus, because the breaker went off. Then the new wonderful computer seemed like it had died!!! I tell you. It seemed like all my hours of editing and layout work were gone!! Scary. I prayed out loud while the guy tried to figure out what was wrong.

Got to go rest. (I took garlic, vitamin C, and goldenseal.)

Love,

Mom

I'm so Excited

Nov 14 , 2006

Hello Wonderful Friends and Praying People,

Thank you so much for your prayers. They are very effective. I was protected and blessed today. And a huge thanks to all of you who write to me. It really helps me not get so homesick to hear from people back home. God bless you.

I walked all over Jerusalem today. I finally got to go inside the Old City for the first time since I have been here. And it felt sooooo wonderful. I felt like I was really, for sure in Israel. It was so enchanting to walk again where Glenn and I and our daughters walked together last Christmas and relive those memories. My heart skipped a beat with the exciting realization that I'm not just a tourist anymore. During my whole walk back to the YMCA where I teach, I kept repeating excitedly, "I live here now. I live here now."

I took some pictures of this nice, long alley between stone walls that I walk through several times a week to and from the bus. I took three pictures that looked really nice. If only I would have been satisfied with those, but I decided to get one more, this time of the entrance into the alley showing the little guard booth (which was empty at the moment). I heard yelling behind me, but I paid little attention because it was far away and I assumed it had nothing to do with me. I just went on photographing.

The yelling got closer and a soldier came running up to me and asked me, in a heavy Hebrew accent, what I was doing. He told me I can not take pictures of this because it is a military sensitive area. I told him, "Sorry, I did not know that." He kindly and gently asked me to show him the picture I took. I showed him. He asked me to delete it. Then he yelled something down the street. He asked me who I was and where I was from. He also asked me to show him the next photo. His boss came and they looked at every picture on my camera and made me delete every single one of that alley!

It was just an empty, black-topped, wall-lined alley! There was nothing to see. I just took the photos to show where I walk every week. But, incredulously, it was some big military deal!!! I guess the little guard house at the entrance and another one on top of one wall half way down the alley should have clued me in. Duh!!!

I was not afraid of them. They were Israeli and they were kind and polite about it all, but I was a little worried that they might confiscate my camera! And I was very disappointed to lose those photos.

Needless to say, I put my camera away and did not feel much like taking pictures after that.

So your prayers kept me safe from that and safe while crossing the crazy busy streets on my walk.

Now, that I know how easy it is to walk to the Old City from my job, I will try to leave early for work and walk there to pray. I have to walk down a little side street, then on some winding paths and stair steps down a steep hill and then up a couple long stairways and a steep street up another steep hill to Jaffa gate. It takes about 15 minutes and it is good exercise. It's probably another 15 minutes from there to the Wailing Wall.

I have the sense that praying on site for Jerusalem and Israel is a big reason why God has me here.

Blessings and protection and healing to you all,
Cheryl

P.S. Charity told me that the alley is beside the American Embassy.

Reply from my sister:
Cheryl, What a great story. You have me smiling and I am in the midst of a menstrual depression.

Safety Safety

Mom,

I just read your letter about being confronted by the Israeli soldiers to delete your pictures of an old alleyway. I didn't have time to read it when I got it. Wow! That's pretty crazy? When I read it I was getting a little nervous for you, hoping your next words wouldn't tell me that they took your camera or something much worse. Of course I had just talked to you on the Skype phone so I knew you are ok. I do pray for your safety. I wonder if that day was a specific day I was emphasizing your safety. Man, and you walk in all those back winding alley ways. Do you walk in the dark alone? I know you said Jerusalem is safe, but just be careful. I love you! It's kinda funny, I'm usually the one getting people reprimanding me to be safe as a young single woman in a city alone, not me telling my Mom!

Dad said we're calling you on Friday when we're all together. Yay!

It's bitter cold here today. I had my double-breasted, blue coat buttoned up tight with a scarf wrapped around my chin walking from the car repair shop to school.

I can't believe I get something that was in your hands across the world tomorrow night.

Love you dearly!

Reply to Sabrina

Oh, Brina, your letters always warms my heart and a smile always makes its way to my face.

I am as careful as I can be in the situation. I AM looking very much forward to Dad coming, because I know he won't let me wait alone for a bus on a dark street. He will be there with me. But Jesus is always with me. And it really is safe here. No one is afraid to be waiting at the bus stops or walking down the semi dark streets, not even old ladies are afraid. People are polite to each other here. And they are very helpful to foreigners like me.

I am praying for a wonderful Thanksgiving for all of you

Love,

Mom

On a More Somber Note

Dear Concerned Friends,

The other week before the elections, I was wondering what was happening in the news, so I took some time to look on the internet. All the news headings were very sad and disheartening. I read the one about the Supreme Court arguing the partial birth abortion case. I couldn't believe that sane, educated, top government people were having to figure out whether it should be legal to suck the brains out of a baby right before it is born. How could this be happening in a civilized society?!!

I decided it is because we really aren't civilized anymore. That is the truth. The American society is no longer civilized. It has actually become barbaric. I could name so many things to prove my case, including the whole thing with Ted Haggard, and the gay movement, and on and on and on. You could name them for me, I'm sure.

My heart became so burdened that I went to my room and cried and wailed for an hour in prayer to Jesus for our broken world.

I prayed for the elections. You all prayed for the elections. The congregations here prayed for the elections. Why they turned out the way they did—why the Republicans lost Congress, I don't know. But I know God has His plan, and nothing messes up His plan.

Grieving and Believing,
Cheryl

Biblical Archeology Display

Nov 18, 2006

Hello Again, Friends
This is important. It is something big God is doing there in America, organized by the people that I'm working for here and other people. I am awed that I am connected at all to people doing such a huge thing!! I actually met the CEO of the whole thing!!

It is a whole, huge display of recent archeological findings that prove the truth of the Bible, along with beautiful artwork and sculptures to bring the Bible and the ancient Holy Land alive for you. It will be touring a few cities in America. It is in Columbus, Ohio right now. It was in Grand Rapids and Atlanta already. It will end up in Texas. Charity, helped set up the one in Atlanta right before she came here in October. .

It is not blatantly evangelistic, but that is the underlying purpose—that and to improve Biblical literacy among Christians. Already there are many reports of people saying their thinking is changed by going through it. One example is an African, Muslim lady who went through it and was shocked to see that Simon of Cyrene was African. She talked to one of the volunteers about it and then asked if she could bring her Muslim fiancé the next day. They said, of course. So, the two went through it together the next day and afterwards they said now that they have seen this, they feel they must give Christianity some serious consideration!! It is also impressing many Jewish people!! (I'm told that most Jews are as illiterate about the Bible as most Christians are—which is partly why we aren't a civilized society anymore!)

So pray for that lady and her fiancé, and for the exhibit to reach tons more.

A street inside the Old City Jerusalem

2.

TRYING TO GET TO THE WAILING WALL TO FULFILL MY MISSION HERE

God is so Personally Awesome

Sat, Nov 18, 2006 at 5:11 PM

Dear Friends,

I want to share this little story. I'm sorry it is long, but perhaps it will be meaningful for some of you.

I have to walk quite a ways to get to the bus stop after I teach classes in the evenings. Classes go until 8:30. The bus comes at 9pm. Usually, because of having to straighten up and put everything away after class, even if I practically run, I miss the 9pm one and have to wait until 9:30.

So, last Tuesday I tried to have most things done at break time so I could get out of class early enough to make it. Then after class I hurried as fast as I could to put all the books and things, including my rain poncho (which I put on top of the books) into the borrowed (from wonderful Charity) backpack, zip it up good and go. I walked as fast as I could, sometimes almost ran. At one point I heard the click of hard plastic hitting the sidewalk behind me. I turned half way around to look as I kept running. I didn't see how anything could've fallen out of the backpack because I had zipped it so well. The sidewalk was very narrow and I was near an iron fence. So, I figured the hanging strap of the backpack had hit the fence and made that noise. So, I didn't stop to take a better look. I didn't want to miss the bus.

I didn't miss it. I even had to wait five minutes. But when I got on the bus and took the backpack off my back to sit down I discovered the zipper was opened all the way and all my books were nearly falling out! I couldn't believe it! The whole ride home I kept remembering things that should be in there and checked to see if they were. Everything I thought of was there. I breathed a sigh of relief. However, one item didn't come to my mind.

The next morning it was raining lightly (Yahoo, Israel needs rain!) and I was asked to walk to the local shop to buy some produce for our Australian chef. So I ran upstairs to get my rain poncho out of the backpack. But it wasn't there! Suddenly I remembered that was what I had put on top of the books! That was what I had heard falling out! I started getting upset with myself for not stopping to look.

The poncho is really important to me here. Winter is the rainy season. So when it is cold here, it rains. My body doesn't tolerate cold very well, so being cold AND wet is not something I want to ever happen to me. With all the places I have to walk and all the times I have to wait for the bus, there might be plenty of times I cannot avoid getting wet if I don't have a rain poncho. My poncho is nice because it folds up really small, making it easy to take everywhere with me in case I will need it. But now it was gone! Buying a new one is not that easy here.

I borrowed a raincoat and went to the store. I prayed all day that no one would pick up the poncho and it would be there when I went back into town to look for it. I couldn't go in until the next afternoon. So I prayed all evening and all the next day. I begged Jesus to have mercy on me and keep it there on the sidewalk for me to find.

While praying, I started to see a lesson in the whole thing. God gave me a warning while I was scurrying down the street. But I didn't take it seriously. I was sure I had secured the bag carefully. I clearly remembered zipping it and double checking it. I was so sure of myself that I didn't listen to God's warning.

I thought about how we do that in life. We think we've covered all our bases and taken care of everything, so we don't pay attention to the little warning nudges God gives us to tell us we are vulnerable to the enemy. We think we have closed all the doors and are safe. So we don't stop and search our hearts to see what God is trying to point out. Thus we find ourselves vulnerable and exposed to worse attacks of the enemy. Just as I was now very vulnerable to being exposed to the cold rain, and could get sick as a result.

Well, the next day I prayed all the way in on the bus ride. "Lord, I know You are going to have that poncho waiting for me. I trust that You will." I walked slowly along that sidewalk, praying hard as I went, but there was no poncho. I started to feel a little afraid of what lie ahead of me this winter. There is no heat in our apartment during the day, and still not some nights. So if I get wet, it might be hard to get warm again.

But then as I thought about who my Lord Jesus is, and how He always takes care of His own, I relaxed and said, "Lord, I don't need a rain poncho to feel safe. I know you will still take care of me. Somehow you will not let me get wet. Maybe You will stop the rain in my spot long enough till I get on the bus. I don't know. But I still pray for rain for Jerusalem, because they need it."

The Lord helped me relax and not worry at all about the problem even as I went on about my wonderful visit with our friends, Shawn and Jane, who came for a tour here. It was soooo wonderful to see them and visit with them. Jane and I walked all over the

Old City together. It was great fun!! (See below.)

Well, guess what? This morning I went to put something in a big bag I have in my room—the same bag I had just previously dug down into to get a washcloth—and there on top to my extreme, jolting shock was the poncho that I had never expected to ever see again.

It is a miracle!! I stood there stunned for a minute. A total miracle! I am in awe of the Lord Jesus!! He did a personal miraculous thing for measly little me. He really loves to take care of us!! So He isn't going to stop the rain for me. He just gave me back my poncho!! ☺

I have thought it through over and over how that poncho could have gotten there! And to me it is just a sheer miracle. You can think what you want. But to me it is a complete miracle. (God did another miraculous thing for me like that before when I was a child, when my wonderful, new clock-radio's minute hand fell off inside the unremovable face, and I was so sad, and then it was suddenly fixed.)

I have also seen many healing miracles in my life. And I've experienced God providing in so many miraculous ways. What else can I say? We serve an awesome, loving God!!!

I'm sure you have experienced God's miraculous, personal care in your life, too. If not, I know you soon will. Just keep spending time with Him, in His Word, getting to know Him. The more you know Him, the more you will love and trust Him, and the more you will notice what He is doing for you.

Blessings of His presence,
Cheryl

Damascus Gate

Shawn and Jane's Visit

Written later from memory

My friends from America, Shawn and Jane, were on a tour in Israel. On Nov. 16, they came to Jerusalem and we arranged for me to meet with them. It was a free day on their tour for shopping etc. Jane wanted to see the Old City. Shawn stayed near their hotel to rest up

I nearly walked Jane's legs off that day. I felt bad and apologized to her later. I was like a bird out of the cage, because except for that exciting jaunt just inside the Jaffa Gate, this was my first to the Old City since moving here. I wanted to see everything again and show it all to her.

The first thing I wanted to do was find the Wailing Wall so I could start going there to pray when I come into town to teach. She and I walked with her group from her hotel to the Damascus gate. I had never been to the Damascus gate before, so I was excited about that. Then we went to the outdoor restaurant where they wanted everyone to meet for lunch. I recognized the restaurant from before when we were tourists, but I didn't know how to get to the Wailing Wall from there. So I took her through the Arab shopping streets back to the Jaffa Gate where I was familiar. We did some shopping on the way. Then I took her down the quiet, walled stone street that I was familiar with. We stopped at a hostel Glenn and I had looked at before. I got permission to take her to the roof to let her see the whole Old City. While there we met a lady from Finland who comes here regularly to pray for Israel (See p. 72).

We headed on toward the Wailing Wall. I showed her many interesting shops along the way, including the Third Temple Institute shop. I got to where I thought the Wailing Wall should be, but I couldn't find it. I felt so frustrated. I took her down several side streets but none of them led to the Wall. I asked several different people for directions. They all pointed in the direction we had already gone. We tried again, but their directions didn't help. I showed her the Jewish Shopping Corridor which she found very interesting. Finally, the time was getting short so we had to head back. I took her down a street I thought headed straight to the lunch meeting place, but it didn't. We ended up in unknown territory. The houses looked very poor, the streets were very dirty and full of trash. It was the Arab section of the Old City and I was lost! I was worried how we would get treated by the Arabs this far away from the tourist section. I didn't dare let anything happen to my precious friend!! I was trying to find the way back as quickly as I could without letting her know I was lost.

We came upon two little, maybe 3-year-old boys who looked like twins. They were darling cute. Jane exclaimed over them. I thought they were adorable, too, but kept on hurrying by, not allowing their cuteness to delay my efforts to get us to safety. Suddenly, I realized Jane wasn't beside me. I turned around and there she was talking sweetly to those wee boys. She was asking the older siblings if they were twins. Of course, they couldn't understand her. She cooed over them, "You are so cute." One of those "cute" little tykes promptly kicked her in the leg. She quit smiling, quickly joined me, and we hurried away, both feeling quite shaken up. An older boy yelled after us in broken English to come and shop in their little store—as if we would shop after being kicked! However, I had the sense it was his way of apologizing.

I kept heading in the northwest direction through mostly deserted streets and finally, we arrived to a street that was familiar to me. I was so relieved. We headed to the restaurant and Jane was greeted warmly by all her waiting friends.

After spending time in Shawn and Jane's hotel catching up on each other's news and having wonderful fellowship together, I walked the long trek to the YMCA to teach my classes. I felt blessed at the time with such good, kind, faithful friends. Jane had even given me some money! But under all the warm feelings, I felt frustrated that I hadn't gotten to see the Wailing Wall! I had been here almost a month and still hadn't found my way there!

Journal Nov. 18 Azal

Zech. 14:4-5, 8 On that day His feet shall stand on the Mount of Olives, which lies before Jerusalem on the east; and the Mount of Olives shall be split in two from east to west by a very wide valley; so that one half of the Mount shall withdraw northward, and the other half southward. And you shall flee by the valley of the Lord's mountain, for the valley between the mountains shall reach to Azal.

Zech 14:6, 8 (CJB) On that day, there will be neither bright light nor thick darkness; and one day, known to Adonai, will be neither day nor night, although by evening there will be light. On that day, fresh water will flow out from Jerusalem, half toward the eastern sea and half toward the western sea....

Zech 14:8 (NRSV) On that day living waters shall flow out from Jerusalem, half of them to the eastern sea and half of them to the western sea; it shall continue in summer as in winter.

Yes, Jesus, Your living water has flowed out to all the world—to the East and the West. And the Kingdom was in the Dark Ages for awhile—hundreds of years—not thick darkness, but also not bright light. And now by evening—by the last couple centuries there has been more light—the Reformation, revivals, the Wesleyan Brothers, Charles Finney, D.L. Moody, Azusa Street Holy Spirit outpouring, etc.

So, we must be near. It must be evening!

We need Your Bright Light, Jesus.

I looked up "Azal." My NRSV Bible says the meaning of the Hebrew is uncertain. The Complete Jewish Bible says "Atzel." I searched the internet for the meaning.

In Arabic it means "morning of eternity"!!

In Hebrew it has the sense of "joining." It also means "near."

Azal is an Arab airlines, and Atzel is the name of some German company with locations all over Europe. I didn't have time to look any further.

Journal Nov. 20 Anger Blazing, Be Fruitful

Hos. 5:15 (God speaking) I will return to My place until they acknowledge their guilt and seek My face. In their distress they will beg My favor.

Hos. 7:6 For they are kindled like an oven, their heart burns within them; All night their anger smolders; in the morning it blazes like a flaming fire.

That anger could be the devil's anger, too! It's been smoldering all night and now it's getting near the morning of Jesus' return and the devil is blazing hot as "an oven."

I've been pondering why Jesus didn't say to the fig tree, "Be fruitful" and this came to me: God did say that once! He said it to Adam and Eve—to all mankind!! And God's spoken Word is so powerful!! That's why we can't help ourselves when it comes to sexual desire because God spoke it and we do it!!! Teeheehee. That's why!!!! ☺

But God wants our spiritual "fruit" to be voluntary!

To Mom and Dad

Mon, Nov 20, 2006 at 7:29 PM

Dear Mom and Dad,

You won't believe this!!! Guess who I met in Jerusalem this evening???? I was walking from the prayer meeting to the bus stop with two other people and I saw some Plain Clothes young people! I was shocked, but I walked on by. Then I started wishing I had stopped them and talked to them. Two minutes later I saw some adults walking my way, so I stopped them and told them I have Plain Clothes relatives and asked where they were from. They said they were from several places, Indiana, Ohio, California. "Indiana!" I said. "I'm from Indiana!" Then guess who stepped out of the crowd and said, "Oh, I know you." It was Cousin, Mike!!!!!

Can you believe it!!!!

I was so surprised! He said they have a group of forty people—him and Gary. They traveled to Greece and saw New Testament church sites and then they came to Israel. He said Gary has been bringing groups here for years.

Wow! It blessed my soul to see them.

Love to all,
Cheryl

From my daughter

Mon, Nov 13, 2006 at 11:32 AM

Mommy,

I miss you so much.

Your letters are great descriptions. They take me back to the stone city of narrow corridors and bodacious Jewish men.

I pray for you everyday.

As for me. It's dreary and rainy and cold. My tummy feels strange. I feel strange. Tired and confused and disoriented. The cause is a mix of future unknowns about next year, another test upcoming that I should have studied for more over the weekend, and maybe more unidentified things (sigh). Sometimes I wish I could just run away into a mountain wilderness with the birds chirping and green fields calling and I could slide smoothly in to the cool blue water under a glorious sky.

I talk with God. But I don't feel fulfilled right now.

I don't know what's going on. I sure hope this phase ends with joy, soon.

My friend would like to be added to your e-mailing list.

-bri

A Funny Story

Hello, Darling Daughter,

Bodacious, now thereäs a word!! (Sorrz, mz kezboard is all messed up. It does y instead of z and ä this instead of apostraphe. Other kezs are messed up, too. A German ladz was using this for German the other daz. I tried the other computer so I didnät have to watch mz ys and zs and make sure I donät use anz contractions all the time, but that one onlz tzped in Japanese because a Japanese lady was using it today.)

What does bodacious mean? (O and the ? and _ are backwards, too. I cannot find the apostrophe anywhere.)

I feel so sad for you. You know, if we could buy that land, you could have those green fields, blue sky and chirping birds, with cool blue water very nearby! Maybe thatäs what you should do. Go be by yourself for awhile where you can shut everything else out and be alone with God and nature.

Do you want to hear a funny story_ oops, I mean ?

(To the reader: This same story is rewritten on p. 67 easier to read)

I was sitting at the bus stop waiting a long time. An orthodox man walked by. He wasnät Hassidim because he didnät have any curls, but he had a black suit and black hat. He zipped right by me. Then he slowed down, stopped and turned around and started talking to me in Hebrew. I told him I only speak English. So he began speaking in heavilz accented English. He asked me in a bit of an excited voice if I was making alyah to Israel. I said no. Then he asked very politely Ä(thatäs a quotation mark, okay?) Is it okay if we talk a little bit?Ä I thought maybe he wanted to practice his English so I said, sure. He then asked me where I was from and what I was doing here. I told him. Then I asked him where he was from. He said he is from France. I asked if he made aliyah. He said yes, I live here. (forget quotation marks.) Then quickly he said uh, excuse me, are you married? I was a little surprised at the question, but I said yes. He immediately stepped back a bit, raised his hand and said, Oh läm sorry, sorry. I said, itäs okay. He waved his hand in front of his face and as he walked away said, No, no, itäs for me, for me. Sorry.

So, I guess, for some strange reason, maybe because it was dark (but still!) I looked like a young, single, available orthodox girl to him. Isnät that hilarious!!! He didnät look that young to me. Maybe in his late twenties or so. So, I donät know if I looked that age to him or what. His parting actions made me feel a little like I had done something wrong, but I was laughing inside all the way home!!

So now I know that if an orthodox guy asks to talk a little bit, it carries a special meaning. Ö) (thatät a smile) I will probably try not to make eye contact if there ever is a similar occurance again.

So, your 50-year-old mom doesnät look old yet!! Hahahaheeheehee. At least not in the dim street lights!! lol!

I just came back from prayer again at that museum-house. I love praying there. It is such a calm, quiet, unassuming atmosphere. No one is trying to impress anyone, or prove anything, or force a spiritual atmosphere. We just sing, and sit quietly to listen to God, and then we pray. Our prayers have the sense of unity and agreement with each other and inspired by the Spirit.

I feel refreshed afterwards.

And in that neighborhood, I really feel like läm in Israel!

I now also help teach conversation English to advanced students three times a week and I'm having a great time with them!. Today they all practiced giving their testimony in English. (They were all Korean Christians. The Israeli didn't come.) It was quite interesting.

I love Zou,
Mommz

The First Rays

Tue, Nov 14, 2006 at 8:25 PM

Oh Mom! You are you a light in my world. How glad my heart is to read your stories and laugh with you as I try to interpret your z's and y's and apostrophe's! What a story to type on a computer of German or Japanese!

I talked with Mrs. _____ about how I was feeling. ... She is very encouraging. She talked about the race in which we press on to take hold of the prize. I am so blessed to live here. God has definitely placed me in this safe haven in this trying time for a reason.

And my 50-year-old Mom attracts 20-some-year-old Jewish men! Hahaha! I always knew you had it! Boy, would Dad be proud, or maybe angry for your safety, not sure which. But if he was there he'd sure prize you to them!

Bodacious-- thorough, blatant, unmistakable, remarkable, outstanding, audacious, bold or brazen

Living on a country homestead in the green and open land does conjure sweet thoughts in my mind. When would this be? In a couple years? Next year? I still have no clue what's going on next year. Awaiting the Lord, . If it's not open, it's not His way.

That prayer/worship time in the museum house sounds wonderful. I love your whole paragraph describing it. The calm, quiet, unassuming atmosphere, where no one tries to impress. No one tries to force spiritual atmosphere. Just to sing, and sit quietly to listen to God, then pray. And to have what you said, the unity and agreement with each other inspired by the Spirit, wow.

I just had a meal of salmon, stir fry veggies, and biscuits with pear preserves with my landlord family. I ate the fish skin they were going to throw away and Mr. ____ asked me if I've always been an adventurous eater. Ha ha. Their kids are the kind that have to be reminded to take at least two pieces of broccoli.

I love Zou, too mommy. And Thanksgiving won't be the same without you.

Re: The First Rays

Thu, Nov 16, 2006 at 12:23 AM

I tried to call you. I'm sure you know by now.

I loved your e-mail. I laughed out loud for ten minutes from the "I love Zou, too mommy." Then I told Charity, and laughed again with her.

Thank you for a good belly laugh. It does a body good!

The keyboard is working correctly now. Thank God!! An American had to do his work on it and I guess he knew how to change the keyboard back to normal. I need to find out from him how to do it. No one else seems to know. I thought I was going to have to wait a month until the repair guy returns from a trip.

Fish skin, yummy. Adventurous eater!! Perfect description of you!

Yeah, Dad was more like worried-angry. He wants me to wear a scarf now, like the married Orthodox women do. lol! (That might have been why the guy thought I was single. I wasn't wearing a scarf over my hair.)

I want to try to call you again on Friday evening (it will be afternoon your time— one or two o'clock.) Will that be a possibility? Charity is being very kind and letting me borrow her laptop skype phone. It won't cost me much at all.

I sent some lightweight, small gifts back with Shawn and Jane. They are all together in one bag with no wrapping. I hope everyone will like them.

I must go to bed.

I love Zou, too, Brina.
Mommy

A Funny Story

(Same story from pp. 64-65 without z's and y's mixed up)

Hey Kids,

Do you want to hear a funny story? (I sent this to Sabrina when my keyboard was typing weird German umlaut letters. It was hard to read. The keyboard is fixed now so I cleaned it up to send to all of you.)

I was sitting at the bus stop waiting a long time. An orthodox man walked by. He wasn't Hassidim because he didn't have any curls, but he had a black suit and black hat. He zipped right by me. Then he slowed down, stopped, turned around and started talking to me in Hebrew. I told him I only speak English. So he began speaking in heavily accented English. He asked me in a bit of an excited voice if I was making aliyah to Israel. I said no. Then he asked very politely "Is it okay if we talk a little bit?" I thought maybe he wanted to practice his English so I said, "Sure." He then asked me where I was from and what I was doing here. I told him. Then I asked him where he was from. He said he is from France. I asked if he made aliyah. He said, "Yes, I live here." Then quickly he said, "Uh, excuse me, are you married?" I was a little surprised at the question, but I said yes. He immediately stepped back a bit, raised his hand and said, "Oh I'm sorry, sorry." I said, "It's okay." He waved his hand in front of his face and as he walked away said, "No, no, it's for me, for me. Sorry."

So, I guess, for some strange reason, maybe because it was dark (but still!) I looked like a young, single, available orthodox girl to him. Isn't that hilarious!!! He didn't look that young to me. Maybe in his late twenties or so. So, I don't know if I looked that age to him or what. His parting actions made me feel a little like I had done something wrong, but I was laughing inside all the way home!!

So now I know that if an orthodox guy asks to talk a little bit, it carries a special meaning. ☺   I will probably try not to make eye contact if there ever is a similar occurrence again.

So, your 50-year-old mom doesn't look old yet!! Hahahaheeheehee. At least not in the dim street lights!! lol!

Happy Thanksgiving. I hope you will all like the little presents I'm sending you through the Shirks.

Love you all,
Your "young" Mommy

Hassidim and Marriage

Mon, Nov 20, 2006 at 4:55 PM

To a Friend,

I found out something the other day that might interest you. Two of the guys, graduate students here, were talking about the Hassidim getting married. One guy said, "Hey, it's the first commandment!" I laughed and said, "There's a commandment to get married?" They both said "Yea, 'Be fruitful and multiply!'" I laughed and laughed as they continued to point out that to be fruitful and multiply you had to get married (if you want to do it God's way). I continued to find it very humorous.

Then another guy said, "No, really, the Orthodox Jews take that commandment very seriously. If one of their young men turns 20 and he still isn't married, the rabbi will go to him and tell him to find a girl and get married." I was shocked and couldn't believe him. But everyone in the room told me it is true. Can you believe it? One girl said that sometimes they give the guy three choices of girls and tell him to choose one and get married! Can you imagine? I wouldn't want to be the girl he chooses, would you?!!!!

I'm still shocked. What a hoot!

So, my friend, maybe you don't need to be so upset with Apostle Paul. He came from the Orthodox (Pharisee) background, you know. Maybe he wasn't so much telling people that you shouldn't get married, as he was telling them it is OKAY if you feel led by God to stay single, that being single can actually be a good thing; that to stay single for awhile is nice because you can serve the Lord unencumbered with family. But that if you desired to get married, that is fine, too. Maybe he didn't mean at all for people to take what he said and swing the pendulum the opposite way to say Christians shouldn't get married! He might have just been trying to get the pendulum to the middle to where it is okay to get married and OKAY to NOT get married, and especially that it is OKAY to get married LATER than your teens!!!!!

That's what I meant by us not being able to hear Paul's tone of voice when we read that Scripture. Whenever any Scripture rubs me wrong, I have found out that if I just pray about it and wait, God eventually shows me the life-giving meaning He intended. His Word is Life-giving and Life-transforming. If we can't see that in certain passages then we just don't have all the pieces yet. "We see through a glass darkly" lots of times.

Hope this makes you like Apostle Paul a little better. ☺

I Wonder if You are Getting News About This in the US

Wed, Nov 22, 5:23 PM

The Palestinian Hamas are still shooting rockets into Israel. Is the news media in America telling you this? I got the following from the ynetnews.com website Pay attention to what the Hamas says in the last paragraph.

Hamas 'very satisfied' with fleeing Jews

Aaron Klein, WND

Ynet News. published: 11.-21.-06. Time: 19:26

http://www.ynetnews.com/articles/0,7340,L-3331070.00.html

(Cont. on the bottom of p. 69)

Journal Nov. 22   Habakkuk
(Tomorrow is Thanksgiving)

The Essenes said Habukkuk is about the End Times, so I studied it this morning and I had the thought light up in my mind that perhaps the last part is more than a declaration of faith in God for natural provision. Perhaps it is also talking about faith in God for spiritual things in the End Times.

The fig tree could be Israel
The fruit on the vine could be the church ("I am the vine, you are the branches…")
The produce of the olive (oil) could be both Israel and the church——the produce of
        having the Spirit in us. (represented by the oil)
The fields — the harvest fields of people in the world
The flock — God's people
The herd — the herd in God's army (They are not in the stalls because they are
        out at war!)

So, we should rejoice in the Lord and exult in the God of our salvation even though Israel doesn't blossom in believing in Yeshua; and there seems to be no fruit among Christians, and the evidence of the Holy Spirit in them seems slim; though there seems to be no harvest from the fields of the world, and Gods people's voices seem to be cut off from the world's media, and Gods Holy army seems to be missing.

Is it true? I don't know. My question is, what 'vision' did Habakkuk make clear like he was commanded to do?

(Cont. from the bottom of p. 68)
Hamas is "very satisfied" with reports here that some Israelis in communities near the Gaza Strip are ready to flee their rocket-plagued towns while students reportedly have been skipping school for fear of being caught in regular Palestinian attacks, a senior leader of Hamas' military wing told WND in an interview yesterday.

Under Fire

Barrages continue: Sderot turns into ghost town. A Qassam rocket which caused severe injury of a worker Tuesday morning was another nail in the southern town's coffin. Market, commercial centers are empty. ….

The terror leader (Abu Abdullah) scoffed at pinpoint Israeli operations carried out the last few months in the northern Gaza Strip aimed at stopping rocket attacks.

"Even if they kill hundreds of our fighters, there is no way (the Israelis) can stop our attacks. While Israel was acting all over in Beit Hanoun, we shot many rockets from Beit Hanoun using new techniques of shooting I will not tell you about."

I've Been Initiated to Jerusalem Now

Wed, Nov 22, 2006 at 6:15 PM

I decided to try a different bus to go into town. I had taken it home several times and it seemed faster. Someone here had told me it was okay to try, but no one had actually done it yet, and no knew the bus schedule for sure.

It was a fifteen minute walk to that bus stop. I waited twenty minutes. Two 10-year-old Jewish boys wearing their kippas (little caps) and carrying their backpacks came. I asked them if they knew English. They nodded. I asked them which bus they were waiting for. They didn't know how to say it. So I said, "32?" They nodded. I said, "Good that's the one I'm waiting for. How many more minutes?" They held out five fingers. Just then the bus came. We all three laughed and got on the bus. They got off a couple stops later. One of them smiled at me and in his heavy accent said, "Goot by." That warmed my heart.

For twenty minutes, the bus wound around the whole huge Gilo neighborhood where I live, which is more like a town than a neighborhood. Pretty soon it was only me on the bus. At the next stop the driver told me to get off!!! He said it was the end of the line. My chin dropped to the floor.

He kindly asked me where I was going. I told him. He took me a few yards to the next stop, told me to get off and wait there for the next #32 bus. That meant I had to pay for another ride and wait another twenty minutes!

That's the initiation to Israel. Everyone here says it has happened to them. One guy said one time the driver made him get off. He pointed out a bus stop just a few feet away for him to wait at. Then a couple minutes later the same bus with the same bus driver came and picked him up!!! But still it cost another bus ticket! Isn't that hilarious?

People Here are so Kind and Helpful to Foreigners.

I waited alone for awhile at that bus stop where I was dumped off, praying for Israel, and praying that I would get to town in time to teach my classes! Finally some people started coming to wait. I asked one girl which bus she was waiting for. It was #32. I sighed in relief. She asked me where I was going and then talked to her father in Hebrew. They told me I needed to get off the next stop after they got off. She asked me if I wanted her to tell the bus driver. I said that I was pretty sure I would know the place when I got there. She told the driver anyway. I didn't sit near that girl and her dad. I sat in front so I could watch where we were and so the bus driver could tell me where to get off.

It took twenty minutes to get into Jerusalem. The bus didn't go the way I expected. I didn't recognize the streets at all. I started to feel very lost, and wondered if I would ever make it to class in time. The bus was packed—the aisles full of standing people. There were many bodies between me and the driver. I think he forgot all about me anyway. I prayed for the Lord to help me. I was looking out the side window forlorn when a strange man knocked on my window. I thought, "What in the world?" Then I suddenly recognized the father, and saw the girl beside him. He was telling me to get off at the next bus stop!

Isn't that so nice?

I have been helped many times by the people here.

People are also honest.

I got shut in the bus door one time!! It was early in the morning when I was headed to visit with Shawn and Jane. The bus was crowded. There were many of us trying to get on. Suddenly the driver decided it was too full to let any more people on. He yelled something in Hebrew and shut the door before I and another lady could get on. (I was last in line.) The lady hollered in Hebrew so he opened the door. She and I quickly darted on. He quickly shut it again, this time on my backpack!! He started whizzing down the street with my backpack sticking out the door!!! I was afraid I'd have to ride that way all the way to town, because he certainly wasn't going to open the door to let anyone else on!! But the same lady hollered at him again, so he opened it and let me come all the way on. We zoomed by the next stop where a crowd of people were waiting. They raised their hands and yelled, but to no avail. They all had to wait another half an hour for the next bus!!

We were all so crowded that we couldn't even get to the driver to pay for the ride. People could have easily just not paid, but they didn't. They all reached through the crowd to pay their fare. One who got on at the back made his way to the front later to pay.

I thought that driver was very rude. But then when I got to town I didn't know for sure where the hotel was to meet Shawn and Jane. I asked him. He didn't know English, but a young lady passenger in the front seat gave me directions, and told him that he had just passed the bus stop where I should have gotten off. So he stopped right there in between stops and let me off. They don't usually ever do that. So I found out he was kind after all.

Ah, the fun of living in Jerusalem.

You should come and try it!!

Pray for My Student

Thu, Nov 23, 2006 at 9:19 PM

Please pray for my Arab student. I lent him my copy of "Parable of the Bridge" that has Arabic and English. It is a parable of the Gospel story. The reason he is studying English is so he can become a tour guide. As a guide he will influence tons of people. So please pray for him.

Happy Thanksgiving.

Thanksgiving

Thanksgiving is not a holiday here, so no one got off work, but Friday night the lady who got me this position, organized a huge carry-in dinner at a church for all the Christian workers she knows here in Jerusalem. And, boy, was it a crowd. Charity and I helped her decorate, set up all the tables and chairs, and set out the turkey and salmon that she somehow miraculously provided. The Australian did his usual extravagant flare of cooking, too. He and I invited our Korean students and they came!! People from many nations came. She asked the blessing to be said in all the different languages present. It was so many: European and Scandinavian languages, a couple different African languages, several Asian languages, Arabic, and, of course, Hebrew.

I got to eat fresh figs. One guy brought a bunch and gave me some to take home. The dishes and clean up afterwards took hours even though a crowd of people helped, but it was a lot of fun! I met so many wonderful people.

Prophecy Coming True! Pray for More to Come True!

Sun, Nov 26, 2006 at 11:14 AM

A Spirit of Grace and Prayer

> Zechariah 12:10 (CJB) *I will pour out on the house of David and on those living in Yerushalayim [Jerusalem] a spirit of grace and prayer.* [NRSV says, *...a spirit of compassion and supplication.*].

Spirit of Prayer on Those Living in Jerusalem

This prophecy is coming true! I am meeting so many people here who have come only to pray. They feel compelled by God to come here to pray. There are tons of Koreans here for that reason. They get up at 5 am every day to pray. When they arrive to class, they bow their heads and pray silently first before they begin talking to us.

Koreans are mighty prayer warriors, I am finding out! (They are also very missionary minded. I am told they have 13,000 missionaries all over the world!!! From tiny South Korea! That's almost as much as America's 15,000, I am told.)

As I told you, Jane and I met a wonderful lady from Finland who comes and stays at a hostel in the Old City for months at a time just to pray for Israel. (She said she also prays for America, including our soldiers in Iraq.)

A Spirit of Compassion

This is also coming to pass. There are so many organizations of compassion here. I learn about more of them every week. Here's a short list. I met volunteers for most of these at the Thanksgiving carry-in. Google them to find out more about them.

Israel Hands of Mercy (helping victims of terror),

Bridges for Peace (helping the poor),

The Joseph Project (giving to the poor, especially Russian immigrants, and starting
        Messianic congregations),

Christians for Israel (helping the poor),

Shevid Ahim (?) (It means: brothers living together in unity.) (They bring Arab children
        needing heart surgery, etc, to Jerusalem for medical care.)

There are many more that I can't remember and that I haven't heard of yet. And those are just the Christian ones.

Another Prophecy Coming to Pass

> Jeremiah 16:14-16 (NRSV) *Therefore, the days are surely coming, says the Lord, when it shall no longer be said, "As the Lord lives who brought the people of Israel up out of the land of Egypt," but "As the Lord lives who brought the people of Israel up out of the land of the north and out of all the lands where He had driven them." ...I am now sending many fishermen, says the Lord, and they shall catch them; and afterwards I will send for many hunters, and they will hunt them from every mountain and every his, and out of the clefts of the rocks.*

This has been coming true for awhile now. Russian Jews (from the land of the north) have been immigrating to Israel by the droves ever since the iron curtain fell. (Our American Messianic Rabbi pointed out to us that this is the fulfilling of this part of the prophecy.)

The second part about "*out of all the lands*" and about the "*fishing*" and "*hunting*" for them is also coming true.

For example, I met a college girl last night from Gibraltar!! —very cute with dark ringlet curls, and very friendly, talking a mile a minute in a heavy British accent. Sometimes it was hard to understand her. She told practically her whole life story in the 10 minutes before service. She was raised Catholic. She was led to the Lord by American missionaries on the beach!! She rejected God when her sister's first baby died, but then came back whole-heartedly. She felt drawn to Israel and last year was planning to move here when she was told by an old friend of her grandmother's that she was actually Jewish!! Her great grandmother was Jewish but converted to Catholicism.

A man I met, also there at the Messianic service, is from the Cayman Islands. He was raised Catholic, too. His grandfather was an Irishman who fled Ireland when he was age 9 by sneaking onto a ship to escape violent persecution. So, to be safe from further violence, when he got to the Cayman Islands he told no one he was a Jew. Instead he lived as a Catholic.

One of my Korean students is a missionary (most of them are). He has worked as a missionary in Russia in Siberia. One thing he did there was to search for Russian Jews. He found many who didn't even know yet that Israel had become a nation! So he told them this great news and helped them do the paperwork to "make aliyah" (move to Israel and become Israeli citizens). He is one of the "hunters" the Scripture is talking about.

On the Israel National News, israelnationalnews.com they tell about finding one of the ten lost tribes of Israel!!! Can you believe it??? They found them in India! A group of several thousand! So there's an Israeli organization that is doing the "fishing" mentioned in the verse!

Isn't it wonderful to see prophecy coming to pass? It fills me with awe.

Prophecy to Pray It Comes True

Since God is fulfilling that part of His Word, let's pray He fulfills this Word:

Zechariah 13:2 (CJB) *When that day comes, says the Adonai Tzva'ot, I will ... expel ... the spirit of uncleanness from the land.*

Pray that He will expel the unclean spirit of homosexuality and the New Age spirit etc., etc.—every spirit that rejects Jesus as the Messiah!! (Homosexuality and New Age are both growing in Israel. The New Age movement is huge here. They have New Age festivals frequently, and I'm told secular Jews attend in hordes.)

Did I tell you that the word "proud" in Hebrew is pronounced "ga-ay"—like "gay" with a slight pause in the middle. I discovered this while studying my Hebrew book. My mouth fell open. "Could that be why they call their marches 'gay pride!?!'" I asked myself. It looks to me like the homosexuals have decided to defile two languages instead of just one—English, the language that is spreading the Gospel all over the world, (They defiled it by throwing the delightful little word, "gay" into the mud.) and Hebrew, the language through which God gave the Torah and the whole Old Testament! They want to defile Jerusalem where Hebrew is the official language, so it is not too far-fetched to think they know what the sound of the word "gay" means in Hebrew.

I asked the vice president of this university, "Why here? Why do all these groups think they have to come here? They have the whole world to choose from, why must they come here to this tiny place?"

He said, "All evil is drawn to Jerusalem, the Holy City, because the devil is trying to make just one of God's promises or covenants to become broken. If he can ruin just one, then all the others would come into question. People would then say to God, 'You broke that promise, now which other one are you going to break?'"

So, that's why. The devil is trying to ruin the prophecies about Jerusalem becoming God's HOLY City!

But he won't succeed, in fact he is going to be expelled! Let's pray Zechariah's prophecy into existence!!!

Pray, pray, pray!!!

Reply From a Friend

Mon, Dec 4, 2006 at 9:10 PM

Shalom Cheryl,

Thank you for the prophecy info. Since the one about finding one of the Lost Tribes thrilled you, listen to this. We just saw a video that showed that they have found not only the one tribe living in India, but 10 tribes out of the 12, as well as the priests -the Cohain. The group in India, the Manashe (Manasseh) are the largest of them, so they have gotten the most attention. They all are as follows:

Name	Tribe	Location
Manashe	Manasseh	India; Burma
Falasha	Dan	Ethiopia
Issahar	Issachar	Bukhara, Uzbekistan
Naphtalites	Naphtali	Bukhara, Uzbekistan
Yuda	Judah, Manasseh	Kaifeng, China
Cohens	Levi	Carthage, Tunisia
Zavola (part of the B'nei Yisrael)	Zebulun	Bombay, India
Pathan	Reuben, Gad, Simeon, Ephraim	Afghanistan; Pakistan; Samarkand, and Uzbekistan (the sub-groups within the Pathan have retained their tribal names) (Note: Samarkand means "city of the Samarians")

They found these groups by studying their ancient writings detailing their travels after they left Assyria. All of these groups have retained their Jewish customs, and most have a desire to go to Israel. Obviously, we are much closer to the end than most people realize. "Lift up your heads, for your redemption draws near." God bless.

My Reply

Tue, Dec 5, 2006 at 10:27 PM

Wow!! That is amazing!! I'm blown away! Thank you so much for sending this to me. It gives you goose bumps, doesn't it? Exciting goose bumps!
Cheryl

Journal Nov. 30
He Will Suddenly Come

Malachi 3:1 See, I am sending My messenger to prepare the way before Me, and the Lord whom you seek will suddenly come to His Temple.

I asked the Lord for a word yesterday and then I opened my Bible and saw that verse!

It goes on to say: The messenger of the covenant in whom you delight—indeed He is coming, says the Lord of hosts.

In whom I delight!!!

But.....

Malachi 3:2-3 Who can endure the day of His coming,
and who can stand when He appears?
For he is like a refiner's fire and like fullers' soap;
He will sit as a refiner and purifier of silver,
and He will purify the descendants of Levi
and refine them like gold and silver
until they present offerings to the Lord
  in righteousness.

O Lord Jesus, please come to Your Temple. Please come suddenly! Please purify the sons of Levi—the natural sons of Levi. Purify them until they offer themselves as living sacrifices in righteousness—in the true righteousness of Your Blood.

O come, Lord Jesus, come. You didn't come with the earthquake that lady dreamed 4 times was coming on November 28 to Galilee—that her whole church was preparing for and kept their children out of school for. But please come! Please bring a great, sweeping revival to all the Jews and all the Arabs here, so You can come.

The Fear of Jewish Scholars

The Jewish leaders in control of the Torah and Tanakh interpretations are working so hard to make sure their people don't see Jesus/Yeshua in their Scriptures. Besides keeping Isaiah 53 out of the prayer books, a professor here who was raised a practicing Orthodox Jew said that in Psalms 22:16 the Hebrew word is "pierced" but it is very similar to "lion." So the Jewish scholars use the word "lion" because they are afraid that if they use the word "pierced" Jewish people will think it is talking about "Him."

We learned last summer that one Jewish woman in New York didn't believe her rabbis would keep any of the Scripture from her. She went home and looked in her prayer book and sure enough it went from Isaiah 52 to Isaiah 54. She became so angry with her rabbis that she left Judaism and promptly became a Believer in Yeshua.

Journal Dec. 1   Age of Scripture Texts

I just found out that the oldest Tanakh (Old Testament) texts besides the Dead Sea Scrolls are from 800 to 1000 AD. So they are from 1000 to 1200 years old. But the Dead Sea Scrolls are 2000 to 2200 years old! That's a whole thousand years older!!

> Ps 87:5-6 And of Zion it shall be said,
> "This one and that one were born in it";
> For the Most High Himself will establish it.
> The Lord records, as He registers the peoples,
> "This one was born there." Let this be so, too, Lord Jesus.

Journal Dec. 2

Muslim Chanting

You know, the way the Muslims pray/chant really can sound very beautiful. Maybe we should learn from them. It sounds like cries coming from the depths of their heart. Perhaps when we allow our own prayers to be so openly sincere like that, maybe then it will be our prayers being broadcast and not theirs.

Jewish Thought

O yes, I heard from the Psychology professor here that Jewish thought doesn't separate the heart and mind but the Greek thought does and this leads to much mental trouble. The Jewish New Testament Commentary by David Stearn talks about that, too. "In Western tradition a scholarly commentary does not discuss modern issues that have no obvious direct relationship to the Biblical text. By contrast, (Jews) seek them out since they see life as a seamless whole" (pp. xii-xiii).

(I just learned that there have been 50 some false messiahs in Jewish history!!)

How do we know if we are abiding in Jesus? By noticing that whatever we ask is being done for us: If you abide in Me and My Words abide in you, you will ask what you desire, and it shall be done for you. By this My Father will be glorified, that you bear much fruit and become My disciples (John 15:7-8).

The Complete Jewish Bible says in John 15:16: You did not choose Me, I chose you, and commissioned you to go and bear much fruit, fruit that will last, so that whatever you ask from the Father in My Name He may give you. I command you keep on loving each other.

Fruit seems to be connected with asking, receiving, and loving, and, of course, abiding.

Journal Dec. 5   The Stones Will Cry Out

...Even the stones will cry out... Luke 28:40 So, are the stones going to cry out?

Maybe they are already!!! The stones making up the buildings and the streets of the Old City are crying out so loud they are bringing pilgrims from all over the world!!

Guess What!

Mon, Dec 4, 2006 at 6:55 PM

Guess what! I ate strawberries from a strawberry tree on Sunday! Imagine that! They were round and small, more like a cherry-shape but rough and no pits!! They were lightly sweet and very good. And there were lots of them. The tree trunk is very red——a red-brown——and smooth——no bark. Quite interesting.

Isn't it funny! God knows I love strawberries, so He brought me to where they have strawberry trees!!!! Ahahahahahahahahaha! It makes me laugh inside with delight. God is always doing things for me that make me laugh!

Re: Guess What!
cHERYL;
   strawberrys do not grow on trees darling, they grow on bushes. Unless, grama, the israelys have invented a strawberry tree. in that case i want them to invent the money tree for me! God is so good to you. you get to exsperiance so much and Lord i want to be there also. cry---cry -- cry---tears tears tears and more tears. I LOVE YOU, GLENN

 ps you are to young and pretty to be a grama and so enough of that my princess. remember this certaint knight is looking for you with a passion never seen or heard before. BE READY AND PREPARED, YOUR KNIGHT

   [My husband was just learning to type with one finger. It shows how much he loved me that he would write to me even though typing each word took lots of time and great pains. That's why I left in what, to me, are endearing mistakes.]

Re: Re: Guess What!
   Exactly my thoughts!! I was thinking that next I will find a money tree!!! That's much more spectacular than a strawberry tree, right???!!!

   (Glenn and I talked about it more on the phone later. I said jokingly, "Since Jesus got money out of a fish, why not us get money off a tree?")

Re: Re: Guess what!   Wed, Dec 6, 2006 at 10:12 AM
INSTEAD OF GRABING MONEY FROM THE FISHES MOUTH JUST COMAND THE TREE TO PRODUCE HUNDRED DOLLAR BILLS, FOR IF WE HAVE FIATH WE CAN TELL THE MOUNTANS TO DIVE IN THE SEA. HA HA

Japanese Gift

From Journal: Dec. 9, 2006

You know what is so amazing?! On December 7, the very next day after Glenn sent me that e-mail, I met with a Japanese lady to give back her Master's thesis I had edited for her. She gave me a small gift and a Christmas card because I had refused to accept payment. After she left I told Charity, "I think she wants me to wait until Christmas to open this card, so I should wait." Normally I have no trouble waiting for things like that, but a few minutes later I said, "I can't wait" and I opened it. It was a beautiful Japanese card. As I opened the card,, out fell a hundred dollar bill! I was completely, totally shocked, flabbergasted, and amazed at the extravagant amount of money! I sat there wondering if I should accept it—wondering if I would offend her if I tried to return it, etc. I was so tired and sneezy, so I went to bed.

The next day I went to the computer room to read e-mail. I re-read Glenn's e-mails and I couldn't believe it!! Glenn could've just said a money tree. But no, he was very specific and said exactly what kind of money the tree gives fruit to—hundred dollar bills! She could've decide to give me much less or nothing, or she could've given it in two fifty dollar bills or five twenties. But no, she gave me a hundred dollar bill!

Jesus, You are soooo amazing! You make our life such a wonderful adventure with all these nice, wonderful surprises along the way!

Tue, Dec 5, 2006 at 10:13 PM

Mom, what are you doing for Christmas?
Melissa

Dear Melissa,

I don't get any days off of teaching for any holidays. The holidays are all on Sunday or Monday. I teach on Tuesday and Thursday. So I don't get any break. Poo! But I'm sure there will be a big meal cooked and we will celebrate somehow. I'm not really in charge of my life here. I just have to go with the flow.

Love you,
Mom

Road Safety, A Court Case, Life Sentence
Mon, Dec 4, 2006 at 12:27 AM

Hi Friends. Are You All Buried in Snow?

News

At prayer meeting tonight, we were told that the Jerusalem Post had all bad news headlines today about Lebanon, the Hizbullah, Iran, etc. Then in the corner it had another small headline that read, "IDF (the Israel military) expects 2007 to be a Year of War" They're saying that with the two recent assassinations in the Lebanese government the Hizbullah could take over in two weeks time. When that happens it will be "legal" (by UN resolution) for the Hizbullah to be in control of southern Lebanon since it will be the Lebanese government. So things could change really fast here.

A Supreme Court Case Here

A married couple is being denied citizenship purely because they are Messianic (Jewish) Believers. They both have lived here twenty years. Both of their sets of parents became citizens before that. The couple's children were born here. Two of their daughters are serving in the Israeli military right now. But the couple, as Jews, accepted Jesus as their Messiah, and now they are in jail—separate jails. They have been denied citizenship, and are awaiting the court's decision.

Rain

It hasn't rained here since the gay pride indoor rally. Up until then it was raining every weekend. Interesting, huh? Their "rainy" season isn't very rainy as it is. But now we haven't had a drop for about three weeks, I think it's been. (I haven't needed my miracle rain poncho yet.)

Safety

I tried to find the Wailing Wall last Thursday by following the main road through a very narrow mini tunnel/roof sort of thing. Cars move slowly through it. I heard something bigger than a car behind me. I looked. It was a van that was about as wide as the road, so I flattened myself against the wall. As it got closer I realized there wasn't going to be room for my head between the mirror and the wall. The van kept coming and didn't move over. I screamed and raced ahead out of the tunnel. When the driver passed me, he said (kindly), "Be careful!"

A similar tunnel

I found it curious and somewhat amusing that he made it seem like it was my fault——as if I should tell him sorry! Was he really going to crush my head??? I don't know! Welcome to Israel, I guess!

I finally discovered how to get to the Wall!! I made it far enough to see it from a distance, but didn't have time to go further. I can't wait to get all the way there next time.

Then I looked for and found a different way back to avoid head-crushing vehicles.

The Wailing Wall

Life Sentence

I found out that most Christians living here think it is like boot camp, because everything is so irritating, and because it is so unwelcoming to Christians. One Christian doctor said he and his wife feel like Jerusalem is a prison. When they hear people say they believe God has called them to come here, he and his wife wonder what "crime" they've done to deserve a life sentence in this prison.

I don't feel that way at all. I'm exhilarated to be here. I still get a thrill running through me when I realize anew that I'm living in Jerusalem. I say to myself, "Wow, I'm almost as old as my grandmother was when I was a kid, and I'm living in Jerusalem!!" My brain almost short circuits because it thinks grandmothers aren't supposed to do wild things like this. It thinks grandmothers are supposed to just stay home and be grandmothers!! This is an adventure beyond my imagination!

I have so much more I want to tell you, but it will have to wait. Oh, my Arabic student thanked me for the book. He said he liked it very much. Pray that the message is germinating.

Any of you would be so much more qualified to witness to him. I feel so unequipped for it. I have had so little success. I tell people about Jesus, but when it gets close to the point of them accepting, I seem to freeze up. I get the feeling I'm persuading them to do something against their will. It's so crazy stupid of me. I have grieved over it. And it has been my constant prayer to become better at it. Even now I feel all my inadequacies. But I pray God will either miraculously use me, or will bring someone else to him to help this man find complete joy in Jesus. So pray for him.

Finally All the Way to the Wailing Wall!!!

Tue, Dec 5, 2006 at 11:22 PM

The Wailing wall

Words cannot describe what I felt as I reverently approached the Wailing Wall today. My spirit was overwhelmed with a sense of awe. To be in the presence of a crowd of people praying in total reverence and complete silence just grips your soul. Many young adult girls were there with their little Hebrew prayer books opened in their hands, as they poured over them intently. Some had the books up to their faces to give themselves a bit of privacy in their praying. Those who could get to the wall were leaning their foreheads against it praying their hearts out desperately, yet silently. Some who weren't Orthodox leaned their arms on the Wall above their heads. Even many young soldier girls were there in uniform with their guns hanging from their shoulders praying and reading sincerely. Dozens of Grandmas were sitting in white plastic chairs scattered through the crowd facing the wall. Normally when you are in a crowd of people, it is noisy. That's why the silence stands out so much.

I've never been to any worship service that felt more worshipful than it felt there. God's presence felt heavy. And I sensed such a solemn spirit of urgency. At first I wondered if some tragedy had happened that I hadn't heard about. One young lady, I couldn't tell for sure which one, even started crying in a continuous low cry.

There was such a different feel there than last Christmas when we came. But back then Israel had been having relative peace. Plus they had high hopes that the security walls they were building were going to bring real peace.

Now they've just gone through a war and they know there is soon going to be more war. Those young soldier girls know they could be killed. The older women know they could lose sons or daughters or grandchildren. You could feel their desperation in their silent cries.

I looked up—way, way up—several stories up to the top of the wall and prayed, "Jesus please come. Please 'suddenly come to your Temple.'" I thought how marvelous it would be if He did suddenly set His Glorious, majestic feet on the top of that massive wall and looked down with tender love upon all of them—with love that these praying people could see with their physical eyes.

I could only stay there ten minutes. People were not moving. Most of the ones who were there when I arrived were still there when I left. My spirit was so touched, even in that short time, that my tears flowed and a sob welled up in my throat as I walked back. I said, "Jesus, your heart must be broken as you listen to them." In a way they are crying out to Jesus. They just don't know it is Jesus. They are praying to the God of Abraham and they are longing for their Messiah. But they don't know that that very Messiah is Yeshua (Jesus).

The last time Jesus spoke of Jerusalem, He was weeping over her. After being there today I'm thinking maybe He never stopped. Perhaps He is still weeping. Today I wept with Him.

In His sacred tears,
Cheryl

Journal Dec. 9 Narkis Street

I went to the Narkis Street church this morning. There are around 3 churches that meet in the building. The one that owns it is Baptist. Today there was a guy from India there who says he's a walking miracle—that 60% of his lungs are gone and doctors told him he would never play guitar again. He has designed the worlds only bongo-guitar. He did marvelous things with it playing Shout to the Lord. He played a very long introduction and then the song once through. It was beautiful and very interesting to watch. He says every day is a gift because he was not supposed to live.

That is still how I feel. In 1997 they thought I would die within two years. But here I am almost ten years later.

At the same meeting an African husband and wife with their toddler son lit the advent candle, and then she sang. She said doctors told her that she would never be able to have children and there she was with a little boy, age one, and very big pregnant with a new baby.

God is so awesome.

Movies in Heaven?

Father, I don't know why there has to be darkness or why Jesus has to wait so long to return, but is one reason so that there will be thousands upon millions of stories of people coming out of darkness into Your Light: so we will never run out of hearing stories—like watching movies—in heaven? Maybe that's why we like movies so much here on earth, because we will be watching them in heaven—only they will be of people's real lives and their real thoughts: and it will be the real truth: and we will be able to experience what it was really like to be inside their minds and bodies. Is that why, Father?

Another Dream

O yes, in my dream last night, somebody in the group I was involved with (I know none of them in real life) was pregnant. We showed people the swollen belly to prove the group was pregnant. At one point it seemed like I was the pregnant one, and while I was the baby moved. We were all shocked and knew then that the time was very near!!

No Rain

Sat, Dec 9, 2006 at 11:53 PM

It still hasn't rained here. It has been four weeks and more now, I believe. Everyone is getting concerned.

The sky has been clear blue every day, with not a speck of a cloud in it. On Wednesday I took a walk. Again the sun was blaringly bright in the expansive blue sky. It was hard to take good pictures in such glaring sunlight. As I turned to go home I glanced up to the sky again and to my astonished surprise there was a little cloud there—off in the distance! I thought, "Well, where did that come from?" It was just a wispy little thing. It looked so out of place. I hadn't seen a cloud in weeks.

My next thought was, "Is it going to rain?!" I realized then why Elijah (besides because he was a prophet) would think that one small cloud the size of a man's hand meant a storm was coming. When a normally cloudless sky suddenly has a cloud, it is an event. It seems like a miracle. It seems like it has to signify something. And Elijah hadn't seen a cloud for three years!

Sure enough, the very next morning (Thursday) the sky was completely clouded over with gray clouds and the air had the feel of the rain everyone was sure was coming! Even the weather man said it. I was sure I was going to get too wet if I tried to walk to the Wailing Wall. But lo and behold by noon the sun had driven all the clouds away and it didn't rain a drop!!

They predicted rain on Friday, too. But it hasn't rained, not since the gay pride indoor rally and small parade.

So, please pray for rain for Jerusalem. Pray for God's mercy that He will send rain.

Praying for Israel

Tonight at church an Israeli young adult girl prayed for Israel. She was the picture of a typical Jewish girl: dark skin, curly, long, black hair, gorgeous face. She's a Messianic Jew. She prayed in Hebrew, of course, with someone translating into English. It was the most beautiful, heartfelt prayer. How touching it was to hear one of God's chosen pray for her own people and her own country. She read from Ephesians about the one new man. Then she prayed for the descendants of Ishmael as well as for her own people, "both a broken people" were her words. She called them "our older brother." She prayed for the wall between them to come down and they become the one new man.

Is this not a new day, that in Jerusalem a Jewish girl who knows Jesus is leading a whole congregation in praying for the salvation of all Israel? To me it is the beginning. To me it is that small cloud in the sky which means the desired storm is coming! Praise the Lord!

Let it rain!
Cheryl

Journal Dec. 10 For Those Who Mourn in Zion

At the service last night they sang a beautiful song in Hebrew that quoted Isaiah 61:1-4

Verse 3: To provide for those who mourn in Zion
to give them a crown of beauty instead of ashes.

To PROVIDE for those who mourn in Zion.

The Lord will provide!

Please provide, Lord. Please provide for all the people You have called to come and mourn in Zion. You have called so many people to come here just to mourn and pray. You are still calling more people. Please provide for them, Yeshua.

Please provide for Glenn and I, too. We also feel called for that same reason. Please provide so we can spend more time just listening to You to know how to pray for Israel and Jerusalem.

And Yeshua/Jesus, I pray again to be delivered from the spirit of fear of evangelism. Last night I saw the Koreans singing, "The Love of God" on Ben Yehuda Street. One of the two playing guitar was from my advanced conversation class. I rejoiced inside that they were singing there. They sounded so beautiful. I admire them so much, but shyness and fear gripped my heart. Then I felt so convicted.

Something is wrong with me!! Please deliver me, Jesus. Heal me of this fear and rescue me from the lies from the enemy that are blocking me from being more evangelistic. Cleanse me. Wash me with Your Blood. Cleanse away the clumsiness of my personality. Heal me of my personality handicap. But Your will be done. Just keep me near You, Jesus. Bring me closer and closer to You.

O Lord Jesus, let there be more evangelism on the streets of Jerusalem. O Yeshua, call more people, equip more people with the gift of evangelism. Use them to bring revival. Call them, equip them, send them.

Bless the Koreans, Lord. Bless them for singing. Bless them for glorifying You. It is part of my answer to prayer that praises and prayers to You be heard in Israel and Jerusalem instead of the prayers and chants to allah.

The Best News and the Worst Kind of News
Sun, Dec 10, 2006 at 10:23 PM

Dear Praying People,

This is about the beginning of an awesome answer to prayer and then a serious prayer need for someone else.

I finally got up the courage last week to go visit the church, King of Kings, here in Jerusalem. I had to go by myself and find the place. That's why I needed courage. I found the right building, but I got there early, so I decided to just have a look around the street outside. Then I decided to explore a different part of the tall building before going into the section where the church is. A guard had to check my bag first. (That is the way it is here at any grocery or department store.) The building looks impressive on the outside. It is a sky scraper, one of only a few in Jerusalem. But when I got inside, I felt like I had jumped back fifty years. It is an old, dingy, dirty place, with dull, grimy floors and unimpressive open stairs. It's supposed to be kind of like a mall. But there are very few shops. Most of it is just dark, closed doors and vacant space.

Before I went back outside to go into the correct door to get to the church, I ventured down to the basement to take a look and soon found myself facing a large opening to a fabulous place with nice, shiny floors. It was such a shocking contrast to the rest of the building, it seemed like I had entered Alice's Wonderland or something. There was a guard at the door, and inside the double doors, well-dressed people were greeting the guests and it seemed like they were checking out their names to make sure they were authorized to enter. I thought it was some fancy ballroom or a high class hotel or elite conference area. I said to myself, "I definitely don't belong there!" and started turning around to high tail out of there. Then my eye caught the name of the place. Lo and behold, it was the church!! I had come in the correct door of the sky scraper after all. The greeters weren't taking names they were just greeting people.

The church has a huge, beautiful auditorium, and it was full.

Prayer Tower

After their very worship-filled service, I took a tour of their Pavilion Prayer Tower. The tour guide was one of the founders we'll call Clay. (He and his wife are in charge of the "Israel Prayer Watch.") This prayer tower is something awesome God is doing in Jerusalem. You can go to their two websites and click on a tour of it for yourself.

kkjc.org and pavilionprayertower.org

The Best News

One of their prayer watches focuses especially on the Ultra Orthodox community which is just blocks away from their tower. The Orthodox held a protest when the King of Kings church opened, I heard. But Clay said that recently an Ultra Orthodox man came to one of their prayer meetings. After being welcomed, he came in, sat down, and respectfully watched them as they prayed. Clay was so overcome with emotions of joy that he went to the other side of the room with his back to the Orthodox man and wept saying, "God, how can it be you brought one of them right here to our room?!" The man only stayed five minutes but he seemed to have a favorable attitude. Since then there have been others who have visited. One time two guys came, but each was surprised to see the other one! Clay says their hearts seemed to be open!

Isn't that just awesomely amazing?!!! Praise the Lord Almighty! Hallelujah!! If the Orthodox come to know Yeshua, then the rest of Israel will follow like a wave, I would think!

Someone told me that one lady does prayer-walking in the Orthodox community. I would very much like to do that. The Orthodox are very much on my heart.

On December 21 the King of Kings is hosting a concert of all the new, latest Messianic Jewish music. They expect to be packed. In January their young adult group, Deepend, is taking a worship tour called One Song (Sheel Echad) all around Israel. They plan to take their music into clubs and all the most sinful places to reach their generation with the LIGHT. So please pray for them!

The Awful News

(This isn't about Israel.) Friends of mine from my childhood church just lost a tiny grandson. He's the youngest of three boys, ages 3 ½, 2 and he was nine months. Yesterday, while his mother was vacuuming he pulled something heavy on himself. By the time she found him he was blue. The ER team after an hour revived him. They medi-vaced him, but this morning he passed away.

Another of my friends, a friend of the family, writes: She is a wonderful mother, who, of course, is now blaming herself. Please pray for the whole family.

I want to pray for resurrection of the baby. What have we got to lose? We certainly won't get it if we don't ask!

Dear Jesus, Yeshua Ha Mashiach, Savior of the world, Son of Man, full of compassion, You looked with compassion upon the widow who lost her son. You were often moved with compassion. Please, Jesus, be moved with compassion for this young mother. And like you did for the widow, give her back her son. I pray for Your resurrection power to enter into his body and revive him completely whole and healthy. Please Jesus, so many mothers today don't want their babies and kill them. This mother wanted her baby. This mother was caring for her little ones with love. Please don't let her suffer this loss any longer. Don't let her suffer guilt any more. Comfort her. Touch her. Give her what her heart is ripping apart in horrific pain for. Spare her, Jesus. Have mercy and compassion on her. We beg you, Jesus. We cry out to You, Jesus. Make your LIFE Power flow into that tiny body. Let the funeral service turn "from mourning into dancing." For Your Honor and Glory. In Your Awesome, Holy Powerful Name I pray. Amen

Re: The Best News and the Worst Kind of News   Wed, Dec 13, 2006 at 10:55 PM

Oh Cheryl I stand with you in your prayer for resurrection life to enter this little one. Cheryl, You are growing so much in Christ!!! Isn't He wonderful!!! And you are right in the center of where all history revolves around. The Nation of Israel.....Oh Lord we ask for the Nations!!!! We ask for you to bring the Israelites to a knowledge of Jesus Christ, their true Messiah!!!! Use your servant, Cheryl, for your glory there in the land of Israel!!! Holy Spirit fall upon her and anoint her with all that You are!!!!!!!!!!!!!! In His lovely name, Lis

Journal Dec. 12   Now I Bring to Pass

Last night, at the prayer meeting for Israel, and again this morning, I was praying Jer. 23:22, namely, for people to "stand in God's counsel" (listening to God's counsel) and council (God's council where His decisions are made) so they can bring His Word that will "turn His people from their wicked ways."

I didn't have much time for devotions this morning, so I asked for a quick Word. I opened to Isaiah 37 and saw verse 26.

Have you not heard that I determined it long ago?
I planned from days of old what now I bring to pass

It seems like it is God telling me that He is bringing Jer. 23:22 to pass! He's going to bring His Word through prophets who have been standing in His council, that will turn His people from the evil of their doings.

Hallelujah! Hallelujah!

Distractions to Praying at the Wailing Wall

Tue, Dec 12, 2006 at 11:24 PM

Nice lady begging

Dear Loved Ones,

Going to the Wailing Wall proves again to be interesting.

It was quite a different experience today. First you have to get past the beggars. Yes, there are beggars there just like in Peter and John's day. Actually there are beggars scattered all over Jerusalem. Some of them are in the same spot every day. My friend says that when she comes back to Jerusalem after being away, the beggars are the first people she recognizes. I told you about the elderly lady wearing dingy clothes and sneakers who sat on a sidewalk near the YMCA. She was very grateful when I gave her something. Some of them don't act grateful. They just beg you to give them more. One guy near the Wailing Wall today actually told me how much to give him for "his baby who has Leukemia." Many of them have heart-wrenching stories. One of my friends asked one healthy, well-fed lady beggar to show her where she lived. She wanted to see if her story proved true. She also gave the beggar phone numbers of places where she could get help. Then before she left she gave her a not-so-small amount of money. But you won't believe what the beggar did. Instead of being thankful, she happened to see that my friend had more money in her purse, so she demanded that money also. Isn't that shocking?

As you can see, beggars here are not the most polite people. Some are aggressive and ungrateful. They hound you and some are actually deceiving you. Because of that I have not had a very good attitude toward them, also because I know there are plenty of places where they could go to get proper help. But one of my Korean students in his very broken English told me that whether or not they are telling the truth, whether or not they are true beggars; that it is not for us to judge. We should still give to them. I felt chastised by the Lord, and have since started giving.

So, now as I approach the Wall, I pray about it in advance. I get my money out of my purse ahead of time and keep it in my pocket, or as today, in my glove, ready to give to them quickly as I pass them by. Thus, I make it past that hurdle. That was the first distraction to getting into a worshipful mood. The second distraction was the very LOUD sound of a huge, crane-sized jack hammer blasting away behind us across the plaza. I could tell it was distracting everyone from entering into the sacred realm of prayer. The whole atmosphere was a little more casual than before. I thought how similar it is for all of us at times trying to have quiet prayer time with God. There can be so many things hindering us even before we get there and other things distracting us from focusing on Him when we do get there.

When I got to the front, though, and leaned my head against the giant stones, I sensed the Lord's presence and communion with me. Yes, I can get close to the Lord anywhere. I don't have to be at the Wall. But there is something so special about touching the same foundation stones that were there when He walked this earth. Perhaps I'm touching the same place where His human hand touched once. There just seems to be instant connection and communion with Him there.

Still, the hammering and pounding distracted me. Then this grateful thought hit me. I prayed, "Thank you, Jesus, that it is not the sound of guns, or of bombs."

I was able then to enter in and pray as if I was all alone until I sensed some commotion beside me and heard a slight giggle. I looked and saw three young, 12 or 13-year-old girls trying to stick little folded slips of colored prayers into the Wall. But the Wall is so full of paper prayers that tons of fallen ones litter the ground. Every crevice and crack is chock full. Yet the girls kept trying. One girl persisted, pressing hard on her orange note squishing and forcing it into different little indentations in the stone, only to have the wad fall out again.

Notice the paper prayers in the cracks.

As I watched, I asked the Lord to answer their prayers.

I prayed as long as I dared, time wise, and then headed back, giving my last coins to another beggar on my way out. I went out past the metal detectors, up the big stairs, and was heading toward the road that runs just inside the city wall when a guard yelled at me in Hebrew. He motioned me to go back into the plaza. I said, "But I'm going this way." He insisted in Hebrew that I go back. He kept yelling, "El a montay. El a montay." (Or something like that.)

I looked and saw other guards corralling other people down to the bottom of the stairs into what looked like a corner. I thought, "Oh, they think I'm part of a certain tour group." But then I noticed they were stopping everyone who was coming out of the Wall plaza. I tried to ask the guards in English what was happening, but they were too busy to pay attention. I thought, "They must suspect someone who was in the plaza of something, and they are going to question all of us and search all our bags, etc, and I will be late for class. My students will wonder where their teacher is. But, oh well, what can I do about it?" I set my mind to be ready for a long wait.

People were hollering Hebrew questions up to the guard above us. He answered in Hebrew. After several attempts, I finally found someone who spoke English, although with a very heavy accent. They told me the guard said there is something that looks like a bomb in a car!! Oh my!

Slowly people started moving off in the opposite direction. That's when I noticed that we weren't in a corner after all, but were on a walkway that led to a gate. (The Dung Gate, I later learned.) We had to go outside the city walls to leave. So I went out the gate. To avoid taking a much longer route by the street, I walked to class up a steep, rugged footpath that runs next to the wall. I listened the whole way, but fortunately didn't hear any explosion. So, either it wasn't a bomb, or they dismantled it safely.

Later I thought how ironic it was that this happened right after I had thanked the Lord the hammering wasn't the sound of guns or bombs!

Just another day in Israel. ☺

God is Good.
Blessings to you all. May you not be distracted from praying,
Cheryl

Re: Distractions to Praying at the Wailing Wall   Wed, Dec 13, 2006 at 10:52 AM
Greetings Cheryl,

Sounds like there's never a dull moment in your days. Thanks for doing such a good job of writing. It's hard to imagine being in your shoes. You do have good walking shoes, I hope.

So, it's December 13 and I haven't heard you mention anything about coming home for the holidays. Do you plan to be in the states soon, with family, renewing your visa, maybe taking Glenn back with you?

.Blessings to you
May God's ministering and protecting angels guard your coming in and going out,
Rhonda

Hi Rhonda,

It's interesting that you mentioned shoes. I was thinking of mentioning the condition of my shoes soon! (See p. 94.) Yes, I have good walking shoes, but they are wearing out. Fortunately I brought another pair.

Our praise report is that Glenn is coming on Dec. 23. I have an appointment to get a long term visa in January, so I don't have to go out of the country. So Glenn and I will be together here in Israel for Christmas. What a nice Christmas present for us both!!!

Journal Dec. 15 Praying at the Prayer Tower

They are telling me this is the first day of Hanukkah.

I went to the Prayer Tower to pray instead of going to the Wailing Wall. I went out on the balcony and looked out toward the Mea Sharim (Ultra Orthodox) neighborhood as I prayed. I had to lean my head out, looking to the right to barely see the Old City. The Prayer Tower is closer for me to walk to, but I didn't feel as anointed to pray there, so I think the Lord wants me to pray at the Wailing Wall.

He Feeds Us

The other day I was pondering the parable where the Master will have the servants sit and He will serve them (Luke 12:37). Then I meditated on Rev. 3:20, "Behold I stand at the door.... I will come in and sup with them." Then I had the thought that Jesus does serve us. He feeds us His awesome Word every day. He already has us sit and He feeds us!

Glenn is coming December 23!!!

Journal Dec. 17   Wait in Jerusalem

Here's what sticks in my mind from my reading today. "Wait in Jerusalem until you are clothed with power from on high "(Lk. 24:49)

I'm waiting, Jesus. Glenn will be here next week. We will wait together.

East Gate

The tourist book says the East Gate, also called The Golden Gate, was sealed up by the Muslims in the 600's AD. Ezek. 44:1-3 says it will be shut and "shall remain shut." (!!!) Ezekiel lived a few hundred years BC! He predicted it almost a 1000 years ahead of time!

Appointed Time

Matt. 8:29 (CJB) The demons screamed, "What do you want with us, Son of God? Have you come here to torture us before the appointed time?"

So, it is an Appointed Time when Jesus will come. (In the Hebrew Torah, the Biblical Feasts are called "Appointed Times.")

In Ezekiel 40, the Feast of Yom Kippur is missing. Thus, the Feast of Trumpets (Rosh Hashanah) and of the Tabernacles (Sukkoth) are the only ones left to be fulfilled. (Yeshua and the Holy Spirit fulfilled all the others exactly on the day and the moment.)

Who knows what year Jesus will come to fulfill the Feast of Trumpets? No one knows. The demons seemed to have an idea, but maybe they are wrong, because "only the Father knows."

O Jesus, help us to be alert and awake so this time does not come upon us like a thief in the night.

The Lord knows what is in the darkness (Dan. 2:20).   So we don't need to search out or study any dark things. God knows what is in them and we know God and He knows us. And He reveals His secrets to (confides in) those who fear Him (Ps. 25:14 NIV).

"I will bless the Lord," David says in Psalms 145 and 146. How do we bless the Lord? He is the One who blesses us!!

How may I bless You, Lord??? You rejoiced in the Holy Spirit in Luke 10:21 when the disciples You sent out reported that they did what You told them to do. They preached, healed, and cast out demons.

May I bless You by doing what You have sent me to do.

THANK YOU, JESUS *for providing for Glenn!! Thank You! Thank You! Thank You! Thank You that he will be able to finish his classes here and get his degree! Thank You that he sold the truck so he could buy the ticket!*

Praise Your Name!

Thank you for all you will do through us here in Jerusalem. Help us to be one with You, Yeshua! Clothe us with power from on high as we wait for You here in Jerusalem.

The Lord Provides

Mon, Dec 18 at 11:27 PM

Hello Lovely Friends,

God has worked an awesome miracle. Glenn got permission to finish his degree independently. So, he is coming here to Israel in time for Christmas!! I'm so excited!! It took awhile for me to believe it was real! (It turned out that he never had time to study.)

Another blessing, I have an appointment in January to get a one year visa. They are getting one for me through the University. So, praise the Lord!!!

Now we are trusting the Lord to provide for Glenn while he is here. Please pray with us. We trust the Lord to provide for us both to stay here as long as the Lord wants us here, to do what the Lord wants us to do. We feel so honored and privileged and richly blessed to be able to be here at all. So we are grateful for however long the Lord provides.

It is cold in this house. Our heat is controlled by other people who hardly ever turn it on. That's just how it is here. So I have been frozen to the bone and have been worn out with sneezing on some days. One volunteer insisted I take his personal electric heater. He wouldn't take no for an answer. So now I am getting better. Praise the Lord. And Glenn is going to bring me more warm clothes! I didn't know I would need them in a warm, desert country!

I have so much to tell you but it will have to wait. I finally met the owner of the museum/zoo/Thomas Kinkaid house. It was so wonderful listening to the prayer burdens for Israel that are on his heart, and to hear him read Scripture and pray. He has a soothing, deep voice with a British accent, and his choice of words are inspiring. It's probably what it would have been like to listen to C.S. Lewis.

I got to go to Qumran and watch an archeology dig! How amazing to get to go to famous places I've only seen in pictures before. (See photos below.) Thank you, Lord!!

Still loving the adventure!
Cheryl

Mon, Dec 18, 2006 at 8:58 PM
RE: The Lord Provides!

Cheryl,
What an awesome answer to prayer!! God was building your faith in all that. I was worried he would have a partial degree again, but God is so awesome!!
I will pray you warm for the next week before Glenn arrives with warm clothes (if his suitcase gets searched, how is he going to explain all the women's clothes—I'd love to be a fly on the wall...not that I expect him to have trouble—it would just be funny).
Your sister,
Jenny

Tue, Dec 19, 2006 at 4:18 PM

You're right that would be funny. I laughed out loud thinking about it! Poor Glenn. What a guy will do for love!!

Looking toward the Dead Sea from near the caves

The two main caves where the Dead Sea Scrolls were found

3.
PRAYING, GETTING ANSWERS AND NEW INSIGHTS

Important Things to Pray for Israel

Wailing Wall on Hanukkah

The Old City was very full and busy today. The street was packed with honking cars; the sidewalks with a mix of hurrying people and sauntering families, many of whom were lost, saying things like, "This isn't the way we came in, is it?" I chuckled inwardly, remembering the fun we had as lost tourists in the confusing maze this Old City is.

At first I wondered why the crowds, then I remembered that this is Hanukkah vacation. All Jewish schools are closed for a whole week. So, besides the growing international Christmas crowd, the Israeli nationals are visiting the Wailing Wall, too.

Around every corner I also met large units of soldiers always heading somewhere quickly. I guess they don't get a holiday. One was obviously a group of novices. Instead of green they were wearing light brown, and they had no weapons—yet. The soldiers don't march in formation here and they don't stay separate from the public. So, several times I ended up right in the middle of them, loaded guns and all. How does a person get used to that? I can't.

There was no giant jack hammer at the Wall today, but with the milling crowd with children in tow, it wasn't quiet. Again, there was a young lady on one side of me wailing very audibly. And on the other side of me came a wheelchair bearing a wisp of a withered grandmother whose granddaughter began to loudly recite prayers for her. It must have been her dying wish to come to the Wall, because she looked very close to death's door. I prayed for Jesus to reveal Himself to her. I also saw two India women dressed in the beautiful, full, traditional sari.

With all the commotion the Spirit was still there. Even though I was being bumped and jostled, I was able to commune with the Lord.

South Side Looks Trashy   This paragraph added later from memory
I left the Wall in the new direction I had discovered when they had suspected a car bomb. I had enough time to go slow and take in the sights around me. I looked out across the archeological garden on the south end of the Temple still inside the city wall. It looked a little unkempt and trashy which surprised me. It hadn't looked that way when we visited a year ago. I walked out Dung Gate again, but instead of turning right to go to class, I sauntered to the left to have a look at the south end of the Temple. Again, I was dismayed at how neglected and trashed it was. There were many tour buses parked along the street, with the bored drivers waiting for the return of their Hanukkah tourists. When I came around a bend, I happened upon one driver just finishing relieving himself under a tree. This further disheartened me. His actions and the garbage thrown over the fence show how little regard anyone seems to have for this area where the former Temple of the Living God stood! This is where throngs used to walk to get to the south entrances of the Temple. Where's the reverence? Where's the respect and awe?

Shoes and Feet
With all my walking, the soles of my shoes are wearing thin. There is no tread left. I don't think that has ever happened to me since I was a child! I usually can wear the same ones for years! It's a good thing I brought another pair with me.

Speaking of walking a lot. In Africa, in 2005, a group of us walked for an hour up a steep mountain to visit an AIDS patient——a mother of three——in her tiny hut. Going back down the hill, my big toes hit the front of my shoes so much that the toe nails got bruised and misshapen.

The missionary lady told me afterwards

An African mother with AIDS who already lost her husband and a baby to AIDS

that she actually lost her toenails that way. Well, I didn't lose mine, but they are only now finally starting to look normal again. This all can make you think of the verse, "*How beautiful are the feet of him who brings good news*" (Isaiah 52:7). I'm not doing that much of bringing the Good News. But many others are, and they are doing it mostly on foot. Their feet may not look so great, but to God they are beautiful. So, when God places a missionary's name on your heart, you might want to add a prayer for their feet and shoes.

In the hut, we prayed for the mother and brought her a new supply of the nutritious porridge that was improving her health. She now felt well enough to get out of bed and sit in the sun for awhile each day (as you see in the above picture).

Political Situation

One Messianic pastor here said, "All the smartest people in the world can't figure out what to do about the situation here in the Middle East." It's true, isn't it?

Another person said, "The UN has spent more time on the Jewish state than any other issue since 1948 (when Israel became a nation)."

The owner of the museum-house, talked at length about the situation here. He thinks that in three months time there will be serious trouble. We prayed and prayed about it in his house which is not far from where Ohmert and Blaire were meeting that night.

Our prayer leader has been an adult for much of Israel's history as a nation. He told us about England's plan of trying to set up a tiny Israel city-state in 1936 which God thwarted; then about the UN proposal in 1948, which the Arabs opposed, which started the war that brought Israel's independence, etc. He pointed out how all these plans of men—including today's "Road Map for Peace"—have been, and are being, brought to nothing. Through it all, he has been leading people to pray the Biblical prophecies over Israel. Through it all, he has seen God take control. He has experienced the power of praying God's Word.

He has also been around. He knows a close childhood friend of James Baker's. And he has met and preached to two sisters of Jimmy Carter. Isn't it interesting? A friend of his, a Holocaust survivor, who has been in the Israeli government says that the situation today is just like it was prior to the Holocaust. He thinks a holocaust is fast approaching, and the world is ignoring it just as they did then. This prayer leader said the results of the midterm elections make him think America may lose its super-power status soon.

People here who are not American who recently visited America are saying they can't believe the heavy anti-Christian atmosphere there.

If there would be a true revival of repentance in America, I'm sure we would not lose our super status. So let's pray, pray, pray.

Abortion

One thing that the U.S. needs repentance from is all the abortions. We all know that. But did you know that Israel does, too?!! I didn't. I was shocked to read in a brochure I got from the Prayer Tower church, King of Kings, that there are 20,000 abortions performed in Israel every year! I am so shocked because I know that the Jews say when you murder a man you are not just murdering him you are murdering all the off-spring he would have had. So how can they think it is okay to take a baby's life? But I have to come to grips with the reality that there are completely secular, non-religious Jews. The pamphlet even said that Israeli female soldiers are given two free abortions each, if needed. I just want to cry and cry.

King of Kings is trying to do something about it. Besides pregnancy centers and ministry to post-abortion girls, they are holding education campaigns for school children with the government's permission!

The brochure says that several people have received a vision that there is a curtain of blood holding back the salvation of Israel. The same curtain is in America!

Original Sin

I learned another startling thing about Jewish thought. Jewish people—even very religious Jewish people—don't see themselves as sinful, but only with an "evil inclination" "...*for the inclination of the human heart is evil from youth*" (Gen. 8:21). *"The Lord saw that ... every inclination of the thoughts of their heart was only evil continually"* (Gen. 6:5). They believe they can overcome it by studying the Torah and obeying all the laws, etc. *"Adonai said to Kayin* (Cain), *'...sin is crouching at the door... but you can rule over it'"* (Gen. 4:6-7 CJB).

> Here's a quote from a Jewish writer, Trude Weiss-Rosmarin: "The Jew rejoices when he can prove his ethical mettle in the unaided battle against the temptation of sin.... The Jew is taught to regard himself always and ever as stronger than sin and the power that draws him to it.... It is a challenge to be exhilaratingly overcome.... whereas the Christian regards sin as an inescapable fate from which the only deliverance is...passive...by a Savior" (Complete Jewish Bible Commentary, p. 368-369).

[It's no wonder Jesus told the parable about the law-breaking sinners and the law-keeping sinners—the Prodigal Son story. (See p. 52.)

The books I'm helping with here are all about the Dead Sea Scrolls. What I am learning is absolutely earth-shatteringly amazing. Here's just one bit of it.

Much of the focus of the Qumran community (the ones who hid the Dead Sea Scrolls) was on apocryphal texts. One such text was the *Book of Enoch*. This book had been lost to the world since the first century or so after Jesus—nearly 2000 years. Both the church and the Jewish community banned it and removed all traces of it. One of the only ways anyone knew it existed was because of Jude mentioning Enoch's prophecy. (They also banned other apocryphal literature.)

Well, in the 1800's someone discovered that the Ethiopian Jews had a copy of *Enoch*. Then a copy was found in an archeological site of an ancient Jewish community in Cairo (where one of the true priests had fled and set up a temple). And then even earlier copies were found at Qumran.

Why is that significant? Well, besides what it could mean about how close we are to the End Times, the *Book of Enoch* and another scroll, *4 Ezra*, point to Jesus, to our sinfulness and to our need for a Savior. *4 Ezra* sounds a lot like Apostle Paul in Romans saying that everyone has sinned. Enoch talks about the "Son of Man," saying things that describe the Messiah! Scholars believe that the *Book of Enoch* was a well-known book in Jesus' time. And it seems like Jesus even quoted from it! If it *was* popular, then people would have known that Jesus was the Messiah because what they had read in *Enoch*, they were seeing in Jesus and hearing Him say.

These books point clearly to Jesus, which might be why the Jewish leaders expunged them. God made sure they were widely known right before Jesus' first coming, so people would recognize Him. Now He is miraculously bringing them to the world once again after they were gone for almost 2000 years. Why? I believe it is so the Jewish people and the whole world will again recognize who Jesus is, and will be ready for His Second Coming—which would mean the End Times are very close!!

The English translations of the Dead Sea Scrolls were published in the 1990's and are just starting to be known. So the Jewish people will discover that their own leaders taught them that they are sinful. They will realize that it is their sin along with ours that "pierced" Jesus, the Messiah, and they will "look upon" Him with the new eyes of people who now know they cannot conquer sin—as ones who do desperately need a Savior.

Doesn't it make your spine tremble?

How the Jews see Jesus' Name

The Jewish people don't use Jesus' correct Hebrew Name which is "Yeshua." They use "Yeshu."

"Yeshua" means "salvation" in Hebrew, even in modern Hebrew.

As soon as any Hebrew speaking person hears the name, Yeshua, they know it means salvation. The meaning is very clear. And to Jewish people the meaning of a person's name is of utmost importance.

"Yeshu" is an acronym meaning, "May his memory be erased."

All Jews use this awful name for Jesus. They've all heard it from little up. (In fact, a friend who is taking Hebrew here said the teacher asked what the word "Messiah" means. A Christian student said it means, "Yeshua." She corrected him right away, saying His name is "Yeshu" and, of course, that the student's answer was incorrect.) Not all Jews know about the meaning of the acronym. But the Jewish leaders over the centuries have been repulsed at calling Jesus, "Salvation," so for a long, long time they have taught their people to call him "Yeshu."

Here's a quote from Answers.com:

"There is some debate over the meaning of "Yeshu." It has been used as an acronym for the Hebrew expression yemach shemo vezichro, meaning "May his name and memory be obliterated", a term used for those guilty of enticing Jews to idolatry and used in place of the real names of individuals guilty of such sins who are deemed not worthy of being remembered in history. Some argue that this has always been its meaning. Indeed the name does not correspond to any known Hebrew root and moreover no other individuals have ever borne this name in Jewish history..."

This is one reason the Jewish people don't recognize Jesus for who He is!

I am telling you this, because I want to tell you some great news. At the church service last Saturday night, a Jewish college student, the same Jewish girl who prayed the wonderful prayer for Israel, gave this report. The Christian college student association of all Israel colleges (which I guess is quite large) has presented a petition to all the college administrations to quit using the name Yeshu for Jesus on all their literature and documents and to change them all to Yeshua. She says they think the colleges WILL do what they are asking!

Won't that be a miracle? Join me in praying for that to happen.

So much to pray for. That's why God needs so many praying people.

Watching the End Times unfold,
Cheryl

P.S The couple I work for here are going to be on your TV! CNN and ABC!!! I can't believe I am connected with such famous people! The wife is so humble. She says it is all because of location. They are a very nice family to be working for. The Lord is good.

Merry Christmas!!!

Journal Dec. 22 Egypt, Syria, Israel

I sent my daughter a long e-mail full of funny quotes about shopping in Israel for her birthday on the 20th. I hope it made her laugh and laugh. My gift to her was laughter. That's a nice gift, isn't it? (I don't have money for anything else.)

The other day while I was combing my hair I was thinking about the prophecy in Isaiah 19:18-25 about Egypt, Syria, and Israel being a highway together of praise to God and a light to the world. I was also remembering Derek's vision about that and praying while I combed that it all come to pass. Then I was thinking about the synagogue in Cairo, started by the true priest who fled there, and that they found an ancient Essenes' Damascus document there; and how the Essenes were in Damascus in Syria before they moved to Qumran and some of their ancient documents have been found there in Syria. Then I thought about how the Dead Sea Scrolls found in Qumran link all these together. Suddenly it hit me that those three places are in Egypt, Syria and Israel!!! My mouth dropped open. I looked up and just stared at myself stunned. I was in so much shock I couldn't even close my mouth! So I just stared in the mirror at my weird, gaping-mouthed self! Isn't that funny?

So the three places are already connected through the whole Dead Sea Scroll findings. It's so awesome! The Dead Sea Scrolls and the Essenes are pointing to God, praising God, and pointing to Yeshua as the Messiah. So, perhaps soon all three countries will begin to believe and worship God together. AND it could be helped by the books Charity and I are working on!!

How Long, Lord?

Psalms 74 is a Maskil of Asaph. Asaph lived when David lived. He was in charge of the singers, if it is the same Asaph. If it is, then the whole psalm is prophetic. It is either about when Babylon or Rome destroyed the Temple. Well, verse 9 makes it clear that it is about Rome because in the time of the Babylonian captivity there was a prophet who knew how long—Jeremiah!! He prophesied exactly how long it would be—70 years!

Psalms 74 is asking the very same question I've been asking God.

> Psalms 74:9 We do not see our emblems;
> there is no longer any prophet
> and there is no one among us who knows how long.
>
> How long, O God, is the foe to scoff?
> Why do You hold back Your hand?
>
> Verse 18 Remember this, O Lord, how the enemy scoffs,
> and an impious people reviles Your Name.
> Do not deliver the soul of Your Dove to the wild animals.
> Do not forget the life of Your poor forever.
> Have regard for Your Covenant,
> for the dark places of the Land are full of haunts of violence.
>
> Rise up O God, plead Your cause
> Remember how the impious scoff at You all day long.

Do not forget the clamor of Your foes,
the uproar of Your adversaries that goes up continually.

This Scripture is so true! The "dark places" of Israel are "full of haunts of violence"! It has been true here in Israel for a long, long time. Right now there is fighting among the Palestinians in Gaza. The Hamas and Fatah are killing each other!!!

(And there was something on the news about eight U.S. soldiers murdering Iraqis!! I don't know if the truth is being twisted again or if we really do have some awful people again for soldiers!! Insurgents in Iraq on the news were deploring the fact that they are not united against the America "for all its atrocities like this." The Iraqis are also killing each other!!)

It Finally Rained, Then it Snowed!!

Thu, Dec 28, 2006 at 11:08 PM

Glenn's Arrival and Rain

Thank you so much for all your prayers. So many wonderful and interesting things are happening. I know it is due to all the prayers.

First of all, thank you for praying for Glenn. He got here safe and sound—and happy! And thank you for praying for rain! God answered your prayers abundantly!

And thank you for praying for me to be warm. The last three days before Glenn arrived it was exceptionally warm. (Just like you prayed, Jenny!) Two days before Glenn arrived we finally got a few drops of rain, but it was just a sprinkling. The next morning everyone was telling me we got a real downpour. They wondered why I didn't hear it. I looked outside and said, "But there aren't any puddles. It couldn't have rained that much." They said the ground soaks it right up. But later I went outside and saw that it was dry under the trees. . The trees here aren't anything like our big maples and oaks at home. They are short, squatty olives, figs, and almonds, etc. It wouldn't take much rain to soak through them. Then I knew that my fellow volunteers had been teasing me. (They like to tease me because I almost always fall for it. ☺)

The day Glenn was supposed to arrive (last Saturday), we finally got a real, soaking rain. The first time I had to use my miracle rain poncho was while I was waiting to be picked up by the airport shuttle to go meet Glenn. It rained pretty hard all the way to the airport. It kept on raining all day and night. So, I told Glenn he brought the rain to Israel. ☺

On my way to the airport on the shuttle bus, I saw an Orthodox couple, (not Ultra) maybe in their forties walking together in the drizzling rain. The man was holding the umbrella over himself. The wife's hair was getting all wet. This seemed to confirm to me that the religious Jewish men here do not treasure and care for their women very well. I felt so sorry for her. But later, I remembered that her hair would have been a wig, so her head wasn't really getting wet at all., and he was probably using the umbrella more to protect his expensive velvet hat than to keep himself dry. I noticed other Orthodox men had their valuable hats wrapped in plastic.

Glenn's Ordeal

The news was saying that the London airport was shut down due to fog. Glenn was coming in from London! Everyone here was sure he wouldn't get a flight. So I went to the airport fully expecting to have to stay there overnight to wait for him. I took a change of clothes, a pillow, my toothbrush, and some books. The British airways internet site said his flight was on time. And the board at the airport also did. So, I started expecting him. But then I waited and waited. A whole hour passed. I saw many happy family reunions. Grandchildren meeting grandparents, children meeting parents, and couples hugging and kissing over and over. I would get distracted watching it all. Then I would be worried that I had missed Glenn.

When I was giving up on him, he finally walked through the door. I ran to him and hugged him, but his hug was emotionless. I was taken aback until I found out why. He was shook up from the ordeal he had just been through.

He had made a mistake in answering the airport official's first question, "Why are you coming to Israel?" His quick response came from what was first and foremost on his mind, "To see my wife." As soon as the words came out of his mouth, he knew he shouldn't have said that. (He should have just said he was a tourist.) The lady questioned him more. "To see your wife?! What's your wife doing here?" At this point Glenn was nervous and fumblingly blurted out, "She works for the University." "She *works* for them?" This made her see red flags.

She made him wait in a holding area. After 20 long minutes they took him to a room where they fired question after question at him. He started to worry whether he would ever get into Israel! They asked him what exactly I do for the university. And, strangely enough, because of the way his last name, Zehr, is spelled, they kept asking him where his ancestry was from. Finally he realized he needed to tell them I VOLUNTEER for the university, not WORK for them. They were finally satisfied, but not until after they had looked me up on the computer and verified my address with the information he gave them. We are still wondering how they had my address in the computer. I never told anyone my address when I arrived. I didn't even know it yet at that point. Interesting, huh?

Snow

Yesterday it rained all day again. Then in the late afternoon it turned to snow!! Real snow!! It was very cold, too; cold enough for the snow to stick. Everything in the whole city came to a halt. Schools and colleges closed. And all the buses stopped running. One of our Japanese workers told us today that she missed the last bus and had to walk the hour walk home in the cold, slushy, falling snow. By nightfall, the ground and even the olive trees were covered with snow. They were still white this morning. The rose blossoms by our neighbor's door were also covered with snow.

So, praise the Lord, hallelujah! Jerusalem is finally getting the water it desperately needs.

Cold

So, the weather has turned suddenly much colder. Yet they still turn the heat on ONLY from 8 pm to 11 pm. Glenn cannot believe how cold it gets in this house. He got froze to the bone himself yesterday! But I stayed warm this time because I am wearing the thick fleece long underwear on top of my other long underwear. And I'm wearing sweaters, wool socks, a scarf, and my goose down long, hooded coat that Glenn brought me. Yes, I wear all that inside the house while I work at the computer! Glenn is going to wear long underwear too from now on.

It's a good thing I learned to live in a cold house in Virginia, or I might not be able to bear this frigidness.

I do hope it will warm up soon, though. It's hard to feel like a real person buried under five layers of clothing! I wear Glenn's big shoes (whichever ones he's not wearing) because mine don't fit with such big wool socks on. So that doesn't help me feel human either. lol! (You should hear the teasing I get about those shoes!)

Christmas Eve

We went with Charity and Todd to Bethlehem on Christmas Eve. We boarded the free shuttle the Israelis are running this year. There were only two other passengers besides us on a huge, luxury tour bus. We found out how close we really are to Bethlehem. It wasn't hardly a five minute drive to the checkpoint. We got through that relatively quickly, but then came upon a traffic jam. There were policemen-like guys redirecting the flow. They weren't letting people go up the main street to Manger Square. The Israeli bus driver found this rather comical. They want the tourism that Christmas brings, but then they scramble the traffic that's heading there.

Our ten minute drive took an hour. We went down some very tiny side streets. It was amazing that the bus could maneuver through them, while still fighting all the traffic. Finally, the driver told us we might as well get off and walk the last several blocks.

We were accosted right away by aggressively begging young boys, maybe around ages 8-10. At the checkpoint we had been given bags of candy to give to the Palestinians to bless them. (They were donated by Israeli churches.) Glenn gave his bag to the first begging boy. He instructed me to do the same, so I did. A third bigger boy, about 12 or 13 years old, saw this, so he begged and begged for Todd's bag of candy. We were walking fast, but he kept right up with us and kept reaching for the candy. He even got ahold of the bag and pulled on it. Todd didn't enjoy being forced to be generous, so he resisted for a whole block. But the kid wore him down until he reluctantly gave in.

As we approached the square, we, and the crowd with us, were suddenly shoved off the street toward a wall, by several Palestinian policemen. I noticed that the crowd was made up mostly of Palestinians. They resisted being pushed aside, but the police persisted. There was obviously something up ahead that the crowd wanted to see. The bus driver had said something about the traffic jam being because the Palestinian president was speaking at Manger Square. So I assumed that was what the people wanted to see.

We weren't sure if we wanted to be stuck there for who-knew-how-long. Before we could decide to leave, it was too late. More people were being herded in and we were trapped. The tension seemed to be high. We squeezed in behind a parked car. We were ready to crouch down for safety in case things turned bad.

Eventually, a motorcade stream of vehicles raced passed. We watched siren-blaring, rushing police car after police car, then an ambulance or two, then zooming, dark-windowed, VIP car after VIP car. Finally, after about 15 vehicles, it was over and we were allowed to approach the central area.

Some sort of peace group was performing a concert of strange music, singing in Spanish. We squeezed through the crowd to find what looked like it could be a post office. I wanted my Christmas cards to be postmarked from Bethlehem. It *was* a post office, but the guy wouldn't take my cards because I had Israeli stamps on them! : (

We were going to meet some Palestinian Christians (whose oldest daughters are my daughters' ages), but we couldn't find them. Another disappointment. The line to get into the church was extremely long and you had to have advance tickets to get in on Christmas eve. A third disappointment. As we were standing around trying to decide what to do, a little boy, maybe age 5, stood in front of us with the most pitifully sad face ever seen, holding his hand out begging. His clothes were dirty. He looked the picture of a lost, abandoned child who would never smile again. My heart was so touched. I took his hands into mine and wanted so badly to hug him and hold him. His hands were so cold. I kept asking him where his mommy was, but, of course, he couldn't understand me. I looked around but didn't see anyone that seemed concerned about him.

Later a girl about age 7 or 8 used the same pitiful face and stance. I could hardly keep from cupping her cheeks in my hands and giving her a loving kiss. Charity pulled out her bag of candy from her coat, which she had somehow miraculously concealed from those earlier aggressive boys, and gave it to the girl. And, my, you should have seen how quickly that girl's sad expression disappeared. She grabbed the candy and ran away, laughing in delight. I thought to myself that if their lives are as pitiful as their begging expressions make it seem, candy wouldn't wipe away their sadness.

Charity and Todd went back to Bethlehem on Christmas day. It wasn't crowded at all anymore then. They said they saw that same pitiful 5-year-old boy. Only this time he didn't look pitiful at all. He was laughing and playing with friends. So they decided that someone must be training them how to turn on the heart-rending look in order to wrench money from people. Glenn hadn't wanted to give the boy money because he is afraid that there is some ring leader guy that the money goes to instead of to the boy or the boy's family. I don't know what the truth is. I was so looking forward to meeting Palestinian Christians so we could find out the truth about the whole situation. I wanted to be able to help the people who really need the help. I'm sure you all would also love to help the poor, trapped people of Bethlehem.

In the Lord's time we will meet the right people and then we will let you know how you can help.

On our walk back to the bus there was a small food shop where they were selling popped popcorn! I was so shocked! It's the first I had seen anywhere in Israel! So we bought a bag. It was the best-tasting popcorn ever. It tasted as delicious as good homemade popcorn!! (For those who don't know, I come from a family-line hooked on popcorn.) Isn't it hilarious? I had to go to walled-in, security-tight Bethlehem for good popcorn!

Before the bus was allowed back through the checkpoint to re-enter Israel, two soldiers had to do a walk-through check of the whole bus. They were just young soldiers. The girl looked only 16, but she was probably 18. There were only us four passengers on the whole empty bus, but they had to look under all the seats and everything.

So, that was Christmas Eve in Bethlehem.

A Worshipping Family

Christmas Day Glenn and I decided to walk to Jerusalem. (You're right. Glenn didn't take much time to rest from jet lag. He hit the ground running. He wanted to see Israel!) It was almost a two hour walk! Public bathrooms are hard to find in Jerusalem. There are none on the buses, nor are there any in the little shops. I don't know what people do if duty calls! Well, duty was calling me. We weren't dressed nice enough to look like we belonged in the fancy hotel across the street, so I decided against trying there. I prayed and asked the Lord to take care of this need, too, and walked on knowing He would. As we got closer to the Old City, I remembered that the Sukkoth Hillel (I think that's the name.) Prayer House was near there. They would have a bathroom!! It was a different direction than we planned on going, but we decided to stop there and pray awhile. The Lord provides!!

The musicians playing were all young. I thought maybe they were a youth group or something. But there was a really little boy playing bongo drums, and an even younger girl sitting on the front row also playing a bongo drum. Other little kids seemed relaxed enough to walk around among the musicians. There were school aged, long blond haired girls in long dresses dancing and waving banners. Soon I realized that all these children looked alike and resembled the four young musician men. Sure enough there were the parents sitting all the way in the back with yet another wee boy.

We worshipped with them awhile, enjoying their relaxing style of music, and their interjected prayers of praise and adoration. I was so amazed and touched to see teen-age boys worshipping so sincerely!

The Prayer house leader presided over communion, and we partook. It was such a wonderful blessing for Glenn to be initiated into Israel this way. I also was brought to that same prayer house only a few days after being here. I felt like it was God letting us know He really does want us both to be here.

As we left I asked the mother of all the children what her name was. They are the Walker family. They have 11 children and they live here in Israel in Ariel. What a privilege that we got to meet them!!

Ultra Orthodox Jewish Mea Sharim Neighborhood

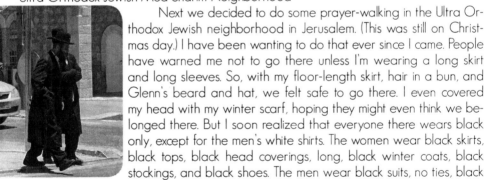

Next we decided to do some prayer-walking in the Ultra Orthodox Jewish neighborhood in Jerusalem. (This was still on Christmas day.) I have been wanting to do that ever since I came. People have warned me not to go there unless I'm wearing a long skirt and long sleeves. So, with my floor-length skirt, hair in a bun, and Glenn's beard and hat, we felt safe to go there. I even covered my head with my winter scarf, hoping they might even think we belonged there. But I soon realized that everyone there wears black only, except for the men's white shirts. The women wear black skirts, black tops, black head coverings, long, black winter coats, black stockings, and black shoes. The men wear black suits, no ties, black shoes, and black hats—all immaculately clean.

Their streets were very quiet. A side street sounded noisy and active. We turned and found a school. The fenced-enclosed, small cement play yard was full of rowdy, black pants-clad boys—all with their side-curls dangling in front of their ears. They were around age 5 or 6 and looked very cute. I smiled at them as we walked by, but they didn't smile back. They stopped playing and stared at us. One boy gave me an angry look and ran toward me, growling, as if to scare me away. I was quite taken aback. My long skirt and covered head didn't fool him a bit!

It really bothered me the whole rest of the day. It seemed so strange to have a little boy treat you that way.

We found their main shopping street. We saw a couple places there that sold popped popcorn!! I thought how like the Amish! They dress like the Amish and they eat popcorn like the Amish! It looked as good as in Bethlehem, too, but Glenn wouldn't buy any.

We were surprised at how dirty the sidewalks were. The farther we walked the more we felt a kind of oppressive spirit. Of course, no one smiled at us or greeted us. No one even urged us to buy their wares as they do everywhere else in Jerusalem. A couple little girls, sisters, walking alone together ahead of us kept looking back at us suspiciously and trying to hurry faster to get away from us. I smiled at them, but it didn't reassure them at all. Smiling didn't seem to soften anybody in that neighborhood.

We found a small bakery shop that sold wonderful pastries dripping with sweetness. The owners were friendly enough there, so we bought a few. Mmmmmm. So delicious!

We headed on to the Wailing Wall from there. We were behind three Ultra Orthodox teenage girls who ended up at the Wall, too. Standing behind them at a traffic light, I noticed they were wearing make-up and earrings! Yes, you heard me. They had all black clothes, and their hair was up and very plain and yet they wore jewelry and painted their faces. Even their eyebrows were plucked. That is NOT like the Amish!! Today I looked closer at the adult Orthodox women on the bus, and sure enough, I saw plucked eyebrows, make-up, and earrings!

Oh, yeah, the Orthodox also drive cars, some of the men dance on the street to guitar music in the open-air mall on Saturday nights, and some of the men smoke. Also all very different from Amish. Another thing is that the Amish believe "cleanliness is next to Godliness." Their farms are usually very neat and tidy. If they lived in a city, their streets would be clean and beautiful. (As are the streets in the Jewish section of the Old City where Orthodox, not Ultra Orthodox, Jews live.)

The actions of the little boy wouldn't leave my head. It reminded me of when I got my friend, Jane, lost in the Arab section of the Old City and the cute little Muslim boy kicked her. (See Nov 16, 2006.)

Both little boys from both sides of the religious spectrum treated us with contempt. It seems so odd, because little children don't naturally treat adults that way. They have to be taught to hate like that, don't they? They both are taught that we are the enemy—that outsiders are bad people. It is so sad. In both places the streets were dingy, dirty, and trashy. In both places the atmosphere feels oppressive. Both sides need prayer equally desperately. May the Lord set them all free.

Glenn and I feel called to do more prayer-walking in the Mea Sharim area. If you pray, too, we will be carrying your prayers with us in our spirits as we go.

May the Holy Spirit continue to direct your prayers for Israel,
Cheryl

Journal Dec. 29   Waiting Expectantly

Mark 15:42 Joseph of Arimathea, a respected member of the council who was also himself waiting expectantly for the Kingdom of God went boldly and asked....

He was waiting expectantly for the Kingdom as we are. He got to see and take part in what he was waiting for. May it be so for us, too!

Journal Dec. 31   Pomegranate

The word "pomegranate" comes from the Hebrew root word "raman" which means "exalt and lift up"!!! So, that is why God instructed the High Priest to have pomegranates on the hem of his garment. (I got this from Bode and Brock Thoene's "Third Watch.")

"Rain" in Hebrew also means "reveal" according to the preacher, last night. So, the early rain and latter rain could be the early and latter revelation.

This morning I was thinking about all this and I opened the Bible to this

Joel 2:12,16,22 Return to Me with all your heart with fasting and weeping ....

Rend your hearts... gather the people...the children...even infants.... I will remove the Northern army far from you ....

Do not fear, you animals of the field for the pastures are green. The tree bears its fruit, the fig tree and vine give their full yield.

Yes, Jesus, let it be so!! Bring it to pass!
You are the vine, we are the branches. We shall give our full yield!
Israel is perhaps the fig tree. It shall give its FULL yield!
The olive tree is both of us. We are grafted in. They will be grafted back in and together we will bear the tree's fruit!!

Joel 2:25 I will repay you for the years that the swarming locust has eaten, the hopper, the destroyer, the cutter, My great army, which I sent against you.

God sent them!!! Not the devil! Is it the army described in verses 2-11?

Journal Jan. 6   Wailing Girl

Lord, You increased my strength of soul (Ps. 138:3)

O Jesus, I need you to do this again for me. Please increase the strength of my soul and of my boldness in You, Jesus, so I will never again shrink back from obeying Your nudging. Forgive me for not going to that girl at the Wailing Wall today.

A teenage girl, in jeans, who was a little heavy-set with strawberry blond hair was wailing openly. She had many friends around her tending to her—all wearing jeans. They were all backing away from the Wall with her as she cried the whole time. A beggar lady walked up to her and motioned that it was good for her to cry. I thought it seemed so rude and intrusive of the beggar lady, who then, even worse, in my opinion, proceeded to beg from the girl's. After they refused her, she actually begged from the grieving girl! Before they left, the girl stopped and wailed loudly some more. (Maybe someone close to her had just died or something.) Her friends were holding her hands and standing around her sympathetically, but none of them were crying.

I sensed that Jesus wanted me to go to her and find out what was wrong and offer to pray for her. But I didn't want to be intruding like the beggar. I was suddenly overcome with shyness. I know my failures in the past—how I botch up those kinds of things.

So, I didn't go to her, Lord, but then at the Wall I didn't sense Your Spirit at all. So, I went back to find her and obey You, but she was gone. I'm so sorry, Lord. Please forgive me. Cover me with Your Blood. Please send another much more Godly lady to her who will say the right things, who will show Your Love much better than I can.

And please heal me from my communication handicaps—from my facial expression, body language, and tone of voice handicaps.

Therefore,…. be steadfast, immovable excelling in the work of the Lord for it is not in vain (I Cor. 15:58).

For these are days of vengeance as fulfillment of ALL that is written (Lk. 21:22).

! ! ! !   *Jesus* said that!!

God is Answering Prayer!

Sun, Jan 7, 2007 at 3:13 PM

Hi Prayer Warriors and All,

I'm sorry I haven't written in awhile, but my excuse is good. I have a husband here to go do things with and to talk to now. ☺ Also, I only had one day off from work for the holidays. But anyway, I'm back and I have wonderful, exciting things to tell you!

Jewish and Arab Friends

On the Sabbath meeting before New Years, the pastor asked people to come up front and thank the Lord for things. Two college girls came up [one a Jewish believer (the same girl who prayed so beautifully for Israel) and the other an Arab believer]. They said they have become very close friends. They both had been praying to find a friend who would have their same zeal for God and for spreading the Word as they each have. God answered their prayers by bringing them together. They clasped hands as they offered prayers of thanks to God for their new friendship.

This is truly a miracle to have a Jew and an Arab working together in unity and love. Together they are taking Hebrew University by storm. PRAISE THE LORD.

Messianic Music Concert

Every two years the Messianic community here has a contest for all the new Messianic music and they play all the winners in a concert usually held at King of Kings. People come from all over Israel. It was to be held the Thursday before Christmas, Dec. 21 at 7 pm. I paid for a ticket but had to come back later to pick it up because they had run out of them.

I had to teach until 8:30 pm, and it is a half-hour walk for me from class. I was hoping maybe everyone in my class would want to go so I could cancel class for it. Or I thought maybe God would bring Glenn to Israel in time to go.

I went back that Thursday afternoon before my class to pick up the ticket knowing now that Glenn couldn't use it. I found out that they ended up selling so many tickets in advance that they were now having two sessions, one at 5pm and the other at 8pm. So I wouldn't miss much if I came to the 8pm one. However, I got a glimpse of their rehearsal and discovered that everything was going to be in Hebrew. All the words on the screen were in Hebrew letters, with no English transcription even. So I realized I wouldn't get much out of it.

I decided I would give the ticket to my Arab student. I thought that would be a wonderful way to introduce him to more about Jesus. But he didn't come to class. All my other first hour students were going to another meeting, so I couldn't give the ticket to any of them. My last class had only two students present, it being so close to Christmas, so we let out early. I went to the concert and was only a little late. There were guards outside the locked door and they tried to turn me away until I showed them my ticket. Then they knocked on the door for someone to let me in. (The guards were necessary because the Ultra Orthodox have sometimes caused trouble at these kinds of events, it being so close to their neighborhood and being Messianic Jewish and all.)

The whole huge auditorium was full, including the balconies and the aisles. I found an empty spot in the back aisle, laid my heavy backpack of books down, and leaned against the wall.

The songs were being done as a performance, not as worship, but one of them was so worshipful that people all over the audience began to stand up and raise their hands in reverence. Many even joined in singing the Hebrew. One was a guy in his soldier uniform. The spirit of worship was so strong that I joined in even though I couldn't understand the words.

As my mind focused on our Redeemer, this realization hit me. If this meeting is packed, then the earlier one was probably packed, too. And if this is all in Hebrew (even the announcements), then that means that most of this audience (and the earlier one) is Israeli and the choir is Israeli; if Israeli, then probably Jewish and thus Jewish Believers—Messianic Jews! If all these songs are in Hebrew, then they are most likely also written by Messianic Jews!

And no one expected to have this many people come to this since they planned on having only one session, which means that the number of Messianic Jews in Israel has at least doubled in two years!!

Then it was as if Jesus spoke to me and said you have a part in this because you have been praying for the Jewish people to be saved. This is the beginning of the answer to all the prayers people have been praying for Israel! Here are hundreds and hundreds of Messianic Jews praising and worshipping Yeshua—even a soldier in uniform!

I was so overwhelmed, I nearly melted to the floor with tears of joy.

Hallelujah! Praise You, Yeshua!

This is the fourth or fifth time Jesus has taken me somewhere to show me the answers to my long-time prayers. He took me to Mongolia to show me that the Gospel is reaching the ends of the earth, and to China and Africa to show me what He is doing there, and to an International House of Prayer "One Thing" meeting to show me what He is doing with American young people, etc, etc. It seems like if you pray for something with all your heart for a long, long time, He likes to show you the answers to those prayers!

Christmas Decorations

Get this. This is ironic, I think. You know that since the secular Jews do not like Jesus, they also do not like Christmas. But God has worked it out that for economic reasons they have to embrace Christmas. Here's why. Israel's main income is tourism, and since many (maybe most) of the tourists are Christians, Christmas is one of the biggest tourist times. Because of the unrest here and the war last summer, tourism has greatly decreased, so the government is doing everything it can to show favor to tourists in order to encourage more people to come. So this Christmas they went all out. They offered free shuttle buses from Jerusalem to Bethlehem as I told you. AND they decorated the whole Hebron Highway from the Old City to Bethlehem with Christmas lights and everything. It was very beautiful!

I have to laugh every time I ride down that road thinking about how it must grate on them to have to put up decorations for something they are so religiously opposed to! Isn't it funny? (The decorations are still up because certain sects of Christianity, such as Eastern Orthodox, celebrate Christmas later in January.)

The Palestinians did the same. Bethlehem was all lit up with Christmas lights. Even with lit up crosses! I was so amazed because it wasn't like that last year. I was so happy that none of the decorations were secular, but then, to my disappointment, we did see a couple Santa Clauses when we were leaving Bethlehem.

Rain, Hail, Fog, Lightning, Cold

It rained two days before Christmas, and it has hailed, snowed, rained, then hailed again and rained again. We have had almost non-stop rain since then. I find it interesting that it all came in around Christmas. On New Years Eve late afternoon a heavy, pea soup fog rolled in. People are exclaiming how fog never happens in Israel, at least not heavy fog. It brought a very eery feeling with it, and it lifted almost exactly at midnight, when the New Year rolled in. (Our New Year, not the Israeli New Year. Theirs is in September or October.)

Friday it was windy and dreary, and it rained all day. Towards evening it really started storming. We had thunder and lightning. People were surprised again. They said they hardly ever get lightning storms. And they were amazed at how the lightning seemed so close.

It hailed, too. Hail was collecting on the ground like snow. Glenn and I were asked to drive to pick up one of the volunteers from the office so he wouldn't have to walk home in the storm. Glenn carried me on his back to the car because the water in the walk way was ankle deep. Charity went with us just for the adventure. As we drove down the road lightning boomed right on us. Whoa, was it shocking!

We are wondering if the unusual weather is a signal of what is to come this year in Israel.

Yesterday it rained all day, too. Today it is cloudy and dreary with a light rain.

The weather has also been very cold. Even Glenn is getting cold. He has had cold hands inside the house for the first time in his life!! So, it is not just me. It really, truly is cold in these stone-block houses where they use no heat most of the day. On one of the coldest days we noticed the neighbors had their big patio door wide opened. We decided it must have been because the outside was warmer than the inside, which often is the case.

Thank you for praying for rain. Keep it up. I don't think a desert can get too much rain.

Well, this is a long enough e-mail. I'll put the rest in another e.

Exciting Blessings to you!

More Answers to Prayer!

Sun, Jan 7, 2007 at 4:03 PM

In Israel Shabboth (Sabbath) is observed. Everyone, even most Christians here, have Shabboth meal on Friday evenings. The tradition is to light two candles, break bread and sip wine with the traditional blessings said over each. Saturday is when the traditional meetings are usually held. We could go to more than five Christian or Messianic meetings per weekend, if we wanted to. Some churches hold their meetings Saturday morning, many Saturday evening, a few Sunday morning, and King of Kings holds theirs on Sunday evening. One weekend I went to three meetings. Most weekends I've gone to two.

Today Glenn and I went to a very small Sunday morning meeting. It was at the museum house. While there, we heard some exciting stories.

Muslims

A Christian worker here, we'll call Chad, said that in Jericho there are so many Muslims getting saved, the Christian workers hardly know what to do. He says the same is happening in Athens with "Helping Hands," a refugee organization. The Arab women are getting saved in huge numbers and their husbands are starting to come to the meetings. In Bethlehem also, many Arabs are coming to the Lord.

Chad said, and the others in the meetings agreed, that it used to be you could count on one hand the number of Arabs that would get saved in a life-time. And many of them wouldn't remain Christian. They would go back to Islam. But now it is different.

Chad said that if these Arabs receive the Holy Spirit and get filled with love for the Jewish people that will really speak to the Jews, and make them believe in Yeshua. When I told Charity, she was delighted. She said it would really provoke the Jews to jealousy like the Scriptures say. Her friend from England, who has just arrived in Bethlehem to do Christian work there, is also telling her that the Arabs (so-called Palestinians) seem very open. He says also that the Arab Christians are not being treated as badly as before by the Muslims. (We will meet him perhaps tomorrow evening. I can't wait.)

Praise the Lord!!

Openness Among the Jewish People

There was a women's watchmen conference last weekend where Chad and a Scandinavian lady, we'll call Katalina, were both speakers. They said there were religious Jewish women who stood just outside the door peering in out of curiosity, but were so intrigued they couldn't leave. Katalina met two young Jewish women in the rest room who asked her questions and gave her their phone numbers.

On the shuttle from the airport when Katalina was returning from Mexico, she was planning on sleeping the whole way, but a Jewish lady kept talking and talking to her. The lady even said she doesn't usually bother people, but she wouldn't leave Katalina alone. She told Katalina she is paid by rabbis and their wives (probably not Orthodox) to read Tarot cards for them. The lady invited Katalina to her home. Katalina couldn't come. Then she asked where Katalina lived and if she was going there now. Katalina took the hint and invited her home. She came. Katalina invited her to her small group meeting. She came. Katalina has talked to her about needing to repent of reading Tarot cards. She says she knows it is wrong. She wants to change. Can you believe it?! They are coming to the Christians, not the other way around!

On the Bus

Another older lady at the meeting said she was riding the bus in the Old City the other day when a very religious-looking Jewish man got on. He obviously knew the bus driver, because he sat in front and began talking to him. They spoke in Hebrew, and the bus driver told the man that he believes in Yeshua. The religious man said, "Well, they say he really did rise from the dead."

Can you imagine? A bus driver in Israel is a believer!! I'm shocked! And the Orthodox now believe that Jesus rose from the dead!! WOW!

The lady said she was so shocked that they were talking openly about this in public, in Hebrew—the language everybody in earshot understood! Chad was surprised also. He said that in the past such a thing would have caused a riot! He said one young guy he knew used to always talk about Jesus everywhere and often got punched for it!

So things are really changing!

And all of you who have been praying for Israel have a part in this!

I'm so excited!

May our prayer bowls continue to overflow,

The Wall and Other Things that Might Interest You

Sun, Jan 7, 2007 at 5:19 PM

The Wailing Wall

It has been interesting how the atmosphere at the Wailing Wall is so different every time. Around Christmas time there have been lots of tourists taking pictures and talking, and of course, trying to put prayer notes in the cracks. However, Glenn and I have both been surprised that it wasn't more crowded during this holiday season. We expected it to be packed, but it wasn't at all.

One time I was thinking about what an awesome place the Wall is. It is open to anyone to come at any time to pray. Anyone of any religion is allowed in. Most come here in a worshipful attitude to meet God. All this without anyone controlling or directing it. I was thinking maybe our churches should be more like this.

But then there is the negative side of the beggars who seem to be getting bolder and bolder, coming closer to the wall to do their begging. Glenn even got interrupted while he was praying! So it would be nice to have someone controlling that.

[We found out that maybe the beggars bug us because we look Jewish. Jewish people, we are told, never refuse to give to a beggar. They at least give them a tiny coin. It's part of their law, and they believe it brings them blessings.]

One day there was rank after rank of soldiers filing in. They were having some huge military/religious ceremony of some kind on the plaza. It was kind of hard to concentrate on praying that day due to their blaring loudspeakers.

Last time I went there, I saw a young mother with a tiny baby boy. The baby was so beautiful! I could hardly take my eyes off of him. I smiled at the mother. She smiled with that motherly pride that is so touching. Then I looked back at the baby and just wanted to gaze and gaze. There seemed to be something that drew my eyes to him. The mother might not have minded. She seemed to know how beautiful he was. I reluctantly pulled my eyes away. It made me think of Anna in the Temple. I wondered if that was a tiny bit how she felt when she looked at baby Jesus.

One day we got there earlier than I usually do, and lo and behold while I was praying, the Islam singing-chanting prayers started from a loudspeaker far above us. I began praying, as I always do, that the Lord will silence their cries to their false god. I always pray for the equipment to malfunction. Glenn says he prays the same thing. We also pray that they will soon be praying to the One True God over those speakers.

I was thinking about the pleasantness of the sound again there at the wall that day. Then I thought about how it sounds so much like mourning. Then I thought about the prayers around me at the Wailing Wall and how they are also prayers of mourning. (Another similarity between the two peoples.) The words, "I will turn your mourning into dancing" came to my mind. This made me begin to pray for the day when they will all worship together, maybe in the new Temple, with rejoicing instead of mourning.

The old Temple was only opened to Jewish people—only the outer court was opened to Gentiles. God wants a Temple that is open to all nations and is filled with joy and praise.

Wailing Wall on the women's side

Soldiers and an Orthodox man with a cell phone in the Wailing Wall plaza

The Talmud

The Talmud is the Jewish Oral Law. Today it is written down, but in Jesus' day it was passed down orally. The Pharisees held the Talmud in higher regard than the Torah (the books of Moses). And they hardly even considered the books of the prophets as the Word of God. The Hassidim still today, even though they give the Torah extreme honor, hold the prophets lower and the Talmudmuch higher. Even some Messianic believers hold the Talmudalmost as high as Scripture. I'm told one Jewish believer said that if another Christian didn't believe in the Talmudhe didn't know if he could call him a brother.

That is why Jesus made a point of saying, "such and such and so, in order to fulfill the Law (the Torah) and the Prophets." He was telling them that the Prophets were on equal level with the Torah and both were higher than the Talmid! He also often spoke against their man made traditions, which would have been this oral law——the Talmud.

Not 400 years of slavery

One more thing. In my studying for the book I am helping with, I discovered I had been wrong on something in the Bible. In case I'm not the only one, let me tell you.

I have always thought the Israelites were slaves in Egypt for four hundred years. And I always wondered why God would let his people suffer so long before He delivers them. I mean, many generations would have died not knowing deliverance! So why?

Well, in studying the time line, I found out that it wasn't four hundred years at all. The 400 years is counting from the time God made the covenant with Abraham to the time of the Exodus. They were in Egypt for most of those 400 years, but they weren't slaves the whole time. It wasn't until a pharaoh came who didn't know Joseph that they were made slaves. That would have been quite awhile. (Just think for a minute how long it would have been in America for someone to not know Lincoln!) It was only the next pharaoh after that whom Moses dealt with for the Exodus. So they were probably slaves for not much more than one hundred years! Moses was 80 years old when he went to Pharoh, so it had to be more than eighty years. But since people lived longer back then, maybe there weren't many of the actual slaves at all who died not knowing deliverance!

God is an awesome God, isn't He? If there is a situation in which it looks to us like He wasn't fair or good, we need to wait for new revelation, because it is our understanding that is wrong, not the Scriptures. When we get the new revelation, we see how wonderfully, marvelously, abundantly good God really is. This has happened to me quite a few times now. ☺

On Singleness

One recent example is about Jesus and Paul elevating the single life——Paul even seeming to say it is better to choose than marriage. Now I see that they were most likely just trying to bring balance to the Orthodox tradition that a man must get married by age 20. (See p. 68.)

Now I think maybe Jesus and Paul are just giving honor to single people, not trying to make a new rigid rule; that they are not lowering marriage at all, but are only lifting up the single life to the same honor as the married life!

I love finding out all these Jewish traditions. It is bringing new revelations and light to the Living Word of God for me.

Blessings of revelations to you,
Cheryl

Oh, One More Blessing

Sun, Jan 7, 2007 at 7:08 PM

God seems to really want us here in Israel. They have decided already to get Glenn's visa. They waited more than two months to talk about getting me mine. Glenn wasn't even here two weeks before they talked about his. My visa appointment is in January. We don't know yet when Glenn's will be. (They have told Glenn they want him to help organize their library. The lady who has been working on that is leaving in February. So Glenn has a month to learn all about it.)

So, praise the Lord!

If you wouldn't mind, you could join us in praying for a laptop. They don't really like us using their office computer for our personal stuff. We had to leave our desk top computer at home, so we have nothing here. Electronic things are quite expensive here. But we trust the Lord will supply, if He wants us to have these things. We have seen Him do so in many miraculous ways. So we expect to see it again.

God is Good.

May He supply all your needs, too,

Cheryl

Journal Jan. 10. 07 Ten Years

This is the tenth anniversary of my stroke!! Thank You, Lord Yeshua, for ten wonderful, bonus, healthy years!! Praise You, Jesus!

Journal Jan. 12 Paid for the Land

Well, Glenn used a credit card to pay for the land from his family farm. His brothers had to meet with the lawyer and needed it. Glenn wanted to use the credit card rather than go back on his word and have his brothers angry at him the rest of their lives—even though the whole process took so long and we are in a completely different financial situation than we were when he made that promise ... This could prevent us from being able to stay in Israel, but we are trusting that the Lord will provide. We are believing that this is the answer to our many times of prayer-walking on his farm before it sold and before we ever dreamed of coming to Israel.

Journal Jan. 20 Devotions Before Going to the Desert

Acts 13:22 God says: I had David...a man after My own heart who carries out all My wishes.

Acts 13:48 All who were destined for eternal life were saved.

Acts 13:49 And the Word of the Lord spread throughout the land.

O Lord, may we be people who carry out all Your wishes. May Your Word spread everywhere and may all souls everywhere, whom You died for, be saved!

Arabs at a bank

God is Doing Awesome Things for the Arabs!

Sat, Jan 20, 2007 at 9:56 PM

Dear Family in the Lord,

Many Muslims are becoming Believers in Jesus!! We met a wonderful Godly man who is an Arab pastor. His church in the West Bank is growing, and it is the first church in this land where the members are all from Muslim background. It is a very new church yet he says there are about 25 adult members, plus children!

I asked him to tell how some of his people are coming to the Lord, and he told some very interesting stories. He said that 70% of the Muslims who come to the Lord, come through direct contact from God through visions and dreams. After they receive the visions or dreams they learn more about God from a Christian.

The most recent is a young man whom God saved from death six times in his life. The first time was after his father left his mother, or kicked her out. In her despair she threw her son, this young man, in a well. The miracle was he didn't die. When he thought it was getting morning, he yelled and yelled, and someone rescued him. That was the first of his six scrapes with death.

Recently this young man had the same vision several times. In it a man asks him in Arabic, "Are you chosen?" In Arabic "Chosen" is a person's name, so in his vision he always says, "No, I'm not." He kept having this vision over and over, and it was puzzling him. Finally he had a different vision. In this one a man came and gave him a drink. He drank and drank. Then the man told him, "You are chosen." He knew in the vision that this man was Jesus.

Then he had a vision in which he was a shepherd leading a flock, when suddenly he saw himself as a sheep, then again as a shepherd. All this was very confusing to him. The pastor gave him an Arabic book, called *The Man Who Changed History*, that has various passages from the NT in it. One of them is about the Lord being our shepherd, another about living water. As he is talking things over week by week with the pastor, his understanding is becoming clearer.

One older gentleman was actually visited by Jesus in person. He was sleeping when someone knocked on his door. He got up and opened the door and saw Jesus. Jesus told him, "I am the one you are looking for. You can read about Me in the Bible."

I asked the pastor what the man said Jesus looked like. He said Jesus was dressed in white with a big smile on his face and wore a white Bedouin Kafi (head thing). Interesting, huh? (This is exactly what we used to pray for in our prayer meetings with Kirk and Daisy in America! Isn't it exciting?!)

This is so exuberantly exciting to me. I just keep on hearing such enormously awesome things, my mind almost cannot contain it. It's just like God promises: I will open the windows of heaven and pour out a blessing you cannot contain (From Mal. 3:10).

Be blessed,
Cheryl

Learning More About Muslims

Sat, Jan 20, 2007 at 11:32 PM

So, we were riding in a van with two pastors of former Muslims. The one I told you about; the other one is from Nigeria. His wife used to be Muslim. We learned so much from both these men. Here are some notes about what they said. (I took notes while they were talking so I could remember everything.)

They said the most powerful Biblical passage to a Muslim is the Sermon on the Mount because it completely clashes with everything they believe about prayer, about enemies, about adultery, etc., etc.

I asked them why Islam is spreading so fast. First, the one pastor said that I shouldn't believe the reports. He said Christianity is spreading much faster than Islam. He said he has a recording of a Sheik's speech saying he's very upset because there are six million Muslims converting to Christianity per year in Africa! SIX MILLION in Africa alone!!

(Chad said once that the Iranian president is upset at how many Iranians are becoming Christian and thinks they need to do something about it!)

The Arab-Israeli pastor says they hold their meetings the same time as the mosques do, so that while the loudspeakers are blasting the angry words, they are praising and worshipping the Lord. (So, here is the beginning of the answer to my prayers that the loudspeakers be silenced and turned into prayers to Jesus!!!)

The African pastor explained how the Muslims spread their religion. They go to the poor people and promise the men four things: that they will give them a lot of money, a house, and a wife; and that they will take them to Mecca. The problem is they don't follow through on those promises.

He says when they try to convert him he says, "What about eternal life?" They tell him, "Allah will decide that." Then he says again, "I don't need those four things. I already have a house and a wife. What I need is eternal life." They tell him again, "Allah will decide that." So he says, "Then you cannot help me because I'm not worried about this life. What I'm concerned about is the next life." That gets them thinking.

He said one African pastor friend of his was taken in by all their promises and denounced Christ. They gave him a wife, but never gave him any of the other things. He already had a wife, so it messed up his family in a big way, and his children all went astray. Years later, he came back to the Lord after one of his wayward daughters turned to the Lord as she was dying. But he is now a broken man.

Morality Among Them

Both these pastors were raised Christian, but they grew up around the Muslim culture. One of them moved to England for awhile in his teens or so. He said he was surprised to find out how good the Brits were. He had been taught by the Muslim culture that non-Muslims are very bad people, but he found them to be kind and honest. He pointed out that in the Western culture it is abnormal for a person to be dishonest. But for his culture it is abnormal for a person to be honest——especially a store owner about his prices!

The Arabic pastor said something like this: "If a Muslim says, 'Tomorrow I will go to a certain place at this certain time to do such and such," and tomorrow he is there at that time doing what he said, this is abnormal! He said to us, "If you are like that, people will think you are a strange person!" (Imagine him saying it jokingly with an exaggerated Arabic accent and you get the picture.)

He said one of the biggest things soon to bring Islam down is that morality in their culture is breaking down so fast. According to their religion they are supposed to be so much purer than the rest of the world, but the morality of the West has slowed down in its decline while theirs is sinking faster and faster. (I don't think he knows what all is going on in America, but anyway I was very surprised to hear about the decline of Muslim morality.)

One of their biggest morality problems is incest. He says that a woman who ministers to a Muslim refugee camp asked the young girls there to write on a piece of paper, without their name, what their worst problem is. She said that out of the forty-two girls, thirty-five wrote about daily molestation from family members.

An Islamic saying is "Eat in a Muslim or Jewish home (to avoid eating pork), but sleep in a Christian home." (Too bad this is not really true since incest happens in far too many so-called Christian homes also.)

Muslim men think morality depends on the woman covering herself. Both pastors lamented the fact that Muslim men don't realize that immorality comes from a man's heart.

In Islam, the woman's salvation depends on her obedience to her husband.

About Marriage
Mohammed gave four types of marriages:
1. regular marriage (of which I think they are allowed more than one)
2. marry her but don't live with her (usually kept a secret)
3. a contract marriage without a sheik
4. pleasure marriage for a week or ten days or so

Mohammed's successor did away with the #4 type of marriage. However, (this was shocking to me) Iran now has such a high rate of homosexuality that they have brought back the pleasure marriage.

Evangelistic Riddle
Here's a riddle one Christian pastor tells Muslim men. He asks them to think about it for a day or so before they give him their answer:

Imagine if you had a very beautiful wife whom you loved very much. In fact, she is so beautiful that all the men in the village want her. Then one day you have to leave the village and you can't take her with you. You have to leave her there. Who would you choose to stay in your house to protect her, Jesus or Mohammed?

Bethlehem Girl
There's a young Christian, Arab girl who grew up Christian, but in Bethlehem in the Muslim culture. So, she has picked up the Muslim way of thinking. She told Charity that she doesn't think Saddam is so bad. Charity asked her, "Well, didn't he kill a lot of people?" She said, "Well, they SAY he did." Then she said that the Koran says the Iraqi's are bad people and that they need a strong leader to keep them in line.

Isn't that funny? It shows how easy it is to unknowingly absorb false beliefs.

The Koran is Disjointed

I asked the Arab pastor if the Koran really says that. He wasn't sure. He says the Koran is written in such a disjointed, disorganized way that it isn't easy to know for sure what it says. It jumps from Abraham to Noah to Jesus to Moses, etc, etc. Thus Muslims often will base a whole theological belief on one isolated verse of the Koran. When they become Christians they have to learn not to do that with the Bible.

Both pastors said that any English translation isn't a true translation, but only a sort of commentary. They said that Muslims have strict rules to the point of death about copying the Koran or translating it, or even (I think they also said) writing any of it down themselves.

They said the Koran is purposely disjointed so that people won't see the discrepancies. Then the Israeli-Arab pastor said this, which I think is the most profound statement from our whole conversation:

"Christianity is very simple but very deep; Islam is very shallow but very complicated."

I'll leave you with that thought.
Cheryl

A Couple More Things About Muslims

It was storming fiercely last night while I was e-mailing you. It even hailed again! It was terribly cold and windy, and it rained all night! Praise the Lord, because it hasn't rained at all for two whole weeks. It was sunny and had gotten kind of warm even. But that changed last night! It is still very cold and windy right now. I'm dressed in several layers again with my long, goose down coat, a scarf, and gloves (with the tips of the fingers cut out) to e-mail you right now.

Anyway, here are a couple more things I remembered about what the two pastors said yesterday.

First, I should have described the two men to you. The Israeli-Arab pastor is a young and handsome, very Arab-looking guy with pitch-black hair cut in the typical Arab way—very short on the sides and back, with the wavy top all sleeked up with gel. He is a very kind and intelligent man. His gorgeous wife is expecting. The Nigerian pastor is a very dark African, rather short in stature, who is very friendly and cheerful. He sang enthusiastically most of the way home. He kept on singing whether anyone joined in or not. He has four little boys and a wife back home. When his wife (raised Muslim) became a Christian back in the 1980's, her family disowned her and her uncle threatened to kill her. She knew what she would face before she converted, so it was very difficult for her to decide to take that step. She heard about the Lord from the Christian family she worked for. Years later her immediate family came to accept her. In fact, he says she is now their favored one. Her uncle, though, still doesn't believe.

The Arab pastor had many things to say about Islam. He says the demise of it will be caused by freedom. As soon as the people are free, it will fall, he says. (Sound familiar??) He says Islam only flourishes in oppressive regimes. When governments have forced Christianity in the past, Christianity stagnated. On the other hand, when there's separation of church and state, Christianity grows, while Islam falls. Islam only grows when it is enforced. He believes that because of the increasing immorality, (not just sexual, but fraud, corruption, piracy, etc.) countries like Saudi Arabia are ready to "vomit Islam."

As we were driving through the dry, barren desert, Palestinian controlled region outside of Jerusalem, both pastors noted that this is what the landscape is like in most of the Islamic countries. They think maybe someone should do a study on what happens to any land after Islam takes over.

The Arabic pastor's church is working on an Arabic website, which is very exciting. A week or so ago, Glenn and I watched a movie in Arabic with English subtitles (put on by CBN on Middle East TV) which told the life of a Muslim terrorist who came to the Lord. He was asked by his terrorist leader to search the Koran and read the Bible and prove that Christianity was wrong. Instead he found out it was true. Then Jesus visited him in a vision and he converted. This immediately put his life in danger. It was a true story. Afterwards an Arabic man gave the Gospel message and invited people to respond. He made sure to point out that although many people do, you don't have to receive a vision to find Jesus.

I was amazed the whole time we were watching it. I thought maybe it was a Christian station, but afterwards it had on silly secular stuff. We haven't been able to catch anything Christian on it since.

May the Lord's fire continue to spread!
Cheryl

Less Frequent E-mail Offer
I offered shorter, less frequent e-mails for the people who didn't like getting such long ones, and I received many responses like the following.

Hi Cheryl,
PLEASE do NOT put me on the SHORTER, LESS FREQUENT list! I enjoy the glimpses. This was GREAT news about the Muslims and Arabs. If I don't have time to read any of your longer e-mails, I either wait till I can, or I don't once in a while. But I read the vast majority and enjoy them. So please keep me on the regular list.
PJ

Tidbits About Life in Israel
Sun, Jan 21, 2007 at 6:46 PM

I want to catch you up on lots of little things. I have been jotting them down so I won't forget to tell you and I have a whole long list.

Gunshots
We have been hearing gunshots. It was the Monday after New Years that I heard the first gunshots I ever heard in Israel. There were two shots coming from the Bethlehem direction. Glenn and I wondered what was going on. My boss said, "The Arabs shoot their guns for lots of reasons. It could have been a wedding." I said, "On a Monday afternoon??" She didn't say anything. Then the next day in class one of my students who

lives in Ramalla (in the West Bank just north of Jerusalem) said the Israeli army attacked near her home with guns and tanks and four Palestinians were killed. My mouth dropped open. She just smiled. She said it was for the prevention of terrorists. When I told Glenn, he said it had been on the news. (He has more time to check up on news than I do.) He said they conducted a raid and found some Palestinians so close to launching a suicide attack that they had the explosive belts ready. He said the IDF did several raids—one in Bethlehem, too. So that could have been the shots we heard.

My student had been absent that day so I asked her if that had been why. She said no it wasn't. It was because she went shopping. I find that very amusing. I guess the incident didn't shake her up terribly much.

The next time I was teaching we heard a gunshot, then later another one. Both times I stopped in mid-sentence. I was shocked because I teach in Jerusalem, not Bethlehem. I teach right across from the King David Hotel, where diplomats and important people stay. The shots came from that direction. I looked over at Glenn (who was sitting in on my class). He looked at me. We waited. Nothing happened, so I went on teaching.

We have learned that you wait. If you don't hear any sirens following the gunshots, then you assume it is nothing.

At prayer meeting one night, the usual sound of ringing church bells in the Old City ended while I was doing the praying. Then I heard gunshots, which also came from the direction of the Old City—a highly tense area, politically. I kept on praying. My thought was that if something really was happening, the best thing to do would be to pray! I expected it to stop after two shots. (I was getting used to that number of shots by now. ☺) But it didn't. More and more shots came. Then there was a big boom, then another. Like a tank, I thought. I finished praying and waited for all the men in the room to start reacting. No one did. No sirens ever sounded either.

After the meeting when I asked, I was told by those who have experience living here that it was fireworks. Besides shooting guns at weddings and celebrations, the Palestinians also like to shoot fireworks. Again I asked, "A wedding on a Monday night?" "Oh yea! The Jewish people have weddings on Thursdays and sometimes on Tuesdays. So the Palestinians could easily choose Mondays."

So there you have it. Expect to hear gunshots in Israel. Actually, we haven't heard any since then.

My Fears

The amazing thing is that I used to be afraid of so many things. One day God told me to list all the things I feared. I did and it was a list three pages long!

One time when I was alone in our house in the country, I heard what I thought was a gunshot close to the house. I was so terrified I nearly lost my mind. When Glenn came home, I ran out to him shaking and crying. When there was a snake in our house once, I ran out screaming at the top of my lungs. I sat down and trembled for a full five minutes. I didn't have my wits about me enough to stop a 12-year-old boy visiting, from running in the house with a shovel to try to kill it! Thank the Lord he killed it without getting bitten.

That was me then—a lady who fell apart in crises—even to the point of having a stroke.

Can you believe it is that same woman, ten years later, who is living in perfect peace here in Israel around all this potential danger? I can't believe it. I would never have believed I could feel this calm in a place like this, but I do. It is an absolute miracle.

After God told me to write all my fears down, He began a five year long deep work in my heart and mind. He completely transformed me. He brought me to the place where I trust Him completely. I know Him now. I know He is the Almighty God who has everything in control and loves each one of us so much. We are totally, completely safe under His wings, no matter what happens around us. Praise His Name.

I hope someday I can publish the whole story of how God changed my fearful, mental-case thinking into calm, confident trust.

Safe in His arms,
Cheryl

More Tidbits

Sun, Jan 21, 2007 at 8:31 PM

A Bus Breakdown

Glenn and I still can't believe that we are actually riding public buses. The other day when we were coming home together late at night after my classes, when the bus got to the mall, where lots of people always get off and lots more get on, the bus motor died. The driver tried several times to restart it, but to no avail. It was one of the very old buses that is two buses attached together—kind of like subway cars. They are huge and they hold a lot of people!

The driver told everyone something in Hebrew. Some people got off, but it was only a few. We asked a girl near us what he said. She told us he said we have to get off, that they would send another bus to get us. He told people again. Well, it was raining lightly outside, so not many moved. One lady started yelling at him—in a polite way, of course. ☺ I mean, she didn't look angry, she was just using a very loud voice. They argued back and forth for awhile. No one moved. No other bus came either.

Glenn wanted to get off and be ready for the next bus. I wanted to stay on the bus until the next one came so they wouldn't try to make us pay another fare, not knowing we were from the broken down bus. I thought maybe that was why the other people didn't want to get off.

We waited and waited. Finally, the driver convinced most people to get off, so we got off, too. Then we waited and waited in the rain a long time. Some people got back on the disabled bus to get out of the rain. One lady called on her cell phone and spoke in English, "Will you come and get me. The bus broke down in the middle of nowhere." We thought that was funny since we were right across from the mall! What she meant was it wasn't in the middle of town where there are other bus stops for other buses right nearby.

Finally another bus came, but it wasn't an empty bus at all. It was just the next bus on the route and it was full of people already!! The nice thing is the driver let us all file past him without charging anything—even more amazing was that we found a place to sit.

Bus Safety

On the first of the eight days of the Hanukkah holiday, the bus door opened and out stepped this man who looked like a guard. He stood right by the door and said something in Hebrew to the people as they got on the bus. I was very curious. After we got on, he got back on and stayed standing there on the steps by the door. He got off at every stop like that.

He was a tall, young, modern, good-looking guy. He didn't wear a kippa and his hair style was almost like the Arab guys. There was a fashionable girl, in slacks sitting on the front seat. Between stops he was talking to her. Sometimes they held hands. Once in awhile they kissed. It wasn't in bad taste or anything. The kisses were quick pecks. It amused me that here in the country where terror actually happens, they take guarding the people so lightly. No one was upset that the guard was being distracted by a girl!

Later she got off. Then he talked to the bus driver. He said a friendly shalom to me as I got off to go teach.

Several days later, the day before the actual Hanukkah Day they had two guards on each bus.

People on the bus

On a bus you are forced to sit next to total strangers. Most people cope by not looking their seat partner in the eye. They ride in unsmiling silence. They don't necessarily like it if you try to start a conversation. But once in awhile you can meet some interesting people on the bus. On most buses they have a section of seats that face each other, so four friends can sit together and visit during the ride. The bad thing is you end up stuck there with total strangers! One time Glenn and I were in that section across from a soldier holding his huge duffel bag, and gun, of course. After riding awhile, I decided out of respect to let him know we appreciate his service. So I asked him if he spoke English. He answered in perfect American English, "I'm from Jersey." We were so surprised. Glenn immediately started talking to him. He is Jewish and is here volunteering in the military to help protect his homeland. I thought maybe he had served in America first, but no he said he didn't care what the American military was doing. We told him we hope the Lord will protect him as he serves. Then he had to get off.

Separate Buses

The other day I was in a store in the Arabic section of Jerusalem (known as East Jerusalem) ordering English textbooks. Afterwards I asked the lady where the nearest #30 bus stop was. She asked if I meant the Hebrew bus or the Arabic bus. I wanted the Hebrew, of course. She said in a bit of a contemptuous voice, "We don't know about the Hebrew buses. We don't have anything to do with them." I was taken aback. I had seen some small vans pick up Muslim-dressed people, out in the country near our home. But I have also seen Muslim women in their scarves get on the buses I ride, so I didn't realize they have a whole Arabic bus system that goes all over Jerusalem. If they do, then I wonder why some Muslims ride the regular buses.

I also wonder if the Arabic buses are cheaper. If they are, then we should take them. The real question is, though, would we be welcome on their buses?

Cats in Israel

When you are taking out the garbage in Israel, watch out for attacking cats. Well, actually no cat has attacked me, but one shot out squealing from the bin after I threw the bag on top of it. I was as shocked as the cat, I think. Now I look before I toss!

There are stray cats all over Israel. They take the place of squirrels. ☺ Apparently rabies is not a problem here.

Business in Israel

Businesses are run very differently here. I am told that this country was started as basically a socialist country and in a lot of ways it has stayed that way. I'm finding that to be true. I bought twenty textbooks through a company in Tel Aviv. Their policy says they deliver in ten to fourteen working days. At fifteen working days I called them. When I got to the sixth person I was told the books had been delayed because they were out of stock but they were in the warehouse now. (Sure. Interesting they are already in the warehouse at this very moment.) She didn't know all the procedures they had to go through in the warehouse (She was the top lady in charge. Why doesn't she know???), but she said they should be there the beginning of next week. The whole next week went by. Still no books. A couple weeks later we finally got them, but two were missing and two damaged. When I called, she told me a salesman, a very nice man, would bring the two missing ones. She wasn't sure about replacing the damaged ones. She asked how bad the damage was. I suggested that the salesman could judge whether they are damaged enough. I looked forward to being wined and dined by the salesman trying to convince me to buy more of their products, because I was interested in seeing everything they had. After all, we had bought twenty textbooks! Well, nothing of the sort happened. He couldn't get out of the door fast enough. I could hardly get him to look at the damaged books. He said I needed to send him an e-mail about it. I did, but, of course, we haven't heard a peep since.

That business place is run by Israelis. The store in East Jerusalem, managed by Arabs, is run much more efficiently. That is why I was there placing an order. I hope we will be able to get the textbooks I want from there.

I am told that the best exchange places are also in the Arab section. Interesting, huh?

About exchanging your money. Nowhere in Israel will you get the correct exchange rate. They skim off quite a bit for themselves. And you don't go to a bank to exchange your money because banks really jip you. Glenn tried once. Besides charging him an exorbitant price, they wanted to see his passport and I think his driver's license. Just to exchange cash!!! The best places are these nice, tiny little shops set up for the sole purpose of exchanging money.

Prices in Israel

Besides lots of things not being available, some of the prices are outrageous. For example, chap stick. You have to have it here. The sun is so blaring! Even in the winter, the sun does a number on your lips. I can't imagine what it is going to be like when it is hot. My chap stick is running out. We looked in several stores and couldn't find much of anything, let alone find the kind I like. Glenn finally found some when he went shopping with someone else, but it cost 16 shekels for a little tube. That's $4.00 for something that costs only a $1.50 in the U.S.! And we will probably go through it pretty fast here.

Customers in Israel

People in Israel don't wait in line very well. I haven't had any bad experiences in that regard yet, but Glenn has. He had put his merchandise on the counter already when someone butted in front of him and bought their stuff. The clerk allowed it!

Glenn and I were starving one night so we went to a little falafel shop we had been told about. When it was our turn, we placed our order. They shouted something to the kitchen help behind them. Then two guys behind us squished in and ordered. They were given their stuffed falafels and left. We gave the workers quizzical looks. They said, with their accent, "Oh, we are making new for you. Nice and hot." We must have looked like we didn't believe him. After all, it looked to us like there was plenty of food in front of him. He promptly took the last two round, fried things they put in the falafels and gave them to us to snack on while we waited. It was worth the wait. Our falafels were scrumptious.

Amazingly enough that was the first falafel I ate since I moved to Israel. It is the most famous food in Israel, so I thought I would be eating them all the time. It is a pocket bread sandwich chock full of choice vegetables (including fried eggplant), a special sauce, and those round fried things, also called falafels.

Christmas

Here in Israel, there are three Christmases. Most Christians celebrate Christmas on December 25. But here in Israel there are several ancient types of Christian religions still being practiced. There are the Greek Orthodox, other kinds of Orthodox (Syrian, Coptic, Romanian, and Ethiopian) and then there are the Armenians. The Orthodox celebrate Christmas on January 6. And the Armenians celebrated just two days ago on January 19. So that explains why the Christmas decorations on Hebron road to Bethlehem are still up. These groups go to Bethlehem on those days for their big events.

So if you have ever wished Christmas lasted longer, come to Israel!!

By the way, did you know that Bethlehem ("Beit Lechem" in Hebrew) means "House of Bread"? The One who is The Bread of Life was born in the House of Bread. And the shepherds who were caring for newborn lambs, many of whom would be sacrificed at Passover, came to see the newborn Lamb of God who would be sacrificed at Passover thirty-three years later as the final sacrificial Lamb for all people.

May you receive from the Bread of Life today,
Cheryl

Just Another Day in Jerusalem

The other day, Glenn and I were walking from the Old City down Jaffa Street to pick up the papers we needed to get our visas.

By the way, God has provided. We both have visas now! They are good until the end of the year. So we don't have to leave the country every three months. We do hope to be able to come home next summer though to see the people we miss—especially our children and our precious little granddaughter.

Anyway, as we were about to cross the street, which was eerily empty, suddenly some police motorcycles came flying up over the hill. There was one lone car stopped on the side of the street opposite us. The car had apparently stalled or something. Motorcycles instantly gathered all around it and the men started yelling at the poor lady inside. She moved the car ahead a little. They yelled at her more and hounded her until she inched down near the bottom of the hill and turned off into a side street. I didn't notice but Glenn, being a man, noticed that those police were loaded with fierce weapons—automatic pistols, M-4's, hand grenades, etc.

There were quite a few pedestrians across from us waiting for the light that apparently was paused. Another couple motorcycles appeared. One stopped to say something to those people. I was so curious what he was telling them. A lady police on foot in the middle of the huge intersection, directing the non-existing traffic yelled something toward that motorcycle. It didn't move. She yelled louder almost screaming. It left the people alone and zipped on down the hill. Glenn and I waited, wondering what strange thing was going to happen next. We decided there must be someone very important coming and sure enough there came a long train of black, dark-windowed Suburbans speeding one after another past us. We wondered who the VIP was. When we got home we found out that Condoleezza Rice was visiting! Do you think when she saw us standing alone on our side of the street, she said, "Look, there's an interesting (or weird?)-looking couple." ☺ I doubt it. She was probably being briefed up for the next meeting.

Did I tell you that one of my students who is from Spain got to meet Condoleezza Rice? My eyes nearly popped out when she told me. My student's husband is a radio journalist for Spain and he got to take her with him to a press conference. My student got to shake hands and exchange a few words with Miss Rice. She said Miss Rice is very nice and friendly. The husband of another student of mine from Spain is a member of the Spanish consulate!

This is close enough to important people for me. If the Lord wants me to ever actually meet high-up, official people, He needs to make me into a more dignified, more refined lady so I wouldn't be an embarrassment for His Kingdom!!!

Never bored,
Cheryl

P.S At the next Messianic church meeting, Glenn noticed that the guy sitting behind us had a weapon on him. So Glenn asked him if he was with the army. "No, I'm with a special police unit." So Glenn asked him if he was with those men in black on motorcycles with Condoleezza's motorcade. The guy said, "Maybe." He said their job is to go right to where the terrorist action is. Motorcycles can go anywhere.

Nazareth and Nazareth Village

Sun, Jan 21, 2007 at 10:33 PM

Last Christmas when we visited Israel as tourists, we had to skip going to Nazareth because we ran out of time. I see now why the Lord had us skip. Besides there being political unrest at the time, we would have never found the places!

Driving to the Nazareth sites is both interesting and complicated. We went by way of the Megiddo valley, which is Armageddon in Revelations. It is a huge, totally flat area, beautifully green with mountains scattered here and there in the distance. Our guide pointed out Mt. Carmel where Elijah had the show-down with the prophets of Baal. There were many, many battles in the Old Testament fought in this area. The road goes across on a natural land bridge. On either side of the road, the land is very marshy, especially during the rainy season. This is where God saved the Israelites once when Sisera's army chariots apparently got bogged down in the mud (Judges 4).

After we crossed the valley, we traveled up a very steep mountain, so steep that the road zigzags up it. The big city of Nazareth is on top of that mountain inside a huge bowl-like crater. (It makes you think it was once a volcano, but they tell me it wasn't.)

They took us through many turns to the Church of the Annunciation. I expected it to be an ancient building built by Helena, Constantine's mother, in the 300's AD like all the other the sacred sites churches. But it isn't. The old church building she built was destroyed.

America

The current one was built in 1966! That is modern times! I was alive then! Very unusual for Israel. It was built by the Catholics, of course.

The most fascinating thing to me is how they involved the whole world by letting the Catholics from every country put up a huge piece of artwork depicting their rendition of Mary. All very interesting. The Japanese used pearls to create her dress. The Americans used a 3-D Picasso style, except not that distorted—actually quite beautiful. Some were done in Mosaic style. Most portrayed her in the traditional dress of their country, which were strikingly gorgeous! In each one you could sense the respect and reverence they have for her. I wanted to gaze longer at each one, to get the feel of that culture's views toward God and toward the virgin He chose for this miraculous event, but we didn't have enough time for that.

The church is built over the archeological finds, of course. That's the way it is in Israel. It was done to protect the sites, for which we should be thankful. There, under the church, we saw a mikveh (ritual, purification immersion pool) and the cave-like place where they say the angel came to Mary.

We ate lunch in a plaza in the same place where, in 2001, the Muslims started building a Mosque. They were doing it against the rules and were basically trying to take over the area. A professor and a few students were standing at the site at the time, watching the builders, looking at the pictures of what the mosque was going to look like, and the professor said he asked the Lord, "God, don't you care?" He says this is the site where the greatest miracle in history happened. Bethlehem is where Jesus was born. But birth is a natural process. Nazareth is where the miracle really happened. And the Muslims were deliberately trying to overrun it. Christians were going to have to squeeze by the mosque to get to the sacred site. He says he felt like God answered, "Yes, I do care." He and the students prayed together right there. He took us to the very spot where they prayed, and we prayed together there again. After they prayed they put their heads together and each delegated who would do what and who would call whom to get a campaign going to bring the building of the mosque to a halt. It looked impossible because the Nazareth government had already tried to stop them, and yet the Muslims continued in defiance. But with God nothing is impossible.

It took two months of demonstrations (getting harassed and pushed around) and petitions to the Knesset and Prime Minister of Israel with the help of many American donors and lobbyists who knew high up people. With that and tons of people praying, God turned the whole situation around miraculously. Today there is a beautiful plaza there.

Nazareth Village Synagogue door overlooking the cliff.

Nazareth Village

Nazareth village is another miracle that the professor has been involved in. There is a small plot of untouched land smack in the middle of the huge Nazareth metropolis. Why? No one knows. It is just a miracle of God! It was owned by the Nazareth Hospital built by a Scottish missionary group. A native doctor there wanted to do something with the land to show people what Nazareth was like in Jesus day.

To shorten the story, the professor was walking over the land one day with, I think, the doctor, talking over the plans for a museum of sorts, when he discovered some artifacts that made him realize this was the site of a terrace farm. They then got all the permits to do an archeological dig and found many wonderful things, including a wine press and a well. So, the committee decided to turn it back into a farm and village like in Jesus' day, which is what it is now. They have done research to make everything authentic, right down to the clothing. They've also built an open-air dining hall where they can feed large tour groups.

As part of their tour through the village, they show you many things that illustrate parables Jesus told and highlight events during His life. There's the hole cut through the roof of one of the homes. There's the cave-like basement like the one in Bethlehem where Jesus could have been born, and the synagogue exactly like the one where Jesus would have read Isaiah 61 to announce his ministry. Then there's the cliff in the distance across a ravine where the villagers probably tried to throw Jesus off. There's the rocky soil, thorny soil, the footpath and the fertile soil. There are also sheep and shepherds, grape vines, and an olive press, etc., etc.

You can be praying for the village. They need much more publicity. It is one of Israel's best kept secrets.—this one-of-a-kind place. No other tourist site in Israel let's you experience life the way it was in Biblical times. They are really hurting for funds because tourism declined greatly since the war last summer. There is so much more they'd like to do if they had the means. You can read more at their website: nazarethvillage.com

I hope you get to come and visit someday!
Cheryl

4.

HEIGHTENED PRAYING AND INCREASED TENSIONS

The Negev Desert, Bedouins, and Nabateans
Mon, Jan 22, 2007 at 2:00 AM

Archeology and Museums

Last Thursday we went to a graduate seminar lecture by the archeologist, Zvi Greenhut. He told us about finding what they think might be Caiaphas the High Priest's ossuary (the small casket for bones). It is elaborately decorated as if for an important official and it has the name "Caiaphas, son of Joseph" on it. It is from the correct time period and was in the correct area to be his tomb, but they are not sure because it lacks the title "High Priest" on it. They found it in 1990 when they were digging for a road. The bulldozer hit the roof of the tomb. They found ten ossuaries—four of them complete—in the tomb, and many artifacts, including coins. Caiaphas's ossuary was completely intact and had 6 people's bones inside! Before they deciphered the writing on the ossuary and realized how important the site was, the authorities allowed the road building to continue. So now the place is buried and ruined!! That's Israel for you.

Now days the Orthodox won't let anyone excavate any tombs. It is against their religious laws. They are notified every time an archeology permit is given out, so no one can do a dig at a tomb without their knowledge.

Mr. Zvi also told us about his most recent dig near the Pool of Saloam where he discovered a rich person's dwelling from the time of Jesus (They call it the second Temple period.) in the place where they previously thought only poor people dwelt. So this is throwing a wrench in things like the current Temple model!! It is also going to change their former boundaries of the City of David.

Negev Desert Trip
Bedouin Museum

One of the privileges or perks Glenn and I have from volunteering here is we get to go on some of the university field trips and we get to sit in on some of the classes—all for free. Today (I mean yesterday, it's tomorrow already--2am!) we went to a Bedouin museum, a Nabatean archaeological site, and a magnificent gorge all in the Negev Desert.

First we went to a Bedouin Museum near Beer Sheva (Beersheba). It is one of the best museums I've ever visited.

The Nomadic Bedouin culture which is ruled by Sheiks is quite interesting. Outside the museum they have a real Bedouin tent that is actually used for certain things by real Bedouins. We sat in that tent and were served by a Bedouin man. He told us about their culture. Our guide translated. She had already told us a lot of it, but it was nice to hear it from him, too. Everything we heard shed light on how Abraham and Sarah, Isaac and Rebekah, and Jacob and his families lived! Here is some of what we learned:.

Museum Bedoun tent model

The tents are made from black goat hair, which expands and contracts with the weather. It takes one year to weave one strip. Then they sew the strips together to make the tent. They make a partition in the middle to separate the men and women sections: men to the north; women to the south.

The women do all the indoor work, while the young boys do the animal herding. The men are the hosts who sit and do business while making and serving their special coffee, from a special coffee bean mixed with cardamom (a spice).

In the desert, when a stranger comes, you must serve him. In turn he must serve you when your journey takes you past his tent. This is necessary for survival in a desert. I found the same rule in the desert country of Mongolia

When a guest or stranger approaches, he must go around the back of the tent (which is always the west side), never in front of the women's section. Standing at the northeast corner, he coughs three times, which is like knocking at the door! A guest is allowed to stay 3 and 1/3 days. If he is going to stay that whole time he takes off his shoes and puts them behind him when he sits down. If not, he keeps his shoes on. A half a day or a day is considered a very short visit. The host (the elder father of the extended family) first serves the dehydrated visitor a glass of very sweet hot tea to revive him. (Yes, they serve hot tea in the hot weather of the desert!) Then he roasts the coffee beans over a fire, and begins the grinding process with a mortar and pestle pounding the pestle in a special rhythm using the side of the wooden mortar as a snare drum signaling to the whole neighborhood that a guest has arrived and everyone is welcome to come for a drink. Each extended family has its own rhythm. So when you heard the sound you immediately knew which tent had the visitor.

Drinking coffee is very important for doing business with Bedouins even today, including the business of giving a daughter away in marriage. (It is also for giving impor-
tant news.) You don't drink their coffee if you don't want to accept their business deal, but not drinking it is also a signal of an end to a friendship. You will never see each other again. The Bedouin told us the coffee is supposed to be black like night, strong like a man, and bitter like married life! The cups are very tiny, almost as small as little girls' play tea cups, and they usually fill them only half full.

They serve their guests three of these half cups of coffee. The first is to the guest's honor; the second is for the guest's enjoyment; and the third is for the full protection of the sword for the guest while he is in their tent. If you shake your cup, this signals you have had enough.

The women do all the cooking. When the food is done, the family elder's first wife appears just beyond the divider at the corner of the men's section and announces that the meal is ready. Then she serves the men. She then eats with the women who eat on their own side, separate from the men. This explains why the three angels who were visiting Abraham could hear Sarah laughing, yet she could deny she laughed. Because of the divider between them, they couldn't see her, so she could claim that it was a servant that did the laughing! (I always wondered, didn't you?)

The story of the three angels visiting Abraham is the most important story in the Bedouin religion, which existed before Islam. Bedouins are allowed to pray anywhere in any direction because they believe God is everywhere. Their sheiks are their government representatives, who must be wise in the laws of the desert.

Many Bedouins are Christian today. They are beginning to live in houses which are very interesting looking. They are four stories high with every other story open to the air. Next to most of their houses you will see a Bedouin tent. This is a sign of wealth, we were told. They consider it an honor to still be able to serve their guests in a traditional tent. The poorer Bedouins live in tin shacks.

In the tents, the men and women sleep in separate sides, too. The women sleep with the daughters and very young sons. The men sleep with the older sons. Most of the time there are extended families living in one tent. The couples signal each other during the day about rendezvousing in the desert at night! That's what our guide told me. It gives you quite a different picture of Jacob and his two wives fighting over him, doesn't it?

Men are allowed to have more than one wife. One Bedouin man's four daughters asked him why they weren't allowed to have more than one husband. He told them to bring him jars of milk each from a different animal: goat milk, sheep milk, camel milk and cow milk. Then he told them to bring a large bowl and to mix the milk altogether. After that he told them to separate the milk again into the individual animal milk. They said they couldn't possibly do that. His reply was, "That's why you can't have more than one husband."

The Bedouins are a nomadic people who wonder around the desert in circular travel according to the seasons to find grazing for their flocks. They have such good systems for packing up their tents that it doesn't take them long to tear down and set up. If they are going to travel without their tent, they pack it up and hang it in an Acacia tree. They know no one will touch it because the laws of the desert are very strict about that.

Nabateans

After that museum, we went to the ruins of a Nabatean town. [See photos on the front cover and at chapters 3, 6, and 8, (pp. 92, 200, and 262).] The Nabateans used to also be a nomadic people. But they traveled in a straight line on a trade route, as opposed to the circular fashion of the Bedouins. They brought frankincense and myrrh from the Yemen area to sell in the coastal area of Gaza. They navigated by stars and had stations along the way where they had secret, hidden wells to water their camels. They are similar to the Rachabites in Jeremiah 35 in that they were forbidden to build houses or plant vineyards. Because they were traders, they weren't supposed to ever settle down. The two might be the same group of people. No one knows.

The Nabateans were very wealthy people. Petra was theirs. The Greeks were jealous of them.

The Romans ruined their trade business when ships became well developed. But the Nabateans were too intelligent to be doomed. They changed their laws and started building towns, planting vineyards, and doing business selling wine. And they did so well that they stayed wealthy. A few centuries back a Christian came to them from Bethlehem and preached that they needed to repent and believe in Jesus. He also prayed for them and miracle healings happened. The people listened and their whole society turned to Christianity. Then they built an elaborate church with a cross-shaped baptistery. Even their ruins atop a desert mountain are beautiful.

Isn't it amazing that one man could help turn a whole culture to the Lord?!

From there we went to this magnificently beautiful canyon-like gorge where there is a stream fed by a desert spring. In the Middle Ages monks dwelt there in caves in order to seek God apart from their corrupt society. It is a marvelous, breath-taking wonder which God created in the middle of the desert.

After all this we feel blessed beyond what we ever imagined!

May you also be blessed thus
Cheryl

Journal Jan. 21

Thank you, Lord Jesus, for the storm! Thank you! You are answering my prayer for a day of rest and for more time to pray. O Jesus, guide me in my prayer time. Give me more time alone with You.

O yes, Jesus, the other day at the Wall you made me think of the verse, "You will be at the top, not the bottom" (Deut. 28:13). O Jesus, please bring the Jewish people back to You. Bring them to You so they can be at the top of the Temple mount, instead of the Islamic religion. Bring both Muslims and Jewish people to You so that they can all be at the top together, worshipping You!!

I began asking the Lord for more people to stand in the counsel and council of God. And now God has us here with people like Chad who do stand in God's counsel!!

Thank you, Jesus. Thank you. Thank you. Thank you.

And now they are having a prayer conference, Yeshua. Please bless it! Let it be a time of a whole group of people standing in Your council and counsel, listening to Your every Word—listening, pondering, meditating, understanding, and obeying—speaking and praying Your Word into existence: praying Your Will into happening. Hallelujah!

Let the prayer conference be heaven-rending and earth-shattering. O Yeshua, tear open the heavens and come down to the prayer conference. Guide the prayers to be the exact strategic prayers You need prayed at this time in history. Tell an angel to take the prayers and mix them with coals of fire from Your altar and throw them down to the earth to cause thunder and lightning and spiritual earthquakes, Lord, to shake all the evil powers until they crumble to the ground, including all religions, with all their sects and divisions that are not of You: and all kinds of human thought, including secular-ism, humanism, New Age, homosexuality, false peace movements, liberalism, and every other kind of thinking that is opposed to Your Word.

Bring to this prayer conference only people who want to stand in Your counsel: only people who want to abide and soak in Your Word: people who want only Your Word and Your Will to come to pass, not their own words, ideas, and will. Bring people who have already been shaken until all that is not of You has fallen away.

Ezekiel 20:40-42 For on My Holy Mountain, the mountain of the height of Israel, says the Lord God, there ALL the house of Israel, ALL OF THEM, (It repeats it like that!) shall serve Me in the land;

There I will accept them .... As a pleasing odor, I will accept you; when I bring you out from the peoples, and gather you out of the countries where you have been scattered;

And I will manifest MY HOLINESS among you in the sight of the nations. You shall know that I AM the LORD....

O Jesus, it seems this would be the time to bring this to pass—very soon it will, I would think. Father, please bring it to pass soon. Now is when all the nations of the world are focused on Israel and the Middle East. And now is when You are bringing the Jewish people back to the Land.

Bring more of them, Father. Bring them all. Bring every lost tribe from everywhere they are scattered. And show Your HOLINESS before all the world. LET YOUR WORD BE!!

From Nov 22, 06 journal: "I must wait to be commissioned." Of course! We shouldn't do anything until commissioned by God. In the military that's the way it is. You just follow orders. You don't run off and do something just because you want to!!

Jesus, help me to be closer and closer to You. Help me to listen and wait and do nothing without Your command and Your anointing.

I am anointed when I pray and I feel anointed when I write.

The Lord certainly miraculously has helped me do color layout!

O Lord Jesus, give me the POWER to comprehend the Breadth, the Length, the Height, and Depth, and to KNOW the LOVE OF CHRIST—of THE MESSIAH—that surpasses knowledge so that (I) may be FILLED with ALL the FULLNESS of GOD! (Eph. 3:16-19)

So, in order to be filled with ALL the fullness of God, we have to know something that surpasses knowledge!

O Lord, increase my capacity to supernatural comprehension, so I can KNOW what is unknowable—what surpasses knowledge! Come, by the power of the Holy Spirit, stretch and explode the edges of my mental capacity. Enlarge it. Grow my mind and my spirit until I can KNOW and COMPREHEND the LOVE OF YOU, JESUS THE MESSIAH—until I can know completely the breadth, length, height, and depth of Your Love, of the FATHER'S heart, of YOU, and of Your WORD.

Oops! It was my test. I spoke negatively about someone to Glenn. And now I just turned the page of my 2005 journal and, lo and behold, it says, "Speak evil of no one" (Titus 3:2).

The good person brings good things out of a good treasure (Matt. 12:35).

O Jesus, forgive me. I was not speaking out of a good treasure. I was speaking out of suspicion. I'm sorry, Lord. I'm so sorry. Please forgive me. Please keep me from getting sucked into negativity, gossip, and suspicion. Please wash me clean, by Your Blood, Jesus. Please don't let this keep me from the Prayer Conference!

Speak evil of no one … be peaceable, gentle, showing all humility to all men. For we ourselves were once foolish, disobedient, deceived, serving various lusts and pleasures, (the lust of gossip and negativity!) … hating one another…. (Titus 3:2-3 NKJV).

(Note from 3/17/07: I prayed for this person instead of gossiping and two weeks later after hearing a convicting sermon about negativity, this person changed completely!! Praise the Lord!)

So, Jesus, do I need wisdom beyond Solomon in order to comprehend the breadth, length, height, and depth of You and Your Love?

O yeah, 2007 is 40 years from 1967, the Six Day War!! (Who said that? O yea, the prophet guy in the e-mail forward my friends sent.)

Oh, I must tell you. Glenn says that one day when he was walking around in the Old City while I was teaching, a young Orthodox Jewish girl, maybe in her early 20's, came up to him and started talking to him in Hebrew. When he told her that he speaks only English, she stood there and stared at him and his beard with a puzzled look for five minutes before she walked away. Isn't that funny?!

Journal Jan. 23.

We went to the Prayer Conference and prayed for Israel. They often had people come to the microphone to pray. I went once and prayed for the Ultra Orthodox. Afterwards some people asked me if I was Jewish! I was surprised! I guess it was because I said, "in the Name of Yeshua HaMashiach!"

Things Can Change Quickly in This Country
Sat, Jan 27, 2007 at 4:02 PM

Dear Prayer Supporters,

Thank you so much for all your prayers for us. They really are helping us. Something happened this week that makes us realize what a miracle it was that we got our visa so quickly and easily. And we also realize now that it will be an ongoing miracle to keep our visas.

The wonderful lady responsible for bringing us here to Israel is an absolutely marvelous lady. She makes friends with everybody. I rode with her through Jerusalem one day and she stopped the car three times to talk with people along the way. Once while waiting at one red light she got out of the car to talk to the guy behind us! She seems to know everyone in Jerusalem. She's the one who had the big Thanksgiving gathering I went to where 120 some Christian workers came and she fed them all!!

She does ministry all over. She just returned from a trip to China and Thailand. On part of that trip she joined a ministry that witnesses to prostitute women.

Here's where the story begins. While she was in Thailand the Israeli Ambassador there invited her to come to the Embassy. She went, and to her surprise, they honored her there, thanking her for her ten long years of service to Israel. She felt very blessed.

A week later she arrived back in Israel at Tel Aviv, via Turkey, and while waiting in the check-in line she heard them call her name over the intercom. She thought, "Wow, I'm really being blessed! They must want to honor me again!" She waited while they called a few others from the line. She didn't pay much attention to that until they were all ushered to a room and told that they were being denied entry into Israel! Their luggage was confiscated and then they were transported to the airport prison!! Apparently they were suspicious of her because she has been here so long, has recently tried to change her type of visa, and because she traveled through Turkey. (It was the cheapest ticket, she says.)

Can you believe it?!!

She promptly called a few friends, but then the officials discovered that her phone can take pictures so they confiscated that, too, in case she had taken any pictures she could have used against Israel! All the other ladies were crying, so she began to comfort them. Then she borrowed one of their cell phones, put her Sim card from her old phone into it, and called more friends. A couple ladies from here went to see her at the prison which is another whole story of how they had to ask special permission to come after visiting hours and then couldn't find the prison, so they even missed that deadline, but they did finally get to see her.

They say that she was taking it all in stride. She wasn't angry at all. Instead she was comforting all the other ladies, and even the policewomen who kept apologizing to her at how their country was treating her. They liked her so much that they let her get to her luggage to retrieve a few things. What a testimony!!

At first the government was going to send her back to Turkey. She told them, "But I don't know anyone there!" Then they were going to send her to Thailand and again she begged them not to. So they sent her immediately back to the States. She was not allowed to leave the airport, so all her things are still here in her apartment!!

Can you imagine?!!

But the good thing is they told her they are not "deporting" her, instead they are just not allowing her entry at this time. Apparently she cannot return for at least a year!! "Deporting" her would have meant she could NEVER come back. She, of course, is going to appeal her case.

To me there is some humor in this. How strangely amusing it is that one day the government can honor you saying, "Thank you for all the years you have served here," and then the next day a different part of the government can slap you in the face, saying, "You have been here far too long. Get out of here!" Isn't it so funny?!! It's like a comedy movie!

Only in Israel!

Another funny thing is that she is the one through whom we found out about this volunteer opportunity, but Glenn has never met her. He was looking forward to meeting her, but she left for China before he got here. Now it will be a long time before he meets her if he ever does.

I heard all about this at church this morning. Some of her friends are talking about contacting the person in the embassy who honored her. Maybe that person can do something for her.

She was planning on moving to America in May. God just decided to move it ahead for her for some reason.

I think maybe God did it to show the world what kind of wonderful person she is through and through. It makes me think of the story

Journal Feb 1
I'm copying verses from Proverbs about the righteous (starting in Prov. 10)
The desire of the righteous will be granted.
The righteous are established forever.
The fear of the Lord prolongs life.
The hope of the righteous ends in gladness.
The way of the Lord is a stronghold for the upright.
The righteous will never be removed.
The righteous are delivered from trouble (11:8)
By knowledge, the righteous are delivered
Those of blameless ways are His delight (11:20)
Whoever belittles another lacks sense, but an intelligent person remains silent.
The prudent are restrained in speech (Prov. 10:19)

of Joseph. First he is honored by his father, then suddenly he finds himself a slave. Then he is honored by Potipher, but then is suddenly thrown into a dungeon. It's like it was a test of his character to see how he would handle it all. He passed the test and then received an extremely highly honored position.

There's also Daniel, highly honored and then thrown in with the lions. Or David, honored by being anointed king and honored again after killing Goliath, but then has to spend years fleeing and hiding from threats of murder. Or there's Elijah, whom God honors by sending fire from heaven, but then he gets chased by the queen and must hide in the desert. So perhaps our friend is headed for a high place of honor in the kingdom, too. She certainly passed this test!

How about you and me? Would we pass such a test? Would we be able to stay cheerful and not get angry if things suddenly did not go the way we wanted them to? Would we be comforting the police who are imprisoning us? That is the question we were asked this morning after they told us all about it.

Only with Christ in us!

May the Lord spare you of any such test, as the New Jerusalem Bible's translation of the Lord's prayer goes: "... And do not put us to the test, but save us from the evil one."

Praying to be spared,
Cheryl

P.S. Just to make sure no one misunderstands. They did NOT slap our friend in the face, nor did they yell at her, or say the words, "get out of here." I was just saying that figuratively. Also, they sent her luggage to America with her. The confiscation only lasted while she was in the airport. I hope I understood everything else correctly from the reports which I heard second hand. I'm hoping and praying that I did not start any false rumors.

Prayer Conference

Sat, Feb 3, 2007 at 7:29 pm

Shabbath Shalom, Everyone,

This is a beautiful season here in Israel. The almond trees are in full bloom. They have no leaves at all. They are just covered in pale pink and white blossoms. It is still winter, yet they are already blooming. It is also olive pruning time.

The Weather is Cold

It was sunny and getting much warmer, but then it turned very cold again. Today it is windy and raining. So maybe the almond blossoms will be gone tomorrow. I don't know. Glenn's whole body including his feet got cold today and he could hardly warm up, even with our new, little heater on. I have never seen Glenn cold before except when he was working outside in subzero weather! It's the cold cement walls and floors. It gets to you after while. And then there is no place to go to warm up. But at least it isn't hot and humid, so we aren't complaining.

Almond blossoms in Scripture

The beautiful almond blossoms explain the verse in Jer. 1:11-12 where the Lord asks Jeremiah, "What do you see?" Jeremiah sees an almond branch. The Lord says, *"You have seen well, for I am watching over My Word to perform it."* In Hebrew the word for "almond" and for "watch" sound the same. So the Lord is doing a play on words here. This word for "watch" also can mean "hasten," I am told. And apparently the word for almond branch also means almond blossoms. When almonds bloom here it is like they are "hastening" spring. They bloom before anything else. They hail in the feel of spring before it is spring. The Lord is telling Jeremiah that in the same way the almond blossoms hasten spring, He (God) is hastening to perform His Word.

And the Lord did "hasten" His Word in Jeremiah's time. Jeremiah got to see the ful-fillment of his own prophecies (and those of Isaiah's from about a hundred years earlier) about the exile of Israel. Interesting, isn't it?! (Remember, I don't know much Hebrew. I'm just passing on to you what I heard at the prayer conference.)

Prayer for Israel Conference
Yes, we went to a wonderful annual intercession-for-Israel prayer conference. The conference happened to be within walking distance of our home here, so we went to all the sessions we could after our work here was done. For everyone who wishes they could have attended with us, here are some of the things we learned.

Hezekiah was besieged by Sennacherib, the king of Assyria in II Chron. 32. Assyria is today's Iran and Iraq. Today we have Iran's Ahmadinejad. (Glenn calls him "the bad pair of pajamas.") (The speaker says he calls him "the bad dinner jacket.") Notice that the devil isn't doing anything new; he is not creative. In Isaiah 37, Hezekiah receives a blasphemous letter from Sennacherib. Hezekiah is at his wits end, so he lays the letter before the Lord and prays. At the prayer conference during the day, they took the typed up words of Ahmadinejad to the real Hezekiah's tunnel and laid them before the Lord and prayed prayers similar to Hezekiah's. Isn't that neat? They want God to answer us today like He did Hezekiah. Sennacherib's army was defeated by an angel.

A couple hundred years later when Persia was ruling over Israel, Daniel is told that the angel has been fighting the prince of Persia and then the prince of Greece will come (Dan. 10:20-21). That was the invisible world then and it is still the same today. The prince of Persia today is Islam that is controlling the thinking of all Arabic countries, and Greece is the Greek (Hellenistic) thought controlling all Western countries! The devil does nothing new!

We need to do intercession like Daniel did. He had no idea the scope of his inter-cession. It even had to do with the Messiah. He couldn't have known that. There wasn't even a Bethlehem in his day. It had been destroyed by Babylon! In the same way we don't always know the scope of all the things the Holy Spirit lays on our hearts to pray

Here's a very intriguing thing. The word used in Jer. 31:6 for "watchman" or "senti-nel" is not the same Hebrew word for "watchman" used elsewhere. This Hebrew word is "notzreem." There's no way that Jeremiah could have known that this word would mean something very different in Modern Hebrew. It says: "For there shall be a day when senti-nels (notzreem) will call.... 'Come, let us go up to Zion, to the Lord our God.'" In Modern Hebrew "notzreem" is the word the Israelis use to mean "Christian." Isn't that amazing!!

Oh yes, a speaker we'll call Winston says he believes God will protect Israel from Iran's nuclear weapons because the Bible says all Israel shall be saved, "and we (he's Jewish) can't all be saved if we are wiped out." (You've got to read that again with a very refined British accent and then you are hearing Winston.) But he says it won't matter to us Christians if we are wiped out because we will be with the Lord. (Listen with a high class

British accent again.) "You will wake up in heaven and say, 'Where am I?' The Lord will say, 'You're in heaven.' You will ask in a daze, 'How did I get here?' The Lord will say, 'I blew you in.'" He got a laugh from that one.

Winston's message was on Daniel. It was fabulous. I wish you could have heard it. The man who introduced him said Winston gives us jewels. He is right. Here's one nugget Winston gave. "Knowledge has to do with facts. Wisdom is knowing how to handle the facts."

He said, "Why does the Lord need us for intercession? He doesn't need us. He can do all things without us. Yet he chooses to not do anything without us. God says, 'I need you because I say I need you.'"

A Mr. Priest quoted the verse that tells us to "make mention to the Lord." He says it is not like we are telling the Lord what to do. It is like a secretary reminding her boss what he has on his schedule.

He believes that just as there was an iron curtain holding back the Jews in Russia from coming to Israel, (Isaiah 43:6 *I will say to the north, "Give them up."*) so there is a "Gold Curtain" keeping American Jews from coming. They like their financial security and comfortable life in America too much. It isn't near as nice to live here in Israel.

Mr. Priest, a Jew, used to be a hippie. He doesn't look at all like one today. He looks like a normal, respectable pastor. He told us that 50% of the Messianic Jews in Israel today are from the hippie movement. He said many of them, like him, were hippies because they were searching for God, not for drugs or an immoral life. They saw through Rabbinical Judaism and were searching for something real. He says he was searching for God, not Jesus, because as soon as you search for Jesus, you find him. ☺

He says it is the same with the Jewish youth today who are into New Age. They are searching for God. They go to the New Age Festivals in droves and a large number of them come to Yeshua at these festivals. We spent time praying for them.

We also prayed for the one hundred Messianic Jews who are in the Israeli military. ONE HUNDRED! Isn't it awesome?! That many soldiers who believe in Jesus are in Israel today! And I know one of them personally! Please join us in praying for them.

One speaker told us that the prophecy in Isaiah 27:6, *"Israel shall blossom and put forth shoots, and fill the whole world with fruit"* is true today. He was in Scandinavia one week near the Arctic Circle and they served him fresh squeezed orange juice from Israel's Jaffa oranges. The next week he was in Australia in Tasmania near Antarctica and again they served him juice from Jaffa oranges! From as far north as you can go to as far south as you can go, Israeli fruit!!! He said that if you look up the Encyclopedia Britannica from the year 1850 or so (I didn't catch the exact date, sorry.) it says there were no more than five hundred trees in the land of Israel! So back then that prophesy would have seemed ludicrous! Today it is being fulfilled in the natural. (It has already been fulfilled on one level spiritually through the spread of Christianity that started in Israel, right?)

The last sermon was by a Messianic pastor from India. He learned English while he lived in America, but now he pastors here in Israel. He gave a wonderful sermon about intercession using the analogy of the High Priest's garments and breastplate. It was so wonderful. And then using the story of Joseph when his brothers come to Egypt, he showed how the brothers had let their father grieve all those years and had never told him the truth. They did not care about the father's heart. But now Judah steps forward to intercede for Benjamin because he finally cares about his father's happiness. Well, for 2000 years the church has not cared about the Father's heart toward Israel. Judah said in essence that he would rather see his father happy and Benjamin free then to have his own freedom. He wasn't going to go anywhere without Benjamin. After that there was redemptive weeping. Mr. "India" says this needs to be our heart about Israel today.

May it be our collective heart.
Cheryl

Shiites and Africa: the Word is Spreading
Sun, Feb 4, 2007 at 3:48 PM

Praise the Lord. God is doing such awesome things.

The last two Saturday mornings we heard a speaker who is working in Lebanon among the Shiites. I want to tell you about that, but first I must tell you about something happening this week in Africa—in Nairobi, Kenya to be exact.

Eric Foster, whose book I edited (*Destiny of Discipleship*), and who is a Campus Crusade missionary, is heading up a marvelous training seminar in Nairobi. He's using a new software that enhances, simplifies, and speeds up the whole process of translating and making new editions of books. It is especially designed to be used in the mission field. It was born out of a Wycliff Bible translator's frustrations, who himself is there teaching the leaders how to "localize" information.

This is all part of Eric Foster's work for the follow-up/discipleship arm of "The JESUS Film Project." Here's an excerpt from him and his wife's newsletters that explains the project:

"... Both of us will be going back to Nairobi, Kenya in eastern Africa.... The goal is to bring the Bible stories to life in a way that makes sense to local people, leading to life-application of the biblical principles. ... We covet your prayers as we leave for the 10 days of teaching in Nairobi, Kenya. .... We are expecting over 60 African missionaries and pastors from many mission organizations throughout Africa to attend, each wanting to be trained on how to use an incredible new software program that will aid them tremendously in producing follow-up materials. Our goal is to enable them to produce quality follow-up resources in 1000 languages in the next 3 years. ... Only God can make that happen! ... We know the enemy will not like it, so please pray for us and for those attending...."

An orphan in Kenya

Just think, the WHOLE CONTINENT OF AFRICA!!! And Eric has been doing follow-up work in India, too. Isn't it exciting? PLEASE PRAY for them this week. May the Lord bring them to your mind often.

Works like this are going on all over the world! We are approaching the beginning of the end of the fulfilling of Jesus' prophesy, "*And this Good News of the kingdom will be proclaimed throughout the world, as a testimony to all the nations; and then the end will come*" (Matt. 24:14) We should be tingling with exuberance! The end is very near!

Now to the Shiites

The speaker's parents are from Georgia, but he grew up here near Tel Aviv. He spoke about his evangelistic work among the Shiites in Lebanon. Yes, I said Shiites, the sect that was with Saddam Hussein in Iraq! This man does overt evangelizing right out on the streets in villages in South Lebanon. He said many Shiites are coming to the Lord since the war last summer. Last week he told how his operations had to stop because of the fighting going on (after the general strike). (The Hizbullah are trying to overthrow the government.) Roads were blocked, etc. He cancelled some plans for the next day. Then he was told that the roads were opened again. He couldn't believe it. People had worked all night removing huge piles of dirt and he was able to get through.

Yesterday he told us more.

He said that when Jewish people become believers they seek out other Jewish believers. He remembers when he was young, the first Jews coming to the Lord thought they were the only ones. They were so happy to find out about other Messianic Jews. They didn't care how far they had to travel, they made time to meet them and have fellowship with them.

However, he says with MBBs (Muslim Background Believers) in Lebanon where they have to meet in secret by candlelight, it is the exact opposite. They are living in danger in the area ruled by the Hizbullah. One day he asked a new MBB if he knew Ameed, another MBB (not his real name). The guy looked at him in surprised shock, as if he couldn't believe Ameed was a believer. He said, "Yes, I know him." The evangelist was excited, "Let's arrange a meeting so you two can get to know each other!" The guy's eyes got real big and filled with fear. "No, no,no!!" He said emphatically. The evangelist tried to persuade him. "Come on. You two could have wonderful fellowship together." The guy flatly refused, "Do me a favor. Don't even mention my name to Ameed!"

That is the fear they live under—fear for their very lives.

This evangelist got to know a Shiite in another village, Hamed (we'll say). One day someone asked Hamed if he knew about Jesus. He said yes he did. They asked more and found out he was raised in Sierra Leone and had studied the Bible there. Later the evangelist asked him what that was all about. "Do you believe in Jesus?" He asked him. "Yes, I do." "Do you believe He died?" (Muslims don't believe Jesus died.) "Yes." "For your sins?" "Yes." "That He rose again?" "Yes." He believed it all!! So then the Evangelist said, "But you're a Shiite!" Hamed said, "That is the culture I live in." They talked on and had great fellowship together. Later Hamed told him, "I'd love to visit you in the city, but after three visits the leaders here would ask me, 'who do you know in the city?'" He said already since he doesn't show up for Friday prayers, they are boycotting his market shop even though it is the only one in their village that wasn't destroyed in the war. (Apparently they go to a market in the next village to avoid his!)

So the evangelist says it is next to impossible to get congregations started in Lebanon. Please pray for them and him.

He says that in Cairo they are having better success. Some MBB's there were arrested. All were expelled from the country, except for one man who was allowed to stay for some reason. He is now the leader of an underground church. He has said that if they had freedom in Egypt there would be a mass defection from Islam.

The evangelist here said he's seen evidence of this in other countries. He visited a lady in Northern Iraq during Ramadan, the time of fasting when no one is supposed to eat. Eating in public during that month is a terrible taboo, yet she was eating in public. He asked her why. She said, "We are fed up with religion."

So, all our prayers for the Muslim world are working. This is the third time now that I have heard this kind of thing. It sounds like Islam is fast becoming an empty shell that is ready to cave in. Keep praying!!!

After the meeting, Glenn and I shook the evangelist's hand and told him we will be praying for his ministry and will tell our supporters to pray. He was pleased to meet us. He knew all about our Bible college. A professor from there, who has recently passed away, ministered in Israel years ago. Referring to the professor, he said, "He's the one God used to bring the Spirit here." It's a small world!

They are not having problems starting fellowship groups in Jericho. I got to meet a lady who is doing ministry there among the women. She said they are at the stage now where the local MBBs can take over leadership. Praise the Lord!!

Do you realize that all this work among Muslims is in the "10/40 window" which the church has been targeting for prayer and evangelism for the last 15-20 years!! We are seeing the results of all those efforts today! Isn't it amazingly awesome?!!

Be encouraged,
Cheryl

Reply From a Friend
Dear Cheryl,
Enjoyed your letter. We also have contact with former Muslims. One who has been a part of our small group. One night we were eating at the table as a group and I had a phone call from another former Muslim who I had been working with and absent-mindedly invited him to come over. After the call I realized what I had done and I told the one eating that I had invited the other young man over. He said, "You did what?" He immediately left his pie and ran out to his car and left. What a terrible way to live with such fear constantly.
May our God give you wisdom in all your ways!

God Answered

Sun, Feb 4, 2007 at 4:15 PM

I just have to tell you this amazing answer to a personal prayer.

To get to the prayer conference, we had to walk forty-five minutes, the last fifteen up a very steep hill, making us sweat. I had been taking my heavy winter coat, but the weather was getting so warm that I was just carrying it most of the time.

The last day we left in the morning to attend all day. The weather was sunny and very warm with not a cloud in the sky, so I decided not to take my coat. They had prayed for rain and snow the first night, so I should've known better, but I didn't even take my rain poncho!

By early afternoon, the weather turned suddenly very cold and windy. It looked like it was going to rain, or even snow! I looked out the window that was shaking from the high winds and I said, "Lord, if I walk home in that without my coat or rain poncho, I will get horribly cold and thus open myself up to getting sick. Please let there be a break in the weather long enough for us to get home." Charity also didn't bring a coat. We looked at each other and said, "Somehow the Lord is going to take care of us." We prayed and decided not to worry.

Most of the people at the conference were foreigners staying at the hotel where the conference was being held. They had come by airplane and taxis. The locals that we knew came by bus. No one had a car. So we figured the only way God could answer our prayer was to change the weather.

Before we left that morning, Glenn and I had read an e-mail from some friends who said there was a couple from Germany, friends of theirs, who were also at the prayer conference, could we try to meet them? We did. We asked all the people whose tags said Germany until we found someone who knew them. We met them and talked together over coffee and hot chocolate. They asked a lot of questions about us and found out we had walked there. We told them we were a little concerned about walking back in this weather. By then it was raining hard. They said, "We have a car. We can take you." "You have a car?!!" we said in shock. They had rented a car because they were planning to go to the Dead Sea the next day! They were probably the only people there with a car.

So the Lord answered our prayer with a ride home. And he answered the prayers for rain! Praise His Name.

God is so good! He takes care of us on all levels. Thank you for praying for us. They also gave each of us a generous gift of cash!!

May the Lord give you interesting answers to your prayers,
Cheryl

Feb 9, 2007

To a Friend:
... People are handing out my e-mails to lots of people. One friend told me she is even sending them to a man in prison who is a new Christian, studying the Bible for the first time. So, please join me in praying for them and for me as I write these things that so many are going to read!!

Glenn sends his greetings.

Journal Feb. 4   Banish the Enemy

This morning as I was praying, this thought hit me about the Lord's prayer. I was praying after reading I, II, and III John again after hearing the teaching that it is about a church split. Here they had church splits already only a couple decades after Jesus' death, resurrection, and ascension. So I was crying out to God that He please return soon. It is too hard for us humans to get along and to understand each other here on earth. Then I thought about why that is and decided it is, as I and II John say, because of the anti-Christ spirit, i.e. the devil. So, I began to pray that the devil be banished.

Jesus, You gave us the keys to the Kingdom (Matt. 16:19). You gave us the authority over all the power of the enemy (Lk. 10:19). So, help us to unite together, take our authority and bind him up and banish him. Come, Lord Jesus. Bring Your Kingdom and banish satan. It's been 2000 years. Why does it have to be any longer? Deliver us from the enemy!

Then I thought about the Lord's Prayer. That's what it says, "Deliver us from the evil one." Jesus was telling us to pray this! And to pray, "Don't let us be tempted, ("tested" in some translations) but deliver us from evil (or the evil one)."

Actually the whole Lord's Prayer could be thought of in this way!

Your Kingdom come (His Kingdom doesn't have satan in it!)

Your will be done on earth as it is in heaven (That would be with the devil gone! He isn't in heaven anymore!)

Give us today our daily bread (Jesus is our Bread of Life—our daily bread. Besides asking the Lord to feed us His Word today, this could also be asking God to give us Jesus today—for Jesus to return to earth today!)

Forgive us as we forgive (This must happen for us to be part of His Kingdom.)

Deliver us from evil (or the evil one) (Banishing him from the earth would be the greatest deliverance!)

So, Jesus was telling us to pray that the enemy be banished from the earth! And to pray that God's Kingdom come and God's perfect will be done.

O Yeshua Adonai, unite the world of Christians and Messianic Believers in praying this! Help us to take our authority and banish the devil to the pit, so the angel in Revelation can be told by You to lock him up in there.

Adonai, Your Gospel is going out to the ends of the earth. Tomorrow, they are training leaders from all over Africa to use new software to begin to translate follow-up material into tons of languages! And Jewish people and Muslims are beginning to come to You!! So, it's time, Jesus. It's time. Bring everything to pass so You can come!

I plead my case before the mountains (Micah 6:1).

I lay my case before you, Father (Job 23:4).

Cut off your hair and throw it away;
raise a lamentation on the bare heights,
for the Lord has rejected and forsaken
the generation that provoked His wrath (Jer. 7:29).

O Father, don't reject this generation, but instead banish the enemy, all the enemy's lies, and all his temptations that are leading this generation astray. Don't let Your people be deceived anymore. Don't let there be anymore temptations on this earth that lure them away from you, Father. Take all the veils away, all the deceptions, and all the lies so people will see Your Truth, Your Beauty, and Your Loveliness and will turn to You!!!!

And Lord, I pray for the type of management here that is very hard to follow. I banish fear in Jesus' Name.

Journal Feb. 6, 07 But there is still hope for Israel (Ezra 10:2).

Journal Feb. 10, 07   A Prophet

Go tell that fox for Me, "Listen, I am casting out demons and performing cures today and tomorrow, and on the third day I finish My work.

... because it is impossible for a prophet to be killed outside of Jerusalem" (Lk. 13:32-33)
Glenn found that verse!

You are Never Going to Believe This!!!

Feb 5, 2007

You are never going to believe this!!! There is a well-respected, well-loved, well-known Jewish Rabbi, here in Israel who died a year ago and shortly before he died he told people that God revealed to him the Name of the Messiah. He wrote the Name down on a piece of paper, sealed it in an envelope and told them not to open it until a year after his death. Well, they just recently opened the envelope, and guess what the Name is?!! He wrote down, "Yehoshua" which in Hebrew is almost the same as Yeshua—too close for the Jews here to feel comfortable about it. Now that this Name has been revealed they are suddenly saying that the rabbi's mind had been declining at the end before he died. Before the Name was revealed they were saying nothing but honorable things about him!!!

God is doing amazing things!
Cheryl

The Wall Today

Tue, Feb 6, 2007 at 11:30 PM

Dear Interested Folks,
    I have to tell you what happened today!
    I am having a break from teaching in between semesters right now so I don't have to go into town. However, I went today to take a free Hebrew class, then to walk quite a ways to pick up ESL placement tests at the YMCA. On the way walking there the Holy Spirit nudged me to go to the Wall to pray. I was a little reluctant because it meant an ad-

ditional long walk there, then another long trek back to the bus. But finally I said, "Okay, Lord, I will go to the Wall."

As I was climbing the hill outside the city the wind suddenly grew strong and cold, and the clouds got darker. I said, "Lord, I can't do this. I'm gong to get cold and wet walking back to the bus." But I felt a stronger nudge. I was tempted to treat God like I used to treat my Daddy. You know, argue with him, and not listen until he has said it five times, then give in with a sarcastic, "Alright, I'll do it!" I almost acted like that (the old me definitely would have), but instead I said, "Okay, Jesus. I have my rain poncho, and I know You will take care of me." So, I went to the Wall and, lo and behold, something was going on!

There were TV vans parked outside the gate. I couldn't see anything different in the distance. But when I tried to enter in the usual place, they turned me away and said in broken English that it was closed. I couldn't believe the whole Wailing Wall was closed! When I asked further they motioned me to go up the stairs.

I was confused because I didn't know there was another way in. As I passed the huge iron gate for cars, it opened up for a small sports car. Some pedestrian ladies were trying to enter there so I joined them. But the guard stopped us. Finally I found the way. It was up a long staircase and down another into a small, single file metal detector area. There was a long line of people. I didn't want to wait, but I did anyway because I was so curious to see what was going on. Three TV cameras and crews were at the top of the stairs. I had looked where they were pointing the cameras and had seen that workers were tearing up the stone walk on the ramp up to the Mosque. I thought they were getting ready to put in a new one. It seemed like a normal thing to me. I had no idea it had anything to do with all this commotion!

There were lots of people milling around in the plaza, including a lot of police. But when I got to the Wall, I couldn't believe how empty it was! In spite of the emptiness, it wasn't quiet at all. Above us loud talking and lots of laughter was coming from the crowd of workers at the top of the Mosque ramp. It seemed very strange to hear men's voices on the women's side of the wall. They sounded so close.

I prayed my heart out in spite of the noise. It was nice not to have to worry about having to leave in time for class. As I waited for a space at the wall, I watched a very fashionable young lady ahead of me in a wheel chair. Every once in a while she reached out and touched the wall, her nails elaborately decorated. All the other ladies around her were plainly dressed Orthodox. She seemed strangely out of place. But she looked just as reverently deep in her praying. It made me think about how Jesus wanted His House to be a House of prayer for all people. And right above us was the very spot where He took the whip and said that!

I started thinking about all the different kinds of people I see at the wall all the time—people from all walks of life and nations—even India women in their saris. It's like the Lord is getting the answer to His prayer now, here at this Wall! It is such a unique place of worship. There is no other place like it in the world, is there? Here, no one is turned away. Anybody can come and they do come! And most everyone approaches with a reverent attitude of prayer.

Then I thought of the Dome of the Rock right above it. People are not welcomed to pray there. In fact, they actually watch Jewish tourists to make sure they don't pray there! So, I started praying that God will do a work until the Temple mount also becomes a House of Prayer for all nations.

After I finished praying, I was surprised to see there were more people at the Wall. It was getting full again. And the plaza was swarming with police, with more and more arriving. Huge earth-moving equipment had arrived and they were now digging up the dirt of the hill and loading it on trucks. I wondered if they were going to make a retaining wall instead of having a sloping hill. But as I watched, I realized most of the "workers" were actually police.

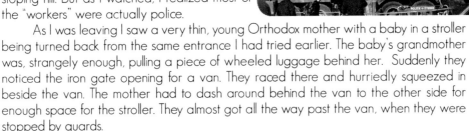

As I was leaving I saw a very thin, young Orthodox mother with a baby in a stroller being turned back from the same entrance I had tried earlier. The baby's grandmother was, strangely enough, pulling a piece of wheeled luggage behind her. Suddenly they noticed the iron gate opening for a van. They raced there and hurriedly squeezed in beside the van. The mother had to dash around behind the van to the other side for enough space for the stroller. They almost got all the way past the van, when they were stopped by guards.

Instead of quietly obeying orders, they argued and tried to get around those uniformed men carrying huge weapons! Can you imagine? A little old lady and a skinny mother fighting with the guards! The young mother soon gave in, but not the older lady. "Why can't we go in here?" She argued angrily in English as she tried to push her way through, "We go this way every day. Why not today?" Finally the calm guard took a hold of her suitcase to keep her from going in. She tugged and pulled and wouldn't give up. It was very comical to watch such a religious looking woman behave in such a manner. (The plain clothes ladies from my childhood church would never act like that!!)

I was going to leave, but I was asking the Lord to guide me. I decided to go back up the stairs to have another look around. I thought it was just me deciding on my own, but now I don't think so. When I got to the top I found the TV reporters were very interested in that young mother. They were talking to her in English. I got as close as I could without being on camera so I could hear. She was asking them what was going on. They said they are tearing down the ramp to the Mosque and they are afraid the Muslims will react violently because the Muslim's feel it is their property.

So, that's what it was all about. Did you see anything about it on the news?

They asked the mother who she thought that piece of land belonged to. She calmly referred to the Torah saying, "It belongs to us, but I don't believe in using violence to take it." Next they interviewed the grandmother when she came sauntering angrily up the stairs. "We never get treated right!" She spouted, aiming her anger at the news crew. The reporter was laughing, "You mean we, the media, are the ones mistreating you?" "Yes, you always say things wrong...." On and on she went, but the reporter soon lost interest. She seemed to not be able to get past herself and see the big picture. (How many times do we do that spiritually. We focus so much on our own little problems that we can't see the big things God is doing all around us.)

The Lord was good to me. I got home without getting wet or too cold. The rain waited until I got home!

I'm so glad I listened to the nudges of the Lord today. I wouldn't have wanted to miss all that! I have been praying for years about my tendency to disobey the nudges. I pray I will have more such victories in the future.

May you have victory in it, too,
Cheryl

P.S. Boy, I sure have been hearing a lot of gunshots while I write this. Perhaps they are angry in Bethlehem about the Mosque ramp.

Jerusalem Clashes

Fri, Feb 9, 2007 at 6:26 PM

Dear Concerned Folks,

Have you seen the latest news about the ramp in Jerusalem? They are tearing it down to build a new, safer, more beautiful one. The old one was unusable. The temporary one is a huge eye-sore and is becoming unsafe. They are digging down all the way to the foundation of the original ramp to start over, that's why the big earth-moving equipment was there.

So, the uproar and violence from the Muslims doesn't make a whole lot of sense.

Charity went to the Old City today with a friend. She said you couldn't go in by the Stephen gate at all. There were police and military all around, plus tons of news reporters. They heard lots of popping and booming from the Temple Mount and saw a man brought out on a stretcher to a waiting ambulance.

So they entered the Old City by the Dung gate. She didn't know if you could get to the Wall or not because she didn't try, but she didn't see any people near there.

We are safe here in Gilo. We haven't heard any gunshots today. We plan to go to the Wall on Sunday. We can't go tonight or tomorrow because the buses don't run on the Sabbath which starts this afternoon. We will be given a ride to church tomorrow evening near the Old City, though.

Thank you so much for your prayers.

Sun, Feb 11, 2007 at 7:02 PM

Mom,

The Newspaper today had a huge article on the front page about building a Jewish settlement in the Muslim quarter, with a flower gate? Is this different than all that you were talking about? It didn't mention the ramp. It's a very informative article. The picture looks just like where we walked on top of some of the houses when we were lost in the Old City. Remember? It was at that one place where there was a tour group with a couple guards and we probably weren't supposed to be there.

It talked about a lot of resistance to the Israeli police and Palestinian's protesting in the West Bank. Is that what you see?

I love you.

Till Jews and Muslims get along on this old earth,

Your Brina

Mon, Feb 12, 2007 at 10:18 PM

Hello, My Darling,

Amen, Until they get along!!

At first, I thought maybe the newspaper got it all wrong. But I found out tonight that it is true. There are Jews that are doing just what you said. They are buying houses in the Muslim quarter of the Old City. The Flower gate is also known as Harod's gate. They started doing it about two years ago, we were told. It is a whole different issue from the ramp issue, though. And there are always Palestinians protesting in the West Bank. That is nothing new.

We went to the Wall yesterday and things were pretty calm. There were lots of police there, but we didn't see any Muslims. Dad wouldn't go to the Stephen's gate where there might have been some problems. I wanted to get close enough to see, but he wouldn't let me. So I listened to him.

This computer is very slow!! I type half a line before it shows up! It is as tired as Dad and I are. We are both feeling very tired lately. Pray for us.

We had a wonderful prayer meeting again tonight. And we had a wonderful time at the Wall. I'll write to everyone about that.

Well, this computer is getting frustrating, so I'm going to go.

Love you until computers always perform perfectly,

Mom

Wailing Wall Open Again

Wed, Feb 14, 2007 at 9:54 PM

Last Sunday, Glenn and I finally had a whole day out together again. We went to the Wailing Wall. It was open again already. They were still tearing up the old ramp, but it was peaceful. There were even children there.

A Bar Mitzvah

Saturday night we had watched a documentary on the FOX channel about how the radical Muslims are educating their children to become suicide bombers. We watched as little kindergartners were singing songs full of hatred. Some of the little girls were singing the awful words with zeal and enthusiasm. It was so shocking! We saw a cleric kindly and gently tell a few innocent little kids a story about how children who are good, who have good parents grow up to become suicide bombers. I was appalled! It looked all so nice and sweet, but the message was so evil!! We also saw little tykes traipsing around, proudly displaying their bomb belts, and some tiny little boys marching together in tight formation, completely in sync. I used to lead children's choir. It is nearly impossible to get little ones to do anything in sync. So I know those boys must be losing their childhood with all the hours of practice it takes for them to be able to do that.

And lastly we saw mothers saying they are happy that their children became suicide bombers.

I went to bed with tears exploding from my heart, nearly ripping it apart, mourning for all those children, begging God to rescue them.

The next day as I approached the Wall, I saw that the area was full of school-aged Orthodox girls all dressed in navy blue, pleated skirts, white blouses, and light blue sweaters. They looked so lovely holding their prayer books and reverently reciting their prayers. There was no room right up next to the wall, so I waited and observed the girls from a distance behind them. I noticed a few who didn't want to comply (as always with children!). About four of them hung back together talking instead of praying. I was standing near enough to hear their conversation, which surprisingly was in perfect American English. Speaking sarcastically, one said, "I told the teacher, 'No, I didn't bring my prayer book. I forgot it at home.'" Another asked, "Let's take a picture. I forgot my camera. Can we use yours to take a picture of you and me." A third, "No, I don't want to be in a picture." "Come on...."

There was a Bar Mitzvah happening on the men's side. A group of men with the honored young boy were dancing in a circle as they sang some very dancy Hebrew songs, some of which were familiar to me. A row of women, relatives of the boy, were standing on the white plastic chairs peering over the fence to watch. Every once in awhile, the women let out their tongue warbling, high-pitched cheers. It was quite interesting.

At one point the "rebellious" girls said about the Bar Mitzvah music, "Oh, I love this song." "Me, too. My grandpa sings it all the time."

As I watched the large number of praying girls, I began to think how wonderful it was that they were being educated this way rather than to become suicide bombers. Tears of joy nearly spilled over at the thought. I closed my eyes and began to thank the Lord, and to pray for them, that they would all come to know Yeshua their Messiah.

When I got to the Wall and squeezed in among the Orthodox ladies and girls into a spot of my own, I covered my face with my scarf and let all the sad tears for the Muslim children freely spill out. I tried to pray, but hardly could because of my tears. It seemed the Holy Spirit just wanted to cry for them through me.

A couple days later we were with someone who works among the Muslims who confirmed that what we saw in the documentary is true. I said to them, "I can't imagine the brainwashing it takes to overcome the natural instincts of motherly love from a mother's heart to cause her to want her children to kill themselves." I couldn't even finish without ending up in tears. The person told me to take the burden I feel to the Lord in intercession because they need it, which is what I'm doing. Will you join me?

Glenn told me about two interesting experiences he had at the Wall. Quoting his words: "After I prayed for awhile standing at the Wall, I was sitting there in a chair reading in Psalms. A man wearing a kippa (Jewish cap) came over and stared at my Bible curiously. He looked and looked. Then he asked, "Are you reading Psalms?" "Yes." "Well, you're not supposed to READ the Psalms. You're supposed to PRAY the Psalms." I nodded and said yes, in agreement with him.

"Later a man brought a group of very little boys. They sat in chairs in a circle and he taught them to say their prayers. I knew the one they said that starts, 'Baruch ata Adonai Elohanu, Melech ha olam....' They all looked so cute and funny sitting there praying together. Then at the end their teacher handed them each a little prayer book, you know, like a church might give little children a small Bible when they graduate from kindergarten or something. I thought how nice it is that here the men teach the boys."

We saw a similar group of boys walking in the streets of the Old City. They were so little (maybe 4 & 5) and so very darling cute. Jewish boys are separated from the girls for their education. Sunday is a regular school day for them. I often see male teachers outside teaching their older groups of boys (ages 9-10). I guess they don't think boys do well cooped up inside all the time for their education. What a concept, huh? Often they are walking and singing camp-type or marching-type songs. Sometimes all the boys are singing together whole-heartedly. Sometimes in another group the teacher is mostly singing alone with only a couple compliant boys joining in. I smile thinking that is just how boys are.

After we were done at the Wall, we went prayer-walking around the south side of the Old City wall. Glenn wouldn't go very far, so we had to retrace our steps. On the way back a TV van rushed by us. When we got to the top of the steps overlooking the Wall, the Muslim loudspeaker prayers began reverberating, this time all over the whole valley. Suddenly a huge group of Israeli soldiers and riot police materialized right outside the Temple mount entrance. We hadn't noticed them running up

Notice the police at the top of the ramp.

there, but there they were. More TV cameras were arriving. We watched to see what was going to happen. While we waited we noticed that workers at the excavation site just below us had their prayer rugs laid out and were kneeling and rising and kneeling again in their Muslim prayers. We thought it rather ironic that if Jewish people did their praying on Muslim ground, there would probably be a riot. But here were Muslims praying right next to the Wailing Wall plaza and no one bothered them. And their Israeli supervisors were even allowing them to do it during working hours!

Immediately, when the loudspeakers prayers stopped, the group of soldiers and police went on into the Temple mount. We waited quite awhile but nothing seemed to happen. If it did, it was at the other entrance which we couldn't see. Glenn wouldn't take the long walk there to find out, either. But since we heard nothing, I don't think anything happened.

So, praise the Lord, maybe the contention over the ramp is quieting down.

Keep praying for both sides. They all need the Lord Jesus.
Cheryl

Journal Feb. 14 Doesn't God's Majesty Terrify You?
I opened my CJB Bible to this

He makes nations great and destroys them. He enlarges nations, then leads them astray. He removes understanding from a country's leaders and makes them wander in trackless deserts. They grope in unlit darkness. He makes them stagger like drunks (Job 12:23 CJB)

Is it for God's sake that you speak so wickedly? For Him that you talk deceitfully? Do you need to take His side and plead God's case for Him? If He examines you, will all go well? Can you deceive Him...? If you are secretly flattering [Him], He will surely rebuke you. Doesn't God's majesty terrify you?   (Job 13:7-11)

...Look, He will kill me—I don't expect more, but I will still defend my ways to His face. And this is what will save me—that a hypocrite cannot appear before Him (Job 13:15-16).

A Hebrew Joke

Wed, Feb 14, 2007 at 10:49 PM

It is a break between semesters here. During this time I am taking advantage of a once a week, free Hebrew class taught by a lady near 90 years old. Her teaching method is full of rabbit trails and is way over my head, but it is free, so I'm not complaining. (The university also loaned me a book and tapes which were made in the 1960s. So, with the two, I'm learning a little anyway!!)

The lady came here in 1948 or so and lived with the daughters of Ben Yehuda, the man accredited with modernizing the formerly "dead" Hebrew language. She learned Hebrew from them, so she knows almost all there is to know about it. She relates almost every word she teaches to the Bible. There is a deep well of knowledge to be gleaned from her.

Here's some examples: Deuteronomy calls the Ten Commandments the ten "words" not commandments. Jesus is the "Word." So He is there in the Commandments!

Many Hebrew words are made out of one root word and they are always connected. For example, "shalom" and "shelem" come from the same root word. "Shelem" means "paid." Because Jesus paid our debt, we have "shalom" (peace), and in Him we are "shalem" (complete) which comes from that same root.

Here's another thing she said that isn't from the language but spoke volumes to me. She pointed out that there are only two chapters about creation, but chapter after chapter about making the Tabernacle. The Tabernacle is very important because it points to Jesus. God said the stones to make the altar had to be un-hewn stones. They were to use no tools because none of our human efforts are any good to help us reach salvation. The sacrifice of Jesus on that altar was sufficient. And there were to be no steps up to the altar because there are no steps or methods to salvation—no "first you do this and then that and that and then He will accept you." You just need to accept what He has already done.

I find that very revealing.

Here's one more interesting thing: "Shem" means name. "Ha Shem" means "The Name"—God's Name. The Jewish people won't say the Name God revealed to Moses, in order to protect themselves from saying it "in vain" as God commands us not to do. They just say, Adonai (Lord), Elohim (a different word for God than what God gave Moses), or Ha Shem (The Name).

Here's a few Modern Hebrew words for you:
Shalom = hello or good-bye (also "peace");
Ken = yes
Lo = no
Lo, ken? = "isn't that so?" or "isn't it?";
Sleekah = excuse me, or I'm sorry.
Katan = little
Gadol = big

So, Here is the Joke.

"Sus" (soos) means horse, and "zuz" (zooz) means move. An immigrant, Jewish man whose Hebrew was still a little shaky was sitting on a bus. Another man came along and asked him to move over a little. "Zuz katan." The immigrant heard, "Sus katan" which means "little horse." So he quickly retorted back in Hebrew, "Hamore gadol!" (You big donkey!)

I have to ride on the bus all the time where people hardly ever talk to each other. I chuckled off and on about that joke all the way home—on the bus.

Lila tov ("night good" meaning "good night") (pronounced "lighla tov." "Tov" rhymes with stove),

From Glenn's Cousin   Mar 4, 2007
Cheryl and Glenn,

I enjoy so much your e-mails. I have printed some of them and passed them on to other people who have enjoyed your journaling. Many of the historical and geographical things you have been sharing I have been learning in seminary. I appreciate your up-to-date accounts of what God is doing. A couple of the professors have contacts with

Palestinian Christians so their stories are not pro-Israel. When you come home, I wish you would come and do a chapel service at the seminary sharing what you saw God doing, and what it was like living in Israel. Would you be interested?

Blessings

Hi Cousin,

We would love to. Because of finances I might be coming home soon and would be in the area to see the kids, but Cheryl will be here till July. God is at work in the Jewish people and there are many Messianic congregations and new ones all the time. We are truly in the last days and it saddens me that people in our denomination are so not with it and so anti-Semitic. Lord, forgive us. There are many Scriptures that the church has disregarded because of Replacement Theology, which is SIN. (See p. 162, A Messianic Polish lady.) But yes, I feel a heavy burden to return and tell the truth about the Middle East. The news is so one-sided. Here's something for thought, Iranians are not Arabs, they are Persians that have been conquered by the Arabs and the Islamic world.
Glenn

Journal Feb. 15
I am reading *Miracle of Miracles* about the wealthy Iranian Muslim lady who found the Lord, then had to flee Iran. (See Journal p. 166)

Journal Feb. 22   Recognized Him
I have been very busy with placement tests and student orientation that I haven't had time to write in here. I was also studying Hebrew. Glenn and I bought some books and cds for learning Hebrew!
Last weekend we went to an Ethiopian/Russian Messianic Synagogue. They are all Jews. WOW!! What a divine appointment! (See p. 162-163.)
We also went to the Mall and ate a Sambuki sandwich. Saturday night Glenn ate a swarmy (or something like that) (Shwarma) sandwich. Mmm!

Matt. 14:34-35 *At Gennesaret*
After the people of that place recognized Him, they sent word throughout the region and brought all who were sick to Him, and begged Him that they might touch even the fringe of His cloak, and all who touched it were healed.

Lord, may the people in Israel
Recognize
You!!!
May they send word throughout the land until everyone wants to touch
YOU!!

A Weekend at the Wall

Tue, Feb 27, 2007 at 11:16pm

(I wrote this on Monday, but our e-mail was acting up so I couldn't send it.)

It seems like it has been a long time since I've written. I've been busy giving English placement tests, grading them, and e-mailing all the results. We had seventy students on the roster for this semester that starts tomorrow. (Their school schedule is quite different here.) Only one student has backed out so far. I don't know if Ali will come back or not.

The amazing thing is that we have four teenage Arab boys registered!! They are all 16-years-old. They say their English classes at their school are not good enough, so they are going to come to our evening classes. I will have two of them. They have names like Achmad and Haled, etc. There are a couple Arab adult men, also, plus a sharply dressed guy from Turkey. With a name like Tazmon, you can't be anything but cool! He's a really neat guy. He won't be my student, though. He is in a higher level class.

Anyway, please pray for these students. Perhaps it is your prayers that brought them to class! It's quite interesting to me that I've had such a burden to pray for Muslims and especially for Muslim children (and told you to pray with me) and then God brings four of them to us. Those four young guys were very polite and kind, and very respectful——quite different from the typical 16-year-olds in the States. These boys are very likeable guys who can have bright futures. When I asked one why he wants to study English with us, he said to get a good job. He was small. He looked more like he was 12. But he was quick with his English. I asked him what kind of job. Without hesitation, he said, "At the UN." I complimented him for aiming high! But, just think, their spiritual leaders' ideal goal for them would be to blow themselves up. It is heart-wrenching to think about.

The funny thing to me is that I was just starting to feel like I was figuring out how to teach Korean adults, and was feeling confident and comfortable, and then God brings me teenage Arab boys! I told you God has a sense of humor. (Well, of course, He does. Who do we think created humor anyway?!)

The Weekend

Glenn and I got away this weekend and stayed in the Old City. It was so wonderful to be in the City over Shabboth. Buses don't run after 4 pm on Fridays, nor all day Saturdays. So living as far away as we do, it is hard to visit the city on the Sabbath. It takes a two-hour walk just to get to the outskirts. By then you are a bit tired for further walking around!

At the Wall Friday Afternoon

We got to the Wall the first time at around 2 pm Friday. We watched as the squads of riot police were packing up to leave. Friday is the big day for expecting trouble from the Muslims who come to the Mosque. It is the so-called "preaching" at the noon meeting that gets them all riled up for action. Apparently the danger is over by 2 pm. This seems so funny to me. It's like there is a riot schedule. It's like some war game with strict rules that everyone is following. From the top of the stairs looking way down below, we watched the police as they removed all their riot gear and packed it away in duffle bags. They put their automatic rifles away in the van, and then someone passed their small handguns out to them. We saw a pile of their grenades. We assume they were stun grenades. They handled them very carefully as they packed each one in its own tube and placed them together in small metal boxes. What we were watching was happening right out in the open on the sidewalk. The Muslims could easily have been watching it from their lookout points on their Mosque roof. Glenn and I said to each other, "You'd think they would see all the soldiers and police leaving, with only a few replacements coming in and would decide this was the time to do something." Glenn decided they must be really dumb. Then we thought maybe they are just normal people who don't care a whit about the rebuilding of the ramp, but when they get into the meeting, they get possessed or something.

(As I watched the last group of soldiers in their well-pressed green uniforms march away, I prayed that none of them will have to be injured or killed this year.)

The ramp itself is now crawling with an archeologist team doing their archeological digging. They carefully go through the dirt that they put into little buckets and then they pour it into big white gunny-sack-type bags to be gone through even more thoroughly later, I assume. The whole little hillside is lined with those big white bags.

Friday Night

After watching the police pack up, have their debriefing in a huddle, and then leave, Glenn and I went to the hostel for a rest. We came back to the wall around 5:30 or 6 pm as it was starting to get dark, and we couldn't believe the change in atmosphere! Shabboth had begun!! We went through the metal detector as normal. A family was entering behind us. The red-head mother was wearing a very fashionable, light green dress, pushing a child in a stroller. Her 12-year-old (or so) son, wearing a suit and a kippa like his dad, walked close beside her as she explained in English how Jerusalem is different from other places, "...because you can feel the spirit of holidays before they arrive, like right now, Purim is almost here and you can already feel the spirit of Purim." The father and older daughter (about 14) were walking within listening distance. The younger children were running ahead. After they all got through the metal detector, the mother and older daughter put on different shoes. They already had on very fashionable ones, but they put on even fancier pairs. I guess because the Wall plaza is like holy ground. I don't know. I found it interesting. The father and older son didn't change shoes, though.

Anyway, the minute we entered the plaza we felt the exuberant atmosphere of joy. The whole place was packed with people—joyful, happy, dancing, singing people. All dressed in their "Sunday best" (in this case, their Shabboth best). There were different groups of young people congregated here and there throughout the whole area. Some were talking and laughing. Others were singing and dancing in circles. Inside the Wall areas, young guys were doing circle dances on the men's side and girls likewise on the women's side. It looked very spontaneous. The circles grew as more and more joined in. It was like one big, huge party as if there was some marvelous thing to celebrate, and all they were celebrating was the Sabbath!!

When I saw the crowd, I thought I would never get all the way to the Wall to pray! There was just no way! The women's side was full of women, children, and baby strollers. But it soon started thinning out, so I actually did get there. I guess the women had to go home to put the food on the table for the special Sabbath meal. I was at the Wall praying for awhile, enjoying the background sounds of joyful shouting, singing and cheerful praying. None of the prayers I could hear were mourning prayers this time. Then suddenly everything grew quiet. I stopped and looked around to see what had happened. I thought maybe everyone had left, and they had! There were still a lot of men on their side, but most of the women had left. It wasn't long until the whole place was empty. It was time for Shabboth meals in their homes. As we walked back through the streets we could see through open doors, people sitting at their elaborately set tables. It's kind of like the fancy Sunday dinners after church with company that I experienced when I was little, only fancier.

Saturday Morning

The next morning Glenn and I came back to the Wall first thing. Again we were amazed! The night before the men's side was nothing but black hats and black suits. Now it was full of men all clad in prayer shawls. Many of which were pulled up over their heads. It was a sea of white. The atmosphere was so awesomely reverent! Yesterday I felt blessed and very much at home seeing all the men wearing black hats and suits, because it is what everyone's daddy in the church I grew up in wore. But this blessed me ten times more.

There were tables set up all throughout the men's section. Men (at least the required ten) were gathered around each table, around Torah scrolls in their beautiful upright Scroll holders, listening to their chanter, reading the Torah in a chanting voice—all in Hebrew, of course. A couple of the groups were young adult men only. At one table with a mixture of old and young men, someone found a pacifier on the ground, and for a little bit they were jokingly passing it to each other—during the reading ceremony!

No one touched the scroll with their hands. Colorful, silky scarves hung from each scroll holder with which to turn the scroll to the next spot. One scarf was teal with orange design. Another was fuchsia and blue. At one table, a small 13-year-old boy was reading the Torah. His mother, grandmother and sisters were listening over the back fence. All the old men were listening closely, with heads cocked, toward the boy's soft voice. Encouraging humming-chanting sounds erupted from the listening men every once in awhile. The boy's father kept looking up toward the mother and sisters with a proud, approving smile. When the boy was done, he received a chorus of exclamations and congratulatory kisses. The men held his face in their hands and kissed his forehead. Some of them, in friendly jest, even slapped his cheeks, especially the couple of boys barely older than him. Glenn and I watched all this together from the behind the fence before we went to the Wall to pray.

I couldn't take pictures. They don't allow it on the Sabbath. One Orthodox man walked up to unknowing tourists and demanded that they put their cameras away.

Sunday Morning

Sunday morning we went to the Wall again. This time there weren't many suits or black hats. It was mostly tourists. Bus loads kept arriving. Most of them were Africans. Then to our joy, we saw another group of cute, darling little boys arriving for a class field trip to the Wall. They couldn't have been older than 4 or 5! (For some reason, I didn't have my camera with me then either!) First they were being taught how to do the special washing of their hands before entering. They were all wearing blue cardboard ties, and cardboard crowns, which, instead of jewels, had Scripture on them. Their teacher then had them hang onto each other's shoulders as he marched them into the men's section.

They went inside the Torah room for awhile. Glenn said jokingly that they were probably going to read II Samuel about being kings! Later they came out and the teacher set up two rows of chairs for them. They sat there holding their big prayer books in their laps repeating the prayers in unison after the teacher. Their childish voices sounded so cute. (I went to the women's section so I could watch and listen better through the divider.) They read through a very long section. It might have been Psalms 119 because it sounded like it was divided in sections headed by alphabet letters the way Psalm 119 is.

The wind blew one boy's crown all the way across the floor and he had to run to catch it.

After they were done, it was funny to watch them figure out how to hold their big prayer books while they carried or pulled their large plastic chair to the back to be stacked. The book would slide off the chair or fall out from under their arm, etc.

Two other such groups of little boys came later. (See related photos on p. 165)

While that was all going on, we also watched a Bar Mitzvah! A very small 13-year-old was going through the ceremony near the back of the men's section. At one point a rabbi laid his hands on the boy's head and prayed for him. A whole crowd of women were lined up behind the fence, standing on the white plastic chairs, watching very NOIS-ILY! They were cheering, shouting, whooping, hollering, and clapping in cool rhythms. Glenn said they had to be Jews from California being that loud! Then he asked one lady, "You're not from Jerusalem, are you?" When she finally understood his question, she said they were from Tel Aviv. Glenn told her he could tell because they "dress different." (I'm glad he didn't tell her the other reason!) (California——Tel Aviv, close enough, hahaha heehee.)

During the ceremony, the ladies and girls, besides cheering, were also throwing wrapped candy at the boy. Sometimes they actually hit him! One man picked one up and threw it back at them. When the ceremony came to a close they really pelted him! But then he was free to defend himself. (See other Bar Mitzvah photos on pp. 292-293)

Later the two classes of little boys were excitedly picking up those candies!

We left the Wall as it was approaching noon. The soldiers and riot police were arriving in large numbers as the Muslim prayers began sounding over the loudspeakers. And so the "game" began again.

Someday may these two opposing sides be united in glorifying and lifting up the Name of Yeshua Ha Mashiach (Jesus the Messiah). Hallelujah! May it come to pass.

Bar Mitzveh blessings to you,
Cheryl

Journal Feb. 28

The so-called Jesus Family Tomb thing has rocked the world. I've been busy doing ESL coordinator things.

The surviving remnant of the house of Judah shall again take root downward, and bear fruit upward; II Kings 19:30)

Shall take root downward ... And bear fruit upward!

The zeal of the Lord of hosts will do this (II Kings 19:31)

Yes, Lord, please do this for Israel today. May they take root downward. May they have good strong roots in You and Your Way. And then may they bear abundant fruit upward—spreading all over the world and upward to You—to give You abundant reward for all Your sufferings and sacrifice and interceding.

And, Lord, please do this for Glenn and me—by Your zeal, do this in our lives!! May we bear fruit upwards to You from deep roots You cause to go even deeper in You and Your Word.

Journal Mar. 3 Devotions on Hezekiah in II Chronicles

The people were encouraged by these words of King Hezekiah of Judah

Be strong and of good courage. Do not be afraid or dismayed before the King of Assyria and all his horde that is with him; for there is One greater with us than with him. With him is an arm of flesh; but with us is the Lord our God to help us and to fight our battles (II Chron.32: 7-8).

God left him to himself in order to test him and to know all that was in his heart (II Chron. 32:31).

Dear Lord Jesus, please do not leave me to myself to test me, because I will fail. Please always be with me and guide me.

The hand of God was also on Judah to give them one heart to do what the king and the officials commanded by the Word of the Lord (II Chron. 30:12).

Jesus, please keep Your hand on me to keep my heart in unity with You, so that I will do all that You have commanded by Your Word.

Please help me now in this position of authority as coordinator. Please help me to honor these Koreans. Please help the Koreans. Now all the ESL rules are getting very harsh and strict when all I wanted was that people don't miss so many classes. Please help me to do right by the two students who missed too many.

Hezekiah's prayer and actions

"...Good Lord, pardon all who set their hearts to seek God ... even though not in accordance with the sanctuary's rules of cleanness." The Lord heard Hezekiah's prayer and healed the people (II Chron. 30:18-20).

... kept the festival ... with great gladness and the Levites and priests praised the Lord day by day, accompanied by loud instruments for the Lord (II Chron. 30:21).

He commanded the people ... to give ... to the priests and Levites, so that they might devote themselves to the Law of the Lord (II Chron. 31:4).

As soon as the word spread, the people of Israel gave in abundance (II Chron. 31:5).

"Since they began to [give] ... we have had enough ... and plenty to spare; for the Lord has blessed His people, so that we have this great supply left over."
(II Chron. 31:10)

I am thinking about telling people to give to the Koreans. Help me, Lord. How can I organize such a thing?

The Koreans

Dear Praying Friends,

The Lord is placing the Koreans here in the Land heavy on my heart. Let me tell you why.

Every Saturday night, after sundown when Shabboth is over, all of Jerusalem comes out to the outdoor mall on Ben Yehuda street. People from all walks of life come there, including curled sideburn, Ultra Orthodox men, both young and old. (But I guess you don't actually see many Ultra Orthodox women, now that I think about it.) The men are usually down at the bottom of the street dancing to their bouncy music drawing a huge crowd gathered around them. It is quite something to see——men, young and old, in black suits and black hats dancing gleefully in a big circle.

Higher up the hill near the head of the street on some steps in the center, a group of Korean young people sing Korean hymns and worship songs to the accompaniment of three guitars. (One guitarist was a student of mine last semester.) They sing with all their hearts loud and clear. The amazing thing is that this draws a crowd every time. Jewish people of all kinds find it a very curious thing. They stop to watch, take pictures, peer quizzically over the shoulders of the guitarists at their music, and stay quite awhile to listen. Many times the young people will stand with the singers or behind them, while they are singing, to have their picture taken.

One time the Koreans were singing in Hebrew. Boy, did that make the Jewish young people laugh.

Glenn and I stood and watched a long time last Saturday. We were praying silently the whole time. I was so amazed at the favor God was giving the Koreans with the Jewish people. There was an older Korean lady standing apart from the singers. Jewish people were going up to her and asking questions. We were standing close enough to hear her skillful answers. People usually ask her what the group is singing about. She tells them they are praising the God of Israel——of Abraham, Isaac, and Jacob. Then she goes on to tell them about the Jewish Messiah, Yeshua. It is so marvelous! Two rabbis at different times each stopped and talked to her——one for a long time. A group of younger people were hanging back a ways, but still listening in on the conversation.

Several groups of young men at different times would be hurriedly heading down the street and would suddenly stop to listen to the singing. They seemed compelled by some force to stop. One guy refused to move on even though his friends tugged on his shirt.

It's like the Jewish people have never heard this kind of music before and they are really drawn to it. That, coupled with the fact that it is Asian people singing the songs, which makes them very curious. When a song ends the Jewish people often clap.

I think God has given the Koreans a special place here. I am so delighted at what this group is doing. I feel compelled to pray earnestly for them.

God is calling so many Koreans to come here to pray for Israel. One lady I gave an English placement test to said she was working on a Master's degree in neuro-biology when the Lord told her to stop and come to Jerusalem to pray. She has been here a few years praying and teaching other Koreans how to pray for Israel. She went to Kansas to the IHOP (International House of Prayer) to study and has started a Korean house of prayer here in Jerusalem. There are so many dedicated Koreans like her.

After seeing that lady spreading the Word on the street, provoking the Jewish people to jealousy, I feel so much more privileged to be teaching English to others like her so they will also be able to communicate the Word here.

Please join me in praying for them. Just think, if it wasn't for what America did for Korea during the Korean war, these people wouldn't be here. They would be stuck back home like those in North Korea. Also remember that the Compassion International organization was started in Korea to help the Korean orphans. (My parents supported Compassion when it was starting.) America has given a lot to help South Korea and now this is one of our rewards—that the Koreans are going to help bring the prophecy to pass that all Israel will be saved.

I am praying that the Lord will bless the Koreans so they can do the work God has called them to do here. Some of them are very young families. One of my student's wives just had their second baby. She had no one to help her, so he had to miss classes to take care of his young family. Here they are in a foreign land not knowing Hebrew or English, no one here knowing their language, having a new baby! How brave they are.

The only way they can be here is on a student visa and the classes are very expensive, as are the apartments. I have been told that some of them have to trust God every day for enough food to eat. I hope the Lord will supply all their needs so they can "devote themselves to the Word and to prayer" (Acts 6:4) as He has called them to do.

And may God bless all their prayers. May their prayers reach heaven and shake the earth. *"And their voice was heard; their prayer came to His Holy dwelling in heaven."* II Chron. 30:27

May people give to them. *"He commanded the people ... to give ... so that they might devote themselves to the Law* (Word) *of the Lord. As soon as the word spread, the people ... gave in abundance."* II Chron. 31:4-5

May the Lord command people to give, so the Koreans can say, *"We have had enough and plenty to spare for the Lord has blessed His people, so that we have this great supply left over."* II Chron. 31:10

Yes, Lord, may it be so for all your workers, including the ones reading this e-mail.

An Encouraging Verse

Sat, Mar 3, 2007 at 11:51 PM

The sky over Jerusalem is a "no fly zone" and I never heard any planes overhead until recently. In January Glenn and I started hearing quite a few planes usually on cloudy days. But one day Glenn caught sight of one and, sure enough, it was a fighter plane. They are preparing for what's ahead, we assume.

The last few days there have been guards on every bus again.

Miraculously, we are not afraid. The Lord is so good. We know we are in His hands. Today the Lord gave me this verse:

Be strong and of good courage. Do not be afraid or dismayed before the King of Assyria and all his horde that is with him; for there is One greater with us than with him. With him is an arm of flesh; but with us is the Lord our God to help us and to fight our battles (II Chron.32: 7-8).

That is why we are not afraid. The One with us is greater than the one with the leaders of Iran, Syria, Hizbullah, Hamas, and Fatah.

Praise the Lord!!!

The same is true for all the troubles you have in your life.

Trusting in Him,
Cheryl

Blessings, Divine Appointment, and Sabbath Peace

Sun, Mar 4, 2007 at 11:52 PM

Blessings

The Lord has been blessing people here. The student from Africa was in dire need, so the head volunteer spent time at the office praying with him. The next day he received a couple anonymous monetary gifts. Then a few days after that someone gave the head volunteer a free car, which he badly needed! It's old and small, but it runs! We get to benefit from it, too, because we ride to church with him, so it saves us taxi fares there and two bus tickets home! Praise the Lord! He is our provider!

Rain

Oh, I want to thank you all for praying for rain. We have had quite a bit of rain here in February. Glenn and I got caught in it a couple times. I found out my backpack is not waterproof! One time we got on the bus just before it started pouring down. Another time it was raining and hailing while we were on the bus, but by the time we got to town it had stopped. May the Lord keep sending the streams into the desert!

A Messianic Polish Lady

I met a cute little elderly lady who is a Polish Messianic Jew. Her family left Poland right after WW II. They ended up in America. She found Jesus in Tulsa, Oklahoma after an accident with her sister. Jesus met her miraculously. She ended up being rejected by her family because the church she went to told her she was no longer Jewish if she was a Christian. She said, "That's what the church did back then! They thought they were grafted in, in place of the Jewish people." I said sympathetically, "I know!" Then she got dramatic. She put her head on my shoulder and cried out. "They took our Messiah away from us!" "I know. It's awful," I comforted her. Then she smiled at me and said, "But we're getting Him back now!" I told her that I'm one Christian who wasn't taught Replacement Theology, that I have always believed the Jewish people were a special people. I told her there are a few churches who don't teach that. In fact, I told her I hadn't even heard of it until recently. She was surprised and pleased. She said, "It's so nice to talk to someone who understands what we went through!"

I have to give credit to my father, who was my pastor, who understood and taught the truth about this from Scripture, and to Rabbi Jim who taught Glenn and me more depth of that truth.

A Lady on the Bus

The other week the Lord gave me a divine appointment on the bus. When I got on the bus, a lady, talking on a cell phone, smiled at me and motioned for me to sit beside her. Those two things, first that she smiled at me, second that she wanted me to sit by her, were both very strange. I almost passed her by because it was so strange. There were other seats available, but I was drawn by a special sweetness I sensed in her. Then she did another strange thing. She started talking to me!! She said she had noticed me and my husband on the bus the night before. We talked further and I found out she is Ethiopian and Jewish. Then she said in a very low voice, "I believe in Yeshua." I didn't catch it until she repeated it. I said, "In Yeshua HaMashiach?" She nodded. "I do too!" I said. Then she felt free to tell me that the Holy Spirit had told her to talk to us the night before but she hadn't, so she had prayed for another chance and there I was!

Anyway, we went to her Messianic congregation made up of all Jews, including many young adults, who are Ethiopian, Israeli, and Russian. They are wildly on fire for Yeshua, let me tell you!!! When they pray the rafters shake!!! There is a nightclub on the other side of the wall of the small room they rent. They drown out the loud dance music when they pray, let alone when they sing. We went to one of their prayer meetings. It lasted until midnight. They prayed earnestly, with all their hearts for Israel!

We are torn about which Messianic congregation to attend now, because they both meet on Saturday nights. We like them both. I like one because they do everything in Hebrew AND English. It helps me learn more Hebrew and it makes me feel a little more connected. At the Ethiopian/Russian one we have to listen to the translation with earphones, which makes it so you can't hear the Hebrew very well.

I trust the Lord will make it very clear why He gave us that divine appointment soon, and to which congregation He wants us to stay connected. One thing for sure, He wanted to show us that more Jewish people are finding Him and following Him devotedly. I had just read in the news how the Ethiopian Jews were asking the government here for the names of Ethiopian Messianics so they could target them negatively. So, I was praying for the Ethiopian Messianics and then I met one on the bus! That CANNOT be coincidental! She is a widow, and has to do housecleaning for a living. Her youngest daughter is only 19 or so, and lives with her. They are struggling financially. The daughter is almost finished with her service in the military.

Celebrating Shabboth

I want to tell you what a blessing it is to celebrate the Shabboth every Friday evening. There is a wonderful blessing God gives when you celebrate His Shabboth. It is one of the Ten Commandments, after all. We have always treated Sunday as a special day. But it never had the same affect we've had choosing the real Shabboth.

Almost every Friday, Glenn and I go through a private Shabboth ceremony in our room. I light the candles and say the blessing, welcoming in Yeshua (Jesus), the Light of the World, then Glenn blesses the bread and the wine and we partake, just like a communion. Then Glenn prays blessings over me and each of our children, then I do the same for him and the children. While we are doing it, we get such a wonderful, sweet sense of God's presence in the room with us. There is just something really special about doing it in God's timing. From sunset on Friday to sunset on Saturday is the time He set apart and sanctified for His people to enter into a rest with Him.

I highly recommend it for all of you. Following are the ceremonial words for you (to which we add our own words as the Holy Spirit inspires us).

May we all find the sweet peace of entering into God's REST,
Cheryl

Shabboth Ceremonial Words
Edited original from friends of mine
(Please add your own words as the Holy Spirit leads.)

"Shabboth" means "rest." It celebrates love, peace, and harmony. The Sabbath begins at sunset Friday and ends when three stars appear in the sky on Saturday evening. Commandments to keep Shabboth: Ex. 20:8, Deut. 5:12 and Ezek. 20:12, 20

Before Lighting the candles, cover the bread, pour the wine and cover your heads. Men use a Tallith (prayer shawl), women use a scarf. Say, "Shabboth Shalom" as a greeting.

Mother: Light the two Shabboth candles eighteen minutes before sundown. Make three circular motions with your hands over the candles to bring in the Shabboth. Then reverently hold your hands over your eyes, like you are shielding your eyes, and recite the Shabboth blessing: "Baruch Ata Adonai, Elohenu, Melech Ha Olam ... Blessed are You, Lord our God, Ruler of the universe, who has sanctified our lives, and has commanded us to keep the Sabbath." (Continue by praying, asking Yeshua/Jesus to bring us into His rest and fill us with His light, etc. as the Holy Spirit leads.)

(Traditionally, the two candles represent the two Shabboth commands: observe and remember. They also remind us of creation: Light and dark; Holy and profane, etc.)

Father and Mother: Spend some time in reverent silence and praying and asking the Father, Son, and Holy Spirit to come and sup with you and to make their home with You (Rev. 3:20 and John 14:23).

Mother: Uncover the two loaves of Challah (special Sabbath bread). They use two loaves to represent the two portions of manna that was to be collected on Fridays for Sabbath. They have them on a special plate, covered with a special cloth. (Glenn and I often use a slice of regular bread, covered with a napkin.)

Father: Lift the bread and say the blessing over bread, "Baruch Ata Adonai, Elohenu, Melech Ha Olam, haMotzi Lechem, Min haEretz." "Blessed are You, Lord our God, Ruler of the universe, who brings forth bread from the earth." Continue with "We remember the broken body of Jesus who said, 'I am the Bread which is come down from heaven' (John 6:41)." Then continue by thanking Yeshua/Jesus for suffering for us.

Father: Tear the bread, and pass it around.

Everyone: Salt the pieces to remember, "You are the salt of the earth" (Matt. 5:13) and God's command to offer salt (Lev. 2:13).

Everyone eat the bread.

Everyone raise your wine glass already poured before the ceremony began. Hold it like a rose. It represents perfection. Wine gladdens the heart (Psalms 104:15). And it represents Yeshua/Jesus' Blood (Matt. 26:28).

Father: Say the blessing over wine. "Baruch Ata Adonai, Elohenu, Melech Ha Olam, Boreh Pri haGafen." "Blessed are you, Lord our God, Ruler of the universe, who creates the fruit of the vine."

Father continues alone or Father and Mother together: (Traditional prayer) "Blessed are you, Lord our God, Ruler of the universe, who has sanctified us through Your commandments and has taken delight in us. You have lovingly and gladly given us the

Holy Shabboth, a reminder of the creation. Shabboth is the first among the days of sacred assembly that recall the Exodus from Egypt. You have chosen us, sanctifying us among all people by granting us Your Holy Shabboth lovingly and gladly. Blessed are You, Adonai, who sanctifies Shabboth."

Father: Feel free to continue by praying and thanking Yeshua/Jesus for shedding His Blood which this wine represents, and pleading His Blood over yourself and your family as the Holy Spirit leads.

Everyone sip the wine reverently.

Father blesses the mother.

Father blesses the children as he and mother hold his Tallith (prayer shawl) over them.

Mother blesses the father.

Everyone eat the Shabboth meal.

Father: Traditional prayer at the end of the Shabboth meal, "Blessed are You, Lord our God, Ruler of the universe, who feeds the entire world in Your goodness——with love, kindness and mercy. You give food to all people because Your kindness lasts forever."

Little Orthodox boys 1. At the stairs above the Wall, 2. On the women's side of the Wall, 3. Just outside the Wall plaza with their two men teachers. (Read pp. 157-158)

Journal Mar. 10   More on Islam and Iran

It's Shabboth!

I'm almost finished reading <u>Miracle of Miracles</u> by the Iranian Muslim girl. In the back she tells the truth about Islam, Islamic history, and the Koran. It's very revealing! The practice of visiting Mecca and circling the black stone are all pagan rituals that predate Islam, she says.

She quotes verses from Apostle Paul and Apostle John that predict the Islamic religion on page 145. Islam means "surrender" or "submission," "surrender to the will of God." Salaam means "peace" which is part of the word Islam. She also talks about the impending collapse of Islam (p. 195).

She and her husband have lived in Virginia since the early 90s! Their ministry, Touch of Christ is based there! (Right near where I lived!)

Their website is touchofchrist.net.

I read an essay about Iran. Iran means the land of the Aryans!! Hitler was all about preserving and purifying the Aryan race! (It gives me the shivers.)

Purim Holiday

Sat, Mar 10, 2007 at 12:36 PM

Purim is quite a holiday here! It's the celebration of God's deliverance at the time of Queen Esther from Haaman's plot to kill all the Jewish people. The Jews here get dressed up in costume for it. On Friday all the children went to school in costume. People waiting for buses in costume performed for the cars waiting at traffic lights. Charity saw one girl dressed as a puppet. As soon as the "puppet" noticed that the people on the bus were looking at her, she put on an act, pulling her own strings to make her leg move, then her head, then arm, etc.

We all went to a modern Messianic Purim party and, oh my, do they know how to have good, clean belly-laughing fun!!! The adults were more into the costume idea than the kids. There were some crazy outfits! One guy held a fork in his hand that was stuck into an outlet with frayed wires. His clothes had holes singed into them and his face and skin was charcoal color to make it look like he had stuck the fork into an outlet and gotten electrically fried. Another guy was dressed as a tree! One of the ladies said her beautiful, ancient Arabic evening gown was the same one she wore at the New Age Festival outreach tent where they witnessed to the Jewish people.

And then they had a talent show. It was hilarious! Exact animal sounds, expert juggling, break dancing and more. One couple came as African-American singers and lip synced the "The Lord's gonna answer your prayer tonight" mimicking the moves of the singers almost exactly!

After the party, we went for a walk down Ben Yehuda street and was that a sight! The Orthodox music was louder than on Saturdays. They had an extra van with extra loudspeakers blaring it out. I could make out the word HaMashiach several times which felt very strange because they are not singing about Yeshua (Jesus), the Messiah. The crowd watching their dancing was bigger than ever and seemed quite inebriated. And there were loud, popping firecrackers going off all the time, which sounded too much like real gunfire! We didn't stick around.

What a contrast to the Messianic party we had just come from!

The actual Purim holiday in Jerusalem was Mar. 4-5, Sunday and Monday. I'll have to tell you about that in the next e-mail. We just got conscripted for an errand!

May the Jewish people come to know
the TRUE JOY of knowing the TRUE MESSIAH!!

What Should We Do Afterwards?
Sat, Mar 10, 2007 at 4:41 PM

East Jerusalem

On Monday we had to go to a book shop in East Jerusalem (an Arab neighborhood) to pick up some back-order books. We went by bus and got off one bus stop past where we were supposed to, so we saw some things we hadn't seen before like a bookstore of Sunday School material, Bible stories, etc., in Arabic right there out in the open in a Muslim neighborhood!! I was shocked! We went into the courtyard through the open gate but the door to the store was locked. The windows were opened and several birds were chirping loudly from a cage right inside the door, but there was no one around.

We went on down the sidewalk to the busy section, walking in among the scarf-covered, floor-length suitcoat clad Muslim women. After going to the bookstore and finding out the books weren't in yet (That's Israel for you. She told me "a couple days." It was a week later and they still weren't in!), we decided to go to the garden tomb since it is close by and we hadn't seen it yet.

The Garden Tomb

The garden is inside a very tall stone wall. Many Arab young people were walking home from school past the wall. I began wondering what they think going past this place every day. Do they know what it is all about? Do they ever wonder what the pull is that draws so many tourists there? Do they feel drawn to it?

We got to the gate and found it locked. We were too early again! Glenn lifted me up and I peered over the wall, but couldn't see much. As we were walking away, the gate opened. We hurried back and begged the guy to let us in, explaining that we hardly ever can come, especially not at the few hours it is opened. He couldn't let us in, he said, because there was no one there, but he offered us a ride to wherever we needed to go.

He was a really nice guy—a young Canadian, father of two children, son of missionaries to Bulgaria (I think he said.). He and his wife are volunteers for the Garden Tomb, hoping to get long term visas for that job.

I asked him about the Muslim young people who live in the area. He said sometimes they come in to look around—mostly girls. His wife gives the girls literature in Arabic and tells them all about Jesus. Isn't that great?!!

He said if guys and girls come together they cannot let them in, otherwise the staff would get in trouble from the parents. He said that when guys come in, they are usually up to no good.

Bus #30

He took us to the Y where we dropped off the books and headed to the bus to go home. Glenn was tired and hungry. He hadn't even wanted to go to the Garden Tomb. As we were walking to the bus, I felt the nudge that we should go to the Wall to pray, since we were in town. I told the Lord I would like to go, but that Glenn won't. I didn't say anything to Glenn not wanting to hear his refusal to go. We waited and waited at the bus stop for bus #30. Many #14's and a couple #7's went by, but no #30. I was getting cold, so I went and stood in the sun a little ways away.

Finally a bus appeared that looked newer like the 30's usually look, but as it approached we saw "OOO" on the front. Glenn shook his head to the driver, but just then I saw #30 on the side and tried to tell Glenn, but the bus was pulling away. It stopped at the traffic light. I ran and knocked on the door, but the driver wouldn't open it for me. I tried to tell him that the front of the bus doesn't say #30 on it, but he paid no heed.

The #30 buses come only every half-hour. We were in despair thinking about waiting another half-hour. Finally we decided that since we have to come back into town for prayer meeting that evening we might as well stay in town. So we decided to go to the Wall to pray and then get something to eat. We decided that it was the Lord who made that bus not say #30 on it!!

The Wall on Purim Day

As we walked through the Old City, we chuckled inside at all the costumed Jews heading off to Purim parties. Most little girls were dressed up like Queen Esther in white prom/wedding-type dresses. Signs all over announced parties starting at 4 pm. It was 3 pm. When we got to the Jewish square, we saw Orthodox Jews dancing to music, with their fringe under-their-shirts garments hanging on the outside, fringes flying in the air. One man was carrying a sleeping baby as he danced.

We also saw young people carrying their opened bottles of wine. Esther served wine at the feast for the King and Haaman, so the Jews drink wine on this day. We have been told that it is seen as a day to get completely drunk—the only day in the year the Jews are allowed to get drunk. They are supposed to get so drunk so that they can't tell the difference between Haaman and Mordecai. (Why in the world, I don't know.) One large young man in a suit was passed out on the stone sidewalk moaning. His friends were all standing around him, one calling on the cell phone. I didn't take it too seriously until I saw another friend off to the side crying. But I saw that they were taking good care of him. When the guy threw up, they turned him on his side and had a pan ready.

With all the festivities in the streets, I thought we would find the Wall pretty empty, but I couldn't believe my eyes! The Wall was buzzing with people—costumes and all!! Dotted throughout the plaza were little girls in their beautiful white gowns. The women's side was absolutely packed! We had never seen it packed before, not even on Shabboth eve. Nor had we EVER seen the women's side fuller than the men's! I decided the women must be praying for their menfolk who were going to drink themselves silly on this day. (It is only the men who do the dancing and drinking.)

After an hour at the Wall (as crowded as it was, I still got my turn for a few minutes at the actual wall), we heard loud music playing. I thought, "Wow, they are actually playing musical instruments near the Wall!" But when I looked, I couldn't see them. Glenn thought it was just from a loudspeaker. We headed up the stairs toward the sound and found a Purim party happening right out on the street. There was a table laden with wine bottles and cups. A band—guitars, keyboard, flute, electronic violin, drums, and all was playing. The flute player and the singers were Orthodox men in black suits and beards! A crowd of reg-

ular crazily dressed, secular-looking Jews along wi̇......... .... fringes and side curls were dancing wildly together. Most of the secular ones were wearing some type of silly clown items. (The only Orthodox costume I saw was one man wearing two hats—a straw hat with a bright red hat on top! That's going pretty far out, I guess, for them. ☺) Several men were dancing with flags with the word "Mashiach" on them. Others danced with their wine bottles in their hands. There was some broken glass on the ground. One guy was already so drunk that his friends had to hold him up as he danced, and his glasses were falling off his face.

The sidelines were crowded with wom-
en, young girls, little children, and even babies in their strollers watching the men in their reverie. Glenn asked one girl why the girls weren't dancing. She just stated matter-of-factly that only men dance. The girls weren't even wearing costumes. At one point one girl did stand up among her sitting companions and begin to move her body enthusiastically to the music, but the other girls glared at her as if she was strange and irritating, so she sat back down.

Some little children got to join in. One father danced, carrying his two small sons in his arms. Another held his son on his shoulders. Still another danced with his little daughter for a few minutes.

Most of the songs were very lively. But for a slow one they called up a young teen boy to come up to announce it.

Singing the mournful song.

I couldn't hear it all, but he spoke in English and said something about a Messiah who was going to come and be with us and live "in us" forever. I couldn't believe it!

It was a slow, sorrowful song. The whole crowd of men (The women didn't sing either.) really got into singing it—the teens especially. They sat on the cold, stone-block flooring in a circle, singing their mournful hearts out. At one point some of them lay all the way down as they sang. (See photo p. 169)

Isn't it amazing, they are singing and expressing their longing for a messiah, not knowing that the Messiah is already here, yearning to live in their hearts for all eternity—the Messiah who loves them and is soon to return in POWER and GREAT GLORY!

So that is what Purim is all about. What an experience! And we would have missed it if that bus 30's sign on front would've been working properly!

As dark was approaching, we went to a tiny Jewish restaurant in the Old City to eat shwarma and falafel. The beautiful, young, Jewish hostess was from Canada, just across the border from where Glenn grew up. She said they drive past his town all the time to visit relatives

Only in Jerusalem!

May the Jews soon find out who the Living Messiah is!
Cheryl

Journal Mar. 14   Wednesday

We are going to a special viewing in Tel Aviv of the documentary about the so-called "Jesus Tomb." The producer himself will be there. (See p. 179)

Journal Mar. 15   Glenn's Gone

Well, Glenn is gone. His dad is showing serious signs of Alzheimer's and everyone is concerned. That's the main reason he went home.

It was raining, sleeting, and then snowing when Glenn arrived here in Israel and it was raining, sleeting, and snowing last night and today when he left. He left at 5:20 am.

I could hardly go to sleep last night knowing that in the morning he was going to be gone. And I could hardly fall asleep after he left. When I finally went to sleep after 6 am, the phone rang. I thought it was going to be Glenn so I picked up right away, but it wasn't him. I was dreaming Sabrina had just arrived here. We were about to hug when the phone rang.

I am alone again. But, I have JESUS!

Thank you, JESUS.

Help me get to work on this cold, blowing, raining, snowing day, JESUS.

Journal Mar. 17   Rest

Last night Charity and I did Shabboth together—candles and all. At first the candles went out right while I was praying about LIGHT!! (They were very cheap candles.) We had to cut the ends of the candles to taper them down. The wicks were drowning in wax!

While Charity was praying, she said something about this time giving God rest. I had never thought of it that way—that our celebrating the Sabbath gives God rest! I guess, if the whole world celebrated Shabboth in their homes, maybe it would give God and the angels some rest! ☺

> Blessed be the Name of the Lord
>   from age to age
> for wisdom and power are His.
> He changes times and seasons   (Dan. 2:20-21).

So, God, please change the times. Please make this be the time of Your return.

5.

EXCITING
ANSWERS
TO PRAYERS

The Arab Boys

Sat, Mar 17, 2007 at 11:07 PM

Hello Friends,

Thank you for praying for the five Arab (or Palestinian) teenage boys and the one girl that we have as students. (A brother and sister joined later.) They are doing very well. My three are participating in class enthusiastically.

In the placement test they had to answer the essay question, "What makes a good family?" I thought you might be interested in some of their answers (mistakes and all):

Omah

First, you should talk to everyone and lesten to him problem and what he feel about him family. after that I tell to every body what he must to do: Fathers: work and get the money to his family and after work....play with him sons (if he not tired) and help him wife in the house work. Mothers: take care to her sons ... and teach them, play with them, and the important thing the mother just to love her sons. Sons: must do what them father and mother told them to do, keep the house clean, don't kick the doors - - - - like this. At the end, I want to told to every family in the world, specialy fathers: "you must love your family and do the empossible to make your family happy.

Mohammed
I think the love in the family make it very good.... And the other thing that making time to talk about their problems. And the better thing will to be good and lisning to the father and the mother that will be very good, and not to give the children a lot of freedom. They will lose them in that way like people in America. I think it's good to go camping with the family in the forests. It will be nice. It will make them strong and love more each other.

Hassam
The family is the basic unit of the socitey. If the family is good the socitey is very good. So we should work to make a good family. There are too many reasons that make a good family: The first one is giving caring for small children. If they got a good caring they would feel they in safty, so when you feel safty you don't harm society. The second one is the money. If you get the basic things, you won't seal or kill anyone or beat or hit him. The third one is the real love. The love is the most important thing for the family. It makes you happey and it gives you an advantage to share people and to serve your socity and more. At last "please think hard when you make family."

Sabra
I have many advises to people to makes a good family. The first one, the fathers and mothers be good, and don't shouting, spechly on your baby.... The second, (you) should make some time to talk to you children and asking them about the problem in their life. Third, children don't afraid talking your fathers about a problem....

Hazem
All the person in the house most work together and speaking together and played and eating together and see the tileving (television?) together and talk together....

Ozman
(a, sharply dressed adult who answered the more advanced essay question, "Why is the family unit continuing to break down these days?") There are very reasons to break down the family unit. As far as I'm concerned, the first reason is the globalization of the world and the changes of our cultures, our habits, etc. ..... These days you can see people live just with wife and husband. And their children when coming to 18 years, they go abroad from the family to work and live his life freely.....

Interesting, isn't it? I hope the Lord prompts you to pray for them that they will come to know Jesus, the source of Love.

East Jerusalem

Sat, Mar 17, 2007 at 12:03 Midnight

Dear Comforting Friends,
Glenn is gone back to America to see his ailing father, and I am lonely and sad. But the Lord is with me, so I am okay. Writing e-mails helps keep my mind off my sadness. It snowed right after he left. I told him that even the weather is sad to see him go.

He came with the first snow of the winter and left with the last snow. (Wouldn't that make a good opening to a novel?)

I am so behind in all the things I could write to you about.

No Fatherly Love

The other week when I was praying at the Wailing Wall, the Lord reminded me of what my Chinese girlfriend told me about the Muslims. She said that they don't know God's fatherly love. They come from Ishmael who was kicked out of his home by his own father and abandoned to die when he was about age 13. In their religion, their god is not a loving father. She said they need to be told about the God who IS their Loving Heavenly Father.

As I thought about this, I began to envision that someday there could be an official apology from the Jewish people to the Arabs, apologizing for how Abraham and Sarah treated Ishmael; and that there would be complete reconciliation between the half-brother nationalities. Wouldn't that be something?

East Jerusalem and Lion Gate

On March 7 Glenn and I had to go to the Arabic East Jerusalem again to pick up some English books. The streets were packed. Their sidewalks had pedestrian traffic jams, filled mostly with women, some in jeans, some in long skirts, some in the floor-length, very dressy, suit-like coats, and young girls in plaid skirt school uniforms, but all had scarves on their heads. All the while we were walking we were also praying.

On our way back we decided to take a long way around and do prayer-walking around the outside of the Old City. We made it to the Lion Gate (also called the Stephen Gate) and couldn't go on without going through a Muslim graveyard. The small gate to it was opened, but Glenn didn't want to try to go through it. I wanted to. I thought if there is any place that needs prayer warfare it is in a Muslim cemetery! But I obedi-

Lion Gate
Notice the carved lions

ently followed my husband into the Lion Gate. We met a tourist with a darling accent who wanted to help us. He told us he was from Ireland. He showed us a quick way from the Lion Gate straight to the Wailing Wall. On the way he showed us where he was staying where Jews and Arabs work together in peace and love. He said it was started by the Catholic Sisters of Zion and the atmosphere there is wonderful. We were glad to have met him.

When we got home that night, I saw on the Israel National News that the night before there had been an attempted stabbing of a Jewish young man by Arabs in East Jerusalem, and that stones had been thrown at a tourist at Lion Gate. The Jewish man escaped and the police caught the would-be stabbers. The tourist at Lion Gate ended up in the hospital. We were at both places the very next morning after these things had happened. We praise the Lord for His constant protection. And we thank you for your prayers.

No Motherly Love

On the 13th we had to go to East Jerusalem yet again. My English ESL cd's on back order were finally in! When we were walking back, a darling, cute, little 2-year-old boy coming our way was getting ahead of his Muslim, fully-covered mother. She was quietly calling his name, but he wasn't slowing down. He nearly ran into me. I thought of stopping him for her, but I was afraid she wouldn't want me touching her child. At that point it looked like she could easily run to catch up with him.

The boy ran past me and the mother walked past me. I turned and watched as the little boy turned toward the street. I expected the mother to start running then, but she didn't. He darted between two cars, but still she didn't shout or run. I thought I was going to see a little boy get killed, so I ran out into the street to go around the parked cars to cut him off at the pass. That way the traffic would see me and stop; whereas, they might not see a tiny little boy. Praise the Lord the approaching, huge bus had slowed down, due to having trouble getting through the narrow street a little ways ahead, and the little boy had paused to have a look first. I got to him just as he decided to race on. I intercepted him and guided him back to his mother who got to us just then. Her expression instead of being gratefully relieved as I expected, was full of shame. She barely glanced at me, took her boy and promptly spanked him.

I walked away a little shaken. I couldn't get over the fact that she didn't run! Her boy's life was in danger, but still she didn't run to save him. I tell you, it seems like their religion truly does rob them of their motherly love. In their religion, it is wrong for a woman to run——and apparently to yell, too.

We need to pray for Muslim mothers!

(Glenn was walking ahead of me and didn't see any of this. He only looked when I started running, saying, 'No, no, no!" He said he wondered what in the world I was running out in the street for. He couldn't see the boy because the boy was in between the parked cars.)

May you come to know our Heavenly Father's personal Love for you more and more each day.
Cheryl

A Jewish Girls' Faith

Sat, Mar 17 2007 at 11:34 PM

We learn many wonderful things at our prayer meetings. One time we learned that the student village at Hebrew University has many Christian students living there this year! Isn't that great?!! One of those Christians is witnessing to a student who came to a church meeting and was very touched. The Christian girl gave her the Gospel of John which she read in one day! But then she got very cold again. So we prayed for her.

At the last prayer meeting a Jewish girl came who accepted Yeshua seven years ago. She is a cute, light-skinned, light, curly-haired, dimpled girl who exudes the joy of the Lord. After the meeting I asked her to tell us how she got saved.

She was raised in a secular Jewish home. Her parents divorced when she was young. For comfort her mother got into Jewish mysticism (called Kabalah). She said it is a very dark religion with witchcraft and everything. Because of it she had what she thought were dead people always floating around her. Now she knows they were evil spirits. When she was a little girl she was very curious about Jesus and the Jewish faith. She asked her mother once if it was possible there was more to the Scriptures.

When she was 16, she was into very bad, dark things, always in trouble. Later she went to Italy on an art tour. There she decided she wanted to start believing in this Jesus, so she went into a Catholic Cathedral to a mass. She did all the things they did like crossing herself, etc. and came out a believer. She bought a cross necklace and wore it. She met a friend who asked her why she was wearing the cross. She told her she believes in Jesus. Her friend gave her an uncle's phone number who was also a believer.

She called the uncle and got his wife who, although she was a Messianic believer, was very rude to her. This didn't deter her. She said, "Let me talk to your husband." He was very kind. Through him she got connected to a congregation and grew in the Lord.

Her dad was very upset with her new faith, but her mom, whom she lived with, noticed that she had new, better friends and wasn't getting into trouble anymore, so she allowed her to continue. A couple years ago, her dad became a believer at a Messianic Passover Seder. Her mother still isn't a believer but the other day said to her, "You went to a prayer conference? Wow, you do such interesting things in your faith." This girl writes devotionals and sends them through the internet to people all over the world! Two people who have read them are Elizabeth Elliot and her husband!!

I was so shocked to find out what Kabalah is. I didn't know it included witchcraft and demons! On the way home, I asked the air angrily, "Haven't the Jews learned anything from the Diaspora? It was witchcraft and idol worship and stuff that made God so upset with them! And here they are into it all again——into Kabalah and New Age, etc!! Ugh!!"

At the same prayer meeting we also learned that the gay pride people are trying again to have a march in Jerusalem. Only this time they are disguising it as a civil rights march, of which the gay rights will be the highlighted one, of course! I forget when the date is, but it isn't far off. So please pray!!!

Charity has been invited by a friend to come with her and some others to meet an Ultra Orthodox young man who is secretly a believer and needs some fellowship. Can you believe it? An ULTRA ORTHODOX!!! Our prayers are working!!!!

Keep interceding!
Cheryl

Iranians

Sat, Mar 17, 2007 at 12:50 Midnight

I just finished reading a book, *Miracle of Miracles* by Mina Nevisa. She is the daughter and granddaughter of well-known Koran teachers in Iran. She became a secret believer. When her group was exposed, she and her husband had to flee Iran in 1980 or so. Their ministry is near Virginia of all places——less than two hours from where we used to live!!! They have a wonderful ministry reaching Muslims for Christ. The story of her conversion is marvelous. In the back of her book she teaches us about reaching Muslims, and then has a section talking straight to a Muslim unbeliever. It is such a great book. You can buy it on her website: www.touchofchrist.net She tells of many Iranians who gave their lives evangelizing for their new faith.

It was so encouraging to me to read this book. I've been praying for the Muslims for years, and here the Lord was answering me——and right in my own back yard, too!!

A lady we know just came back from a visit to Iran with a group of ladies. They took Farsi Bibles in. (Farsi is the Iranian language.) They met young college students who pleaded with them, "We don't support the nuclear program. Please don't bomb us." They were very open to listening to the ladies.

So, keep praying. God is doing great things.

Being a praying Christian is such a wonderful adventure, isn't it?!!

Glenn

Sun, Mar 18, 2007 at 2:56 AM

Okay, Faithful Friends, this is my last e-mail tonight and then I have to go to bed.

Glenn is back in the States. His father's mind comes and goes. (He has early Alzheimer's.) Glenn is helping his mom pack for the move to the retirement center. This move is really making Glenn sad, but apparently his parents are handling it okay.

A Jewish Lady and a Jewish Girl

The day before Glenn left, there wasn't much for him to do here so he took the bus into town. He prayed for a couple hours at the Wall and then walked around the Old City. The Lord gave him an opportunity to witness to an Orthodox lady. It was in a shop. A customer started talking to Glenn about being a convert to Judaism and how a person needs to study the Torah and obey all of it. Glenn told him, "It's not about religion, it's about relationship." The customer went on talking his own spiel and soon left, but the owner seemed interested, so Glenn asked her, "Don't you see what's happening?" She responded with, "Why, what's happening?" He explained, "There are so many Christians moving here. Don't you ever wonder why?" She said, "It's because they love Israel." Glenn countered her, "It's more than that. They love the God of Israel and He is telling them to come here to pray. Don't you read the prophets? It is a fulfilling of what the prophets said." She said she doesn't have time to read the prophets. She started to act uncomfortable because there were some people outside within earshot, so Glenn left her, telling her to read the prophets, "Especially read Isaiah 53!"

He came home encouraged, feeling like he finally got to do what we were called here to do.

On the plane to the U.S. Glenn sat between two Orthodox Jews, an old man coming to the States for the first time who didn't know hardly any English, and a 13-year-old girl. The girl was very talkative. Her first question to Glenn was, "Why don't the married Christian women cover their heads like they are supposed to?" This opened a conversation that lasted four hours. She taught Glenn many things about her Jewish faith, and he asked her questions to raise her interest in Yeshua.

She said they can't build a new Temple. Why? Glenn asked. Because they have to wait for their Messiah to come, but they don't know who he is, or what he will look like, or when he is coming. "Then how will you know when he comes?" Glenn asked her. "The rabbis will tell us," she answered. "Well," Glenn asked further, "if you don't know who he is, or what he looks like, or when he is coming, is it possible he came already and you missed him?" She had no answer.

Her father is a doctor in NYC. Her mother and all her many brothers and sisters live in Israel near Jerusalem. Her father is very wealthy and comes home constantly and regularly. She is a rebellious girl. She doesn't like her mom's rules. She has watched many forbidden movies with her friends and has seen things on the internet. "You would be surprised what kinds of things I've seen," she told Glenn proudly. (I feel so sorry for her mother!!!) She has been kicked out of school, so she was going to live with her father who was getting a private tutor for her.

Glenn talked to her about having a personal relationship with God, being sure of His love for her, and knowing that He will never leave her. He said he could tell it was touching her because her eyes got a little teary.

I am so proud of Glenn!! I pray the Lord will cause these seeds Glenn has planted to be watered and to take root and grow. Join me in praying for these two precious Jewesses.

Koreans

One of the new Korean students is a computer programmer who used to work for Samsung and then started his own business. His business was going strong when God suddenly told him last August to move to Israel. So he sold his business and his home and moved his family (his wife and two almost grown daughters) to Israel. They moved to a Jewish neighborhood instead of to French Hill where most of the other Koreans live. He said he still is not sure why God brought them here. They were not in church work or ministry before at all, so the whole thing is still a mystery to them. They just knew they needed to obey God. Isn't it amazing?!! God keeps calling more and more Koreans here! All independent of each other. They meet and become friends after they get here.

About the So-Called Jesus' Family Tomb

The night before Glenn left, we were taken to a special reception for a special viewing of the documentary about the tomb. The film-maker himself, Simcha Jacovinci (?) was there. ("Simcha" means "happy" or "joy.") There is one good thing about this film. For all Jews who watch it, they can no longer tell themselves that Jesus' Name isn't Yeshua (which means "salvation"). The whole premise of saying the tomb belongs to Jesus is based on the inscription reading "Yeshua, son of Joseph." So the Name, Yeshua, was said repeatedly and written repeatedly throughout the film.

During the question time afterwards, someone in the audience corrected Simcha, saying, "Yeshu!" (This is the derogatory name they use for Jesus.) Simcha said, "No, Yeshua!" I found it very funny. Here is a Jewish guy trying to disprove the resurrection of Jesus, but instead he is proving the True Name of Jesus!! He did use the derogatory name himself a few times during the questioning, but his film never used it!

They don't like to use the Name, Yeshua, because they don't like to be calling Jesus, "Salvation." Yeshua still means "salvation" in their modern language today. (See p. 97.)

So, praise the Lord! This has been one of our prayers for the Jewish people—that Jesus' True Name will be revealed to them. What a way to have it proven! But praise the Lord!! Whatever it takes!!!

Now, I believe I'm caught up. Oops! There's one more thing.

Baptist Jews!

We are getting to know a Christian leader here, a very Godly, self-sacrificing man, who was raised in Michigan and, as a young adult, went to a church an hour from where I grew up! It's such a small world here in Jerusalem. He was raised Baptist, but found out he was a Jew when he was a teen. Can you imagine?!! He has been serving here in Israel for most of his adult life.

❋   ❋   ❋

Praise the Lord, He is our provider!! I just found out that you wonderful people are giving us a brand new laptop for Glenn to bring back!!! Praise the Lord!!!

God is Good. May He provide for all your needs also,
Cheryl

P.S. We haven't heard planes overhead for awhile.

P.S.S. The snow that came on the day Glenn left was so bad that in Hebron there was an accident between a city bus and a van, killing the parents of eight young children!   It is so awful! It's a huge deal here because accidents from weather are extremely unusual in Israel!! Actually this is the first bad accident of any kind that we've heard about here.

Journal Mar. 20 Solomon's Prayers

✏️(I've heard four jets flying overhead while I've been doing my devotions just now.)

I Kings 8   Solomon's Prayer

Verse 23 O Lord God of Israel,
there is no God like You
in heaven or on earth beneath.

Verse 15 Blessed be the Lord, the God of Israel
who with His hand has fulfilled
what He promised with His mouth.

Verse 24 You promised with Your mouth
and have this day fulfilled with Your hand.

Verse 35 When heaven is shut up
and there is no rain
because they have sinned against You
and then they pray toward this place,
confess Your Name and turn from their sin
then hear in heaven, forgive
and grant rain in Your land.

Verse 38 Whatever prayer, whatever plea
there is from any individual or from all Your people....,
all knowing the afflictions of their own hearts
so that they stretch out their hands toward this house;
then hear in heaven ... forgive, act and render
to all those whose hearts You know—according to all their ways

Verse 41 ... (See p. 182)

I was not going to go to the Wall to pray today, but God is telling me to GO so Solomon's prayer can be answered!

Yes, Lord, I will go. I will pray the prayers the Holy Spirit inspires me to pray—that He prays through me—the same Holy Spirit who inspired Solomon to pray his prayer!

The Lord appeared to Solomon and spoke directly to him!!

II Chron. 7:3 Now My eyes will be open
and My ears attentive to the prayer
that is made in this place.
For I have chosen and consecrated this house.
So My Name may be there forever
My eyes and My heart will be there for all time! ...   (See p. 182)

Encouragement for Praying at the Wall

The other day I felt tired and under the weather, so I wasn't going to go to the Wall to pray. I hadn't had much time for devotions lately either, so I felt a bit discouraged. I asked the Lord to guide my Bible reading since I hadn't been able to be doing any systematic study.

The Lord reminded me that I had been studying about all the kings for the book I had been working on, so I decided to read II Kings again now that I knew so much more about each of them. I didn't want to read about Solomon since I already knew about him, but somehow I ended up reading about him anyway, and it soon became clear why.

Solomon's Prayer of Dedication of the Temple

> I Kings 8:23 *O Lord God of Israel, There is no God like You in Heaven or on earth. ... Verse 38 Whatever prayer, whatever plea there is from any (ANY!) individual ... forgive, act, and render to all those whose hearts You know....*

> *That was all great, but here was the clincher!*

> Verse 41 *Likewise when a foreigner who is not of Your people Israel comes from a distant land because of Your Name ... Your Great Name and Your mighty hand and Your outstretched arm, ... prays toward this house, then hear in Heaven... and do according to all that the foreigner calls to you so that all the peoples of the earth may know that Your Name has been invoked. (II Chron. 6:33 says: ...Do whatever the foreigners ask of You in order that all the peoples of the earth may know Your Name and fear You.)*

> II Chron. 7:15, *God answers Solomon's prayer with these words:* Now My eyes will be open and My ears attentive to the prayer that is made in this place. For now I have chosen and consecrated this house so that My Name may be there forever; My eyes and My heart will be there for all time.

Wow!! I knew right away, God was telling me He wanted me to go to the Wall to pray that day. So I went and I boldly prayed that God would answer Solomon's prayer, by answering all the prayers of foreigners, whom He has sent from so many distant lands, America, Korea, China, etc., to pray! I also prayed over the folded prayers right in front of me stuck in the crevices.

Today I read further:

> II Chron. 7:19-22 *But if you turn aside and forsake ... My commandments ... and serve other gods ... then I will pluck you up from this land; ... and this house which I have consecrated for My Name, I will cast out of My sight, and will make it a proverb and a byword among all peoples. ...everyone passing by will be astonished, and say, "Why has the Lord done such a thing to this land and to this house?" then they will say, "Because they abandoned the Lord the God of their ancestors...."*

So, I felt discouraged a minute, until I saw that God didn't say He would take His eye, or ear, or heart, or Name away from this place, He just said He would cast the house away. And He certainly has fulfilled that prophecy!! God does not go back on His Word or His promises. The Wailing Wall still bears His Name today. People don't come there to pray to false gods, or to put prayers in the cracks for other gods. They know they are praying to God! And verse 14 is the famous verse, "*If My people who are called by My Name humble themselves and pray....*"

Speaking of Foreigners Praying Here

There are four Houses of Prayer in Jerusalem, two of which are full-time 24/7 places of continued prayer. Guess where they are located? One is on the west side of the Old City, called Succat Hillel (Tabernacle of Praise) and the other is on the east side of the Old City, on the east side of the Mount of Olives. It is called the Jerusalem House of Prayer for All Nations.

East side....west side.... There's a startling Bible verse about that.

Zech. 14 : 8 *On that day living waters shall flow out from Jerusalem, half of them to the eastern sea and half of them to the western sea; it shall continue in summer as in winter.*

This prophecy has a physical fulfillment that will someday come to pass—soon I hope. But it looks like it could be coming to pass spiritually through these Houses of Prayer!! Interesting, isn't it?

There's an article in the magazine, *Israel Today* (Jan. 07), about the people who pray through the night watches at Succat Hillel. They comment that their prayers are being answered, that "many times they read the results of their prayers in the newspapers the next day." (This has happened to us in our prayer group! We have read about it in two days.) One main prayer of theirs that has been answered is "there have been no terrorist attacks since 2004 in Jerusalem, the most spiritually contested city in the world."

So God is answering Solomon's prayer!!!

Of course, God is everywhere, and He hears everyone's prayers no matter where they pray them. He answers all believing prayers everywhere from all sincere hearts. But it is neat to see that He is also answering prayers from this site where He promised He would.

May the Lord give you special encouragement in your praying today.

The New Believer

Sat, Mar 24, 2007 at 1:47 PM

Dear Praying Partners,

Have you been praying for the Jewish people? Well, God is answering. Charity saw the believing Orthodox guy (as in Ultra!!) the other day. Here is his story. He is the son of a rabbi. (That in itself is amazing!!!!) He is number nine or so of thirteen children. One day at the yeshiva (a school where they study the Torah and the Talmud, etc.) he read that Yeshua had five disciples and got kicked out of every synagogue. He asked his teacher/rabbi about it, who told him, "It's an awful story. You don't need to know about that," and refused to tell him anything. (Why do they say only five disciples? Maybe because if they said twelve, it would look too much like a good, Jewish thing?!!)

The young man really wanted to know about this Yeshua, so he went to a big protestant church in the Old City. The people there connected him with a Christian family who led him to Christ and mentored him. Way to go, Church!!!

That was two years ago. Since then he has remained a believer, but secretly. He has to be very careful so his father doesn't find out, otherwise he might get sent to a psychiatric hospital and given drugs. That is what they do, he says. Charity says she actually knows a guy they did that to!!! Can you believe it?!! They do it because they say, that if you believe in Yeshua, you must be insane. How horrible!

He said he told his mother one day that Yeshua is the Messiah. She said, "Yeshua? Who's Yeshua? You mean Yehoshua (Joshua)?" (The two names are very similar in Hebrew.)

Pray for him. He needs more fellowship in the Lord. And, of course, pray for his protection. His name was... I forget.... Joseph, I think. Maybe it's best you don't know his real name. God will know who you mean. Pray that his whole household comes to know their Messiah! I may get to meet him soon. I hope so!

I wonder how many more "secret believers" there are among them! This really makes me feel encouraged and empowered to continue doing prayer-walking in that neighborhood!

May this be the beginning of a complete revival in that whole community!!!

Praise His Name!! God is awesome,

Another Interested Jewish Guy

Sat, Mar 24, 2007 at 10:09 PM

Tonight we heard that the Christian and Messianic college students here in Israel had a special weekend conference. A Jewish man attended who is a kosher inspector. He inspects the meat to make sure it is killed and butchered the kosher way. To be qualified for that they have to be trained as rabbis, I believe. Anyway, it means he is a serious Jew. He said to her, "Do you really feel that God loves you?" She gave an enthusiastic, "Ken! (Yes!)" He responded, "Wow! I've never felt that. I wasn't taught that." He asked a lot more questions and is getting close to believing in Yeshua.

After the Israeli college student told us this she prayed another very earnest prayer for her country.

So there are religious, Jewish people who are hungry and longing for more. Our prayers are being answered, and prophecies are being fulfilled!

Exciting, isn't it?

Healing, and Young Boys at the Wall

Sat, Mar-24, 2007 at 3:09 PM

Healing

The other night I could feel a terrible sore throat and headache coming on. Others around here had it. I knew by morning I was going to be very sick. I prayed and prayed, telling the Lord that I wouldn't be able to teach if I got that sick. I laid my own hands on my throat and pleaded the blood of Jesus, rebuked the sickness, claiming that "by His stripes I'm healed." I didn't feel very full of faith. I woke up later and it hurt to swallow. I prayed hard again.

Then I woke up in the morning feeling fine!! Praise the Lord. This same thing happened to me in December one night. Thank you, Lord Jesus.

But a few days later, I felt on the edge of sickness again. Thursday, at the Wall, I felt so weak that I pulled a chair up to the Wall and sat on it to pray instead of standing up. Before I had left the house I had Charity lay hands on me and pray for me. That evening during my third hour of teaching, I was healed!! Praise His Name. Hallelujah!!

A Class of Boys

While I was praying, sitting in the chair, I heard young boys being coached by a teacher through their prayers. He would say a line and then they would repeat it. I moved to another chair close to the separating fence and peered through the cracks, now and then, to watch. These boys were older—fourth or fifth grade, I'd say. Their teacher wore the typical black suit, black hat, and had an untrimmed black beard (but no sideburn curls). The boys, however, were wearing colored sports outfits (long pants) and baseball caps. Each one had a small, paper prayer book in hand. They looked like regular American boys. The teacher and the students oddly didn't match.

It was nice to see Ethiopian boys in the group. At one point a couple white boys said something and laughed. It was an Ethiopian boy who said, "Shhhhhhh."

Near the end, I could understand what the teacher was telling them to say. He said in a loud voice, "Anachnu! (We!)" They repeated, "Anachnu!" " Rotzim! (Want!)" "Rotzim!" "Mashiach! (Messiah!)" "Mashiach!" He said another word at the end that I didn't know. Then he lowered his voice and said what apparently was, "That wasn't loud enough. Put your heart into it." He started again, "Anachnu!" And they yelled in unison very loudly, "ANACHNU!" etc. It was very cute.

After they were done reciting, he said something and suddenly they all produced folded up personal prayers and started finding places in the wall for them, helping each other so that no prayer would be left behind!

After they were gone, I prayed that they will come to know this Messiah they were crying out for. And I prayed that they will see the Lord return in all His Glory before they grow up.

When I had entered the women's prayer section, I had passed some cute little Ethiopian girls dressed in the Orthodox long skirts playing while their mothers prayed. They spoke Hebrew to each other. How refreshing, yet strange it seemed to me to see them so modestly and conservatively dressed. Their skirts were bright and colorful. One tourist was taking pictures of them.

My Continuing Prayer for Muslims

Lord Jesus, please have mercy on all the Muslim people. They long for love. Some don't know love in their own lives, yet they know there is love; they know there should be love. The ones who do know love, as soon as they begin to question the Koran, find that the love was conditional. They find themselves being threatened to be banished from their families. Reveal Yourself to them as their Heavenly Father who loves them better than the best fatherly love they could ever imagine, who wants to be with them always and take care of them. Reveal yourself to the mothers who are being robbed of their natural motherly love. Be with that one mother I saw, who couldn't break free of the strict rules and chains of religion enough to rescue her son. Reveal Yourself to her and set her free. Set all the women trapped in Islam FREE! Give them true freedom in You, Jesus, and fill them with Your Love. Thank you, Lord, that You are answering our prayers!! Thank you that You are bringing special revelations. Bring more!!! Praise Your Name!! Amen.

Will you join in the chorus of prayers going up for them? If you're already part of the chorus, thank you, thank you

May the Lord let you personally see the answers to your prayers!
Cheryl

Journal Mar. 24   Psalms

Charity and I celebrated Shabboth together again. I could sense God' Spirit again. It is so awesome!

This morning, for encouragement, I read all the praise Psalms I have marked in my Bible. Some of the verses around them stuck out to me.

Psalms 37:23 Our steps are made firm by the Lord when He delights in our way.

Psalms 27:4 One thing I ask … and seek after to behold the beauty of the Lord!

Psalms 57:2 I cry to God Most High who fulfills His purpose for me.

Psalms 71:18 O God do not forsake me until I proclaim Your might to all the generations to come. *God answered this prayer of Davids! His Psalms are still proclaiming Gods might!*

Psalms 66:19 Truly God has listened. He has given heed to the words of my prayer.

Psalms 26:8 O Lord, I love … the place where Your Glory abides.

Psalms 100:5 One who secretly slanders a neighbor, I will destroy. *Help me, Jesus, not to slander people, not even secretly!*

Psalms 33:8-9 Let all the earth fear the Lord. Let all the inhabitants of the world stand in awe of Him. *I am so happy to read Davids proclamation here! So, it is okay for me to pray it, too, if David prayed and declared it! Here's my cry:*

LET ALL on the earth
TURN to JESUS/YESHUA
and WORSHIP and
PRAISE HIM.

May JESUS/YESHUA receive the
REWARD HE deserves:
that ALL people who ever lived
will BELIEVE in HIM!!
         and that satan will get NO ONE!!!

Journal Mar. 25 Give Them One Heart.

II Chron. 30:12. The hand of God was on Judah to give them one heart to do what the king and officials commanded by the Word of the Lord.

So, if ever there are people doing things with one heart, according to the Word of the Lord, it is because the hand of the Lord is upon them. No credit should necessarily go to the leader! Besides, it would also be the Lord who gives the leader favor and lifts him up in the people's eyes as He did for Joshua.

Here's something I learned about the kings of Israel and Judah. Jehoshaphat was one of the best kings of Judah. The only wrong thing he did was to be friends with the evil king, Ahab. He even let his son marry one of Ahab's daughters. His grandson also did, so the evil got all mixed up into Jehoshaphat's family and kingdom. As a result, most of his offspring were killed. That's why God tells us to not be yoked with evil.

The Lord healed my sudden aching knee! It hurt so bad I was limping around late last night after everyone else was in their rooms. I didn't know how I was going to walk to the bus to get to the YMCA to teach the next day, but in the morning the pain was gone. He has also healed the sharp needle pain that for years has been in my heel whenever I hyper-extend it. Here in Israel it has been hurting without bending it at the end of the day after I walk on it a lot. But now it is healed!

Bless you, Lord.
Praise You, Lord.
Hallelujah!

Jesus, help me this morning. My sense of security in You is being shaken, partly by how Glenn is being shaken by what's happening to his father. Partly by my apprehension about going to the New Age Festival. Help me, Jesus. Bring me back into Your security. Bring me back into You. Help Glenn to find you as his solid Rock of comfort. Thank you, Jesus. Everything is in You.

Isaiah 46:9-10 I am God and there is no other;
I am God and there is no one like Me,
declaring the end from the beginning ...
My purpose shall stand!

Journal Mar. 31 New Church, and About Kings

I went to the Israeli/Ethiopian congregation prayer meeting last night. I think they forgot the time change. We didn't get there until 10 pm and it still hadn't started. They all help clean the church afterwards. I had to wait for my ride home, so I helped. I didn't get home until 3 am.

Studying Israel and Judah's Kings

King Asa was being threatened by the Ethiopian army of one million men and 300 chariots. Here's Asa's prayer:

II Chron. 14:11 "O Lord, there is no difference for You between helping the mighty and the weak. Help us, O Lord our God, for we rely on You, and in Your Name we have come against this multitude. O Lord, You are our God; Let no mortal prevail against You."

The Ethiopian army fell until only one was left alive and there was a great quantity of booty!! (See verse 13)

So, it is no different to God to help Glenn's volunteer boss or Glenn, to help Joyce Myers or me, to help Billy Graham or my dad, to help President Bush or our son. No difference to God. He is happy to have any of us turn to Him. He is happy to be found by us and to help us!!

King Jehoshaphat was facing an army made of Moabites, Ammonites and some Meunites—a great multitude. Here's his prayer.

II Chron. 20:6-12 "O Lord, God of our ancestors, are You not God in heaven? Do You not rule over all the kingdoms of the nations? In Your hands are power and might, so that no one is able to withstand You. ... They ... built You a sanctuary in Your Name, saying, 'If disaster comes upon us, the sword ...or pestilence, or famine, we will stand before this house, and before Your Name, for Your Name is in this house, and cry to You in our distress, and You will hear and save.' ...Our Lord God, will You not execute judgement upon them? ...for we are powerless against this great multitude that is coming against us.... We do not know what to do, but our eyes are on You." Meanwhile all Judah stood before the Lord, with their little ones, their wives and their children.

Later, as the army went out, Jehoshaphat stood and said to them, "Listen to me, Believe in the Lord your God and you will be established (II Chron. 20:20).

The great army against them was completely destroyed by the Lord. No one escaped!! Verse 25: They spent three days taking the booty because of its abundance.

(They) returned to Jerusalem with joy for the Lord had enabled them to rejoice over their enemies ... with harps and lyres and trumpets (II Chron. 20:27-28).

And the realm of Jehoshaphat was quiet, for his God gave him rest all around (II Chron. 20:30).

II Sam. 14:14 (from the woman sent by Joab to King David about Absolom) "...but my lord the king has wisdom like the wisdom of the angel of God to know all things that are on the earth." So, maybe David was as wise as Solomon!!

At church, they prayed for the ones going to the New Age Festival. The ladies behind and beside me laid hands on me as they prayed and that was when the heavy spirit of insecurity lifted off of me. PRAISE THE LORD!!

A Dream-Like Meeting in Africa
Apr 1, 2007 at 6:49 PM

What occurred in Africa at Eric Foster's meetings in February was the realization of several people's dream. It was Eric's dream. It was the publisher's dream. The whole reason he started his little company was to get discipleship materials translated and published into small languages. [He is in partnership with Eric for this project.] And it was the realization of the life-long dream of the Wycliff Bible translator, the creator of the software.

God is the fulfiller of dreams!!!

Here is Eric Foster's report:

The time was amazing. We had about 70 participants to be trained on using the software called "Shellbook" to "localize" follow-up materials into local languages, using local expressions and phrases, so the Biblical stories and principles come to life for the reader or hearer. It was great!

We ended up with booklets in 23 languages in 4 days! All of them were written or re-written by local missionaries and pastors, developed especially for their target audience. The responses were overwhelming. They were so excited about the process and ease of the software. Even though we ended our lessons at 5:00, many stayed into the late evening, working on their books and creating brand new books to reach their targets.

We are working on a proposal to make the software and training available to all missionaries and church workers worldwide and develop an online library of resources that they can easily download and customize to their needs. Our goal is to develop—in partnership with our staff and partners—follow-up materials in 1000 languages in 3 years. It is a daunting task, but the Lord is able.

Isn't that great??? So, how about you? Has God given you a dream? Don't give up. These men had to wait. The Wycliff worker has worked hard and waited almost eighteen years for this day!! So, keep waiting and praying. God will fulfill your dream, too. Especially if the dream is directly from Him, like these men's were!

God is both dream maker and dream fulfiller.
Cheryl

What's Happening in India!
Sun, Apr 01, 2007 at 7:02 PM

I thought you might also be interested in what is happening with The Jesus Film follow-up in India. I am so excited about what Eric is doing that I am almost bursting. And I can't believe that this is someone I actually know!! Here's his newsletter, in case you'd like to read it.

Happy reading,

...On Easter Sunday, Eric, along with two of his teammates, is heading to northern India for the premiere of the Indian edition of "Following JESUS" -the follow-up video series that he has been producing for the last year. ... (H)e has already been to India twice—once last February to meet with the Campus Crusade staff in India to create the outline for the videos and again for two weeks in October to actually film the videos. Well, after months of editing and working with the film studio in Mumbai, the videos are finally ready to be released! Praise the Lord!

In some ways, this trip is even more exciting than the last two trips! Eric will spend 2 weeks touring around northern India with our Campus Crusade staff, hosting 8 separate video premieres. At each premiere, there will be between 50-100 pastors and Christian leaders from many Christian agencies that work in India.

The plan is to expose these 400-800 leaders to the video series and make it available for them to use within their ministry. We are so excited and humbled at the chance to be involved in a project that has a scope of this magnitude. It is only by His grace that we have been able to produce a product like this over the past few years. To be a part of this project has truly been a blessing.

As Eric plan ... is to lip-sync the video series into about 20 other Indian languages over the next year or two, making the lessons available to millions throughout India. In addition, he has already begun working on the second version of "Following JESUS" for India—one that will teach more in-depth topics and prepare new believers to further be witnesses for Jesus in a land that worships countless gods and goddesses. Please continue to lift up Eric and his team as they work on this next version for India, as well as versions for Africa, Latin America, the Middle East and beyond.

.... Pray for our staff in India—that they will be strengthened and be able to continue to fight the good fight, bringing His message and Word to over 1 billion souls. Please pray for the new believers who will see these videos—pray that the Lord uses these videos to ground them in the principles that are taught and that they will go out into their villages to share the Good News of Christ with others....

May God bless you and keep you.
In His love,
Eric and Allison
ericandallison.org

Just think, all this from a guy who used to be a chef!
Isn't God amazing?
Cheryl

India Baby and Mommy praying
(my daughter, Melissa West's, photo)

Some Heavy News

Sun, Apr 01, 2007 at 7:12 PM

Dear Prayer Warriors,

Don't read this if you aren't good at handling ominous world news. But do read it if God has called you to pray about these scary End Times.

The new Palestinian so-called "united" Fatah and Hamas combined government doesn't acknowledge Israel's right to exist, and hasn't even hinted at denouncing violence from its own people. I've been informed by Hebrew speaking people here, who are much more aware of the situation than I am, that according to the Hebrew news here, hundreds of Hamas men have been sent to Iran for terrorist training. Hamas is building bunkers and stockpiling anti-tank and anti-aircraft missiles in Gaza, as the Hizbullah has been doing in Lebanon—all with Iran and Syria's help, of course. Syrian military maneuvers have been noted near the Golan Heights. Hizbullah is rebuilding and stockpiling weapons right under the noses of the UN peacekeepers.

So Israel is at risk on three fronts!!!

I've also found out that this so-called "peaceful" new government of the Palestinians has forced an Arab Christian bookstore and radio station in Gaza to shut down, and their new textbooks teach high school seniors that it is their religious duty to destroy Israel!

Christians here are reporting that an Arab Christian pastor here says the Mediterranean Sea in his grade school textbook map was red. He asked the teacher why, and was told, "It's the color of blood because we will slaughter the Jews." So, this attitude is nothing new. Another news item being propagated here is that a new Hamas video shows a 4-year-old child being told that her suicide bomber mother did a very honorable thing. The preschooler then vows to do the same. Can you believe it?!! Why our government wants to support such a government, I don't know.

✳   ✳   ✳

Now for some good news. Our good friends in America write:

Dear Cheryl,

The "Night To Honor Israel" in our city last Sunday was extremely moving. I think about 1500 people were there—Jews and Christians. $25,000 was collected to send to humanitarian aide in Israel. Robert Stearns was one leader who spoke so wonderfully with anointing.

I thought you'd like to know that our friends in Israel's church ... say a team of twenty will be at the New Age Fest you mentioned. Maybe you can meet up with them.

They write, "Our team will be camping out in tents, and sharing their faith with Israeli seekers, many of whom are open to hearing about the Lord. The organizers of the festival are expecting 50,000 people to attend. Pray for holy boldness, along with divine protection, for our team and the other teams coming from several other Messianic congregations in Israel. In the midst of the idolatry taking place in this festival, we are asking the Lord to manifest Himself as the Lord of lords and to confirm His Word through signs and wonders...."

Blessings and Prayers

Education From Our Prayer Meeting

Sun, Apr 1, 2007 at 8:39 PM

This is an educational e-mail. Almost every time I attend our weekly prayer meeting, I get more education on the situation here. This is what we were told two weeks ago.

Last year, I think it was May, Ahmadinejad wrote a letter to President Bush. Do you remember? (You can find it on google. I found it and read the whole thing.) In the letter he invites President Bush, and all the American people, to convert to Islam.

Why is that important? Here's what we were told.

The Muslims have to try to convert their enemy before killing them. If the enemy refuses to convert, then they have the obligation to kill them. (!!!!!)

"But that was last May and nothing has happened," you say.

Well, Muslim's have a lot of patience, we were told.

For example: Muslim culture comes from the Bedouin culture which has a law of revenge that lasts to the 5th generation. A generation is twenty years, so that is a hundred years!!! That's a long wait.

Speaking of revenge, we are only fifty-nine years out from the Israeli independence which happened in 1948. So they still have forty-one more years in which to carry out their revenge against Israel for that.

Muslim Peace:

Muslims cannot make peace for more than ten years. Mohammed made peace with some country or someone (I'm not sure with who) for ten years. They cannot make peace longer than he did. So, their peacemaking is with a deceitful peace.

The Fatah-Hamas union is false:

Think about it. In their recent in-fighting of the last six months there were four hundred deaths. That means there are four hundred new needs for revenge!

Fatah is secular and Marxist. Hamas has the same goal as Al Quaida, just different tactics.

Now About the Rest of the World:

The whole world has had one goal for a long time: to internationalize Jerusalem, i.e.: to divide it up. (This is NOT GOD'S goal, most Christians would say.)

This goal was sought:

in Madrid in 1991;

in the Oslo Accord in 1993

at Camp David in 2000

and in the Road Map in 2003 (I'm quoting someone here, so I hope I got the names and dates correct.)

The other world goal is to set up a Palestinian state, but you knew that.

Do you feel better educated now?

Use the knowledge to pray for Israel and for the Muslims, please.

Thank you,

Cheryl

A Rabbi and an Ethiopian

Abomination that Desolates

I've been studying all the kings in the Bible and making a timeline. Wow is it educating and fascinating, but also very disconcerting. It is disheartening to see how little time the Hebrew people actually ever followed God. The worst thing for me is to see that at least three kings of Judah actually defiled the Temple by putting up idols to other gods and sacrificing to them on God's Altar!! So they set up their own *"abomination(s) that desolate!"* (Dan. 9:27)

Weeping

Anyway as I was reading I came across where Elisha looks long and hard at the servant of the king of Aram and then starts weeping bitterly because he sees what atrocities this servant is going to inflict on the Israeli people in the future (II Kings 8:11). We were at prayer meeting asking Jesus to give us His heart. As we waited in silence, I had the thought that when Jesus wept over Jerusalem, it was a similar kind of seeing and weeping (Lk. 19:41). Besides seeing the past history of Israel—how they could never stay faithful in following Him, as He says, Jesus could have also been looking at the future. If so, He saw what Rome was going to do to Jerusalem. He saw the Christians start Replacement Theology in 300 AD and the Jewish persecution proceeding from that. He saw the Golden Dome. He saw the Holocaust. He saw what is happening today. And He was deeply saddened by it all—deeply, deeply grieved. The thought made me begin to inwardly weep with Him.

Banishing satan

I have been thinking for a long time about how Jesus tells us in Luke 10:19 *"See, I have given you authority ... over ALL the power of the enemy."* If Jesus gave us this authority over ALL the enemy's power, then perhaps we Believers can band together and banish him completely from the earth! I often rebuke that way, "Be removed from the earth and be cast into the Lake of Fire!"

Well, the other week a preacher preached something similar. He said, "Let's not just cast the evil spirits out of our own lives. Let's cast them off the earth." He said his son who had been molested as a child had become a homosexual. When he was helping his son be delivered he cast that demon completely away into hell fire never to bother anyone ever again! So maybe we have to do it one demon at a time. But let's do it. Let's take the authority that Jesus has given us and banish satan and all his hosts from the earth.

A Rabbi Who Came to Know the Lord

I heard a sermon by a former Orthodox Rabbi who had been on the anti-missionary organization here in Israel, who later left Judaism and became a New Age positive thinking writer and speaker before he became a believer. (He said a lot of Jewish people who leave Judaism go into New Age.) He said he lived in Hawaii and got paid more for one speaking engagement than most people get paid for a year of work. I think his name was Peter Hirsch. (They don't use bulletin's here, so I never saw his name written down.) He knew a lot about Christianity due to being in the anti-missionary organization. Thus he knew how to use just enough Scripture in his speeches to get Christians interested, so he could deceive them and get them off track. A lot of Christians followed him around the country from seminar to seminar, he said.

He was very rich and proud of it. His wife said to him one day, "You should thank God for how much He has blessed you." He answered, "God didn't make me rich. I did it myself."

God responded by soon afterwards taking away all his riches through a law suit. This brought him to the end of himself. He contemplated suicide because financially he was worth more to his family dead than alive. As a last attempt before taking his life, he got on his knees (which was a major deal because he said Jews don't pray on their knees, except maybe at Yom Kippur). He cried out to Jesus, "If you are really real, show me now!" Immediately, he heard a voice. He knew it was Jesus and it changed his life completely.

Hallelujah!!!

Ethiopian Jewess
I have met several Ethiopian Jews. One is a gorgeous, bright eyed, smiling, young adult girl, we'll call Shri. She told me in her slightly broken English about how she came to the Lord. Her parents made aliyah (immigrated) from Ethiopia. To do so they had to be immersed in a mikveh and to denounce Jesus. Her mother had been a Believer, but they told her not to ever mention His Name. Her mother was very broken and sad inside because of it. Her parents remained somewhat religious, but Shri turned out to be a total party girl. She had a friend she hung out with all the time, drinking, dancing, and everything.

Then she lost contact with that friend for a couple years. When she saw her friend again Shri was very excited, wanting to go drinking with her again, but the friend said, "I don't do those kinds of things anymore." She invited Shri to her house. Later Shri brought a new cd and wanted her friend to listen to it. Her friend said, "I don't listen to that kind of music anymore." Shri asked her why. Her friend said, "I believe in Yeshua now." Shri said, "So, you believe in Yeshua. So what? What does that have to do with drinking and music?" Her friend then tried to tell her about Jesus, but Shri didn't want to listen. She said, "I don't believe in anything but the Tanakh and the Torah."

Well, her friend kept inviting her to meetings in her home. She went and finally she started getting interested. Then when she attended a church meeting for the first time, the leader kept saying, "The Holy Spirit is here and is going to touch people tonight." Shri wondered what the Spirit of God has to do with people! But she prayed silently, "Yeshua, if you are real I want to be touched right now. Not later. Now!" Suddenly her hands went up and she started crying. The leader called her up front. They prayed over her and immediately she fell to the floor. So she knew that Jesus was real and she has served Him ever since. That was three years ago. She says she can't remember what she was before. It seems like that girl never existed.

Her friend who led her to the Lord told Shri she had always felt a connection to Jesus, even though she was a Jew. She somehow knew that Jesus had something to do with Jews. So when she met a believer she just soaked it all in.

Shri's brothers and sisters came to the Lord, too. When they all did, her mother was happy and said, "Now we are back with Him!"

I asked Shri if she has led any of her other drinking friends to the Lord. She said they all think she is crazy. But she is still praying for them.

Rain

My friends, Kirk and Daisy, have been actively praying for rain for Israel ever since I met them which was a couple years ago. Maybe many of you have been praying, too. Well, the prayers are working!!! Two weeks ago a guy came back to Israel who has been coming here regularly for years. It was raining when I saw him. He was bemoaning the fact that he didn't bring his umbrella because he didn't expect it to rain anymore till next winter! Last night it rained nice and steadily again. There were many rivulets in the streets. Many people were caught unprepared, including me. Fortunately I was wearing my heavy coat and scarf and I didn't have to walk too far, so the rain didn't soak all the way through. Also it wasn't too terribly cold, so I was alright. All the way walking home, I was thanking the Lord for the rain, and asking Him to send more.

So, maybe this is the year the desert will blossom as a rose!!! I pray so, because it would mean the fulfilling of another prophecy, and it would mean that the end is really near!

A First in World History!!

This week they are performing Handel's "Messiah" in Hebrew for the first time ever in history!! I bought a ticket because I want to support the people who have worked hard to make this happen!! Just think, Hebrew people are singing about their True Messiah, in Hebrew (His mother tongue) at Passover time!! The end must be really, really near.

Passover is tomorrow, April 2. This Biblical holiday lasts a whole week. (But I only have one day off this week and then another next week for Easter.) I have two invitations to Pesach Seders (Passover meals). One is earlier than the other, so I can attend the one for a little bit and then go to the other one. I was praying for an invitation and the Lord gave me two!

Hakh semayakh! (Happy Holiday! (Actually, Holiday Happy!)
Cheryl

The Passover plate and the fancy cloth holding the three pieces of Matzah

The Passover Lamb

Sun, Apr 01, 2007 at 9:31 PM

In the sermon last night the young Messianic Jewish, believing lawyer/preacher pointed out to us that the head of the household had to inspect the Passover lamb for three days, running his hands carefully through the wool to make sure there were no cuts or sores or blemishes of any kind. The people in the household didn't have to be perfect, but the lamb did.

He said he is glad that God, the head of our "household" is inspecting Jesus, our Passover Lamb and not inspecting us!

I'm glad, too. Aren't you?

Thank the Lord! I'm very, very glad He is not inspecting me!!!! Thank you, Jesus, that Your sacrifice is enough for all our sins—for all the sins in history!!

He pointed out that Abraham prophesied about Jesus, the Lamb. Abraham said, *"God will provide Himself a Lamb"* (Gen. 22:8). What God provided in the bush was a ram, not a lamb as Abraham had said, so Abraham was actually speaking about the Lamb of God: Jesus.

Also in the sermon, he said that just as the ram was the replacement for Isaac, and the lambs at the first Passover were the replacements for the firstborns of every Israeli household in Egypt, so Jesus is our replacement, saving us from death and destruction.

Thank you, Jesus. We can never thank You enough. May all people come to realize what You have done. Amen.

Passover blessings to all of you,
Cheryl

Journal April 1   Hezekiah's Plea Mocked

I'm pondering the kings and how God often (3 times at least) had all the descendants of a king killed off because of the king's wickedness.

But here's an interesting thing about a righteous king. King Hezekiah sent word out for all of the Northern Israel Kingdom people to come and celebrate the Passover with Judah (the Southern Israel Kingdom). He urged them that if they turn to God His fierce anger may turn away from you. For as you return to the Lord, your kindred and your children will find compassion with their captors, and return to this land, …

> … For the Lord your God
> is gracious and merciful
> And will not turn away
> His face from you
> if you return to Him (II Chron. 30:8-9)

This was maybe about ten years after the Assyrian king had taken many of the Northern people captive and carried them away during the reign of King Pekah. It was only 4-5 years before the Assyrian king came back and took them all captive (See II Kings 17:5-7 and II Kings 18:9-12.)

You would think the people would've been ready to turn to God and beg for mercy!! But I guess ten years is a long time and people tend to think everything is going to be okay. Anyway, they laughed at Hezekiah's messengers and "mocked them to scorn" (II Chron. 30:10). Only a few of them listened and went up to Jerusalem (30:11).

So, God gave them a chance to repent so He could save them, but they refused. Of course, they hadn't worshipped God for almost two centuries.

Journal April 3 Shalom

I went to two Passover Seders yesterday. I had to leave the one before it actually got started to get to the other one. The first one was very late getting started.

Jesus is telling me to spend these almost three weeks off from teaching (for Passover) with Him and not to worry about fulfilling the forty volunteer work hours per week——that He will take care of that.

This morning I felt I needed to get back to Jesus Words, instead of about the kings, in order to abide in Him again, so I read John 13-16 again.

Later I read the CJB commentary on the verse where Jesus says, "No one comes to the Father except through Me." I love the strong, powerful stand the commentary takes on the Name of Jesus!!!

John 14:21 (NKJV) He who has My commandments and keeps them it is he who loves Me; and he who loves Me will be loved by My Father, and I will love him and manifest Myself to him.

John 14:23 (NKJV) If anyone loves Me, he will keep My Words, and My Father will love him and we will come to him and make our home with him.

This is talking in the singular—one person. The Father and Jesus will make their home in one person!! In me! In you!

We often ask Jesus to reveal Himself to us or to others, but this makes it look like we should instead ask that we keep His commandments because if we do, He WILL reveal Himself to us automatically! And He and the Father will make their home in us individually!

So, Jesus, do I have Your commandments? Are You just talking about those in the written Word or are You also talking about current ones You speak to us into our ear?

Having Your commandments could go with abiding in Your Word and letting Your Word abide in us, couldn't it?

John 14:27 (NKJV) Peace I leave with You My peace I give to You.

(CJB) What I am leaving with you is Shalom—I am giving you My Shalom. I don't give the way the world gives.

Shalom: tranquility, safety, well-being, welfare, health, contentment, success, comfort, and wholeness (from the CJB commentary). We heard in a sermon in 2005 that Shalom has healing, prosperity, and salvation included in the meanings of those words "health, success and wholeness" above.

Thank you, Jesus, for Your Shalom! Thank you! Thank you! Thank you!

Passover Seder (Meal)

Written April 22, 2007

I must tell you about Pesach (Passover). The word "seder" means "order" but it means the whole meal and ceremony. Last year I went to my first Pesach Seder in the U.S. (See photo.) It was very wonderful. I expected this one to be similar but it wasn't. This one was not as elaborate and it was much more Jewish. It was also all in Hebrew, with no English interpreting! The Seder book, called the Haggada, had English and Hebrew, though, so I could follow along somewhat. It was at a very small Messianic congregation. (Yes, another one! That makes about eight Messianic congregations in Jerusalem that I know about now, four of which I have visited.) I'd say this one is more Jewish, because the Seder included a lot of quotes from ancient rabbis. Some of their quotes are interesting and meaningful, but for a couple of them I wrinkled my brow. I guess you have to be Jewish to see them as profound.

Here's an interesting one from the part where the children are supposed to ask the four questions which the sages believe implies there are four types of children:

Messianic Passover Haggada by Keren Ahvah Meshihit (p. 25)

The wise (son) thus expresses himself: what meaneth these testimonies, statutes, and judgements which the LORD our God hath commanded us? Then shalt thou instruct him in all the laws of the Passover.... The wise son is not satisfied with stories of deeds, but rather he asks regarding matters of law and judgement. He seeks to know more and more....

The wicked (son) expresses himself thus: what do you mean by this service? By the expression "you," it is clear he doth not include himself ... (T)his one leaves the faith and removes himself from the congregation.

The simple (son) artlessly observes, what is this? ... The simple son ... sees the adults doing things that he never saw before and asks in simplicity.... There is no use in expanding things for him that are above his intelligence, and it is sufficient for him the story of action.

But for him who hath no capacity to inquire thou must begin the discourse....

Here's one that had me baffled (from p. 23).

Rabbi Elazar the son of Azariah said: "Verily, I ... have hitherto not been able to prove that the narration of the departure from Egypt ought to be related at night, till expounded by the son of Zoma; for it is said, that thou mayest remember the day of thy going forth from the land of Egypt, ALL the days of thy life." From whence he observed, that the expression of the "days of thy life," ... include the nights also.

One older man who sat near me, brought with him what looked like a very big, hardback children's book. It was a Hagadah that his mother gave him when he was a child. He showed us the medieval-looking drawings in it. During the whole ceremony he read VERY LOUDLY along with the leader, from his book. And he made sure that all of us around him did the proper pouring of wine, dipping of vegetables in salt water and later in the sweet charoset; and that we covered and uncovered the matzah at the appropriate times, etc., etc. It was really quite cute. The fact that he could read along in his old book told me this was a very traditional Seder.

After the afikomen hunt [where the children find the middle matzah piece that was broken, wrapped, and hidden (pointing to Jesus being wrapped and placed in the tomb)], the children were each given a little bag of gifts which included noise makers, and, boy, did they make noise! Then everyone had fun singing a song which is similar to "The Twelve Days of Christmas" but is about real-life things: one God, two tablets, ... five books of the Pentateuch, ... eight days before circumcision, nine months of pregnancy, ... and twelve tribes of Israel. The leader and his 12-year-old adopted son had fun seeing who could sing it the fastest.

(I found it very interesting that this old song included the pregnancy bit. What a difference from the Christian tradition I was raised in where everything about pregnancy was hush, hush! Both traditions are very religious, plain-clothed, and conservative. There are so many similarities between the two, but this is one big difference!)

I was invited to this Seder by one of my Korean students. She has been a missionary here for eight years and has been serving at this Israeli-Jewish congregation the whole time. Also visiting was a group of men from Singapore. They were pretty big, hefty guys for being Asian, and their hair fashions were sort of like the late seventies, you know, feathered! The tallest one with the broadest shoulders, who was wearing a leather jacket and looked like he could be from a Harley motorcycle gang, was their pastor! The Japanese and Koreans sitting near me expressed their surprise at his attire also. At the end of the ceremony, the leader asked if anyone had anything to share, so this Singapore pastor shared a wonderful message that really touched my heart. It was about our youth being renewed like the Eagle's (Ps. 104). He said it is a wonderful combination—an old mind in a young body. He also said, "Don't retire, re-fire!"

Only in Jerusalem would you end a Jewish Seder done in Hebrew with a Chinese accented English message from a Singapore, biker-looking pastor.

The Passover ceremony has so many things that point to Jesus. It gives you goose bumps. There's enough things to fill a whole book. I strongly suggest you find such a book and learn all about it. Many Jews get saved each year at Messianic Seders. I hope and pray many were this year also.

[2008 I found out that this Singapore pastor was none other than the famous Joseph Prince!! My friend in New York was telling me about an absolutely fabulous sermon she heard on the internet by a Singapore pastor. As she described him to me, I got more and more excited, telling her I think I saw him in Israel!! And sure enough, we looked at a picture and it was the same man! I told my friend that I even shook his hand and talked to him. She screamed excitedly in astonishment, "Get out!!"]

6.

ACTION
WITH
PRAYING

Please Pray!

Wed, Apr 4, 2007 at 10:32 PM

I'm leaving for the festival in the morning. The first thing to pray is that I find my ride. I'm not sure I understand where to meet them, and I don't have a cell phone!

I'm praying for big things at the festival. Join me in praying big prayers.

I just came from the very first ever in history Handel's Messiah sung in Hebrew!!! It was so amazing. They gave the references in English, so I followed along in my Bible. It is astronomical that they were singing those Scriptures in Hebrew here in Jerusalem!!! Surely it meant something in the Heavenlies. Surely it is a sign of the End Times!

It was at the King of Kings church and the place was packed with many standing in the aisles and sitting on steps. They will perform it again tomorrow night. I'm sure it will be packed again!

Praise the Lord. He is good!

When I get back remind me to tell you about my new Ethiopian friend and her daughter. Their story is amazing!! (See p. 204)

Cheryl

The New Age Festival

A Huge Big Thank You to All Who Were Praying!!

Here's a quick summary for those who don't have much time to read. There were thirty people from our congregation who went, twenty more from another, and smaller groups from many others. There were so many of us that we had two separate camps set up. And that is besides all the "Jews for Jesus" people, and the twenty Koreans.

Here's the praise report: From just the witnessing done from our campsite, there were at least twenty-seven who committed their lives to Yeshua! That is definite commitments. There were hundreds of others who were given reading material and Bibles who are considering making a commitment. I haven't heard yet, how many Bibles were handed out this year. Last year it was 6000. We also handed out bumper stickers that said in Hebrew, "God is Love" (Elohim hu ahava) and "God Loves you" (Elohim hu ahav atem). They became the rage! Kids stuck them on their clothes—even on their bare skin. I saw those stickers all through the crowds! It was great!

Thank you for praying for me specifically. God really answered in so many ways. The main one was that since I was too shy to approach anyone, God had a guy come to me and start asking me questions! He had such a sweet spirit about him. He was Jewish and he sincerely wanted to know what I believe. Another young man also asked me, but his friend cut him short and pulled him away. Both were Jewish. Almost all of the 50,000 attendees were young Jewish Israelis.

Astounding, isn't it?

The other very interesting thing was the anti-missionary Jewish team, Yad Veshem, that was determined to keep the kids from listening to us, or taking our stuff, or at least from reading it! There were two young guys doing this anti-Yeshua work. One was thin and bearded in a white dress shirt and black pants, the other was in jeans and a baseball cap. Sometimes they worked together and sometimes alone. They were full of zeal, let me tell you! At first they were actually knocking the books out of people's hands! But then our guys got them involved in conversations to keep them away from our booth, also trying to evangelize them, but they were impenetrable. The next day I joined a group who formed a circle in front of our booth, alternately praying, then singing and dancing. This kept their guys away for awhile, too. The people walking by were very curious about what we were singing. We also prayed for our two opposers. At one point they brought in a couple rabbi-looking guys to help them figure out what to do. They never gave up to the very last hour of the festival!

One of them—the thin one—told us that the Jewish court has decided that Messianic Jews are Christians ("Christian" being the condemning word here). He said it in a very serious tone. I think he expected our mouths to drop open. He told us he is doing God's work, saving Jews from becoming Christians. He was so sincere! If only God would show him that he is kicking against the goads!

The last day, he stood farther away from our booth where our guys didn't notice him. I came upon him when I was doing my prayer-walking and saw him talking to a young couple holding literature. I stayed back and watched. (Remember they were talking in Hebrew so I couldn't understand much.) I wanted to see if he really had any influence on the people, because we had been praying that what the enemy meant for evil God would turn to good. I was praying it would only make the people more curious to find out what was so forbidden by these guys. We were the only booth in the whole place of all kinds of heathen religious booths that these guys were trying to keep the people away from!! The couple listened intently to him. After he left, they talked quite a bit to each other, I was afraid they were talking about throwing the New Testament away like the guy told them to. They seemed to come to a conclusion, and began walking on, New Testament still in hand. I followed from a distance for a long time to see if they would throw it away and they didn't!! Praise the Lord!!

Oops! This was supposed to be the short version. So, anyways, you can see that your prayers were needed and were effective!!

Cheryl

Journal April 8 RESURRECTION Sunday!!

Titus 3:2-3 (NKJV) Speak evil of no one, … be peaceable, gentle, showing all humility to all men. For we ourselves were once foolish, disobedient, deceived, serving various lusts and pleasures, … hating one another.

So, there's the list of all the evils we humans say about one another: He's so stupid. He only thinks about one thing. She's so blind. She's so hateful!!!

But we are to show ALL humility to ALL men (!) because we ourselves were once like them or maybe still are!!!

So, Jesus please help me. Guide me. Live in me. I must show humility and gentleness to him. But I'm so disappointed and embarrassed!

Journal April 9 Monday Parables Foretell

I remember the new thing God is showing me, that the parables foretell things. I need to study the parables!

The Israeli guy's manuscript tells how the Old Testament stories foretell—foreshadow things. For example, Abraham was sacrificing Isaac; God did sacrifice Jesus. Joseph's identity was hidden from his brothers just as Jesus' identity is hidden from the Jews today. And Joseph was saving the whole world, just as Jesus is!!

So, the whole Old Testament is full of parables, too. The people's lives were like parables that foretell!! And Jesus' parables are foretelling things, too.

Some of the sins I still need to be cleansed of:
wanting to be famous
wanting everyone to like me (At Boombabella, I found myself wanting to talk to people to make sure they weren't mad at me!! Just like all my life! Ugh!)

My Ethiopian Jewess Friend

Mon, Apr 9, 2007 at 10:46 PM

Before the New Age Festival, my Ethiopian friend and her young daughter invited me to their home to eat with them. They live in a tiny apartment near the top of a tall building. I walked there. Hadassah (we'll call her) told me her story in broken English. To help me understand, her daughter, Reetha, often clarified in almost perfect English what Hadassah said.

Hadassah is Jewish, but came to know the Lord in Ethiopia. She learned about Charismatic Christians when she became gravely ill. After a C-section, the surgeon left a sponge in her. She got very ill and didn't recover even after they removed the sponge. She went to a Charismatic healing meeting that was so packed she was outside. Her wound was still open and draining. The speaker gave a prophetic word that described her. In her shock, she immediately passed out. People carried her up to the front, and she was healed. She says the newspapers even wrote about her.

Years later, her son, I believe he is the one born from that very C-section, was kidnapped one evening. He and his friends were playing together in her back yard when they were all taken. He was sixteen. She has never seen him since. They believe he was stolen by Muslim soldiers and possibly taken to a different country. The police would do nothing to look for him. She says it is such a common occurrence in Ethiopia that no one does anything about it.

The next year her husband died. After that she immigrated to Israel to protect the rest of her children. In Ethiopia she was a respected midwife. But here in Israel, due to the language barrier and discrimination, she cleans houses instead. She did deliver a few Ethiopian babies here, though, she says, and also helped raise a few orphaned children.

The immigration officers told her she dared not mention Jesus here, so she kept her Christianity at a low profile. Her daughter, Reetha, was still young and was so influenced at the religious school that she became an ardent Ultra Orthodox Jew and completely rejected Jesus!! Hadassah says she cried so many tears and prayed so many prayers about that.

She came here for safety, but then in 2002, when Reetha was the only one still living at home, all the bombing started here. There were a couple times when Reetha missed the very bus that was bombed! This was too much for Hadassah to take. So to protect Reetha, Hadassah sent her to America to live in the Midwest with an aunt. Hadassah joined them later. They lived there for a couple years.

In America, Reetha was convinced to believe in Jesus, but then suddenly went party wild! So again, Hadassah cried and prayed!

Now they are back in Israel, and the Lord led Hadassah to this wonderful on-fire Russian-Ethiopian congregation. (The fact that Russians and Ethiopians worship together and are such close friends is a new, miraculous phenomenon here, they told me. Other people are so surprised when they visit.) Later she convinced Reetha to come to a meeting and God met her. Reetha is now very strong in the Lord.

It is wonderful to hear Reetha tell the story of her conversion. She says she was so strongly religious before because she loved God so much. She was faithful to Him in wearing the conservative clothes and eating Kosher and everything because she wanted to please God, even though the religious community she was a part of discriminated against her, saying she couldn't be a real Jew because she was black. (She says the less religious Jews accept the Ethiopians, but not the strict religious ones.) She stayed determined and made a lot of friends in spite of the discrimination. She showed me the pictures of her and her friends all dressed in the same pattern of long dark skirts and long-sleeve, high neck, white blouses.

In America, after her aunt talked to her over and over, and took her to church, she says that the blindness was lifted from her mind and she suddenly just wanted to believe in Jesus. But then no one taught her anything further, so she just went wild, because she didn't know how to function in the real world, and she didn't want to be abnormal anymore.

When she came back from America wearing pants, her religious friends' parents wouldn't even speak to her or let their daughters speak to her anymore. She is now banished from their community.

Now Reetha is in the army. (She was home for the holiday when I saw her.) She has two more months. She wants to study to be a surgeon, but she wonders if any hospital will take her since she is black.

Anyway, now Hadassah has finally found some happiness, but still her heart aches for her lost son, Reuven.

Will you please pray for Hadassah that God will bring her son back to her, and that there will be no more tragedies or sadness in her life!!

Oh, and the other exciting thing is that in America, in Reetha's ESL class, there were Palestinian, Iraqi and Iranian students. On her first day, during the introductions, she proudly and boldly declared that she was Israeli, not realizing where the other people were from. They all looked at her in shock when she said the forbidden word "Israeli." (The Arabs from Israel call themselves Palestinian, even though they are from the same country as her.) She says her teacher feared for her safety. At first she and the other students had some heated arguments, but eventually they all became good friends. One Palestinian guy kept in touch with her for a long time afterwards. When she went into the army, he named several hot spots for her to stay away from because he cared so much for her safety. Isn't that marvelous?!

Anyway, I thought you would be interested in their story and would like to pray for them.

Another Great Jewish Story

Mon Apr 9, 2007 at 11:24 PM

One of the pastors at the Festival is the grandson of a Holocaust survivor who helped set up the Forest for the Righteous Gentiles at the Holocaust museum (Yad Vashem) here in Jerusalem.

This grandson was telling his story to a German lady and me in our dining tent right after we spent a couple hours praying. I wanted so badly to tell him to wait until I could go get my notebook to take notes, but it seemed kind of rude to do that. So I hope I remembered the story correctly.

His whole family was sent to the concentration camp during WW II. Most of them were killed. His grandfather had three very close, miraculous calls. He was a lawyer, I believe. First the community he was in was told to pack one suitcase to be ready to leave.

Then they were all taken out and shot. But one gunman decided to hide him. Another time, he was caught and was going to be shot, but for some strange reason, the officer asked him what his last wish was. He said he'd like to warm up in a warm room. So they put him in a warm room with another officer for awhile. The other officer for some reason took a liking to him. He gave him a lot of money and told him to give it to the one who was going to execute him and they would let him go. He asked how he could ever repay and the man said it was a gift. Another time he hid at a Catholic lady's house. She gave him and the others with him enough food for a few days, put a necklace with a big cross around his neck, and told them to escape to Russia. As they were walking down the road an officer saw them, pointed his rifle and yelled, "Jews!" In his shock, his arms flew open. The officer saw the cross and said, "Oh, you're okay." He let him go, but shot all the others.

Somehow he later got his wife and son out of the camp where they were and they escaped to Israel. The Gentile Forest at the Museum is in honor of people like those who helped him.

Anyway, this pastor who is the grandson, grew up full of anger and hatred towards the Germans, yet it was in Germany where he first met God. He was in Italy in Medical School, and had to go to Germany for some reason. I forget. But there he met a German man who was so full of love and knew so much more about the Scriptures than he did that he was provoked to jealousy. This man convinced him to go to a meeting. He went but was not interested at all. In fact, he laid down on a back bench and slept through most of it. Near the end someone woke him up and said, "She is talking about you." He awoke to hear a lady speaker saying something like this, "There is a young man here who is full of hate, but God is going to do a work in your heart and you are going to do a lot to bring His people back to Him." (I'm sorry I can't remember. It was much more specific than that.) He was so shocked because it exactly described him. He didn't turn to God right then, but later, God met him and all his hatred was suddenly gone. He went on to become a medical doctor with an emphasis in psychology, but now he works only in the ministry.

Isn't God just soooo marvelous?!!
Cheryl

My Thoughts After the Festival
Mon, Apr 9, 2007 at 12:00 Midnight

My thoughts have been swirling around since the festival. There is so much to figure out about the Jewish people. First of all, I was so shocked to see that almost all of the thousands and thousands of young people there were Jewish. And in talking to them and listening to them talk to others, I found out that even though they come to this very hedonistic, ungodly place, where the main god was pleasure and lust, they still think of themselves as Jews. They don't see themselves as leaving their faith to come to such a decadent place. They still say they believe in God and Moses!

The festival was being held during the sacred week of their sacred Passover. You would think desecrating their religion like that would make them feel like they were abandoning their faith, but it doesn't.

And the religious, anti-missionary guys that were trying to protect them from becoming Christians didn't seem worried at all about them getting into any of the New Age stuff. None of the anti-missionaries were standing outside the transvestite-homosexual-teaching booth, for example!! When I told this to a professor here, she said, "Oh yea, Jews can do anything they want to, except believe in Jesus."

There was a big open tent set up by the Ultra Orthodox Jewish sect that believes in this rabbi who lived in New York. (They thought he was the Messiah and that he wouldn't die, but then he did die, so now they think he is going to come back again.) This group is perhaps the only evangelistic sect of Jews. They were passing out free, homemade matzah (the unleavened, Passover bread). I took some. It tasted really good! So, here's these bearded, black hat, black suit, side curls, very religious men and their dark, long skirt, hair-covered-with-wigs wives standing there passing out religious bread to guys wearing shorts sliding half off of them, and girls decked in mostly only navel rings and strategically placed tattoos, and, well, maybe a little fabric, too. The religious men always asked the boys to let them put their hands on their heads and bless them. Many of the boys allowed them to do this.

The amazing thing to me was the attitude of the scantily clad, fun-seeking, young people towards these extremely religious people. The great majority was very respectful toward them and even seemed really pleased that they were there. After being blessed the boys would walk away smiling, gobbling up the matzah. I only saw a few young people refuse the matzah. And I only saw a hint of disdain on a couple girls faces as they refused.

Also, the attitude of the religious people towards them was not one of disgust or condemnation or even judging. I only saw them smiling and talking very kindly to them. They even allowed the bikini-clad girls to sit in groups inside their big, open tent to rest. They didn't seem to be worried that their two little boys wearing kippas, long curls, and the fringes under their white shirts were seeing things they shouldn't see.

Can you imagine how American teens would react if Amish people came to an amusement park or music festival to try and convert them? The Amish people would be mocked, to say the least. They would probably be scorned, and possibly manhandled by the half-drunk crowd.

That's another thing. I never saw anyone staggering around acting truly drunk, although they were, of course, all drinking. I expected to find people passed out all over, or people who looked stoned, but I didn't see anyone like that. They weren't even doing the laughing, teasing, whistling, mocking thing to any of us as we walked around much more covered than most of them. The two who talked to me had very nice, kind personalities. There was no hint of the anger that most American teens have. And as I told you, they seemed almost apologetic that they weren't allowed to believe what I believe in. They seemed to have a longing and a wish that they could. And I'm praying for them that they soon will!

Now for the not-so-good stuff. The music was unbearingly loud and it never stopped. It went all night long and continued into the day, although one day it stopped for an hour between 9 and 10 am. Many in our group had trouble getting any sleep at all because of it. I needed so badly to give my ears and brain a break. I tried to find an escape by walking away from the blaring band's loudspeakers, but as soon as I was getting out of earshot of one band I began hearing the next one. I even walked all the way to the water's edge, but not even the waves could drown out the sound.

The porta pots were filthy with dirty toilet paper and unmentionable stuff strewn all over inside. It didn't seem like people even tried to hit the hole. I saw many girls open a door, turn up their noses and close it quickly again. It was just too disgusting to enter. One morning at 9 am when not many of the campers were up yet from their all night reveling, workers hosed down a few of the toilets. I was so happy to be able to use a clean one. But by noon those were filthy again, too. So, the whole weekend, I tried to not eat or drink much to decrease the number of times I had to use the facilities.

The whole camping area was maybe the size of a huge shopping mall and its parking area, or maybe even two shopping malls including parking lots. It was a sea of silver tents with wide alleyways dividing the huge sections of them. The parking field, a 15 minute bus ride's distance away, was equally as huge. The tents were pitched practically on top of each other. Our small camp was in the middle of one tent section. To get from our tents to the alleyway, we had to step over tent after tent, trying to avoid all the garbage scattered everywhere, and the two pairs of feet sticking out of many of the tent doors.

At one point when I was doing my prayer-walking around, I thought one good thing was that there was no judgment there. Anything goes. No one judges anyone, I thought. Then one guy walked by me wearing a T-shirt with English writing on it that made fun of being a virgin. And I realized that they do have their rules and condemnation. Virgins are scoffed at and condemned. And I suppose refusing to drink or take drugs would be frowned upon, too. Who knows what other twisted kinds of lines get drawn. I know there will be many babies created from that weekend, and there seems to be no hint of shame at snuffing the new life out immediately. I heard one of our ladies trying to convince a girl to keep the baby that was inside her. Our lady was saying the most wonderful things about the girl and her baby. The girl seemed mesmerized by the beautiful words, but her boyfriend beside her was shifting nervously.

It wasn't an amusement park. The only really fun things were the one bungee jumping crane; a tiny little flat, square skate boarding place; and then the beach, of course. But the water was so cold that not many people went swimming. No one was doing any surfing of any kind.

So, boredom was setting in. Apparently young teen boys can only do so much lusting, and then they have to get to the real fun. Boys will be boys. ☺

There was a huge group of boys camping beside us. Our group had invited many of them to eat with us and hear about Jesus, and most took the offer, I hope their hungry bellies weren't their main driving factors. ☺ All they had in their camp to eat was cups of Ramon noodles. Well, there was another huge group of boys up on the slope above us. The second day there erupted a mini war-game between the two groups. The ammunition wasn't paintball guns. It was sand-filled plastic soft drink bottles! Some of the bottle-missiles were landing too close to our dining tent, so the men in our group whistled at them and got them to stop. But the next day it started again. They were enjoying themselves immensely. The air was full of the flying bottles! I was in the kitchen area, sitting in a lawn chair, shredding carrots into a big bowl when one bottle came crashing through our roof almost hitting the girl standing at the table in front of me chopping onions! Our men were upset, but couldn't get them to stop this time, only to quit throwing them in our direction. I thought we should just let boys be boys and have their good, clean, physical, drug-free fun. But later the police came on dune buggies and motorcycles and forced them to stop.

The main thing God taught me there was that God's calling to do the prayer-warring is just as important as His calling to do the witnessing. There were so many who were awesomely gifted in evangelism. I was awed and blessed, listening to the ones who spoke in English. Their words truly were like "apples of gold in settings of silver." And their listeners were captivatingly interested. But God made it very clear that the prayer warriors were of equal value. He showed me by letting me become friends with a dear, German lady who was beating herself up because she found it so difficult to witness, yet she was such a loving support to the whole team, and was a valiant praying soldier! It was important that everyone take their turn praying, but some people are drawn to that task, and are given a special talent and revelation for it. She was always saying to me, "shall we pray about such and such?" "Would you like to pray with me for so and so who is witnessing?" or "Should we pray right now about that?" One time a man came up to us and asked where the 3 o'clock prayer watch group was. We both told him we were it. He said to her, "But you are always praying. I mean where are the ones assigned to this prayer watch slot?" What a compliment to her!!!

And Jesus was so kind to let me feel important in taking one great witnessing lady's prayer watch spot, so she could continue witnessing to a boy who was showing a lot of interest. He came back three times to learn more, and then rode home with us, and is going to start coming to church!! (He slept most of the way home. And her unsaved neighbor talked non-stop, loudly in Hebrew the whole way, so I didn't get to know the young boy at all.) (A beautiful, young, smiling African/British girl, also gifted in witnessing was riding along. She and I talked quietly in the back seat, buried under our sleeping bags and backpacks. She told me her conversion story and the awesome vision God gave her of Jesus coming to the Temple in all his bright, white glory!!)

God is so awesome!

Here's a list of the people we were praying for on the second day:

Ines and Dagon: shopkeepers and their family for salvation and deliverance from witchcraft

Jane: South African Jew staying in Jerusalem one year. Will meet up with this person in Jerusalem after the festival

Leigh and Savir: soldiers—Jewish from Jewish homes. Don't believe God has a relationship to offer them, but are interested. Would like to come back tonight.

Stav and Rishon: 17-year-olds, both received Yeshua

Juli: was given a Gospel of John

Alex: was Messianic but has been deceived. Came for dinner.

Omri: soldier in the territories, was given a New Testament and a dog tag with Psalms on it. Was very open

Elan: Believes in New Age, but has an open heart. Was given a New Testament

Dror, Noa, Mayan: 16-year-old soldiers

Omin: 22-year-old IDF tank driver. Given a New Testament

Gai: given a Gospel of John

Sheer and Kiki: from Germany

May God answer all our prayers,
Cheryl

P.S. Thank you for praying that I find my ride. I was waiting at the wrong spot and almost missed the whole New Age Festival!! Charity's cell phone helped, but I couldn't get ahold of the leader until it was very late. Then he could hardly figure out where I was, to be able to tell me which way to walk to meet them!!!

Journal April 10 Wed.   Pondering Parables

Passover week (8 days) is over. : (

O yes, I learned at the Pesach Seder that the first commandment to the Jews was to do the Passover—to kill the lamb, and then to keep the Passover yearly.

Pondering parables

Matt. 13:10 "Why do you speak to them in parables?" "… to you it has been given to know the secrets of the Kingdom of Heaven   ."

Matt. 13:35 I will … speak in parables, I will proclaim what has been hidden from the foundation of the world.

Matt. 21:43 The Kingdom … will be taken away from you and will be given to a people that produces the fruits of the Kingdom.

Matt. 22:1 … A king who gave a wedding banquet for His Son.

Matt. 22:7 The king was enraged. He sent his troops, destroyed those murderers, and burned their city.

Matt. 21:21 Not only will you do what has been done to the fig tree …if you say to this mountain … it will be done.

Matt. 24:32 From the fig tree learn its lesson: as soon as its branch becomes tender and puts forth leaves … summer is near. … this generation will not pass away until all …taken place.

Journal April 11

Rom. 3:19 *(The Torah was given)* that every mouth be silenced. (!!!!)

Journal April 13 Awesome Time with the Lord

Hezekiah's prayer

II Kings 19:14-19 and Isaiah 37:16-20

O Lord God of hosts, God of Israel,

who are enthroned above the cherubim,

You are God, You alone,

of all the kingdoms of the earth;

You have made heaven and earth.

Incline Your ear, O Lord, and hear;

Open Your eyes, O Lord, and see;

hear the words of Sennacherib,

which he has sent to mock the Living God.

…so now, O Lord our God, save us, I pray you,

from his hand, so that all the kingdoms of the earth

may know that you, O Lord, are God alone.

God answered through Isaiah:

I have heard your prayer… (II Kings 19:20)

Isaiah 37:33, 35 He shall not come into this city, shoot an arrow there … or cast a siege. I will defend this city to save it.

Isaiah 37:36 When morning dawned, they were all dead bodies.

From Romans 11: 33, 36:
O the depth of Your riches
and wisdom and knowledge,
       O God.
How unsearchable are Your Judgments
and how inscrutable Your Ways.
… For from You and through You
and to You are all things,
to You be Glory forever, Amen.

WOW!! God just led me into a most marvelous spectacular time with Him!

Lately, I was beginning to feel a little lost and depressed, wondering what I'm doing here in Israel. I think going to Boombamella really did me in.

I felt impressed to look up the calling God has given me. But first I spent time looking at the three kings' prayers: Asa, Jehoshaphat, and Hezekiah (see his above), and prayed them. I verified that out of all the kings after Solomon (twenty kings of Judah, where the Temple was, and nineteen kings of Israel), there are only three kings whose prayers are recorded. Only three!

Then I spent time crying and praying for a couple of my children who are drifting from the Lord and from me. I was really allowing myself to cry—to let all my heartache out.

Then the impression to look up where I'd last written down my calling increased, so I got my 2005 journal out and began reading, and instantly the power and presence of the Holy Spirit came upon me.

It was awesome.

After reading and being overwhelmed with powerful emotions from His presence and praying in tongues, and praying that the different pieces of the call come to pass (one of them being that I will learn to agape God), I started reading in the following pages about AGAPE love.

Then I noticed on another page that right after I wrote questions asking God where to go in China as a missionary, I wrote verses about Israel being saved!!! That was like God confirming to me that He wants me here instead of China right now, and that the time for Israel's full inclusion is at hand.

Then somehow in reading and praying over all the stuff about AGAPE love, I suddenly realized that the Israeli people are, and have been to Jesus, as many teens and young adults are to their parents—as I was to my mother—as a couple of my children have been to me. Suddenly I knew Jesus' pain. Suddenly I knew why he wept over Jerusalem!! He was experiencing the pain of rejection!! They didn't recognize Him or accept Him. They had cut themselves off from Him. Suddenly I wept and wept. I felt more tenderness and love to Jesus than I ever have before.

I know the pain He is going through. Suddenly I have a stronger desire and zeal than ever to pray that the Jewish people will turn to JESUS, because I want His pain to be over with. I want His sorrow to be turned into joy. I want for Him what I desire for myself, and I seem to want it even more for Him!! Somehow I find it easier to feel sorry for Him than for myself—especially since I helped cause my own pain, but Jesus did nothing to deserve His rejection!!

Journal April 15   May His Suffering End

Having Israel turn to Jesus will feel as marvelous and wonderful to Jesus as I will feel when my children return to me—only on an infinitely greater scale!!!

Prayer

O Jesus, I understand your awful pain. I'm so sorry you have to have such pain. You have suffered soooooooo much pain of rejection for soooooo many thousands of years! I'm sure You look at Your people and wonder how they could be what they are—people You created and love and gave Your life for. They don't look at all like You planned they would be. Oh, the sadness they must bring to Your heart. Oh, the pain!! Your deep, deep pain.

Oh Jesus, they keep on rejecting You and ignoring You! They completely disregard Your teachings! They have gone their own way! All those thousands upon thousands at the festival and all the thousands of Orthodox and Ultra Orthodox.

O Jesus, may the time of Your suffering come to an end!! May You have the extreme, unsurpassing JOY of seeing Your children turn to You and love You and respect and honor You and believe in You and follow You and become Your friends.

Almighty Father, open the eyes of ALL OF THEM and let them see who You really are. Let them see that You LOVE THEM and that You are the MOST HIGH GOD above all gods and that You sent Your Son because You Love them with ever-lasting, covenantal, sacrificial LOVE. O Jesus, remove the shroud over them that they may see that You are wise above all; that Wisdom comes from You—that You are the WAY—the ONLY WAY; the TRUTH—the THE ONLY TRUTH; and that YOU ARE LIFE—ALL LIFE; that ALL LIFE comes from YOU!!!!

O Jesus, Yeshua, bring them all to the place where when You remove the veil they will have hearts ready to repent—that their mourning over the One they pierced will be Godly sorrow that leads to repentance and to accepting You, believing in You, and DEVOTING themselves to You—DEDICATING themselves—surrendering them-selves—giving themselves as living sacrifices to You!!!

Whatever it takes Father. Whatever it takes to make this happen—to turn them to You; to turn the whole world to You.

However long it takes. How long will it take, Father? How long?

O Jesus, Yeshua, You have suffered soooo much. But it will soon be over, won't it? The time is very near, isn't it? Very, very near.

O Father, You are so much better a parent than we humans. We make so many mistakes. But You, Jesus, You are PERFECT in every way and yet Your children spurn You. It's soooo wrong of us, Your children!!!!!! My children have good reasons for rejecting me. But we—Your children—have NO reason to reject You!!!!! You absolutely DO NOT deserve the treatment You have been getting over the centuries!! You don't deserve having an enemy who tears Your children from You—who lures them away, feeding them lies, making them believe lies about You—especially the lie that You don't Love them AND the lie that You aren't even their FATHER and MESSIAH!

That must be the worst pain of all—that they believe the LIE that they aren't even Your people or Your children; that You aren't their REAL Messiah or their REAL God; and that they go after other messiahs and other gods!!!!

But that is soon all coming to an END!!! Hallelujah! Very soon the enemy with all his lies is going to be banished from the earth! Amen, Hallelujah! Very soon his shroud—his dark, dark, heavy, thick covering of lies that he has pulled over the people is going to be gone and You will have the wonderful, awesome JOY of reconciliation with ALL Your children!

(Wow, it's raining and there was even tiny hail for three minutes!!! Thank you, Jesus for the rain!)

O Jesus, what do I need to do to help bring this reconciliation? Little, tiny me though I am, show me what You need me to do and to pray!!!

꙳   ꙳

As I was looking over an old journal earlier this morning (it's 10:29 am now) I came to the part about Ezekiel being sent to a rebellious house and how I thought it described us Americans. Well, it describes Israelis also!! It describes their attitude toward Yeshua, that's for sure!

(Well, the rain has stopped already!! Such short showers here in Israel!)

(Oh! Now the sun is coming out!)

So, I need to find all the prophecies about the Israeli people reconciling to God and to their Messiah, so I can pray them into action!

Oh Jesus, let them see that they are kicking against the goads!! Shine a bolt of Light down upon them like You did Saul!!

I must do more prayer-walking—pleading the Blood of Yeshua—around the Temple and the Old City and around modern Jerusalem.

꙳   ꙳

Well, I asked God to show me what to pray and He gave me a whole long list of Scriptures to pray from Zechariah and Malachi. Here are a few of them.

Zech. 3: 8 I am going to bring my servant the Branch. … and I will remove the guilt of this land in a single day. (Jesus did that on the cross! But maybe it will happen in a different way when they receive together as a whole nation—in one day—what He did for them).

Zech. 3:10 On that day, says the Lord of Hosts, you shall invite each other to come under your vine and fig tree. (!!!)

Zech. 4:1, 6-7 The angel … came again and wakened me as one is wakened from sleep.
… Not by might, nor by power, but by My Spirit, says the Lord of Hosts.
What are you O great mountain? … you shall become a plain. (Jesus said, "If you say to this mountain, 'Be removed and cast into the sea'....)

Zech. 4:7 (cont.) ... and he shall bring out the top stone amid shouts of "Grace, Grace...."

Zech. 5: 1-4 ...flying scroll... curse that goes out over the face of the whole land; for everyone who steals ... swears falsely ... shall ... consume (house), both timber and stone.

Zech. 1:11 "We have patrolled the earth, and lo, the whole earth remains at peace."

Zech. 1:20 Four blacksmiths ... " these have come to terrify them, to strike down the horns of the nations that lifted up their horns against the land of Judah to scatter its people."

Zech. 2:1 ... a man with a measuring line ... to measure Jerusalem ... "I will be a wall of fire around It, says the Lord, ... and the Glory within it."

Zech. 2:10-11 Sing and rejoice, O daughter Zion! For lo, I will come and dwell in Your midst, says the Lord. Many nations shall join themselves to the Lord on that day and shall be My people, and I will dwell in your midst. And You shall know that the Lord of Hosts has sent ME. *(Yeshua!)*

Zech. 2:13 Be silent all people, before the Lord, for He has roused Himself from His Holy Dwelling.

Zech. 6:12-13 Branch ... shall branch out ... build the Temple of the Lord ... bear royal honor, ... sit and rule on His throne ..... .

Zech. 6:15 Those who are far off shall come and help to build the Temple of the Lord; and you shall know that the Lord of Hosts has sent Me. *(Yeshua!)*

Zech. 8:20 The inhabitants of one city shall go to another ... "come let us got to entreat the favor of the Lord and to see the Lord of Hosts; I myself am going." Many peoples and strong nations shall come to seek the Lord of Hosts in Jerusalem and to entreat the favor of the Lord.

Zech. 8:23 Ten men from nations of every language shall take hold of a Jew, grasping his garment saying, "Let us go with you, for we have heard that God is with you.

Zech. 9:6-7 Philistia will also be a remnant for God——like a clan in Judah.

Zech. 9:9 Your king comes to you triumphant and victorious ....

Zech. 9:14 Arrows go forth like lightning and the Lord God will sound the trumpet.

Zech. 9:16 ... flock of His people; for like jewels of a crown they shall shine on His land.

Zech. 10:1 Ask for spring rain from the Lord who makes storm clouds, who gives showers of rain to you, the vegetation in the field to everyone.

Zech. 11:9 I will bring them to Gilead and Lebanon until there is no room.

Zech. 12:5 The clans of Judah will say, "The inhabitants of Jerusalem have strength through the Lord of Hosts, their God." *(Why does it say 'their' God?)*

Zech. 12:10 And I will pour out a spirit of compassion and supplication on the house of David and the inhabitants of Jerusalem
            so that
when they look on the One whom they have pierced, they shall mourn for Him.

Zech. 13:1 On that day a fountain shall be opened for the house of David and the inhabitants of Jerusalem to cleanse them from sin and impurity.

Zech. 13:2 I will cut off the names of the idols from the land, so that they shall be remembered no more, and also I will remove from the land the prophets and the unclean spirit.

Zech. 13:9 They will call on My Name and I will answer them. *(Yeshua!)*

Zech. 14:9 And the Lord will become King over all the earth; on that day the Lord will be one and His Name one. *(Yeshua!)*

Malachi 1:6 A son honors his father, and servants their master. If then I am a Father, where is the honor due Me? And if I am a Master, where is the respect due Me? (!!!!) *(Jesus is our/their Master!)*

Malachi 1:11 For from the rising of the sun to its setting My Name is great among the nations, and in every place incense *(prayers?)* is offered to My Name and a pure offering; for My Name is great among the nations. *(This wasn't true at all when Malachi wrote this! It is prophecy, and it is true today!!)*

Malachi 2:10 Have we not all one Father?

                Has not God created us?

                Why are we faithless to one another, profaning the covenant...? *(Good question for the Jews and Arabs to ask each other?! May it soon come to pass.)*

Malachi 3:3 ...and refine them like gold and silver, until they present offerings to the Lord in righteousness.

Malachi 3:6 For I the Lord do not change; therefore you ...have not perished. (!!)

Malachi 3:8 Do not rob God ... I will open the windows of heaven for you and pour down for you an overflowing blessing ... then all nations will count you happy, a land of delight.

Malachi 3:18 Then once more you shall see the difference between the righteous and the wicked, between one who serves God and one who does not serve Him.

Malachi 4:4-5 Remember the teaching of My servant Moses, ... Lo, I will send you the prophet Elijah before the great and terrible day of the Lord comes. He will turn the hearts of parents to their children and the hearts of children to their parents....

Malachi 3:1 See, I am sending My messenger to prepare the way before Me, and the Lord whom you seek will suddenly come to His Temple. The messenger of the covenant in whom you delight——indeed, He is coming. (!!)

(added on 4/21/07) Isaiah 62:10 Go through, go through the gates, prepare the way for the people .... to the end of the earth.

Isaiah 40:3 A voice cries out, ... prepare the way of the Lord, make straight in the desert a highway for our God. *(Israel is in the desert!)*

Journal April 16 Monday
Virginia Tech Massacre. The Korean student killed thirty-two people and himself !!!!

Journal   April 17   Unapproachable Light

I Tim. 6:13-16
In the presence of God,
Who gives LIFE to all things
And of Christ JESUS
Who in He testimony before Pontius Pilate
Made the good confession,
I charge you to keep the commandment
Without spot or blame
Until the manifestation
Of our Lord Jesus Christ
Which He will bring about
At the right time.   *(Pray for the right time to come!)*

He who is the
BLESSED and ONLY
SOVEREIGN
The King of Kings
And Lord of Lords

It is He alone who has immortality
And dwells in unapproachable

LIGHT   *(This is said by the man who was struck down by that Light!)*
Whom no one has ever seen or can see,
To Him be HONOR
And eternal dominion
AMEN

Take hold of the LIFE
That really is LIFE! I Tim. 6:19

Journal April 18 Wednesday   Do Not Fret

Ps. 37:1-2 Do not fret because of the wicked …wrongdoers
for they will soon fade like the grass….
Verse 10 Yet a little while and the wicked will be no more;
Though you look diligently for their place,
They will not be there.
Verse 13 …the Lord laughs at the wicked,
For He sees that their day is coming.

Lord, I pray this comes to pass ASAP!! Let the devil's day come!!

Ps. 37:5 Commit your way to the Lord;
Trust in Him and He will act.

It's saying what Jesus said—that if we believe what we pray, it will be done—
God will act!

And here, too!

Ps. 37:3-4 Trust in the Lord and do good;
So you will live in the land and enjoy security.
Take delight in the Lord,
And He will give you the desires of your heart.

What a Terrible Tragedy, the V-Tech Massacre
Thu, Apr 19, 2007 at 12:35 Midnight

I am in shock over here, just as you all are over there. I've been staying up late so I can watch Fox news and CNN. (Those are the only two American news programs I can get here.) I have been praying and shedding tears with you all. It seems too close to home for me, especially since our daughter went to the sister college, UVA (University of Virginia), and she had several friends who graduated from VT (Virginia Tech).

It also hits home because I am friends with two Laotian families whose sons also have felt like outcasts from American society, and they have caused their families so much grief, ending up in Juvenile detention. I sat beside the parents to comfort them and pray with them so many times. The one boy has a sister who is doing marvelously well. Both these boys were raised in church, but it didn't help. So this makes me feel a special connection to the killer's parents. I have shed tears for the families of the victims first of all, but also for Cho's parents, and for Cho and other lost boys like him who don't feel like they are a part of any community or culture.

The Lord comforted me about it at the Wall today.

I teach South Koreans. When I told them that I am very sad about this whole thing, I heard several of them suck in their breath, and there was suddenly a very awkward silence. The feel of sudden shame and apprehension filled the room. I was very glad that I could tell them how much my heart goes out to the Korean family and to what this boy has gone through feeling so alone in America. It helped bring warmth to the room again right away. So I thank the Lord for that.

One very interesting thing, which really makes you think, is that the incident happened exactly on Holocaust Remembrance Day which here in Israel is a very important day. So, while they were remembering the victims of the Holocaust, a Holocaust survivor became a martyr, making international news——sacrificing his life to save all his students lives at VT!

That cannot just be coincidence!

God's hand has got to be in it!

And it is for some significant international reason, I'm sure. What the devil meant for evil, God will use for great good somehow.

It all makes one's thoughts spin around and around, because it is just too much to bear or to make sense of. So I find the best thing is to read Scripture and just be silent before Him.

Be silent, all people, before the Lord; for He has roused Himself from His Holy dwelling (Zech. 2:13).

Be still and know that I am GOD (Psalms 46:10).

For lo, I will come and dwell in your midst, says the Lord... (Zech. 2:10-11).

...until the manifestation of our Lord Jesus Christ, which He will bring about at the right time——He who is the blessed and only sovereign, the King of Kings and Lord of Lords (I Tim. 6:14-15).

Dear Jesus, please come and rescue us. Please come and dwell in our midst in all Your Majesty and Glory and "unapproachable LIGHT" (I Tim. 6:16) ——Your Light that overcomes the darkness. In Your Holy Name, Yeshua. Amen.

In silence,
Cheryl

Re: What a Terrible Tragedy!!

Fri, Apr 20, 2007 at 7:05 AM!

We're doing OK.

It's absolutely terrible... hard to imagine.

I don't think I knew personally anyone who was killed, but my 8th-grade Spanish teacher was shot in the shoulder and in the back of his head, By God's good grace, he was released from the hospital yesterday morning! They're calling it a miracle... even the doctors!

You can read about it here:

http://www.dnronline.com/newsdetails.php?AID=9816&CHID=1 (Guillermo Colman)

Today is "Hokie Pride" day. People across the nation are being encouraged to wear "Hokie Colors" (orange and maroon) to show their support.

Keep praying for those who were injured and for the safety of people across the world. We're already hearing rumors of threats of copycat crimes.

These are evil times.

Israel sounds pretty safe right about now.

Much Love

Reply

Thank the Lord you are all doing alright.

What a story!! Someone else sent me the link to WSJV's story about Gil, too. I read and watched it all. I will keep praying.

Yes, these are evil times. But may the Lord bring awesome good out of this, like maybe a sweeping revival. Already there has come a sense of community, it looks like—— with wearing the colors and playing the church bells and all.

Yes, I feel oddly safe over here in Israel, in spite of the ever-present threat of war!!

Much Love to you,
Cheryl

April 19, 2007

To One of My Very Concerned Korean Students,

Hi, this is your teacher. I heard that you were quite shaken by the recent killings in America at Virginia Tech. I, too, was very shaken up by it. I am still very sad. I feel sad for all the families of the victims, but I also feel very sad for Cho and his family. I feel very sorry for what happened to Cho in America. I have written an open letter to all Koreans to apologize about that. I think America should be apologizing to Korea, also, not just Korea apologizing to America. And I hope and pray that no Korean will suffer any discrimination because of this. All the Koreans I have ever met are wonderful people!

The letter is attached. Please read it.

Blessings and comfort to you,
Cheryl

My Dear Korean Brothers and Sisters and Friends,

I apologize to you on behalf of my country, America, for not being warm and welcoming enough to the Korean immigrant family of Seung-Hui Cho to make him feel wanted and loved in his new homeland.

I apologize for the school children who instead of being kind and friendly to him, teased, rejected, and ignored him. I apologize for the parents, teachers, and school officials who may have tried, but were not able to prevent or stop this. I apologize that no one was able to help this lonely, hurting little boy to find solace and inner healing.

I apologize that a family who left your country to find the American dream, who was able to work hard enough to send their intelligent son to one of our prestigious universities, could not also find for him the sense of community and feeling of belonging and purpose that every human being needs.

I apologize that America, the world super power, has no "super" answers for the parents of a troubled youth. I apologize that our society is not open and compassionate enough that the parents of such children do not find it easy to ask for the help they need.

I apologize that my America which once helped your country fight communism and once sent loving letters and support money to your orphaned children, even adopting many of them, evidently did not extend that same help and care to this immigrant family.

I apologize that, though they may have tried, there was no church or group of Christians that was able to provide what Seung-Hui Cho needed the most: the transforming Love of Jesus conveyed in a way that he could understand and receive it.

Please, I beg of all Koreans to find it in your hearts to forgive us Americans for this failure to one of your own.

With all my heart,
Cheryl Zehr

P.S. Please pray that
    the Lord God
    of Heaven above
    will have mercy
    on America.

...REND YOUR HEART, AND NOT YOUR GARMENTS, AND TURN UNTO THE LORD YOUR GOD Joel 2:13

Journal   April 20   Friday   Prayer-Walking

I need to tell you about the prayer-walking I did on Sunday.

I started at the Wailing Wall and went south out the Dung Gate and around the south side of the Temple, praying—pleading the Blood of Jesus all the way. I came to a gate to a Muslim graveyard. The other side of the same one Glenn refused to walk through before. I hesitated and thought about turning back, but had such a sense of urgency that I was supposed to do this. So, with much trepidation I entered—praying hard! There was a small guard house there. It looked empty at first, but then I saw someone sitting inside. I looked at him. He looked at me. I kept walking, as if I knew what I was doing. He didn't move or say anything, so I went on past.

It is a huge graveyard—so much like the Jewish one on the opposite hill—the Mt. of Olives!! Isn't that something? Both religions want to bury their dead here in almost the same spot!! I know the Jews bury their people on the Mt. of Olives because of Zechariah 14 where God says His feet will stand on the Mt. of Olives. I suppose the Muslims are doing it because they believe Mohammed ascended from there. Anyway it really struck me.

When you look at the Temple wall you can see the outline of the Eastern Gate, also called the Golden gate, which is completely sealed and closed in with concrete.

[I later learned that the Muslims put the cemetery here for the sole purpose of defiling the site for the Jews. They closed the Golden Gate to prevent Christians from entering the Gate Jesus came through upon His Triumphal entry and to prevent Him from entering there upon His return!! (Unholy War by Randall Price, Harvest House Publishers, 2001, p. 228)]

There was a very nice, newly constructed walkway through the graveyard. When I came to a kind of tent thing over the walkway I met two families—two women, covered head to foot with only their faces showing, each with a few small children. When they saw me, they smiled very brightly as if they were very pleased to have me there. (I was expecting the total opposite and was worried as I approached them!) One lady said, "Shalom." I said, "Shalom." They brightened even more. One little boy came and kissed my hand then put it to his forehead. I giggled in surprise and said, "Oh how sweet." Then another boy did the same. Then I took the first boy's hand and kissed it. Then he kissed mine and put it to his forehead again. (That time some of the snot from his runny nose got on my hand.) All this time the two mothers were smiling and seemed very pleased as if I was a celebrity or something. But I was wondering why in the world they were treating me like this. I figured that if they knew at all what I was doing there, they would change their mood immediately!! They acted like they wanted to talk some more to me, but I figured it was because they thought I was a Muslim sympathizer or something. I didn't want to disappoint them after they treated me so nicely, nor did I want to see their mood change into anger at me, so I said good-by and walked on.

As soon as I did that I felt guilty, like I should've found out what it was they wanted from me. It felt like they had been expecting me. I don't know. It was just so strange how they were so happy to see me. And their little boys were treating me so the opposite from how the cute twin Arab boys treated Jane—one of them kicked her. It was just so strange. I've got to find out from someone what they would think an American is doing walking through their cemetery, and why it would make them so happy. But I don't want anyone to know that I walked through the cemetery—not even Glenn—so I don't know how I will ever find out.

Anyway, I just take it as a gift from God—that God is very pleased with me doing the prayer-walking.

After I entered Stephen's Gate (also called the Lion Gate or the Sheep Gate) and walked past the Temple entrance and on down the Via Dolorosa, a white, middle-aged guy started boldly talking to me. I didn't ignore him, but was trying to politely keep the conversation to just be greetings. But he kept on talking, telling me he just came back from being a missionary in India. Well, then I couldn't bring myself to cut him off. He followed me all the way back to the Wailing Wall telling me all about his trip. I felt a little uncomfortable, but I was so excited by all the stories he was telling about what was happening in India. He told me he led the owner and principal of a private Hindu school to the Lord!! This happened after he prayed for the lady principal's son who had hemophilia. The boy was healed and didn't need his blood treatment the next day! The school has three hundred children and thirty teachers. He showed me a picture of all the teachers and some of the children sitting on the floor.

In one of his revival meetings, three people were miraculously healed—cancer pain was one of them. So then he gave an altar call and thirty-five people came to the Lord.

He also taught for six weeks at a new Bible school he and a local pastor were starting. Then he gave them all bicycles to take the Word to the villages.

Three of his new converts were young wives who were kicked out of their Hindu homes, so he rented a place for them and bought them a couple sewing machines so they can earn their living. Another lady is going to teach them how to sew.

Isn't it great?!!

He plans on going back, he said.

He said he was from Alabama. I said I was from Virginia. Later he said he moved to Alabama from Indiana. I said, "Indiana? Where in Indiana?" It was my home town!! I was shocked!

Here he is from the Glory Church! (an on-fire church that turned too fanatical in the 1970's.) He's the second person I've met here that is from the Glory Church. After he told me his name and that he used to run a repair business, I recognized him!! I thought he had looked familiar! I learned a lot about the Glory Church from him.

After he followed me back to the Wall, he wondered where he could find a church service that evening. I directed him to King of Kings. The directions were too complicated so I took him there. He was one of those kinds of people who are a little uncomfortably bold and persistent. But it seems those are the kinds of people who make very good evangelists. I'm too shy and timid, and too worried about making sure I'm being polite to be a good evangelist.

Journal April 21 Good Confession

We had Shabboth meal at the university president's house. The Australian volunteer, told them about all the things the Koreans are doing for the Lord, including that they have been granted a room in Hebrew University for holding their Sunday services, which is absolutely amazing—Hebrew U being a secular Jewish university! The president's wife said, "Maybe they think that since the service is done in Korean, they don't need to worry about their Hebrew speaking students being influenced by it." But they don't know the power of the prayers being sent up weekly by the Koreans right there on the campus!

Before he told about the Koreans, he told about how the Muslims are taking over Australian neighborhoods. He said that first they start vandalizing a neighborhood over and over until people are so fed up and afraid that they start moving out. By the time they decide to move they are forced to sell their homes at lower prices because no one wants to buy a home in a neighborhood known to have vandalism. The Muslims then buy up the cheap homes until it becomes a completely Muslim neighborhood. Apparently this has happened in many Australian city neighborhoods.

They stopped our meal right there and prayed for Australia.

I Tim. 6:13 Christ Jesus who in His testimony before Pontius Pilate made the good confession.

Here is JESUS' Good Confession:

John 18:33 Pilate: "Are you the King of the Jews?"
Jesus: "Do you ask this on your own, or did others tell you about Me?"
Pilate: "I am not Jew, am I? Your own nation ... has handed you over to me. What have you done?"
Jesus: "My Kingdom is not from this world.
If My Kingdom were from this world, My followers would be fighting
to keep Me from being handed over to the Jews, but as it is
My Kingdom is not from here."
Pilate: "So you are a king?"
Jesus: "You say that I am a king.
For this reason I was born
and for this reason I came into the world,
to testify to the TRUTH.
Everyone who belongs to the TRUTH
Listens to My voice."

[Then I listed most of the verses again from April 15 that I felt inspired to use to pray for Israel, emphasizing the words that stuck out to me, and adding a few new verses.]

Zech. 5:1, 4 Flying scroll...curse...shall enter into the house of the thief (the enemy!!)

Zech. 10:12 I will make them strong in the Lord and they shall walk in His Name, says the Lord. (His Name, says the Lord! It has to be talking about Jesus—Jesus' Name!)

Zech. 9: 6-7 Philistia shall be a remnant for God—like the clan of Judah. !!!

(May 10, 07 Yes, Lord!! Let the Palestinians be a remnant people for You!! —a chosen clan for You!!!!)

Zech. 10:11 ... and the waves of the sea will be struck down and all the depth of the Nile dried up. *(Nile: perhaps false religion)*

Zech. 12: 3, 4 On that day I will make Jerusalem a heavy stone for all the peoples; all who lift it will grievously hurt themselves. ... I will strike every horse with panic ... every rider with madness ... horse ... with blindness.

Zech. 12:5   The clans of Judah will say, "The inhabitants of Jerusalem have strength through the Lord of Hosts their God. *(May they say 'our God.')*

Zech. 4:7 What are you O great mountain? ... you shall become a plain.

Mark 11:23 If you say to this mountain. Be taken up and thrown into the sea....

> Isaiah 57:14 Build up, build up.
> Prepare the way
> Remove every obstruction
> from My people's way.

> Isaiah 58:1 Shout out, do not hold back!
> Lift up your voice like a trumpet!
> Announce to My people their rebellion
> to the house of Jacob their sins.

> Isaiah 59:2 Your iniquities have been barriers
> between you and your God.

> Isaiah 18:3 All you inhabitants of the world, you who live on the earth,
> When a signal is raised on the mountains, Look!
> When a trumpet is blown, Listen!

Isaiah 27:13 On that day a great trumpet will be blown, And
those who were lost in Assyria and Egypt will come and worship the Lord in Jerusalem.

Zech. 10:6 I will bring them back ... and it shall be as though I had not rejected them.

Israel Independence Day, 2nd Prayer-walk, Cleaning Lady

Sun, Apr 22,-2007 at 12:59 Midnight

Hello, my battle weary friends, weary from your prayer battles for your own country!

Tuesday is Israel's Independence Day. Monday is Remembrance Day to remember their fallen soldiers and victims of terror. Their days start the evening before so the Memorial ceremonies started this evening. When I got to the Wailing Wall today it was blocked off and tons of chairs were set up with a podium, sound system, and everything getting ready for the evening ceremony. There were still plenty of people facing the Wall and praying—lots of women, but they were far away from the Wall standing behind the blue, metal barricade fences. What dedicated people!!

I did another prayer-walk around the Temple as I did last Sunday. Because of the metal barrier fences I couldn't start my praying at the actual Wall, which frustrated me a little. I walked and prayed unhindered around the south side past the Archeological Garden. (I mentioned on 12/19 that things looked pretty rundown and trashy. Well, they cleaned things up before the Passover/Easter holiday. So it looks nice now.)

Outside the Old City wall I prayed aloud earnestly along the deserted sidewalk, looking across the gully to the two long stairways leading to the two ancient doors that once led into the Temple's huge gathering area called, Solomon's Porch. I tried to imagine how magnificent it must have felt to enter one of those doors. I saw a couple Arab men looking at me from way up at the top. I looked at them and thought to myself, "Won't that be the day when we can stand and praise the Lord from there?" I walked on into the Muslim cemetery which was empty. I wasn't stopped by any family this time. Again I gazed at the cemented Golden Gate, trying to imagine it being opened again and Jesus entering there in all His Glory, praying for that day to arrive soon.

I exited the cemetery and entered the Old City through the Lion/Stephen Gate, and prayed under my breath as I walked along the narrow, cobblestone street amidst the crowd. I got passed the place where I had met the missionary from India last time. Whew, I thought, I'm getting through this time without interruption!

Suddenly I heard a man in a thick Arab accent yelling from quite a ways behind me, "Ma'am, you dropped something!" I turned around to see what I had dropped. There was nothing there. I said, "No, I didn't drop anything." He said, "I mean yesterday." I hadn't been there yesterday. It was a lie. Immediately I realized he was a shopkeeper using another trick to get a shopper's attention. It worked, too, didn't it? By then he was close to me and he pleaded with me to come into his shop. When I refused, he told me that I could come up to his top floor and look into the Dome of the Rock, no charge. I asked, "Really, no charge?" He promised. "But I won't buy anything," I emphasized. He assured me he doesn't expect me to buy anything.

I figured he was lying, but curiosity made me willing to suffer through his further pleas I knew would be coming. He took me through his store and up a big stone stairway, telling me all the way about the year this building was built and how his family came to own it. We came to a landing and there it was, a big opened window that looked out over the Dome of the Rock and the huge platform area around it. Children were playing there. It looked like maybe they were having recess from school or something. Too bad I didn't have my camera.

When I came down, he accosted me again with pleas to "just have a look." He had many beautiful carpets and a jewelry counter. I couldn't buy any of it because of the price. I did look at the jewelry to see if I could buy something for our middle daughter who is graduating with her bachelor's degree. I wanted to buy something as a thank you to him for letting me look out his window, but I couldn't. His prices were just too high. So, I walked on and continued praying.

I wanted to find a street that went next to the Temple Wall. I tried two side streets, but each time I came huge closed doors and guards who told me I couldn't go that way. They told me I have to come in the morning to be able to enter there. I thought that was very strange. (Later I realized they were gates into the area around the Dome. They wouldn't let me in because it was closed for Muslim prayer time.) So I had to continue my praying down the terribly noisy, shop-lined, people-packed street, forcing myself to ignore the cajoling shopkeepers, "Excuse me Ma'am." "Ma'am I'm talking to you!"

At the metal detector/check point for entering the Wailing Wall, they gave me a little trouble because it beeped. I pointed to my barrette which usually satisfies the guard, but these guards weren't satisfied. They ran their wand over me, pointed to my waist and asked me if I have something there. I said no. But they found a safety pin in my skirt waist that I had forgotten about. How embarrassing.

In the evening when I got back home, the memorial siren sounded for one full minute. When it sounds you are supposed to stop everything and be silent in remembrance. Buses and cars are supposed to stop driving. This siren also sounded at 10 am on Holocaust Remembrance Day. Since I was at home both times, I didn't get to see if people actually do stop everything. This time I opened our kitchen window so we could hear the siren better while we stood silently. I tried to keep my mind on the fallen Israelis but mostly all I could think of were the Virginia Tech fallen and the church bells that were tolling for them last week. (I happened to have the news on at that exact time and I wept as I listened to the bells ring. I'm sure you all did, too)

With the growing number of fallen students in America perhaps we should have a special Memorial day for them, and make it a tradition for church bells to toll for a few minutes.

America

On the news it looks like America has been getting bombarded ever since the massacre!! Floods, more shooting, tornadoes, forest fires, plane crashes, etc., etc. Goodness sakes! It makes you wonder what America has done to bring all this upon itself! If it has anything to do with their treatment of Israel, then it might be because of America recently giving a huge amount of money, along with weapons, to the Palestinians, and/or it might be from America pressuring Israel to give away more land. Some people believe there is almost always a link like this to American disasters and they have list after list to prove it.

Actually, the news across the whole world looks pretty ominous. I don't remember having this many bad news reports in one day ever, do you?! There are so many urgent happenings the reporters don't know which ones to focus on. Perhaps the End Times really are here. One of my Korean students gave two of his young children names that mean "the great commission completed." Interesting, isn't it?!

Israel Security

The Hamas is calling for new violence in Israel. So who knows what will happen. Already for a couple weeks there have constantly been guards on the buses. On one bus they actually had two guards, one for the back door and one for the front. At most of the bus stops in town now they have at least one security guard. This is the most heightened security since I came here.

I visited a hospital today with a friend. We had to have our bags checked and go through metal detectors at two different locations before we could enter the hospital. At the mall and at any really large shopping building, at the Wailing Wall, and the Hebrew University you also have to go through metal detectors and have your bags checked. At parking garages, cars are thoroughly searched. You have to open your trunk and glove compartment and everything. This is all just routine here. The extra guards is all that is visibly new.

So, with all this security will Hamas be able to increase the violence here? Our prayers are that they won't.

Glenn

Glenn is coming home in two days!! So he will be here to help pray against the violence. And my battle against loneliness will be over! He has had a trying time in America. The latest is fighting the stomach flu!!

Cleaning Lady

My Ethiopian friend, Hadassah, whose son Reuven was taken, cried when I told her that my friends in America are praying for him. I found out today that one of people she cleans house for is Ohmert! She works for a cleaning company and he is one of the clients! She used to clean for Prime Minister Sharon. She loves Sharon. She says he was so kind to her. He would always smile and say hi. And when he went on trips, he would bring gifts back for her. She says she prays for him every day. But Ohmert is much different. He never speaks to her at all. He doesn't even look at her! What a difference, huh? I asked her if he pays her well. She said it is the company that pays her. She told me what the pay is and it isn't too great. But no one in Israel gets paid very well. Wages are low here, while prices are high.

Orthodox Dress and Community

When I first saw the Ultra Orthodox Jewish men with their very long side curls, I thought they seemed a little strange, but some of the Orthodox Christian Greek, Armenian, etc., groups that were marching around in the Old City during the Easter holiday have very outrageous clothing! Each group dresses in their identical garb, including their elaborate, tall head gear of the special (strange) shape and color. One sect's priests even wear white lace on top of their long, dark, flowing robes! (The Jewish men watched them with puzzled looks on their faces!) I was pondering this today, wondering why people would agree to dress so oddly—men especially. My son and his peers thought it a terrible torture if their clothes were different at all from the fashion. I think the answer is the feeling of community and belonging that people—men especially—seem to need so badly. Men will join all sorts of clubs and organizations to find community and will do all kinds of strange things to be a part of them. (Take the Masons, for example.) It is the feeling the Virginia Tech Seung-Hui Cho, sadly, completely lacked.

But with Jesus, we belong to the most close-knit community of all!! I was made aware of that again today as I was visiting a Chinese friend. She told me about a couple other Chinese ladies whom God is calling to come to Israel to pray. One of them is focusing on the End Times in her praying. They are from the other side of the world, but God is telling them the same things He is telling me!! There is no better feeling of connection than that.

Resurrection Sunday Morning I got to go to the sunrise service at the Garden Tomb! That was really wonderful!

Praise the Lord, He is risen. And He is returning to earth soon in all His Glory!!!! The sooner the better, right?

Commit your way to the Lord, trust in Him and HE WILL ACT. Psalms 37:5

Journal April 24

Glenn is coming today. Lord, I pray things will go better for him this time.

Isaiah 48:6 From this time forward, I will make you hear new thing; hidden things that you have not known.

As I was reading this verse I suddenly realized I should be praying this also for the Jewish people!!!

O Jesus, make the Jewish people hear new things. Make them!!! Just like that rabbi giving them the Name of the Messiah!!!

Charity, Derek, and I went to one of my Korean students birthday party last night. They showed us their prayer center. It is sooooo nice! They pray 24/7 for Israel and the Jewish people!!!

Glenn is Here Safely!!!

Wed, Apr 25, 2007 at 6:22 PM

Dear Loved Ones,

My darling Glenn is here safely, but he is very sick with stomach flu. He was in the emergency room in America Sunday night getting 2 bags of IV and Phenergan. By taking Phenergan all day Monday and on the plane on Tuesday, he was able to make it here. He slept through the whole flight. He says it was the shortest 12 hour flight he has ever been on. One of his suitcases didn't make it with him, but they brought it today.

He is very weak and has been sleeping most of the time since he got here. I made garlic and onion soup for him.

He brought the WONDERFUL, NEW, LAPTOP!! Thank you to all you lovely, GENEROUS people who contributed to make this possible for us. I still can't believe it is ours. Both of us are hesitant to touch it——sort of like being hesitant to hold your brand new first baby!! ☺

THANK YOU again, sooooo much!!

Please pray for Glenn. And pray that no one here gets his illness.

Love,
Cheryl

7.

AMAZING CHANGES
IN NATURE
AND IN LIVES

Finding an Orthodox Messianic congregation and Seeing a Korean Prayer house

Sun, Apr 29, 2007 at 11:17 PM

Dear Friends and Family,

Attached is the account of our latest Jerusalem adventure. I hope you don't mind getting them as attachments now. This way I can save them on my amazing new gift of a laptop!

Discouragement

God is soooooooo good! Lately the realization has been hitting me of how long I've been here and how little time I have left before I go home for the summer. (I have to see my granddaughter. She turns two in June, and I haven't seen her since she was 14 months! She was just toddling and could only say a few words. Now she can run, and she talks all the time!) Friday night Glenn and I were both feeling very discouraged about how little we have done while we've been here. I've been here six months and we don't even know one Orthodox Jewish family personally. Both of us were crying out to God. We were crying about other things, too, including family matters. We were feeling so useless and like failures to the Lord. (It was a terrible attack from the enemy.) Finally I told myself, it isn't me I have faith in, it is the Lord Jesus! With that I was able to fall asleep.

Early on last fall, I had been asking everyone if there are any Messianic congregations that still do all the Jewish things, like wear the Talliths (prayer shawls), etc. I found out about a couple but was told their meetings are on Shabboth mornings twice a month and that everything is in Hebrew with no translation, both of which were huge barriers to me. First, since no buses run on Shabboth, I would have to pay the expensive Shabboth taxi fare. Second, since I knew only about 10 Hebrew words, I would hardly get anything out of the service.

The Long Search

Well, yesterday we decided we didn't care about the expense or the language problem, we were desperate to get more involved in the culture here. So we decided we were going to take a taxi and visit one of these congregations. We decided to start walking to catch a taxi since that is cheaper than calling for one on the phone. Well, we walked quite a ways without seeing one, then one came, but we didn't see it until it went speeding by. We waved but it didn't stop. We walked all the way to Hevron Road, which goes straight into Jerusalem from Bethlehem. As soon as we crossed the road an Arab bus came along. We backed out of its way because it seemed to be turning right in front of us. But then we realized it was stopping for us!!! (We didn't think they liked picking up non-Arab people!) We had no idea what route it would take or the price, but we decided to take our chances and get on. The price turned out to be very cheap—even cheaper than an Israeli bus!! An Israeli bus is a little more than 4 shekels with a multi-punch ticket. The Arab bus was just a little more than 2 shekels! A taxi would have been 30 some shekels!

So that was the first God-thing that happened. We felt God did it to comfort us and to show us He was with us and was pleased with what we were deciding to do. He made sure we missed the first taxi, so that we didn't miss the Arab bus He was sending to stop for us! I have walked along that road with others on Saturday mornings many times and no Arab bus has ever stopped for us! I felt very comforted by God.

An Arab bus

The Arab buses are very small—about the size of a big van. This one had about 4 rows of seats—2 seats on one side of the tiny aisle and one seat on the other side. We sat in the very back row which was 4 seats across. There were only men on board. When a young Muslim woman got on, all the seats were full except the two beside us. We quickly switched sides so she could sit next to me instead of next to Glenn. We knew that would be important to her. She said a very sincere, "Thank you" and then was very friendly to us. I told her it was our first time to ride an Arab bus. She said, "We are very happy to have you!" Her friendliness felt like another comforting gift from the Lord.

We had to walk several blocks from where the Arab bus let us off. This was bad because Glenn wore his Sunday shoes, thinking a taxi was going to take us right to the door. He got several blisters by the end of the day!

We were looking for #56 on the street. I knew where #55 was because I went there for the Passover. So, it should have been a cinch. But in Jerusalem the numbers are not right across from each other like they are in America. The numbers on the other side were getting higher and higher and still we didn't come to #55. In fact, there were no odd numbers to be seen. This back street was empty. We asked an Ethiopian guy walking alone. He didn't know. We came to a guard at a gate and asked him. He didn't know English, so I used my terrible, beginner Hebrew. He said he didn't know, but he told us his place was #53. That helped quite a bit. Finally we came to #55. It was where I had been for the Thanksgiving gathering! I was so new to Israel then, that I hadn't known where we were! It is a nice little church which several different congregations use at different times on the weekend.

So, I thought we had arrived but we hadn't. There was a Korean worship team practicing there. One of them was a new student of mine. She was so delighted to see me as I was her. I asked them if they meet every week or every other week. No one understood what "every other week" meant, but they said they meet every week. They had no idea about a Messianic congregation.

So now we were stumped! And Glenn's feet were hurting! We prayed and I decided to walk all the way to the end of the street to see what we could find. Glenn said he could tolerate it. The street was very quiet even as it neared the main thoroughfare. No cars. No buses. Very few people on the sidewalks. And all the stores were closed. That's how Jerusalem is on the Sabbath. We passed a few Orthodox families walking somewhere, some mothers were pushing strollers, but how could we know if they were Messianic? I didn't want to ask them about a Messianic congregation if they weren't Messianic, because they might be very angry about the very existence of Messianic congregations! So we got to the end of the street, finding nothing.

We crossed the big, but empty, Jaffa street to ask at the King of Kings prayer tower. Someone there would know. But the Israeli guard at the wide open door of the shopping center building said they were closed and wouldn't let us in. So we sat on a bench to rest and then decided to go to the Wailing wall to pray. Glenn said he would just bear the pain of walking.

But just then a lady came along whom I knew! She was on the way to her congregation (which doesn't wear Talliths, she said). She thought, too, that the congregation we were looking for was at #55 or 56. So, she told us about the only other one she knew of, but said it would be too impolite to go so late. She also wasn't sure if this was the week they meet.

Well, we decided we'd like to at least find the place so we would know for next time. Poor Glenn. It meant a lot more walking.

On the way, we passed an open gate where we saw two little Jewish boys dressed in black dress pants, white shirts, and kippas, sitting on the front steps of an apartment building. One had a prayer book opened on his lap and was loudly chanting his prayers. It was so cute. I didn't take pictures because it is against their custom on Shabboth. I didn't want to offend.

Finally Found It

Again, because of the strange way they do house numbers here, it was hard to find #16. We walked right passed it the first time. It was a small building inside a stone fence. We entered the darling little courtyard. Through an open window, we heard the reciting and chanting of Hebrew prayers. It sounded beautiful to us! We looked in the open door, but could only see a stairway. Outside in a little garden, there was a young adult girl with gorgeous, curly hair dressed in a long, pretty skirt sitting on a bench under two large bushes reading her Hebrew Bible or maybe it was her prayer book. It was a very picturesque scene. It didn't seem right to disturb her. So we sat on a ledge near the church door and decided to just enjoy the service from outside.

Suddenly a blaring air conditioner came on, drowning out the chanting. We moved closer to the door, but still couldn't hear very well. I got up the courage to approach the young lady. She was very sweet and encouraged us to go in. She said people many times come late due to wrong information or not being able to find the place. But she said it is very full today so there might not be a seat. Still we hesitated.

A mother came out with a young boy and sat near us on the low ledge. Then out came a guy we know—the Hands of Mercy guy!! He told us to go on in although there aren't any seats. The mother beside us urged us to go in and take the two seats she and her son had just vacated. She said it was near the interpreter. (So there was interpretation into English!!) She sensed our hesitation so she walked in with us and pointed out where the seats were.

Again, I felt like God was working things out to comfort us and to tell us we were doing alright.

To my surprise, I could understand more of the Hebrew than I thought I would. Still I would've missed too much without interpretation. We were close enough to the interpreter to hear most of what was said. We enjoyed the service so much. I especially loved the part where the husbands extend their Talliths over their wives and recite a blessing.

I had been told that this congregation wasn't very friendly to new people because they are so used to people coming just out of curiosity, so you have to come many times before they befriend you. But that didn't seem to be the case after all. We were greeted warmly afterwards by the leader who invited us to stay for the lunch they were serving. (The Lord even gave us lunch!!) A Korean couple was there who seemed to be well-known and well-loved. The husband is a student in one of our advanced ESL classes. They have been going to this congregation for three years, they said! I was really impressed.

Another wonderful thing from God was that afterwards there was a group of European tourists who asked the guy who gave the message (who is the one who started this congregation, I found out later) to tell them more about the congregation and about Israel. He spoke to them in English! So we got closer and listened. Here are the things we found out.

• They have a soup kitchen almost every day where they feed the new immigrants and the poor of Jerusalem.

• They tell Jerusalem about Yeshua every day on their radio program!

• They have had 20 young people from their congregation who have gone into the army. 19 of them have received the president's award which is given to only 100 people in the whole army (per year, I assume)!

[The next thing he told us is very important. It embodies the reason why I put together this book.]

He told us that Israel *will* turn to God as a nation because the Scripture says it will. He said solemnly that it would happen sooner if all the missionaries would go home. ***

He thinks the nation will accept Yeshua when Yeshua becomes a Jewish problem, not a Christian-towards-the-Jews problem. He says when the Jews are confronted with Yeshua so much that He becomes the topic of discussion in every home around the Shabboth dinner table every week, then the nation will accept Yeshua.

And he says this is beginning to happen! He said many Jewish scholars are writing about Yeshua. He showed us the English translation of an article by a respected person just last week in the HaEretz newspaper that talked about Yeshua rising again 3 days after He died! He says that lately there has been something like this almost every week!

He says that Jewish archeologists have more respect for the historical value of the New Testament than the Christian archeologists do. He thinks the day is here that was predicted by a famous Rabbi when the Jews will defend Jesus to the Christians!

He said that in 1993 there were only 50 Jewish believers in the Land, and some of them were strange people. Now there are (I think he said) 4000 believing Jews who are normal Jews. He said the Jewish leaders respect him because he has never stopped being a Jew. Here's an example of their respect for him. Recently a Belgium family who had converted to Orthodox Judaism and had joined a kibbutz had been discovered to be secret Believers in Yeshua. The Yad Vashem (the anti-missionary organization) asked him to help them with this family—to get them to leave the community and help them get settled in Jerusalem.

Again God was comforting us! Hearing all that he was saying was emphasizing to me how important praying for Israel is. According to him, it was more important for us Christians to pray than to evangelize. (***He was talking about the nation as a whole and the religious communities as a whole accepting Jesus. Evangelism to individuals, especially secular individuals, is still very important and very productive. I saw that at the festival!) So God was trying to encourage me to keep on doing spiritual warfare praying. He was showing us that all the prayers for Israel are having affect!

We hope we can help people through their soup kitchen or wherever God leads.

Grace

That evening at our regular Messianic congregation, we heard a message on how hard it is to receive God's Grace. (How timely!!! That's exactly what we were having trouble with the night before!!!) The pastor ended with this thought: He has discovered that the prerequisite for being able to understand and receive the message of Grace is failure—complete and utter failure. (!!!) I could hardly hold back a flood of tears! I have failed so many times and so utterly. And it did take failure to get me to see God's Grace. But how many times do I have to keep on failing to keep a hold of this concept?!!! I seem to need a renewed revelation of it quite frequently!! May the Lord give me a more powerful, more astounding revelation of it, so it will stick longer! His Grace is so delicious; it is too hard for us humans to believe it is really true.

Korean Prayer House

Getting back to prayer, I got to visit one of the Korean prayer houses. I was invited to a birthday party for one of my students right before Glenn came back. We were served delicious food. Then afterwards we got to see their prayer house, and, oh my, do they ever know how to make a prayer house!! They have turned an apartment into this fabulously beautiful, reverent, holy place. They have a healing room, which when I stepped inside I could hardly keep from crying tears of joy, the Holy Spirit's presence was so strong and so sweet in there. It was beautifully decorated with velvety red-wine-colored curtains from floor to ceiling, and pillows scattered on the floor for sitting. It had a very quiet, calm feeling. Then there was a tiny prayer closet for personal prayer time. And most importantly, there was the main, 24/7 pray-for-Israel prayer room. It was a little bit bigger than the healing room. All four walls were lined with exquisite silky, crinkled curtains of soft, mute, relaxing colors, like cream, pale orange, tan and such. A lady was sitting on the mat-covered floor doing her watch, playing on a bongo drum to the cd music. The room felt very worshipful and holy.

The Koreans are like the Japanese in one way, at least. To enter the prayer house, you had to take off your shoes and put on slippers. There were shelves full of slippers at the door. My student quickly picked out slippers for us and herself. When we got ready to leave we took our slippers off and placed them back on the shelf. Lo and behold, Charity was trying to put my student's shoes, which looked a lot like slippers, back on the shelf! Here Charity had been wearing those shoes, instead of slippers, all through the prayer house!

After seeing that elaborate prayer house, I was more impressed at the Koreans' sacrificial faith. The home we visited was crowded and very sparsely furnished, with nothing decorative on their walls nor curtains on their windows. They live in very humble, poor homes while they keep the Lord's house beautiful and luxurious. What sacrificial dedication!

I hope I get to spend some prayer time in that special house. I'm not sure how that can happen, though, since it is more than an hour's bus ride away from where we live. But the Lord will work it out if it is His will. I haven't been able to spend much time in the Sukkoth Hillel prayer house either because at the times I could go, they are having special groups doing their special prayer times and the public is not invited. But the Lord will take care of that, too. If we lived right in town, all this would be taken care of. We'll see. We will just keep on praying.

May God give you wonderful, comforting encouragement, and the message of Grace, too, whenever you are feeling like a failure.

Cheryl

To a friend visiting Jerusalem:

On May 1 we went to a Jerusalem city-wide prayer meeting. It was awesome!! I invited my Korean students to come and they did!

On April 30 we went to the Samaritan Passover and didn't get back until late. It was very interesting. It's too bad you couldn't come.

Samaritan Passover

Added in 2008 from memory

We were told that the Samaritans living in the West Bank still observe the Passover the way it would have been done in Jesus' day, sacrificing real lambs and all, and that the public is welcome to come and watch! So I excitedly helped organize things so our whole English department, with all the Koreans, could go, together with a small Bible College in East Jerusalem. We ended up filling two big tour buses!

This was my first time to the West Bank (besides Bethlehem), so it was exciting and scary at the same time. We made sure all our students and their spouses and children had all their passports, and that we had copies of all their passports just in case. But, thankfully, nothing untoward happened.

The last leg of the journey was up a steep, narrow mountain road. It was amazing that the buses could fit on the road, let alone take the sharp turns. Our buses soon joined a whole mountain load of buses! We had to park far from the village along side the road, and join the throng walking the rest of the way.

Naublus (Biblical Shechem) is a small, country village with a few tall apartment buildings along with some single family homes. There was nothing commercial about it. Not even any shops, at least not on the streets near the Passover area. It didn't take long to walk through most of the streets, past every house, noting all the sheep penned in the yards waiting for the slaughter. We headed outside the village through uncut meadows, over fences, to the lookout point that overlooked the two mountains, Gerizim and Ebal, where Joshua carried out Moses' command to have blessings and curses recited there (Deut. 27:11-13 and Joshua 8:30-35). It was interesting to try to visualize the three million Israelites shouting the blessings and curses at each other across the deep ravine.

We then walked through the area where the Passover was going to be held. There was a long stone-lined trough in the center with trash buckets ready for the slaughter. Pits stood gaping nearby. Young boys dressed totally in white were gathering and preparing wood for the roasting. One boy, when he noticed me pointing my camera at the long

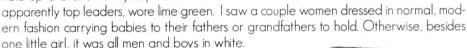

trough, placed himself into every picture I tried to take. No matter which way I turned, he quickly ran to that side. He seemed to be enjoying the "game." We smiled at each other. I waited until he was occupied with something else and wasn't watching me to get a picture without him as the center piece.

As it neared sundown, men dressed in white pants and shirts began to appear and started ushering tourists out of the fenced-in area. (In the Bible, priests wore white robes.) Soon a huge crowd of white clad men in round colorful hats filled the area, some wearing high white boots. I assume they are the ones who will be near the slaughtering and flow of blood. One of the booted men held up a branch of hyssop for all to see. A few men, apparently top leaders, wore lime green. I saw a couple women dressed in normal, modern fashion carrying babies to their fathers or grandfathers to hold. Otherwise, besides one little girl, it was all men and boys in white.

One surprising thing I noticed was one elderly Arab man in traditional Arabic garb——white, cloth head-gear and all——was brought in and given a seat of honor. An elderly Samaritan man in white took him lovingly by the arm to show him around the place. I also saw a young couple, the lady wearing a Muslim head scarf, who were allowed inside the fence. This was very puzzling to me. Apparently there is no animosity between Samaritans and Muslims——only between Jews and Samaritans, I guess. I saw no Orthodox-dressed Jews there.

The massive multitude of spectators who didn't get seats in the bleachers squeezed up against the fences surrounding the area. There was even a group of African nuns watching

As dusk set in, the sheep were led in one by one and the excitement began to build. Later, when the darkness was lit by fires in the pits, the long row of lambs were slaughtered to the sound of the throng of men chant-singing. The place was so crowded we couldn't actually see the lambs, but whenever a throat was slit, a priest standing next to it would give out a yell, to which the whole crowd of men would whoop and holler and clap.

After the slaughtering, there was more sing-chanting. Then one by one the big lambs began to appear up in the air, pierced through from tail to head onto the ends of long sharp poles, skinned and ready for roasting. Each lamb was raised high above the crowd this way. I hadn't expected to see this.

It made me think of Jesus being lifted above his people in an eerily similar manner.

More about the Rabbi Giving the Name

May 7, 2008

We read an article that tells much more about this rabbi giving the Name of the Messiah. It's all very amazing!! He wrote the Name in Sept. 2005 and died in January of 2006. Here are a couple quotes from the article. Go to the link and find out much more!

Rabbi Reveals Name of the Messiah
Israel Today, Monday, April 30, 2007
http://www.israeltoday.co.il/default.aspx?tabid=128&view=item&idx=1347

... A few months before he died, one of the nation's most prominent rabbis, Yitzhak Kaduri, supposedly wrote the name of the Messiah on a small note which he requested would remain sealed until now. When the note was unsealed, it revealed what many have known for centuries: Yehoshua, or Yeshua (Jesus), is the Messiah.

...his last wish was to wait one year after his death before revealing what he wrote.

... A few months before Kaduri died at the age of 108, he surprised his followers when he told them that he met the Messiah. Kaduri gave a message in his synagogue on Yom Kippur, the Day of Atonement, teaching how to recognize the Messiah. He also mentioned that the Messiah would appear to Israel after Ariel Sharon's death. (The former prime minister is still in a coma after suffering a massive stroke more than a year ago.)

... Kaduri's grandson, Rabbi Yosef Kaduri, said his grandfather spoke many times during his last days about the coming of the Messiah and redemption through the Messiah.

... Kaduri was not only highly esteemed because of his age of 108. He was charismatic and wise, and chief rabbis looked up to him as a Tsadik, a righteous man or saint. He would give advice and blessings to everyone who asked. Thousands visited him to ask for counsel or healing. His followers speak of many miracles and his students say that he predicted many disasters.

When he died, more than 200,000 people joined the funeral procession on the streets of Jerusalem....

... Rabbi David Kaduri, the 80-year-old son of the late Rabbi Yitzhak Kaduri, ... confirmed, however, that in his last year, his father had talked and dreamed almost exclusively about the Messiah and his coming. "My father has met the Messiah in a vision," he said, "and told us that he would come soon."

Added Later

After his note was opened, the Jews began to say that this rabbi's mind had been declining near the end. Before the note was opened they were saying no such thing. Telling, isn't it?

The Chinese Church

May 8, 2007

Dear Prayer Warriors,

Thank you all again for giving so much for us to have this laptop. As I look over the names again and read all the notes on the card, I feel blessed to the depth of my soul!! Thank you. Thank you. Thank you!

We've been very busy. We have spent all our free time visiting new places. We visited another Believing Jewish, Tallith-wearing synagogue. We had to walk an hour to a meeting place to be picked up and then were driven another 45 minutes to the synagogue. It is in a town on the way to the Dead Sea. We also went back to the one I already wrote to you about, and visited a Chinese church. In between all that Glenn got very sick again! I had to be a nurse! But praise the Lord, He is the Great Physician. He has now healed Glenn completely!! Hallelujah.

Chinese Church

I had wanted to visit the Chinese church for a long time. Finally there was a week that my Chinese friend , Lila, could be there to introduce me and interpret for me. They meet on Friday nights when there are no buses, so we had to take an Arab bus and walk quite far. It is located near the Mea Sharim neighborhood. It is hard to find because its gate is in between prominent signs for other things, like a Polish convent. No sign says, "Chinese church," because they are just using another church's buildings.

I looked disappointingly at the huge locked iron gate and at how far away the buildings inside the complex were. I wondered how we would get anyone's attention to open the gate, as not a soul could be seen. But then Glenn checked a little pedestrian entrance and found it unlocked.

We discovered we had arrived long before it was time for the service to start. That's why there had been no one around. While waiting, I got to know a mother from Taiwan, where my wonderful friend and college roommate is from. The Taiwanese family has been missionaries here for several years. They have a heart for Israel, but their main ministry is to the many Chinese construction workers here.

The little church filled up with mostly men. Israel allows them to work here up to five years, but won't allow them to bring their wives. Apparently, Israel does not want Chinese babies to be born here who could then claim citizenship. Many of these men are new Christians, having met the Lord while here in Israel at this Chinese church. There is a similar church at the southern tip of Israel in the town of Elat, where Lila, travels every week to help out. I wanted to go with her to help, but it never worked out with my teaching schedule. I was very disappointed.

She says these men face extreme loneliness. And once she spent hours doing a teaching on forgiveness and answering questions afterwards. Some of their wives have cheated on them during their long absences and they find it hard to forgive them.

The Chinese all welcomed us warmly. Lila interpreted for us. The second time we came she wasn't there. But I was surprised how much I understood anyway with my limited Chinese. I tried to fill Glenn in as best I could, but he didn't get much out of it.

The Chinese men were picked up and taken home by a driver from Scandinavia who does this as a Christian service. He kindly took us home also, since the meeting ends long after any buses run. We were very grateful to him! Walking home more than two hours in the dark would have been quite dangerous!

Isn't it wonderful how the Lord provides?

Journal May 8   Help Me Know and Have Grace

God was making me think hard last night while we were walking from our prayer meeting to the bus. I was feeling condemned because I was afraid I had offended someone important. (I apologized later and it turns out I had not offended. Thank God!!) I was asking myself why I always feel condemned, when the Bible is all about Grace. And why do I respond in anger when loved ones don't listen to me? I got angry when Glenn wasn't listening to me when he was having diarrhea. Why can't I just stay calm? Huh?

Jesus, please deliver me. Thank you, Jesus, that you don't condemn. Thank you. Thank you. Thank you. Help me to understand Your Grace, so that I can have grace. How could I have responded to Glenn in grace? He was having a potentially life-threatening—or at least a going-to-the-hospital-threatening—illness (going to the hospital here in Israel!! Who wants that?! And how would we have paid?!!) and he wouldn't do what I, his health-care provider, was telling him he must do. Help me learn how to respond calmly in Grace and Love.

Another time at the Wall

Journal May 10　　Finally, Time Alone with God

Thank you, Lord, for this time with You today. Please protect it. Please put Your wall of fire around it. [I was asked to sit in the university's main office to answer the phone. I meant for the Lord to keep the phone from ringing or anyone from coming in, because I was so hungry for time alone with the Lord.]

The verse I got this morning. (I'm writing it from memory.)

Micah 7:7, 9 I will wait for the God of my salvation ... until He takes my side....

Yesterday it was a verse from Hosea. I can't quite remember it. I didn't bring my Bible because it is so heavy to carry. This notebook is heavy, too. [The long walk to the office is up a rather steep hill the last third of the way.] [I left space for the verses and wrote them in later.]

Hosea 4:1-3 ... There is ... no knowledge of God in the land.
... stealing and adultery break out; bloodshed follows bloodshed.
Therefore the land mourns, ...even the fish of the sea are perishing.

Last night Derek had a long talk with us. He wants us to go to China with him....

If you want us to, Lord, then speak clearly to us and provide miraculously and abundantly as You have done before for us.

O Jesus, I pray that You will make Israel know new things—hear new things, hidden things that they have not known. This whole thing about the rabbis forbidding Jewish women to attend the Woman to Woman Conference put on by Bridges for Peace, I pray even this is causing them to hear new things.

I'm having time to pray. Hallelujah! Praying and praying...

Oh, yes, the news the other day: the dollar is below four shekels!! At first I was tempted to be scared. I told Glenn we'd better draw out money and exchange our U.S. dollars now before it falls more. But he was uncharacteristically optimistic! He said, "Don't worry. The Lord will take care of it!"

Later at the prayer meeting, God entered my thoughts and made me realize the shekel going up is a blessing for Israel. It is the beginning of the answer to my prayers for God to bless Israel!! So, I don't need to worry at all. If God blesses Israel, we will be blessed, too—the whole world will be blessed!

So, Lord, I pray for more blessings upon Israel! Provide for Israel. Fulfill all the prophecies about the wealth of the nations coming to Israel.

Isaiah 57:14 Build up, build up. Prepare the way. Remover every obstruction from my people's way. (Yes, Lord, may every obstacle be removed!)

Isaiah 58:1 Shout out. Do not hold back. Lift up your voice like a trumpet. Announce to My people their rebellion ... their sins.

Isaiah 59:2 Your iniquities have been barriers between you and your God.

O Jesus, who will do this declaring? Raise up the right person to do this declaring and announcing—a person who can do it while also announcing Your message of GRACE and SALVATION!!!

O Jesus, please show us how to pray for these things. Show us what obstacles to pray to be removed. Please remove the obstacle of Israel's rebellion against You, Yeshua. Please remove their rejection of You. Remove their blindness and their being deceived. Remove those who are trying to deceive Israel. Remove them! Remove every last deceiver. Remove the Deceiver himself. AMEN Hallelujah! May he be removed and cast into the Lake of Fire!

Isaiah 18:3 All you inhabitants of the world, you who live on the earth, when a signal is raised on the mountains, Look! When a trumpet is blown, Listen!

O Yeshua, blow Your trumpet! Let it be time, Father in Heaven, for the trumpet to be blown—that Yeshua/Jesus, may return in all His Glory!

Isaiah 27:13 On that day a great trumpet will be blown and those who were lost in Assyria and Egypt will come and worship the LORD in Jerusalem. (Yes, let this come to pass!)

Zech. 10:6 I will bring them back ... and it shall be as though I had not rejected them.

Yes, Yeshua, please bring this day. Father in Heaven, bring Israel to You. Help them to receive their Messiah, so it will be as though You had never rejected them.

Zech. 8:21 ...many ... saying, "Come let us go to entreat the favor of the Lord...."

Yes, Father, we seek You and we beg for Your favor—on us individually and on Israel—and on this university and on all the volunteers here.

(Wow! Thank you, Jesus!! I'm getting paid to pray! Praise Your Holy Name! Well, not paid in money, per se, but in volunteer hours! The phone hasn't rung!)

Ezekiel 44:15-16 (Those) who kept (My) charge ... shall come near to Me ... enter My sanctuary ... approach My table (and) minister to Me.

O Lord Jesus, O Father, help me to minister to You!! The other night at the Messianic synagogue they read in Leviticus about ministering to You and my heart was tugged. Right now my heart is tugged again.

What was for You in the inner sanctuary? The Bread was for us. The Light for us. What was for You? The incense!! The fragrance—the fragrance of prayers—the fragrance of us giving ourselves to You!

Yes, Jesus,. I will join a prayer house, if that is what You want. I will make it be my 'work' to pray. I will trust You to not let it become a legalistic thing to be required to pray at certain hours for certain lengths of times. Provide, Lord! You are providing for me to pray today! It is the sign of things to come, isn't it?!

O the Holy Spirit is filling me!!!!!

Where the Spirit of the Lord is there is freedom (II Cor. 3:17).

Jesus' spirit was and is complete submission and obedience to the Father. He did nothing on His own—even His Words were not His own (John 12:49 and 14:10).

Isaiah 56:6 Foreigners who join ... to the Lord to minister to Him ... I will bring to My Holy Mountain ... make them JOYFUL in My House of Prayer.

/ / / /

My house shall be called the House of Prayer for all people.

The House of Prayer is His TEMPLE!!!

You have brought me here to Jerusalem where I can go to Your HOLY MOUNTAIN—to Your House of Prayer—frequently!! That's where You want me to pray, not at a prayer house. And that is what Glenn and I have felt all along!

Zeph. 3:14-16 Sing aloud ... rejoice .... The Lord will take away your judgments ... fear no disaster (!) do not let your hands grow weak.

Zeph. 3: 14 ... you will not bear reproach ... I will deal with your oppressors.... I (will) restore your fortunes before your eyes.

Lk. 21:36 Strength to escape. ... (Strength) to stand before the Son of Man.

Yes, Jesus, you have brought me here to stand before You on Your Holy Mountain.

Heb. 11: 6 (NRSV and KJV) Must believe ... that He rewards those who diligently seek Him.

Thank you, Jesus. You have taken away my accusers and my oppressors. Thank you. Thank you.

Now, I pray, Your accusers will be taken away; those who reject You; those who give You a cursed name; may they be silenced and removed!

May You be able to come to Your own and your own receive You!

I silence all Your accusers, by the Power of Your Holy Name, Yeshua! I take the authority You gave us over all the power of the enemy and I silence him and all the Jewish people accusing with him. I silence their thoughts, their tongues, their pens, their filming cameras, their computer keyboards, their internet websites, their publicity access, their news access—I silence it all!!

I silence their words of authority over people. I demolish their authority in the Name of Yeshua, the Name above EVERY NAME. *Let all Yeshua's accusers, disrespecters, and rejecters be taken away. Let their authority be demolished. Let their deceptive hold over people be lifted.*

May Yeshua have the JOY *of being accepted, honored, loved, and respected by His own people!!!*

AMEN, HALLELUJAH. *Let it* BE SO*!*

Zech. 3:9,10 I will remove the guilt of this land in a single day. ... On that day you shall invite each other to come under your vine and fig tree.

Yes, Lord, bring it to pass that we who are Your vine will invite those who are the fig tree to come and fellowship with us and vice versa!

Zech. 4:1 Wakened from sleep. *(O Yeshua, awaken Israel from its deep sleep!)*

Zech. 2:1 *(Be the wall of fire around Jerusalem and the Glory within it!!)*

❧   ❧

O, yes. After reading the prophecy, Derek showed us from a guy while he was on the Isle of Patmos, just like John, I was thinking skeptically again as I often do—thinking, "But it is only him writing about it—only coming from him. No one else saw it." But the Lord said, "Well, that's the same for all the prophets and for John in Revelations." It's true. We wouldn't have any of the prophets if they wouldn't have written about what they and they alone saw!!!

So, maybe it wouldn't be wrong for me to write about my visions of angels and seeing Jesus!!! I saw and Felt *Jesus standing by my bed!! I felt Him more than actually saw Him (a couple years after my stroke).*

Even Jesus when He was among His accusers and people who rejected Him didn't do many deeds of power. So, a person doesn't need to feel condemned for that either. He did His works of power for people who believed in Him—where there was an atmosphere of belief and honor and respect for Him.

Journal May 11 Job Offer
I got an e-mail from the Bible college asking if I would like to be a teacher there for the writing department!!! What an honor!!
We now have three choices before us. Find a way to stay in Israel. Go to China. Go back to Bible college.

Psalms 25:12 Who are they who fear the Lord? He will teach them the way they should choose.

Psalms 25:14 The friendship of the Lord is for those who fear Him, and He makes His covenant known to them.

A Twist From the Lord

Sat, May 12, 2007 at 11:14 PM

Dear Powerful Praying Warriors,

It was raining tonight when we got out of church. (Yes, raining in the middle of May!) A group of us were riding together, giving a young mother and her toddler daughter a ride. Her husband and little boys were riding in another person's car. (The cars are too small here to fit their whole family in one person's car.) Well, because of the soaking rain, the car we were in wouldn't start.

So we all piled out, got the stroller back out, left the car sitting there parked on the street, and took the long walk to the bus. We couldn't all fit into one taxi, so the bus it had to be. I chatted with the young, Jewish mother all the way, listening to her awesome testimony.

She's from England. Her parents divorced when she was young and she became a totally messed up girl. Finally, her unbelieving, Jewish mom told her to come to Israel to get straightened out. At a kibbutz she amazingly heard about and met Yeshua, her Messiah. Still she needed a lot of help, spiritually and emotionally. She found this church thirteen years ago. They have "parented" her into spiritual maturity and deliverance.

Her husband came to Israel as a young, Godly, American man who felt called to serve God in the Land. He is not Jewish. He sold everything and left an excellent aerospace job to come here. They met at church. They have really struggled financially here, but they will not leave because they know this is where God wants them.

We waited and waited for the bus. Finally, since it was getting colder, still drizzling, and her daughter was getting restless, we convinced her to let us get a taxi for her. I was going to ride with her, but the taxi driver was so rude, we asked Glenn to go along, too, for safety's sake.

The driver seemed very impatient the whole way, and he spoke only Hebrew. We were a little worried about her getting home safely after he let us off. (We couldn't convince her to have him let her off first because she said it would've been a zigzag route for the driver, which would cost us more.) Obeying God's nudging, Glenn gave the driver a big shekel bill, and told the driver it was for her ride, too, and to give her the change. Later when the phone rang and it was her, I was so relieved that she was home safely. I was also relieved that the driver had given her the change and hadn't pocketed the extra cash. It was almost 11 pm by the time everyone got home.

So there's the end of an unfortunate night that turned out okay.

Right?

NO!

She had a surprising, super great ending to tell me about. After we paid her fare and left, the taxi driver asked her who we were. She told him we were friends who go to the same congregation. He wondered why we would pay for her fare. She said, "Because we are believers in Yeshua and that makes us all family." He wanted to know how to become a believer in Yeshua. So she told him you have to open your heart to Him and ask Him to come in. Then he asked a typical, but very important Jewish question. "Who put Yeshua on the cross?" She told him that we all did, but that really He willingly gave His life and then took it back again. Then he told her that someone had given him a New Testament one time. He read some of it, but then some Ultra Orthodox leaders took it away from him. She said he was VERY open to everything she told him, asking questions and everything!! She got his name, etc, too.

Isn't that awesome?!!!! It looked like a night gone wrong—even to getting the wrong taxi driver!! But God's hand was in the whole thing! And God was so kind to let Glenn and I be a part of the seed planting just by doing a simple act of kindness!! God is so awesome! I feel so blessed and encouraged.

And you have a part in it, too. It is your prayers that helped cause the events to occur just at the right moments.

So be encouraged with me,
Cheryl

Rain

Sat, May 12, 2007 at 11:01 PM

Dear Powerful Praying People,

You have been praying for rain for Israel, and your prayers are being answered here in Jerusalem! On May 4 it rained for about 10 minutes, then again a little later it spit out some huge raindrops for 2 minutes. The raindrops were very dirty. They dirtied every car with big blotches of raindrop footprints. It wasn't much rain, but still I was thanking the Lord for the miracle of rain in May. On the bus one lady told me irritatingly, "It isn't supposed to rain now. It's because it is too hot." The weather had suddenly turned from chilly to very hot for two days before it rained. It got hotter as time progressed. It was so hot that sweat poured down when you were just standing still. If it gets hot enough for me to sweat, you know it is hot!!

Then on May 10 it rained again. It was a sort of drizzle that lasted quite awhile. It made the sidewalks and patios quite wet. I actually needed my rain poncho!! So I was really praising the Lord, because this was really unusual for Israel! But the miracle of rain wasn't over! Today the weather turned cold again, and it has been raining all day——a nice, heavy, soaking rain off and on the whole day!! (It is midnight now.) My rain poncho was a necessity today! It is a real, bonified miracle. Everyone is very surprised!!

It is a physical sign of the spiritual rain of righteousness and revival that is coming to Israel!!

Keep up the powerful praying!!
Cheryl

A Couple Ideas for Praying for Israel
Sat, May 12, 2007 at 12:01 Midnight

Dear Powerful, Israel Intercessors,

Using Scripture to pray is so powerful, because it is agreeing with God that His own Word comes to pass. Jesus said, "*If two of you shall agree ... as touching anything, ... it shall be done*" (Matt. 18:19), which shows that there is power in agreement. And if one of the two who are agreeing is God, how much more powerful is that? How about if more than one of us agree with God?!!! It gets exponential!!

So, in light of that, here are some Scriptures God has been giving me to use to pray over Israel.

This first verse is one we like to believe and pray for ourselves. But one morning God prompted me that we should be praying it for Israel, too, because Israel REALLY needs to hear things that are hidden from them:

Isaiah 48:6 NRSV "*From this time forward, I will make you hear new things, hidden things that you have not known.*"

Isaiah 57:14 "*Build up, build up, prepare the way, remove every obstruction from My people's way.*"

Here's a little, short prayer to help get you going:

Dear Lord Jesus, Yeshua Messiah, we pray that You will cause Israel to hear new things—marvelous, new things about You, their Messiah. Reveal to them the Truths about You that have been hidden from them; that up to this point they have not known. Give them new revelation about You. Show them that You fulfilled every Messianic prophecy except the ones about Your second coming. Cause them to hear Your True Name. Cause the Life-giving sound of Your True Name, Yeshua, to penetrate into the depths of their souls. Remove every obstruction that keeps them from knowing Your Powerful Name, and receiving You. Send more Kingdom workers to build up the Way and to help remove the veil of deception that blocks them from believing in You. Reveal to us what all the other obstructions are that keep them from turning to You, so we can pray the exact strategic, prayers You need us to pray. Teach us how to prepare the way so Your people as a nation can believe. Let these Words come to pass for Your people, Jesus, by the power of Your blood and Your Holy Name. Amen.

May the Holy Spirit anoint you and guide you as you pray,
Cheryl

Journal May 13 Staircase and Car Dreams

This morning I don't feel as confident as I did last night about plans we were considering for next fall. Yesterday I felt sure it was what God wanted. It felt so right in my soul and spirit. But I had a couple scary dreams last night. In one dream I was hanging on the outside of a circular staircase and couldn't walk my hands up to where I could get on it. I thought I was a goner. It was a very long way down—bottomless almost. Then suddenly I realized that it was swinging (yes, a moving staircase!) to where I could drop off to safety on the stair landing below.

In the second dream I was driving beside another car and I almost hit a skunk—a huge, fat skunk. The other driver hit it. It looked like some of the smell was going to get on my car because he was driving so close to me.

The third dream was about me teaching (English, I think) and having to leave the students to study by themselves. The administrator found the TV's left on to bad stations, and thought I did it, so I was in trouble. Weird!

This is very strange, but I woke up from these vivid dreams afraid to go ahead with our plans. They were great plans with good people, but Glenn has been having doubts, too, and the final decision is his to make anyway.

Parashah reading

Lev. 25:18 You shall keep My statutes and faithfully keep My ordinances so that you may live on the land securely.

Lev. 25:21-22 I will order My blessing for you in the sixth year, so that it will yield a crop for three years. When you sow in the eighth year, you will be eating from the old crop; until the ninth year, when its produce comes in, you shall eat the old.

Lev. 26:3-4 If you follow My statutes and keep My commandments and observe them faithfully, I will give you your rains in their season and the land shall yield its produce

Man, just read Leviticus chapter 26—all the judgments if they don't follow God's covenant!!! And still the rabbis (we were told yesterday in the synagogue) have ruled that these Sabbath laws and Jubilee laws are too impossible to follow!!! Even when God says He will increase the harvest in the sixth year!

Even when God says in Lev. 26:6-8 CJB I will give shalom in the land—you will lie down to sleep unafraid of anyone. …The sword will not go through your land. You will pursue your enemies, and they will fall before your sword. Five of you will chase a hundred, and a hundred of you will chases ten thousand…. (!)

Verse 9 I will turn toward you, make you productive, increase your numbers and uphold My covenant with you.

Verse 10 You will eat all you want from last year's harvest and throw out what remains of the old to make room for the new.

Verse 5 Your threshing time will extend until the grape harvest, and your grape harvesting will extend until the time for sowing seed. You will eat as much food as you want and live securely in the land.

What promises!! What Blessings!!
Don't they believe in their GOD and in His promises?!!!

And look at what will happen if they don't follow them!!!

Lev. 26:16 CJB ... I will bring terror on you—wasting disease, chronic fever to dim your sight and sap your strength.

Verse 17 ...your enemies will defeat you, those who hate you will hound you....

Verses 19-20 I will break the pride you have in your own power. I will make your sky like iron, your soil like bronze—you will spend your strength in vain....

Verses 25-26 ... you will be huddled inside your cities, ...dole out the bread ... you will eat and not be satisfied.

Verse 33 ... your land will be a desolation and your cities a wasteland. Then at last the land will be paid its Sabbaths.

Verse 36 ...anxiety *(on the ones left)* ... the sound of a driven leaf will frighten them so that they flee ... and fall when no one is pursuing them.

Verses 37, 39 ... you will have no power to stand before you enemies.... ... your enemies will devour you.

All this because they do not give the land its Sabbath rests!

So here is one of the obstructions in God's people's way!! The rabbi rulings!! The rabbis deciding these commandments of God are too hard to follow so they don't have to follow them!!

So we need to pray and pray for Israel to be delivered from Rabbinic rule!!! And pray that they figure out a way to obey the Sabbath and Jubilee year laws.

God's laws are all framed in with rest—Sabbath rests!! Rest every week; rest on all the holidays—which come every couple months and are 2-8 days long; then a whole year of rest every seven years!!

No wonder God calls it His rest! (Heb. 4:3)

WOW! Look what Jeremiah says in the Half Torah Parashah reading!

Jer. 16:19 O Lord my strength and my stronghold, my refuge in the day of trouble,
to you shall nations come from the ends of the earth and say,
"Our ancestors have inherited nothing but lies,
worthless things in which there is no profit. (!!!!)

Hallelujah. May it come to pass!! May we all come to this place to realize that in our flesh we have inherited only lies!! May we be delivered from all lies!

John 14:15-21 *(The Brit Hadasha reading)* If you love Me you will keep My commandments ... If you keep My commandments, you will abide in My love.

I John 2:8, 15-17 *(also part of the reading)* I am writing you a new commandment.... Do not love the world or the things in the world.... ...the world and its desires are passing away, but those who do the will of God live forever!

Jer. 16: 21 *(I forgot to write down this part)* "Therefore I am surely going to teach them, this time I am going to teach them My power and My might, and they shall know that My Name is LORD."

O yes, Lord, bring it to pass! Teach Israel. Bring them teachers. Teach them directly. Illuminate Your Word to them as they read the Parashoth readings—each one personally. Send them the Holy Spirit to teach each one, that they will all come to know that Your Name, Yeshua, is LORD!

Jerusalem Day Celebration

Fri, May 18, 2007 at 10:20 PM

Dear Fun Friends,

Boy, do the Jewish people know how to celebrate!! I went with Charity to the Wailing Wall Plaza to the Flag Dance. The place was packed with twice as many people as I ever dreamed it could hold. All I could say at first glance from the stairs was, "O MY WORD!! O MY WORD!!" for five minutes! It was quite an experience! In the midst of all the cheering, singing, loud music, and dancing (guys separated from girls by big dividers), there was mournful praying still going on at the Wall. I spent a few minutes praying there, and was touched by the contrast just a few feet from each other. All of them, the dancers and the wailers, were young people.

Everyone was carrying big, beautiful blue and white Israeli flags all the same size on these thick, heavy long poles. Hence the name, Flag Dance. Surprisingly, I noticed some flags lying on the cement plaza floor. Girls laid them down while they danced in circles together. But some of them looked abandoned. Many of those had been stepped on and didn't look too good anymore. I was amazed they were being neglected like that. I rescued a couple that were still nice and I felt so blessed. I waved them in the air to the music, having a grand time joining in the wonderful festive rejoicing.

I was hoping no one would claim the flags so I could take them home. Then a young girl did, so I had to give them up. But then when people began leaving there were more and more flags lying around. I thought I had hit the jackpot. What nice flags I could take home with me, I thought! I had been wanting a big Israeli flag. I happily carried as many as I could handle (about three!) toward the gate, planning how I would gladly share them with the other volunteers. But when I got near the gate a Hebrew-speaking man tried to take them from me. I resisted, telling him in English, which he couldn't understand, that I want them. Then I noticed he was with a group of guys collecting all the flags. Here the flags had belonged to no one! They were city flags! No wonder people were just letting them get ruined on the ground!

They have the Flag Dance every year in May. Watch for it on, israelnationalnews. com In a video titled: "Jerusalem in Blue and White," it showed the march (which I had to miss), the music, and everything. Try to catch it next May!

Enjoy!!
Cheryl

The nice things about the Flag Dance

Fri, May 18, 2007 at 11:34 PM

I wanted to tell you that the Flag Dance celebration was kind of like Purim, only on an exponentially larger scale AND without the alcohol. There was absolutely NO alcohol involved, and still they were all having a blast—mostly young people.

It was also like the New Age festival as far as the loud music and the festive feel about it, but everyone was dressed VERY modestly. All the girls had long skirts, and all the boys had suits and white shirts, yet that didn't stop them from getting wild and crazy!!

Both Charity and I had the thought that this could easily be what the celebration will look like when Jesus returns! At the Wall, I was praying that soon they will be celebrating just like this, but singing praises to Jesus and God, not just to God.

Keep praying this way. It is soon to happen.

I want to tell you so much more (about the rain storm and flooding!!!), but I must go to bed. We are going on a long field trip tomorrow. We have to get up early.

We almost got to visit a family in Bethlehem, but at the last minute the timing didn't work out. They went when I had to teach. Glenn couldn't go either because he had to work. .

We live right next to Bethlehem and we've only been there twice. I want to visit the Bethlehem Bible college really badly. It feels a little disconcerting to be so tied up with work that I can't do these very important things. But the work I'm doing is important, too. And soon we will be able to visit there, I hope. Please pray that we will get to go next week. I will be off because of the Shavuot (Feast of Weeks) (Pentecost) Holiday.

Boy, When You Guys Pray!!!

May 20, 2007,

Dear Powerful Pray-ers,

You have been praying for rain, and oh my, did God answer your prayers!! We had a rainstorm here like I didn't see in their whole rainy season which is in the winter. In fact, this rainstorm has all of Jerusalem puzzled! There was thunder and lightning, which is very unusual! There was wind and hail, and most shocking of all, there was flooding in Jerusalem!! My Arabic student who is a paramedic and is around age 40 said he has never seen a storm like this in his entire life. He believes Jerusalem has never had a storm anything like it ever. He said that because of the force of the flood, water from a drainage pipe in the Old City shot up more than 5 feet in the air! Go to this link for pictures and more information:

http://www.ynetnews.com/articles/0.7340.L-3400959.00.html

I hope it is a sign of the spiritual outpouring soon to come!!

The rain caused the military celebrations for Jerusalem Day to be canceled. One of our professors here said she thinks it is because they were celebrating the victory of 1967 as if it was their own might that saved Israel. But it wasn't by their own might. It was only by the miracle of God that Israel won that war. She also said that most of the flooding was in East Jerusalem where they were against the whole Jerusalem Day celebration. My Arabic student told me that to Arabs it is a black day. (But he didn't seem to have any anger about it. He is a very sweet, always cheerful guy.)

I don't know about any of that. I am just praising the Lord for the rain that is so miraculous that all the Jewish people have to say it is God.

The rain storm didn't stop the parade the night before. And the heavy rain stopped just in time for the flag dance that very night.

I was watching the beginning of the rain storm from our patio. I saw lightning over Bethlehem. The following thunder was very loud. Suddenly the traffic on the highway disappeared. I thought, "My word, are they afraid of a little thunder that they all quit driving?" But no, it wasn't that. Soon along came bikers in the bike race for Jerusalem Day. A van with a loudspeaker blaring the Jerusalem song followed the first bunch of bikers. Glenn and others joined me in watching. We watched the bikers getting soaked in the warm rain.

When it started to hail. Glenn said, "Hey Bikers, I have one question. Doesn't that hail hurt?" It must've hurt, but they were tough. Only two of them took rides in the van. The rest kept on bicycling!!

The wind blew the rain into our open windows. That NEVER happened in all the other rain we've had! It was a bit shocking to have a rain-soaked floor!! We had to close windows and begin mopping! Very unusual here!!

Dusty Sky

A few days before the rain, the sky had been brown from the dust being blown in from the desert. There is a name for this desert wind——hamsin, the Arabic word for 50 (I don't know why 50!). The Koreans have their own word for it. They get the same kind of dust-wind from the Mongolian and the Chinese desert every year. They were surprised that schools weren't closed because they said it brings disease. Today, the sky was dusty again. The brown sky makes me think of the curse God says he will send if the Israelites don't obey His commandments.

Lev. 26: 19 NRSV I will make your sky like iron and your earth like copper.

Deut. 28: 23 The sky over your head shall be bronze, and the earth under you iron. The Lord will change the rain of your land into powder, and only dust shall come down upon you from the sky....

But your prayers are bringing them nice, clean, washing rain! Be encouraged. Keep praying for the salvation of Israel, and for the RAIN of the outpouring of the Holy Spirit, and for physical rain. May the people living here be astounded and turn to God!! May the desert blossom as a rose both spiritually and physically by the Power of the Blood of Jesus!

May God grant that we see miraculous answers to other prayers in our lives also! Cheryl

Journal May 20   Israelite Judges

I've been studying the Judges of Israel. I figured I might as well know a little about them since I've been studying the kings so extensively, making a chart and a couple time lines, etc. for the book I'm working on for the university.

My thoughts on the Judges:

Israel turned away from God right after Joshua died—and even worse right after Gideon.

About Samson: Even though it was the Angel of the Lord (whom a preacher told me is always Jesus, so maybe it was Jesus Himself!) who prophesied Samson's birth and his mother wasn't even supposed to drink any wine or grape juice or eat any unclean thing, and Samson was supposed to be a Nazarite—even with all that he turned out to be a rebellious man who was very selfish, immature, and had a temper!! He failed God his whole life and didn't humble himself until the very end!! And that was only after being captured, imprisoned, and made blind!

As a parent I would've been really upset with God and wondered what in the world was going on. And I would've been blaming myself—thinking I had ruined the special child.

But Samson's parents are not condemned or judged anywhere in the Bible.

❧   ❧

I know one obstruction God is showing me to pray for!

We must pray that the control of the rabbis be removed from Israel! They put their opinions above the Word of God, and even above the judgment of God. They raise themselves above God.

This morning when I was studying Joshua and Judges I reread in Deuteronomy 27 about the blessing and cursing on Mt. Gerizim and Mt. Ebal.

The curses are scary!!

Disaster, panic
Frustration in everything you attempt to do
Pestilence until you are consumed
 Consumption, fever, inflammation
Fiery heat and drought
Blight and mildew
The sky over you will be bronze and the earth iron
The lord will change the rain into powder, only dust will come down upon you.
Go out one way (to fight your enemies) and flee seven ways
Be an object of horror
Boils, ulcers, scurvy, itch of which you cannot be healed
Madness (insanity), blindness, confusion of mind
Unable to find your way
Continually abused and robbed without anyone to help
Engaged, but another will lie with your woman
Plant vineyards but not enjoy the fruit
Sons and daughters given to others while you look on powerless to do anything
Driven mad (insane) by what you see
Gather little crops because the locust and worms eat them
Sons and daughters into captivity
Trees—cicada shall take over.

Deut. 28
The Lord will scatter you from one end of the earth to the other
No ease, no resting place
The Lord will give you a trembling heart
Failing eyes
Languishing spirit
Your life will hang in doubt before you
Night and day you shall be in dread with no assurance of your life
In the morning you shall say, "if only it were evening!"
At evening, "If only it were morning!"
Because of dread and because of the sights your eyes shall see, your heart will fail.

The Lord will bring you back to Egypt by ships and you will offer yourselves for sale as slaves but there will be no buyers. (I don't know if this ever happened. I pray it never will have to happen. But maybe it happened when they were fleeing Babylon. Some fled to Egypt and forced Jeremiah to go with them. Or maybe it means trying to get jobs!)

Jericho and an Author

Sun, May 20, 2007 at 12:13 Midnight

We had the awesome privilege of going on a field trip on Saturday. We got to see where Samson lived and where the oxen brought back the Ark of the Covenant. Then we saw where Joshua began taking over the Promised Land. We saw the hill of Ai, with the hill of Gibeon right near it. Then we descended down, down, down to Jericho.

Here's the beautiful city of Jericho looking toward the Dead Sea.

Below is the outskirts of Jericho looking away from the Dead Sea.

Can you believe the three places are right next to each other?!!!

When we got back to Jerusalem, we got to see and hear the famous author, Joel Rosenberg. And boy, does he have some interesting things to say about the Middle East situation!! For example, did you know that never, ever before in history have Russia and Iran made an alliance together? And did you also know that just a few decades ago Iran and Israel were friends; and that Israel got all its oil from Iran then?

We feel sooooo blessed by all these experiences!!

Our cups are gushingly running over!!!

Thank you for your prayer and financial support that helps us be here!

Thank you, Lord. Thank you. Thank you. Thank you!!
Cheryl

Remove Obstructions

May 20, 2007

Dear Prayer Warriors,

Isaiah 57:14 NRSV ... "Build up, build up, prepare the way, remove every obstruction from My people's way."

I've been praying for the Lord to reveal to us what the obstructions are that are blocking His people's way. Well, He is answering!!

Last Saturday, at the traditional Messianic synagogue, they read the Parashah (weekly Scripture reading that all religious Jews follow) from Leviticus 25 and 26. As they were reading it in Hebrew, I read through it all in English. It is all about giving the land rest every seven years and keeping the Year of Jubilee. (See pp. 246-247).

To keep the Sabbath Year laws you would have to trust God's promise to make the harvest in the sixth year so abundant that it will be triple——enough to hold you over until the ninth year when the 8th year's harvest is coming in. You would have to trust completely in God's promise of provision for this in Leviticus 25:21-22 (See p. 246)

And to keep the Year of Jubilee laws would require a complete break from the pursuit of riches and from greed! Again, you would have to have complete trust in God to take care of you financially. (I heard once that there is no record of Israel ever keeping the Year of Jubilee)

Chapter 26 gives all the blessings if they obey these laws and the curses if they don't. The blessings are blessings of abundance, etc. The curses are awful! Some have happened to Israel in the past, for example:

Verse 33 *"And you I will scatter among the nations, and I will unsheathe the sword against you; your land shall be desolate, and your cities a waste."*

Obstruction #1

Well, guess what? Here is an obstruction! They told us at the synagogue that the rabbis have decided (I'm not sure how long ago——years, or decades or what) that since the economy is no longer an agricultural economy, the Sabbath Year laws don't apply anymore and that the Jubilee laws are too impossible to keep so Israel is exempt from them.

I couldn't believe my ears! I had just read the horrible curses realizing that some have happened to Israel a couple times already, and still they are not going to keep these laws!!

They have not based this decision on the Grace of Yeshua, nor on any Scripture that exempts them, but rather on their own opinions! They put their own ideas and decisions above the Word of God, and think that the curses written in that Word for doing that exact thing will not come upon them!! The audacity of them!!

[Sept. 23, 2007: Good news!! Rabbi Jim says they are now, this year, trying to obey these laws. They are telling farmers in Israel to not farm this year, and they are even giving them money to help them through the year!!]

Here's another decision by the rabbis. At the New Age festival, the anti-missionary guy told us the rabbis ruled last year that Messianic Jews are Christians, a despised label, meaning that they are no longer Jews. This removes all the privileges granted to Jews in Israel from Messianic Jews, which is why the one couple I told you about was put in jail.

The most recent ruling of the rabbis is that they have forbidden Jewish women from attending the "Woman to Woman" conference this year. This conference is put on by Bridges for Peace every year and lots of Jewish women usually attend—even leading Jewish women. The reason for the new rule? The rabbis say Bridges for Peace is doing missionary activity—even though that organization makes a point of not evangelizing! (The policies and goals of Bridges for Peace are to shine the Light of Jesus to Jews quietly through humanitarian means, and to educate Christians on the Jewish roots of the Gospel.) Some rabbis came out in support of Bridges for Peace pointing out all the good they have done for Israel, but to no avail. The ban still holds.

The conference started already and continues this week. Last night I talked to a Bridges for Peace volunteer. She said one of the scheduled Jewish speakers is the wife of a rabbi, so she had no choice. She had to cancel, and many others are not showing up.

So let's pray that this obstructing mountain of rabbinical control over Israel which is preventing them from coming to Yeshua will be removed and cast into the sea.

Obstruction #2

We just found out at prayer meeting last Monday that all the Israeli Prime Ministers have been Free Masons. We had heard this before we came here, from an Israeli, but I couldn't quite believe it. Apparently almost all Western world leaders are. It's all very mind boggling. I also heard it once from a distant relative who is a member (which shocked me, having had no idea he was). He told me all kinds of shocking things. So this is about the fifth source we are hearing this information from and it is being forced from the back of our brains to the fore-front. Why? I believe it is so we can all band together to pray for this obstructing stronghold also to come crashing down.

Prayer Against the Obstructions

Here are the beginnings of some prayers for removing obstructions.

Prayer #1

Dear Heavenly Father, We pray that the rabbinical control over the Jewish people will be loosened. Break the chains in which they have bound the people. May those chains fall to the ground. I pray that all the lies the rabbis are propagating to keep people from believing in Yeshua will be uncovered and proven to be false. By the power in the Name of Yeshua, we pull down every rabbinical argument that "*raises itself against God,*" (from II Cor. 10:5) so the Truth can be revealed ...

Prayer #2

And, Father, we don't know how to begin to pray for the huge stronghold of the Free Masons over the whole world and particularly over the Israeli government. Please show us how to pray. Holy Spirit, please pray through us. We pray that You will expose this evil network. Expose their secret practices. Expose their membership. Expose them going to the secret meetings. Let what is "*whispered be proclaimed from the housetops*" (from Matt. 10:27). Expose their true nature for all the world to see as you are exposing the true nature of the Islamic religion ...

Glenn's Vision

Also at the prayer meeting last Monday night (May 14) Glenn had a vision. He saw a big, old-fashioned, open kettle over a big fire. Written on it was the word "Arab."

This pot was boiling over. Anger and strife were spewing out. Glenn believes the vision means that the Arabic nations will soon have strife among themselves and will begin to turn against each other.

The vision goes along with Hosea 7:6-7 *"For they are kindled like an oven, their heart burns within them; all night their anger smolders; in the morning it blazes like a flaming fire. All of them are hot as an oven, and they devour their rulers."*

We spent quite a bit of time praying about that. We prayed first for salvation to come to the people in those nations. Then we prayed for protection for the Believers in the midst of the heat, just as Shadrach, Meshach, and Abednego were protected in the fire.

There had been strife in the Gaza strip before, but the next morning there was more of it reported on the news. I said to Glenn. "Wow, your vision is coming true!" He said, "But my vision was about all the Arab countries fighting against each other, not just the Palestinians." Then yesterday's news quoted a Palestinian spokesman as saying their inner fighting is to be blamed on the whole world (including the Arab world) except for Syria and Iran!! (It shows you plain and clear who is backing them, Glenn says!) Now today the news is telling about more unrest among the Arab nations! Amazing! May the Lord Jesus' Name be lifted up through whatever happens in this region. May the Lord's will be done as it is in Heaven.

In praying about these kinds of things, we can keep in mind Joel 2:13 CJB *Turn to Adonai your God. For He is ... willing to change His mind about disaster."*

Something Wonderful to Pray For

I am also praying for this passage to come to pass: *Zech. 9:6-7 I will make an end of the pride of Philistia...; it too shall be a remnant for God; it shall be like a clan in Judah.*

Can you believe it? Philistia!! A remnant for God!! As if it is part of the tribe of Judah—the best, most special tribe!!! The tribe that David was in, and the tribe through which Jesus came!! Hallelujah!!! I was so surprised when I first read it. I had to read it several times to make sure I wasn't reading it wrong. The Palestinians are not actually descendants of the Philistines, but they are living in the Gaza strip which is the land where the Philistines lived (or part of it anyway). So I am claiming this verse for the Palestinians! It makes me so happy to find a good prophesy specifically for them in the Scriptures.

Blessings on your praying,
Cheryl

Political Stuff

Sun, May 20, 2007 at 8:58 PM

Dear Friends,

For those of you who like reading political things here is a paragraph from an article about a recent Middle East visit of Condoleezza Rice's. America is giving millions of dollars to Israel's enemy!!

The Fruits of Hizbullah's Victory

By Caroline Glick ,
THE JERUSALEM POST   May. 4, 2007
http://www.jpost.com/servlet/Satellite?pagename=JPost%2FJPArticle%2FShowFul
l&cid=1178198606866

"... So too, in recent months the US has embraced the Palestinians. Although the speaker of the Palestinian legislature Ahmad Bahar just made a televised appeal to Allah to kill every Jew and American on earth, Rice insists on transferring $59 million in US taxpayer money to the Palestinian security forces. So too, last week the State Department dictated a list of security concessions that Israel must make to the Palestinians over the next eight months regardless of whether the Palestinians themselves cease their attacks on Israel, or for that matter, regardless of whether the Palestinians maintain their commitment to annihilating the Israel and the US. ..."

For those of you who believe the verse that says of Israel, "*I will bless those who bless you and curse those who curse you...*" (Gen. 12:3), this article makes you think there might be a reason for many of the recent disasters and troubles in America. The day we read this, the news anchors were having to go from one American breaking news situation to another!! —Fires, floods, tornadoes, shootings. How much more can America handle?? How much does it take for America as a whole nation to repent??? Why doesn't Bush get it about Israel????

Here is how some politically expert Israeli Christians, who wish to remain unnamed, have summed up the situation here:

... On April 27, the front page headline in the Jerusalem Post read: "Massive IDF [Israel Defense Forces] Drill Prepares for Syrian Attack." The article described one of the largest [military] drills in Israel's history with hundreds of tanks, and thousands of troops taking part in a Golan war simulation.

Syria has a full-time standing army of approximately 400,000 soldiers, about twice the size of the IDF regular troops. This neighboring enemy on the other side of the Golan Heights has also been training new terror and commando units. They have witnessed the bloody successes of the "insurgents" in Iraq, many of whom they have aided. They also have a massive artillery force, and stockpiles of rockets and missiles, ... which come from Russia, including their advanced SCUD and other ballistic missiles (some with multiple warheads and capable of carrying chemical warheads), are able to hit all the major cities of Israel. CBN has broadcast TV footage showing at least three sophisticated, hardened missile sites built recently in Syria. June 11 will mark the 40th anniversary of Israel's liberation of the Golan Heights during the Six-Day War.

... Hamas is stockpiling sophisticated weapons, which are streaming across the Egyptian border (vacated by Israel) into Gaza. They, too, continue to train and prepare for war. Persecution of Christians is growing in Gaza. The Bible Society shop and two internet cafes used by Arab believers have been bombed. The American international school in Gaza was also recently blown up. Please stand in the gap for our besieged Arab brothers and sisters. "

Yes, let's pray, pray, PRAY!!!
Cheryl

Jews and Arabs Getting Together!!

Sun, May 20, 2007 at 9:17 PM

I know of two different places where they are working to make bonds between Jewish and Arab young people.

One is at the Bethlehem Bible College. They have been arranging camping-type meetings in the desert in a political neutral place between their college students and the students of the Israel College of the Bible from Jerusalem.

The other is the YMCA. In the big room outside my little classroom they have pictures on display of their project. Sixteen teenage girls, both Palestinians and Jewish, participated in the two-year program. They did many things together that helped them become fast friends. The last project was for each of them to host the group in their homes and for everyone to bring a camera and takes pictures of all the things that interested them. The girls learned to see things from each other's viewpoints this way. The project was a great success. These girls are lifelong friends now.

They already started the program again with nineteen new girls. They have another similar program for mothers—twelve are participating. (I've seen them because they meet on a night that I teach!) They also have a mixed group of teenage boys and girls doing things together, with twenty involved. And they have an Arab-Jewish choir with twenty-five members!

Isn't it great?!!
Cheryl

The famous, beautiful, Jerusalem YMCA lobby

The Jerusalem YMCA walkway

Today is a Biblical Feast

Tues, May 22, 2007 at 9:34 PM

The Biblical Feast Shavuot (Pentecost) started this evening and ends tomorrow evening. It is a celebration of the receiving of the Torah on Mt. Sinai. We went to the Wall earlier and just came back from a Messianic synagogue where we ate cheeses of all kinds, heard the book of Ruth read in Hebrew, listened to a Torah teaching on the festival, and then tasted all the cheesecakes entered into a contest. Tonight Jewish people all over Israel are staying up all night to read the Torah all the way through to prepare themselves anew for the celebration of receiving of the Torah. (They say it is because the Israelite people didn't prepare themselves well enough for receiving the Torah the first time that caused them to make the golden calf at Mt. Sinai.) After the service, after dark when we were walking the several blocks to the bus, we saw group after group of young people heading to the Wailing Wall for this all-night vigil.

At the synagogue, I met a Jewish woman from California who has an amazing story of how she met Yeshua. I will tell it to you later. (See next e-mail below.) I must go to bed. Tomorrow we are going to a large Shavuot picnic gathering of Jewish believers from all over Israel.

Next Sunday, on our anniversary, we've been invited by one of my Korean students to visit an Arabic church in Ramallah. I'm excited!

So much keeps happening here. There are things I don't even get a chance to tell you—like the university's old car breaking down for Glenn in the middle of a very busy street right outside the Old City. The first thing that happened was all the cars started blaring their horns at him!!!! That's what they do here. Finally, a construction worker came over with some tools to help him get it running again. When he was half way home, he picked up two Jewish men hitchhiking, one an Orthodox. Glenn didn't get but a mile down the road when the car broke down again!!! The Orthodox guy immediately said, "Bye. I'm leaving." Glenn said, "Wait. Please let me use your cell phone first to call someone to come and help me." As soon as he was done calling, the hitchhikers both took off!

Hagsamayach (Happy Holiday),
Be sure to celebrate by eating cheese and cheesecake and reading Ruth,
Cheryl

California Jewish Lady's Story

(From my June 7, 2007 journal))

I must write this story down, before I forget it, about the Jewish lady I met at a traditional Messianic synagogue in Jerusalem. She was raised as a practicing Jew. She believed in God, but she thought God was in heaven, not here on earth. She believed you only get to meet God when you die. She didn't believe in the devil. She didn't think evil was real at all. The only evil she thought existed was the evil actions of people. Let's call her Jeanette.

As a youth, Jeanette got heavily involved with the hippie movement. One day a guy wanted to take her to his commune. She had just met this guy, but he was so demanding and persistent that she agreed to go. She got worried as soon as she got in the car with him. Something wasn't right. She got the feeling he wasn't taking her to a commune at all. He took her somewhere in the middle of nowhere and started talking to her. She began to feel evil all around her so strongly that she suddenly knew there was real evil outside of people. The feeling of the evil was so horrible she started passing out. She could see that the guy was still talking to her, but she couldn't hear him anymore.

She cried out, "God help me." God came to her. She knew it was God and He spoke to her. Since she thought you only meet God when you go to heaven, she asked God, "Am I dying?"

God said, "No, you're not." Then she revived enough to demand that the guy take her home. I guess he was freaked out enough by it all, that he obeyed and took her home.

After that she wanted to find God. She went to many rabbis, but found out that some of them weren't even sure there is a heaven!! Finally, she gave up the search.

Years later she and her secular Christian husband got into New Age. But deep in her heart, she still wanted to find God.

One day a little lady knocked on her door and asked her, "Are you looking for God?" Jeanette was shocked.

"Yes!" She answered eagerly, when she could speak.

"Have you ever read the New Testament?" The lady asked.

"No, I'm Jewish. We don't read that book."

"Well, here is one. If you want to read it, start in John." The lady handed her a small New Testament and left.

Wanting to remain a good Jew, Jeanette wasn't going to read the forbidden thing. But then she was awakened in the middle of the night with a sense of urgency that she must read it. So she went to the kitchen and started reading John just as the lady had told her to do.

After reading several of the chapters about all that Jesus had done, she began to feel really sad. She said to herself, "This Jesus is such a nice man—healing people and everything. Why have I been so mean to Him all these years?"

Then she got to John chapter eight and she realized she had to decide if she believed Jesus was God or not!! At chapter thirteen, the devil told her to stop reading. She tried to continue, but couldn't. She kept trying and was able to get to 14:1 *"In my Father's house are many mansions...."* It was so beautiful to her that she said out loud, "I believe!" Immediately she was thrown across the floor. She lay there on the floor laughing, crying, and screaming all at the same time, which, of course, woke up her husband.

The next day her husband called his Christian mother and told her, "Jeanette has found Jesus!"

She told him, "You've got to take her to church!" The church he took her to was Seventh Day Adventist! She didn't know anything about churches, of course, so she didn't know any better. Later, they moved to a new town and there was no Seventh Day Adventist church in that town. She says that was God. She found a wonderful church there and has grown in the Lord immensely since.

She told me she was thinking seriously about making Aliyah (immigrating to Israel) She kept asking me over and over whether I thought she should or not. She said she has been praying and praying about it. I told her she should, that Israel needs her and her testimony!!

Journal May 23 Shavuot!! Given as a Covenant

The Lord led me again to these verses in Isaiah. This time in reading them I am impressed with the fact that they are written to the Jewish Nation.

Isaiah 49:8-13 I have kept you and given you as a covenant to the people, to establish the land, ... saying to the prisoners, "Come out," to those who are in darkness, "Show yourselves."

Isaiah 42:6-10 I have given you as a covenant to the people, a light to the nations, to open the eyes that are blind, to bring out the prisoners from the dungeon, from prison those who sit in darkness

Isaiah 51:16 I have put My Words in your mouth and hidden you in the shadow of My hand

We should all be fulfilling the above scriptures together today—Jewish and Gentile believers—in unity together!

Ephesians 4:3 Making every effort to maintain the unity of the Spirit.... There is one body and one Spirit, one home ... one Lord, one faith, one baptism, one God and Father.

Verse 13 ...until all of us come to the unity of the faith ... to maturity ... full stature of Christ ... we must grow up in every way into Him...

For the Shavuot Festival, they wear flower wreaths and bring baskets of fruit as offerings to the Lord. (Read a tiny bit more about this picnic on page 277)

JPost Article About the Karaites

Friday, May 25, 2007 10:14 PM

Dear Praying Folks,

We just prayed together for the release of the rabbinical control over Israel and the Jews, and look what article showed up in the Jerusalem Post!!!! It is about the Karaites who are Jews that follow only the Bible and not the rabbinical rule!! It talks about holding the Word of God above the word of man!!! Can you believe it?!!!

Here are few short quotes from the long article:

Laying down the (Oral) law
By Joshua Freeman
JERUSALEM POST
May 22, 2007 6:42 Updated May 22, 2007 10:34
http://www.jpost.com/servlet/Satellite?pagename=JPost%2FJPArticle%2FShowFul
l&cid=1178708657471

... Although the Karaites accept all 24 books of the Bible as holy, they staunchly reject the divinity of the Oral Law (recorded in the Talmud) as well as the authority of the rabbis, and view many aspects of rabbinic Halacha [rules] as contradictory to the pshat, or plain meaning, of the Torah.

... Rabbi Moshe Firrouz of the Karaite synagogue in Beersheba. ... says ... you can't say on Judgment Day that the rabbi told me this or that.... Every person's decisions are on his head and that's why each person should read and try to understand the Torah."

.... Born the son of an Orthodox rabbi, Nehemia Gordon, [an active Karaite in Jerusalem], who ... attended Jewish day schools in Chicago, ... [says] "I studied the Torah, which is God's book and then I got to the Talmud and it says 'Rabbi Akiva says this' and 'Rabbi Meir' says this. I went to my teachers and I said, 'One is the word of God and one is the word of man; shouldn't we accept the word of God over the word of man?' And they said, 'No, that's horrible. You can't say such a thing—that's what the Karaites say!' And I said, 'Well, who are these Karaites?'" ...

... "I found that throughout history there have always been Jews who believed only in the Bible and not what the rabbis call 'the oral law' and I realized that I am a Karaite and this has been the path that I've been on ever since."

Use the link under the title above to go on the internet and read the whole article. It gives people a Karaite website even! Read some of the "talkback" comments, too, if you can. This article is making the Jews do some thinking. One guy wrote, "Maybe I'm a Karaite, too."

If more Jews start reading the Torah for its "plain meaning" as Rabbi Firrouz said, maybe they will _plainly_ see that it _plainly_ points to Yeshua as their Messiah!!

This is why it is sooooo exciting to serve God!!!!
Cheryl

8.

HEAVEN-SENT
CULTURAL
EXPERIENCES

To a Church in a Danger Zone
Written on new laptop, Mon, May 28, 2007. E-mailed May 29 at 9:50 PM

Dear Precious Ones,

Can you believe it? It rained again tonight!!! Glenn and I walked home in thunder and lightning, wind, and some sprinkling of rain!!! This is certainly a different summer for Israel!!

Showers of blessings to you all!

Increasing Unrest

Last Tuesday morning after the increased unrest in Gaza and the trouble in Lebanon, we took the Arab bus into East Jerusalem, because we needed to go to the Travel Agent there. When we got to East Jerusalem, an Israeli Soldier entered the bus and checked everyone's passports and visas before letting us off the bus.

We have been carrying our passports around with us everywhere because they say you might have to show them at any time, but we never needed them until now—ever!!—not when we went to Shechem (Naublus today) to the Samaritan Passover; not when we went to Jericho; not the two times we went to Bethlehem (all of which are in the West Bank)—never!! It's another sign of the unrest that Israel feels.

The day we went to Jericho, we passed through two checkpoints. On the way into the West Bank, the Palestinian guards waved us on without even stopping us. It was only when we came back into Israeli territory that the guards or soldiers actually stepped onto the bus and eyeballed us all. It was the same when we went to Bethlehem. That is because it isn't the Palestinians who have to fear normal civilians coming into their territory to kill them. Only the Israelis have that to fear.

Saturday afternoon, we saw on the news that two Israeli guards had been shot at a checkpoint in East Jerusalem, and that, in their wounded state, they had shot and killed the two gunman, and sadly also a bystander. We were shocked for two reasons: first, because this is the first incident in Jerusalem since we have been here; second, because East Jerusalem was where we were headed again the next morning!!!! We had second thoughts about our plans. We prayed about it. We talked to people here. They thought the border would be closed and we wouldn't be able to go into the West Bank anyway, so we decided to check it out at least.

To the West Bank

So, Sunday morning, we went by Arab bus to East Jerusalem to meet two of my Korean students. While waiting for them, near the Garden Tomb gate, we got to watch Arabic life happening around us which was quite interesting. We saw mothers covered completely in their black robe-like dresses and scarves with brightly clothed, little daughters holding their hands, dressed in completely modern fashions. The contrast was so stark, it almost made you think they were stealing the children. One little girl had a pretty dress and hat, she looked to be dressed for Easter Sunday in America! I tried to get a picture without the Muslim-ly clad mother noticing, but couldn't. One father was dressed almost exactly like the genie in the Disney movie Aladdin, big sword and all, yet his two children wouldn't have looked out of place on an American street.

The Koreans took us to the Arab bus station across the street to get on another Arab bus. Now I finally know where it is!! Off we were headed to Ramallah (which is in the West Bank) to attend a little church there where another of my Korean students lives and works. Sure enough at every checkpoint we had to show our passports and visas to an Israeli soldier. I found it interesting that the Israeli soldiers, not Palestinian guards, were checking everyone going into the West Bank, too, not just those coming out.

On the way back out, before we got to the checkpoint, the bus stopped and ¾ of the people got off. Then the driver asked all of us in English and in Arabic if we had visas. He yelled in Arabic at one lady as if he didn't trust that she had one. She yelled right back at him. Finally he proceeded ahead. Obviously, he didn't want the scene that would happen if someone on his bus was visa-less. The Israeli soldier that came on to check us was just a tiny wisp of a teenage girl, her trusty gun, which was almost bigger than her, was dangling casually from her shoulder, bumping the seats as she passed. I kept wondering how in the world she could possibly handle things if someone resisted her. But, of course, there were a couple more soldiers outside the bus watching, and a few more on up ahead.

Since Ramallah is in the West Bank, I expected it to be like the little village of Shechem——small with not much going on——no real shops or commercialism. But I was wrong. It was a busy, bustling city. The main street was lined with shops with their merchandise spilling out onto the sidewalks which were crowded shoulder to shoulder with Arabic people. Some of the women were modernly dressed, but most were in their

scarves and long garments. The streets were lined with rows of brightly colored orange-yellow taxi vehicles—some cars, some vans—waiting, as if expecting passengers. You would think it was a hot tourist town!! But it isn't at all. Most tourists won't venture into the West Bank. By the time we left, most of the taxis were gone, so they must have found their passengers! To me that means there must be people of means in that town, somehow.

We walked down a rather deserted side street to a little Baptist church. A few Arab teen boys followed us most of the way, asking all kinds of questions, in English. When we started to tell them about the Lord they left. At the church, we were greeted in English from the pulpit by an elderly Arabic man. We heard familiar hymns sung in Arabic, had communion led by a Korean man, listened to a sermon by him in English which was translated into Arabic by an older woman, and watched a children's song and dance program led by an American-looking woman and my Korean student.

Afterwards they gave us little plates of snacks and cups of delicious lemonade. Everyone thanked us profusely for coming, and urgied us to come again.

Then, because I'm their teacher, the Koreans took Glenn and I to a nice, tiny restaurant and fed us delicious Arabic food. The Lamb on a shish kabob stick was fabulously delicious!! (The owner/waiter ran to a tiny shop across the street to get our drinks. We found that amusing.) What a nice early gift it was for Glenn's birthday!!

I'll have to tell you more about the little church next time. I've got to get ready to teach.

More About the Ramallah Church
Written June 3, 2007

My Korean student (who is only in her early twenties, I think) and a Korean couple are working together as missionaries at this church. Here is her description of the history of the church which she wrote for her English journal assignment.

This church was built about twenty-five years ago. The lady who was sent by God from America, moved to Ramallah bout fifty-five years ago. She was born in Virginia. After she moved here she has never left the Holy Land since. [Actually, if I understood her husband correctly, she spent several years in America so her sons could go to school there.]

She always looked after people and taught them the Bible, English, music and many other things. Everyone loved her. She married a Palestinian man. They had two sons who are now lawyers in America. Now she is 81 years old and she has dementia. When she was in good health the church was crowded with many people (about one hundred). But after she got ill, many people left. When my friends and I first came, we could see only a few old people.

We who heard the church history were sad. So we decided to work for the church. We are dreaming to revive our church again. We always pray for our church and the Holy Land. We look after them and teach the Bible like her, like Jesus. I love our church, our church people and the Holy Land.

The little church was about one-third full when we were there. It was mostly older people, but there were a few younger ones. There was a baby crying. A beautiful little thing. She fell asleep later. An elderly Arabic man was leading the service. He greeted us from the pulpit in English and started saying things that made me think he might ask us to share something. So I was frantically looking in Glenn's Bible for the verse I would want to use. I hadn't thought about the fact that this is a mission field like Africa where they expect visiting Christians to have something to say!! But in the end, we weren't asked to share. He talked to us afterwards and we found out that he is the husband of the founding lady! He was very happy to have us there and begged us to return.

The Korean man gave the message in almost perfect English, which a lady translated into Arabic. After we took communion, all the children came in to give a performance led by my Korean student. They sang and danced and recited Arabic Scripture. One boy, with sticking up hair, belted everything out boldly. He was so cute. A couple other boys were too shy to go up front. All her coaxing didn't work. They looked so cute sitting forlorned in the back with their little brother.

The Korean preacher talked to me afterwards. He showed me pictures of how rundown the church looked when they first arrived. He said they had to work hard to clean trash out of the building and fix it up. Now it looks lovely. They have flowers planted out front and even a vegetable garden out back!! He said the attendance went down not only because of the leader's illness, but also because of the Intafada (when the Palestinians started doing suicide bombings against Israel). When the Koreans arrived no one even knew this was a church anymore. When people tried to find it, no one knew where to tell them to go. So he decided they should put a cross on top of it. He said the members didn't want to, for fear of persecution. He finally convinced them, and they have not suffered at all for having it there.

He showed me a picture of the crowd that came when they gave a Christmas program last year. The church was absolutely packed for the special candlelight program. He said when they have special programs people come. Otherwise they either don't go to church at all or they go to one of the other churches: Catholic, Greek Orthodox, Coptic.... I forget the rest, but they are all the types of churches where you just sit to enjoy. You are never asked to serve. Sometimes the people even receive financial help from those other churches, he told me. So the people aren't used to a church that asks them to become a part of it, take ownership in it, and serve in it. He says when they ask people to help clean, no one comes. He wants to raise up local leadership for the church, and has finally been able to get the church to elect a board. The elderly Palestinian man is on that board.

The Korean leader asked me to pray for their work in this church. I told him I would pray and I would also ask my friends in America to pray for them. So if the Lord lays it on your heart, please pray for the little Baptist church in Ramallah.

In my next class an Arab student told me that rich Arabs live in Ramallah. It is the capital of the West Bank. I told him about all the taxis. He said all the people from the surrounding villages take taxis into Ramallah for everything: shopping, going to the bank, going to the doctor——everything. He said there is nothing in their villages. He was very curious as to why I went to Ramallah. Suddenly, I realized that I could be putting the Korean missionaries in danger and wished I hadn't told him that I went there. I said, "To visit someone." I wanted so badly to say that I visited a church there.

Speaking of him, he wrote me a journal about his Muslim faith and how he wishes the whole world wouldn't think that Islam is a violent religion. I wrote a response to him, saying that if all Muslims were as kind as he is, the Middle East would be a different place. I wrote a little about Jesus and mentioned that Jesus has the answer to the world's problems. I asked him if he has ever read Jesus' words. I don't know what his reaction will be. I'm praying for him. I hope he will take a Gospel of John that I have and read it.

May God Bless the Korean missionaries in Ramallah and missionaries like them all around the world,
Cheryl

An Absolutely Fabulous Sermon From a Messianic Preacher

Sun, Jun 3, 2007 at 12:45 PM

Dear Wonderful, Praying Children of God,

Yesterday was an extremely important day in my life. Not only did we have the marvelous privilege of visiting an Orthodox Jewish synagogue (in a very rich neighborhood, no less!!) and to eat a meal in a wonderful, young, Orthodox couple's home, but we also heard a life-changing sermon by a Messianic preacher on forgiveness and grace. At the end of the sermon, I just sat there with tears of thankfulness and joy streaming down my cheeks. God is answering my prayer for more revelation of His Grace to enter my brain and sink into my being. And I pray, the Lord will not let this new revelation slip away from me, but will keep it alive inside my heart forever that it may bear much, much, much fruit!!!

It was absolutely an awesome sermon!! Everyone says so.

When I saw that it was going to be a sermon on Matt. 18, I thought, "O, I've heard hundreds of sermons on Matt. 18. This probably won't be anything new." But I was WRONG!!

I want to make sure I don't let this increased revelation of Grace slip away from me, so I'm going to write the sermon down. I think you will be awesomely blessed, too!! In fact, I pray you will.

Dear Lord Jesus, please cause Your Word in this sermon to shine Your light on new revelation and insight about the awesome Truth of Your Grace into every person who takes the time to read this. I pray, Lord, that it will touch them to tears and then cause their hearts to leap with new Joy in the Freedom of Your Grace! May it increase the Joy they already have one hundred fold!! In Your Holy Name, Amen.

Here's the sermon. The words in [ ]'s are mine.

Fabulous Sermon on Grace

Matt. 18: 21-22 "... How often should I forgive? As many as seven times?" Jesus said to him (Peter), "Not seven times, but I tell you, seventy times seven."

Verse 35 "So My Heavenly Father will also do to every one of you, if you do not forgive your brother or sister from your heart."

Jesus didn't mean 490 times. Otherwise my marriage would be over because I passed 490 a long time ago. [Everybody laughed.] Jesus meant an infinite number of times. Verses 22 and 35 give a commandment from Jesus with a story in between. The commandment is:

YOU MUST FORGIVE EVERYONE....FOR EVERYTHING....FROM YOUR HEART.... FOREVER! [He repeated that several times.] We are supposed to pray without ceasing and forgive without ceasing.

Why did the man in the parable fail at this? As we read the parable I want you to ask the question, "What is wrong with this picture?"

[We read the whole parable.]

The man was forgiven for $10 million American dollars, but wouldn't forgive his fellow slave for $20. Why? I always thought it was just because he was a bad guy——just a nasty, cold-hearted guy. But if that is true then why did he wait until after he was forgiven to get so mean with the guy who owed him? Why wasn't he mean before he was forgiven? And why did he put the guy in prison? He's not likely to get the $20 that way.

I don't think it is because he was a bad guy. I think there was a different reason. Let me explain.

In the beginning of the parable four new revelations were given to this man:

1. The time had come when the King decided to settle accounts. [After hearing this sermon, I think maybe the guy didn't even know he had an account with the King.]

2. He owed the King $10 million dollars. That's $10,000,000!!! This was the revelation of his sinfulness.

3. He would never, EVER be able to pay it.

4. The PENALTY!! Everything of his, including himself, his wife, and his children, will be sold. Actually, the real punishment is much worse. It's a terrible punishment of eternal burning in hell.

So the man was given four revelations, but he understood only three of them. He didn't understand the third revelation. He didn't fall on his face and say, "Please have mercy on me!!! I will never, ever be able to pay you back!!"

He missed that revelation. Instead he thought he could pay, if he just had time. What pride!! He thought he could actually pay $10 MILLION dollars back!!!

Since he missed that revelation, he also missed the next revelation that was given to him: the revelation of GOD'S LOVE AND GRACE!!

God was moved! He was touched by this man's plea. We have a High Priest who can feel what we are going through!! [The amazing thing to me also is that even though the man spoke with pride saying he would pay the debt, God still had compassion on him and forgave him anyway!!!! What an awesome, forgiving God.]

God not only forgave the slave, He also set him free!! [The man was no longer a slave!!! He walked out of there a FREE man!]

So what happened? Why did he immediately go and grab the guy who owed him money?

I believe it is because of what Jesus said in the last part of Luke 7:47. "*The one who is forgiven little loves little.*"

"But the slave was forgiven a lot, not a little," you say. Yes, he was forgiven millions, but he didn't know it.

I was a terrible sinner when I was young. I did terrible things. I'm not proud of it, but I probably broke all ten of the commandments. I didn't need anyone to tell me I was a sinner. I knew I was a bad SINNER! But some of you GOOD sinners didn't do all the bad things I did. And thank God you didn't!! But because you have been good all your life, you have a hard time realizing how much you have been forgiven. You also have been forgiven millions, but you don't realize it.

Max Lucado says, "Many are forgiven little, not because the Grace of the King is limited, but because the faith of the sinner is small." [He read this very slowly two or three times.]

This slave had received the revelation of the debt and the punishment, but he had missed the Grace. He had received the revelation of sin, judgement, and hell, but had missed the Forgiveness. He had fear! He had become religious.

Grace had taught his heart to fear, but he hadn't been released from that fear!

What was he afraid of? Maybe he was afraid God would change His mind. Maybe...... But I think he was afraid of something else.

I think maybe he was afraid that next time he would have to pay. Maybe he went out of there thinking, "Whew, that was a close one!!!! I almost lost everything!!!! What if I have to pay next time?!!! I had better be ready!!!" He began to believe in works!

Many of you sitting in this room are thinking the very same thing. You know that you were forgiven much when you got saved. But now that you are saved it's up to you. You'd better not screw up now!!! Don't screw up now or you might end up in hell!

[This is where it got to me!! I have struggled with this all my life! I think it is a terrible thing to fail now that I've been saved because I should know better!! I'm not afraid I'll end up in hell, but that God will be terribly disappointed in me!]

This slave was scared to death!! He had to be, because the very first thing he did— It was the FIRST thing he did!!!!—was to grab the guy and choke him!!! [As an illustration, the preacher put his hands around his interpreter's neck and shook him!!! Glenn laughed and laughed.]

So...

How forgiven are you???

Though your sins be as scarlet, they shall be as white as snow (Isaiah 1:18 KJV).

Your sins aren't pink! [He paused for the laughter.] They weren't pink and they aren't pink! They are white! They aren't off-white. They are as pure white as snow.

He removes our sins as far as the east is from the west

This was written when they didn't know that the earth was round. It means that God told you to go east and your sins to go west on a flat earth. The two would never, ever meet again!! And this is after He made your sins white as snow!

I will forgive their iniquity and I will remember their sin no more (Jer. 31:34 KJV).

After he made our sins white as snow and sent them as far as the east is from west, He also forgot them!!

Matt. 18: 33 "Should you not have had mercy on your fellow slave, as I had mercy on you?"

Jesus gave us the commandment to forgive without ceasing, innumerable times (verse 22) from our hearts (verse 35), just as He has had pity on us! (verse 33)

So
God will forgive us without ceasing..... innumerable times ....forever ....from HIS HEART!!!

Love the Lord your God with all your heart, with all your soul, with all your mind, and with all our strength (Mk. 12:30).

Why does God give us this commandment? Because GOD LOVES US that way!! He Loves you with all His heart!! With all His soul!! With all His mind!! With all His strength!! How much strength does God have???? [How big is God's Heart?!!!] [By this time he was getting exciting and we were being greatly moved!!]

Do you think that every time you sin, God weighs it and has to decide whether he will forgive you this time???? The older we get as Christians, the more we think this way!!! I'm a pastor. I'm supposed to be better than perfect! I can't have a bad day! Maybe God doesn't forgive pastors.

I tell you God has already decided to forgive your sins!!

Romans 5:8-10 God proves His Love for us in that while we were still sinners (That was before) Christ died for us. MUCH MORE SURELY THEN now that we have been justified by His Blood, will be saved through Him from the wrath of God. For if while we were enemies, we were reconciled to God through the death of His Son, MUCH MORE SURELY, having been reconciled, will we be saved by His Life.

[Somewhere he said this:] (If anyone thinks I am talking about a license to sin, I am not. Grace is not a reason to sin. Grace is the most wonderful, awesome, amazing ...... [he used lots of other marvelous words] .....REASON NOT to sin!!!)

Freely receive, freely give.

You can try to forgive everyone always for everything, but if you haven't received forgiveness completely, then you cannot truly forgive. You cannot give what you have not received. [Quoting someone] "Only a healed heart can forgive, and only a forgiven heart is a truly healed heart. The experience of Grace is the MOST powerful aspect in healing." Not the doctrine of Grace, not the knowledge of Grace, but the experience of Grace.

You can forgive someone for the worst kind of thing because you have been forgiven millions!

He went on and told us that we can be forgiven even if we murdered someone, or raped someone, or even if we are a homosexual..... if we've received Jesus in our life as Lord.

He also said we can even forgive a parent who has mistreated us—even if they beat us until it almost cost us our life and it didn't just happen once, but thousands of times—because Jesus forgives us of an insurmountable debt....

That's the sermon. It was soooo awesome. We spent a lot of time in prayer receiving God's forgiveness and forgiving others. He had us forgive ourselves first. He had us tell ourselves out loud that we forgive ourselves!!! I was praying and crying, because I realized that I was exactly like that slave in the story. The people I have done the most "choking" to have been my own children!!! I had flubbed up sooooo much as a young adult, which was after I grew up a Christian and should have known better. God had been merciful to rescue me from that. But I was believing the lie that if I flubbed up with how my children turn out, I really won't make it!!!! And my O my, did I ever flub up! God was ministering to me in that again. It was sooooooo wonderful. I was praying and praying that I will now be able to extend grace and forgiveness always to myself and others—really and truly from the heart!!

People were on their knees and on their faces. I was surprised when I opened my eyes and saw them!! I had been in another place with the Lord and hadn't even realized what was going on around me!

Praise the Lord!!! I believe this is the beginning of the fulfillment of this prophecy:

"And I will pour out on the house of David and the inhabitants of Jerusalem a spirit of grace and supplication." Zech. 12:10

I believe it because that was the most powerful message I ever heard on Grace in all my life. And I have never, ever heard that parable explained in such a personally touching way before. And it is being preached in Jerusalem by a Messianic Jewish Believer pastor!!! The message and spirit of Grace is being poured out in Jerusalem!!!

Hallelujah, we are FORGIVEN for EVERYTHING, EVERY TIME, from God's heart FOREVER!!

2008 added note: Here's the link to a podcast of the sermon: http://www.shemensasson.com/sermons.php?y=2007

Non-Messianic Synagogue Service

June 3, 2007

As I said, we visited a regular, non-Messianic Jewish Synagogue. It was a nice, big synagogue in a well-to-do neighborhood. The men's side was huge and elaborate with a very high ceiling. The woman's side was small and crowded, and had a low ceiling. I couldn't see the men's side very well because I had to look through a lattice that was on top of a low wooden wall separating us. I felt pretty jealous of Glenn sitting over there among the men and being able to see everything clearly.

Being separated wasn't so nice, but everything else was WONDERFUL!!

I followed the chanting as best as I could in the English/Hebrew prayer book. When I didn't know what they were reading, I just looked through the prayer book to see what it was all about. Some of the things in it are pretty amazing!

Part of the time a man read in a chanting way. Then the congregation read in response. The women read very quietly. But every once in awhile the whole congregation chanted together. It was half way between singing and chanting without any musical instruments, but with a definite beat. At those times some of the women really belted it out. For most of this "singing" we had to turn to face the East wall—the direction toward the Temple.

The lady who took us there said to meet her to walk with her at a certain time. We came to her house on time, but when we got to the synagogue, the meeting had actually begun. In fact, they had already brought the Torah out of its special place called the "ark" and were already saying the blessings over it. We are not sure why she goes so late, but it seemed to be very normal to be late. Women were trickling in, coming and going throughout the whole service. Glenn says even a couple men came in after him.

Jewish meetings aren't the same as Christian meetings where everyone has to arrive on time and sit so silently. The children didn't have to sit still. They walked back and forth between the men and women's side through a gate/door in the low separating wall. Yes, little girls are allowed to go to the men's side to sit with their daddies. (It's the same at the Wailing Wall.) No one minds that the children are walking around during the meeting. Mothers did tell their children to keep quiet, though.

Many of the women talked to each other in whispers or even low voices during different parts of the service. Sometimes it made it difficult to hear what the men were saying. Suddenly, I could see why Paul wrote what he did about women being silent in church! It's because since the women are so separated, they can feel like they are not a part of what's going on, so it is very tempting to start their own conversations. And Paul was talking to synagogue congregations who had new Gentile believers who hadn't grown up in the Jewish culture. So perhaps these new believing women who lacked the Jewish boundaries were standing up and leaning over the divider to ask their husbands questions. Perhaps they even argued with the speaker! So that could be why Paul made rules about it.

After the reading of the Torah, they paraded it around the room for everyone to touch reverently—the men with their Talliths; the women with their prayer books, reaching over the lattice work. I was looking forward for them to bring the Torah through the separating "gate" to the women's side but, sadly, they didn't. That really surprised me.

Then there was a teaching on the Torah reading. And much to our delight it was given in English, with Hebrew occasionally sprinkled in. The message was very good. In fact, there was more meat to it than there has been to the teachings at the Tallith-wearing, traditional Messianic synagogue. We were nicely surprised at that. We had expected it to be really dull and lifeless.

The message was about why Miriam was punished more severely than Aaron for their opposition to Moses. He gave the reason that it was because Miriam was the oldest and Aaron was the baby. He pointed out that Miriam had changed Moses' diapers! He said, though, that Miriam was cured because her punishment was according to her whole life, not just for that moment; and that the whole camp waited for her because she had waited and watched Moses in the basket. It was neat how he tied the two things together like that.

He stayed on the point about how punishment should take into consideration the person's whole life, not just the present situation. It made me wish I would have thought more that way each time I was disciplining my children.

Of course, the sermon lacked the message of the redemption through the blood of Yeshua where all our sins can be wiped away completely and where we do not get the punishment we deserve.

At the end of the meeting a young boy, maybe age 12 or so, sang/chanted and the congregation sang/chanted in response to him. His voice was a beautiful boy soprano. My friend pointed out his mother, an elderly lady, who had moved next to the divider and was leaning close to the lattice to peer through to watch him. He was an orphan from Russia that she had adopted.

Sense of Sacredness

For some of you modern women, all this separation stuff would make you feel furious inside. But it doesn't do that to me because in my young childhood my family was in a church where men and women sat on separate sides of the church. It feels normal to me. In fact, the whole time during the service, I kept thinking about my childhood church with very warm feelings towards it. The atmosphere of reverence at the synagogue was the same as at that church. In fact, even though things were done differently in many ways, the whole meeting felt so familiar to me that it makes me wonder if the heritage of my ancestors isn't Jewish. I wonder if their meetings weren't originally fashioned after synagogue meetings. Perhaps many of them were Messianic believers. The "Shema Yisrael" song sung at the beginning of every Jewish service is one song in particular that always makes me think of my childhood church. It ends with the exact same cadence as many of the my childhood church songs end. It touches my heart in a very special way every time I hear it.

After the meeting they had delicious, high class food outside under a big canopy. We were urged to stay and eat. The food was catered in by two Filipino ladies. I spoke a little with the one who could understand English. They looked very out of place wearing low-ride pants among the Jewish ladies all dressed in very formal, modest, long skirts.

This was an Orthodox congregation, but not very strict in their dress. The ladies had very fancy, fashionable, long dresses on. The older ladies wore hats. Some of them were big hats similar to mine, so I didn't feel out of place at all. The younger mothers were wearing pretty scarves wrapped around their head the very Jewish way. They looked much more conservative than the older women, which I found very interesting.

Afterwards Glenn got to talking to this very friendly young man, who in the end, invited us to his home for lunch. We thought we were already eating lunch, but I guess that was just a snack. It was called "Kiddush."

Added Notes on the Non-Messianic Synagogue
Written Monday, June 18, 2007 12:08 Midnight

Just a couple extra things about the synagogue meeting for those who might be interested. I tried to write about it during the day this time instead of staying up until 1 or 2 in the morning to do it. But I got interrupted several times while I was writing it and forgot to include a couple things.

I wanted to tell you that on the women's side there were about five rows of benches with a narrow aisle in between. In each row in front of the benches were long slanted "desks" with a ledge where the ladies could prop their opened prayer books in front of them to read from. (I don't think the men had these, but I couldn't really tell.) After the service the ladies lifted the tops of the desks and put their prayer books away underneath them. We two ladies got our prayer books out of a cupboard with glass doors in the wall on the side of the room, and we sat down on a bench along that same side. So we had to hold our prayer books and our big, heavy Torah reading books in our hands.

About women and men being separated: I said I don't mind it and I don't, but I am glad that in Jesus there is no male nor female. I'm glad that in Jesus we women can go all the way to the front of God's throne right into Jesus' arms.

Eating in a Jewish Home

June 3, 2007

It was the most wonderful thing to have this awesome privilege of eating in an Orthodox Jewish home. Glenn had told the young father that we are very interested in learning about Judaism. So all the way on the long walk to his house (They don't drive on the Sabbath.) he told us about many of their customs. It was very interesting. Then as we ate with them, he explained every custom as we did them.

When we got near his home a friend of his joined us. This friend was more Orthodox with a black suit, a hat, and sideburn curls. He introduced his friend to us and I held out my hand saying, "Nice to meet you," but the young man didn't shake my hand. Our friend explained that Orthodox customs do not allow a man to touch any woman except his wife. I embarrassingly withdrew my hand. It was a little disconcerting, but our host was so kind and nice that my embarrassment was immediately dissipated.

Our host's wife hadn't come to the synagogue. She had stayed home with their baby who wasn't feeling well. He told us on the way home that when other young men had talked about how pretty a certain girl was, he told them, "You don't go by that. You are supposed to go by what is on the inside." Later, when he found a girl with inner character, he had the added benefit of outer loveliness, too. He said when he was ready to get married, a friend introduced him to a girl—who is now his wife—and he thought she was the most beautiful girl he had ever laid his eyes on. He said her inner beauty shined through to the outside. When we met her we saw immediately that he was right. She exudes beauty—a rare beauty that is calm, pure, intelligent, and reverent. She looked reverently elegant in her long, flowing skirt, her pretty Orthodox scarf, and her earrings.

It was such a blessing to be in their tiny home. They are a young couple with only a baby daughter. He is from South Africa and she is from Ohio. They have both made aliyah. She was raised Jewish, but not strictly religious. His mother is Israeli. His father met her when he was visiting Israel.

They had another young adult Jewish woman staying in their home a couple days as part of a visit Israel program for American Jews, so they had to put an extension in the table which then filled their living room.

After the lovely wife and her guest sat the food and extra plates on the table, we all took part in the ceremonial hand washing. They had a special tin cup with two handles, just like the ones at the Wailing Wall. You must fill the cup from the faucet and pour it out onto your hands one by one. No soap is involved. You are to have already washed your hands with soap before this. There's no wiping of the hands, nor any shaking them off. You just hold them up reverently and walk quietly to the table.

As we ladies sat at the table waiting for the men to be done, I felt obliged to fill the silence with polite conversation, so I told the hostess that I admired her for being able to accommodate so many unexpected guests. (Telephone calls are forbidden on the Sabbath, so there is no way she could have known her husband was bringing guests.) She didn't answer me, but looked at me kindly and smiled sweetly. When the men sat down, the husband reverently said the Shabboth blessing over the food, "Baruch ata, Adonai, Elohenu, melech ha-olam...."

When he was finished he explained that the rule is no talking between the hand washing and the blessing over the food, so that was why his wife could not answer me. Again, I was embarrassed, but the wife immediately spoke and put me at ease. She said, "Now that I can talk, you see that we have plenty of food, and I am very pleased to have you as my guests."

We had a delightful dinner conversation while eating the delicious food. They told us how they can "legally" keep the food warm without lighting a fire which is forbidden on Shabboth. She explained when I asked how the rules against working on Shabboth, still allow you to wash dishes.

The men got to the subject of politics and I was amazed at the Godly wisdom of the husband. He said the reason some of Middle East policies are not working is because we are in a sense worshipping democracy instead of worshipping God.

Later they showed us photos in a history of Israel book of a Jewish martyr purposely shot and killed by the British military when the Arabs were trying to take over Jerusalem, soon after Israel's independence. (This was before the Arabs started calling themselves Palestinians.) This lone soldier shot a missile from the side of the hill toward the advancing Arabs. He happened to hit gasoline barrels which caused a huge explosion. This scared the Arabs thinking there was a whole brigade shooting at them and they began to retreat. That is when the Israeli guy was shot from a tower behind him by the British.

Our hosts told us that it could have looked like an accident, but he was still alive and when the ambulance was there and men were carrying him on a stretcher, another shot was fired at him from the same source and he was killed.

We asked them in disbelief, why in the world the British would want to kill an Israeli soldier! We thought the British were always allies with Israel. They didn't say much to us, sensing our ignorance, but since then we have learned a lot more about how the British tragically turned against Israel during WW II and in the following years. England did not want an Israeli nation to form at that time.

I helped them clear the table. They refused to do the dishes while we were there. We continued with the pleasant, interesting conversations and part of the time I played on the floor with their darling daughter. I told the wife about my granddaughter in America that is about the same age. She wondered if there was a chance my daughter and her husband would make aliyah. Then I realized they thought we were Jewish. They thought they were helping Jewish people learn more about their faith. That is why they were so eager to open their home to us. I was afraid that if they found out what we really were, they would feel as though we had misled them and their attitude toward us might change. I began to feel very guilty for not being completely open and honest with them.

They were such a sincere, Godly couple, I believe they are *"not far from the Kingdom of God"* (Mk. 12:34). I continue to pray for their eyes to be opened for them to see their salvation in Yeshua. I later bought them a nice, Shabboth tablecloth from the Orthodox Mea Sharim neighborhood and asked our friend who lived near the synagogue to give it to them along with our thank you note. I hope she didn't forget. She had discouraged us from visiting the synagogue ourselves again, so as not to jeopardize her long time relationship with the people there.

Eating in an Arabic Home

The University has an old car that they are hoping Glenn can keep from going to car graveyard. Someone they knew had another car just like it, junked. They wanted Glenn to go get parts off of it. Well, it was in Hevron, which is in the West Bank, from which the IDF has been arresting terrorists. Glenn was not too keen on going there. I prayed for him and off he went last Friday with the old friend of the head of the university, Mr. Wiley.

(Glenn is telling me about it as I write.)

It turns out that the car was sent to a recycling place years ago, but God richly blessed Glenn for going there. The family who had the car is Palestinian. They live right on the edge of the border inside the West Bank. It was a two-family home, but with only one kitchen and bathroom in the center. The grandparents sleep on one side and one married son and his family on the other side. Another son lives just down the road who also came for the meal. In fact, he was the main guy Glenn and Mr. Wiley talked to.

There is a building down the hill and across the road from their house which was a hospital and a resort area built by Americans. The grandfather of the family had helped to build the hospital. During the Intafada, it was totally abandoned and all the trees around it were cut down by the Hamas and Fatah. Now it is just a deserted place with weeds and everything.

The way they ate was just like the Bedouins, as we learned on our fieldtrip to the Bedouin Museum (See p. 130). First they served a little glass of pepsi (a slight change from Bedouin culture). An hour or so later they brought a little glass of sweet hot tea. Glenn says it was sweet enough to send him to LA and back. Then an hour later they fed them lunch. The elderly grandmother brought the drinks and food in and then went back into the women's side of the house. Only the men ate with Glenn.

The woman brought rice in a huge serving bowl. It had spices and seasoning in it that made it yellow, and it was delicious. They had plain cooked chicken, and then soup that was kind of like potato soup. You took the watery part out and put it on your rice. Some of the men also crushed some potatoes onto their rice. When Glenn's soup bowl was empty, the woman took it. Glenn thought that was nice that she took his bowl because he was done eating, but then she brought it back full of more soup. So he had to eat that, too!

Glenn had started a long fast three days before which he planned on keeping. But he didn't dare refuse their food, so he had to break his fast!!!

As soon as they were done eating they served Arab coffee in the traditional tiny little cups. It was strong enough to send them to the moon and back, Glenn says. That's about when their conversation turned from cars to politics. The Arab men said right away that they will not accept a two-state agreement. They want it to be all Palestinian. And, of course, they blamed all the world's woes on the Jews and the Americans.

These were regular Arab people. They claimed to be Muslim, but they weren't very religious. All the women were wearing pants, one even jeans, and only one of the women wore a scarf—one of the younger ones. The older woman had a Western style hairdo. The men looked like normal men. They were not radicals. They were not Fatah or Hamas or anything, yet this is what they believed.

Glenn told them that the reason America is in Iraq is because in the 1930's America signed a treaty with Saudi Arabia that we would help them build their oil fields. They would give America the right to buy their oil, but in return America had to agree to protect Saudi Arabia. So when Saddam Hussein took Kuwait and was headed to Saudi Arabia, they asked America to come and help. They were semi favorable to Glenn about that. They agreed that the Arabs aren't all in agreement on things. But still they somehow twisted it around and blamed the Jews for it.

The topic turned to the Oslo Accords, when Arafat was offered everything they had before 1948 except for 2%—everything they wanted except Jerusalem, and yet Arafat wouldn't sign it. Glenn and Mr. Wiley talked about how silly that was. But the Arab men told them the 2% was very important. However, Glenn says that in listening to them he sees that the bottom line is it has nothing to do with the 2%. The bottom line is they don't want a Jewish state at all. They only want a Palestinian state. (Mr. Wiley told Glenn during the car ride that in their school books their maps have everything labeled with Palestinian names. Jerusalem is not labeled as Jerusalem. It is given a different name. On their maps there is no Israel. He knows because he used to teach in Hevron.)

Mr. Wiley told the men at the table that they are suffering today because Arafat wouldn't sign the agreement. He said, "Look what you have now. Nothing!" He told them that they are living in a fantasy world if they think that they will get that 2% now. In fact, he told them they will never get an offer like that again. Then the son who has four kids, who had lived in California for eight years and worked for a Jewish guy there as a mechanic, looked Glenn right in the eye, and pointing with his finger said, "I hate all Jews." His facial expression and tone of voice was full of vehemence and fury. Glenn couldn't believe it.

Yet, even though that guy talked that way, he wasn't upset with Mr. Wiley or Glenn. They have been friends with Mr. Wiley for years. At the end of the four hour visit, they warmly invited Glenn to come back and eat with them anytime! (It was on a Friday which is their Sabbath. That is why they could visit so long.) Glenn didn't have a camera with him, so I'm sorry there are no pictures.

Kibbutz, Carved Stone, Shavuot Picnic

This stone with a verse carved on it (below) with a big statue beside it (see p. 219) is at a Messianic Kibbutz not too far from Jerusalem. It's not a farming Kibbutz. It is a Christian lodging and conference center. A rich man from Finland shipped wood in from Finland to build all the buildings. I think it is the only Messianic Kibbutz in Israel. If not, then it is one of very few. We were there in May for a nationwide Messianic picnic on Shavuot (Pentecost). There were maybe around 500 people there. (See photos p. 260)

Thanking People

Sun, Jun 3, 2007 at 8:13 PM

Dear Wonderful, Praying, Supportive Folks,

Ever since we got this laptop, I have been trying to figure out how I can thank everyone properly. (2008: It is the same laptop that allowed me to make this book) I want to thank everyone who gave money for the laptop and everyone who prayed that the Lord would provide one. I want to thank my Mom and Dad for being the ones to get the ball rolling, and my sister Jenny's husband, Dwight, for being the expert to know what kind of computer and special outlet plug we needed, and Jenny for working out all the ordering details.

I also want to thank everyone of you out there for being such a wonderful support to us. I especially appreciate all your interest in my e-mail reports and for the many notes of encouragement you send me from time to time. It has been such a joy to have people interested in what we are experiencing here.

Thank you, thank you, thank you,
Cheryl

Journal June 8 Gods Kingdom

Derek gave me a paper he did for one of his seminary classes. It is very enlightening.

Page. 8 To the Jews, the Torah emerged as a major concept ... linked to the power and presence of God, as the operative power ... used in the act of creation ... with the creative power of wisdom. [But, the Jews thought] God's presence was so elevated beyond the extremities of heaven ... He needed intermediaries ... [namely] the Torah, wisdom, and angels.

Page. 10 Jesus declared the New Age [the Kingdom] was near! *Jews believe in a New Age that is coming.*

Page. 11 (Quoting George Eldon Ladd) The kingdom of God is His Kingship, His rule, His authority. The Kingdom is not a realm or a people, but God's reign. ... We are to receive the Kingdom as little children (Mk. 10:15). What is received? The church? Heaven? What is received is God's rule here and now.

The kingdom of God is His Kingship
His rule, His reign
His authority!
His Glory!

Thy Kingdom come. Thy will be done On earth as it is in heaven.

"Apart from the reign of God,
Heaven would be meaningless."

Except a grain of wheat die...
He who loses his life for My sake...
Take up your cross and follow Me....
He who does the Will of My Father is the one who loves me...
Unless you become as a little child....
Humble yourself as this little child....
God resists the proud and gives grace to the humble.
One of the three things God hates: pride.
Abide in Me and I in you...
I give you authority over all the power of the enemy.

So,

The kingdom can only come to a people who are completely humbled and completely surrendered to God and to His Will; only to a people who have died to themselves and are totally submitted to God; to a people who have no will of their own, who only want Gods will to be done.

Humility, surrender, submission, death to self, not independence, but total dependence upon God; completely, totally trusting God for everything; not worried about anything.

We listened last night to a sermon by John Piper on the internet. He had a couple interesting points: There is no light in our human body. Light comes in through the eye. Gods Glory (which is **LIGHT!**) comes in through our spirit (through our spiritual eyes).

But people trade Gods Glory for a copy of a copy of a copy. Why would we do that? Why dont we want the real thing—the original?

Glorify thy son
So that I may Glorify you.

That those whom You have given Me
May be with Me where I am
To see My Glory.

You have given Me authority over all people.

I have made Your Name known to them
And I will make it known
So that [Your] Love may be in them
And I in them. (from John 17)

He spoke with authority.
His Kingdom is GLORY.
It is Forgiveness of all our debt.
It is being set free from slavery.
It is being washed clean, pure, and white in His BLOOD.
It is being forgiven of our present and future sins.
It is the Father and Son coming to us and making their home with us.
It is Jesus coming and supping with us.

It is LIFE & LIGHT & HOLINESS
—— & ROYALTY ——
Treating each other like Royalty!

Oh, the other day Glenn said that God didnt just arbitrarily decide what things He would have the Jews do so they would be different from all other people on the earth. He didnt say, "Okay, let me see. What should I make them do to be different? Um.....lets see..... I know! Lets make them wear a garment with fringes, and .... Um ......"

"No, God didnt do that," Glenn said. "He made them do those things because they are being done in Heaven. Jesus is wearing a Heavenly Tallith in Heaven! The Temple is designed like the Heavenly Temple."

As he talked we began to realize that doing all those things: wearing the Tallith, eating kosher, etc., wasnt for their salvation or cleansing from sin at all because they still had to constantly make sacrifices for their sins!

Sderot

June 10, 2007 at 11:55 PM

Okay, Friends, I want to know who was praying for us on Sunday (from 1 am to 12 noon your time). God kept us safe from Palestinian rockets in Sderot. There were two of them that landed in the fields near a lookout where we gazed at Gaza on the horizon, but not while we were there. There had not been many rockets at all for a week before that. So you all must have been praying and your prayers were powerful!!! Keep on praying whatever the Holy Spirit lays on your heart!!!

I will send a couple pictures and tell you more next time.

More Detail on Sderot   Written in 2008 from notes taken during the trip

Let me start at the beginning and tell you all about it.

Sderot is the city that has been under siege the whole time since I came to Israel—the city where Jewish people are being bombed by the Palestinians nearly every day! We have longed to go for quite awhile to help in some way, or at least to show our support and give comfort. The terror victim organization leader wanted to take a group to sing in hospitals there, so I asked the Koreans to come. They were interested, but the Koreans are not all from one cohesive group, so permission had to be obtained from different leaders which took time. Then we couldn't get a date set that suited everyone. I was very disappointed figuring all hope for going to Sderot was lost.

Then we saw a trip to Sderot advertised on the Israel National News website. http://www.israelnationalnews.com/News/News.aspx/122666   We signed up immediately, but were told we were only on a waiting list. We figured there were thousands who would want to go to Sderot with this famous TV station, Arutz 7, so we assumed we didn't have a chance.

That's why we felt so extremely privileged as we chose our seats on the huge tour bus. They had informed us only two days before that we could go! We were so early we were the first ones there. I was relieved that we had found the correct location and the correct bus. We were going to Sderot!!

Surprisingly, the bus did not fill up! There were several rows of empty seats in the back. Only about twenty-five people came. I felt sorry for the Sderot people that so few were thinking of them. It turned out that About ten of us were Christian. The rest were Jewish, mostly Orthodox. Our leaders, also Orthodox, were fascinating people.

On the way to Sderot, one of the original directors of the Arutz 7 station welcomed us. He was a tall, big built, full bearded, jolly, Orthodox man—father of nine. Then one of their reporters, a short, blond pony-tailed, purple kippa'ed, very dedicated young man, briefed us on all the latest news from Sderot.

It is a tiny city in southern Israel that has the terrible misfortune of being near Gaza. It was first settled in 1953 by Jewish people returning to the Land from Iran and Iraq, and most recently by Russian Jews.

The Palestinians have fired 1600 Kassam rockets at Sderot since November 2006, the same month they signed the so-called cease-fire agreement with Israel. There are an average of

1.8 attacks per day, but lately that number has increased. A storm of 293 or so bombs fell in May, twenty falling in one day, one time!!

The Sderot people live in constant, daily fear. They must be ready to run to their bomb shelters every moment of every day. Many sleep in their shelters at night. When they hear the siren warning that a bomb is coming, they have less than two seconds to take shelter. That is why people get killed.

The amazing thing is that there have been only ten deaths!! This is because the bombs often miss Sderot and land in the open fields between the city and Gaza.

(Quoting the director further) "The Israeli government said when they forced all Israeli citizens to leave the Gaza strip, that if one rocket falls, we will retaliate. But since there are so few casualties, instead of stopping the bombing, the government has done nothing except evacuate. Sixty-five percent have been evacuated since May 15. The whole Ethiopian Jewish community, from the northern section where the city has been hardest hit, has been forced to leave. The homes and buildings that have been damaged are receiving no help from the government for repairs, including a synagogue that was hit three weeks ago."

During the three-hour drive, we all introduced ourselves and then were interviewed by Arutz 7's beloved talk show host, Walter. He was a soft-spoken, kind-faced older man with white hair and a nicely trimmed white beard. We were all very excited about the possibility of our interview being used in his online radio talk show, and that we might be chosen for a longer live interview in Sderot. When he found out we were Christian he said something like, "Aren't you here just to convert Jews?" Glenn then really started witnessing to him. I said excitedly that we just want to introduce the Jews to their Messiah. At that he moved on to people seated behind us.

The first place they took us to was on the edge of town where all the exploded bombs are stored, each one marked with the date it fell. We saw shelf after shelf of these empty iron rocket shells with their noses blown open, ripped like cloth. They said we could hold one. I tried but they were so heavy, I could barely lift them, however, Glenn, with his big muscles, made it look easy.

Next, as they drove us through the town, we were sobered by the ghost-town feel. Many homes were empty. Damaged houses with gaping holes in their roofs sat unrepaired. Some streets were completely empty, others had cars parked in them, but there were no pedestrians on the sidewalks. Lawns weren't mowed.

The elementary school with part of the roof protected

The playgrounds were empty. Swimming pools in the backyards on this beautiful summery day sat there eerily empty and quiet, even after school was let out.

We went past the school while it was still in session. No kids were on the playground. The sports fields were unused. Part of the school was protected by a special, very thick steel roof. The reporter told us only grades 1-3 were protected. The older students had to race to take cover every time a siren went off. He wondered out loud whether those children felt very valued by their government.

He told us he has spent a lot of time in Sderot reporting on it, trying to let the world know what is happening there. He has seen the terror in the people's faces as they rush to take cover yet again for another incoming. He said he has seen not only women, but also grown, normally calm men screaming in terror as they try to get all their little children to safety in time. He said the psychological damage to these people is massive.

We stopped at an outdoor market place, which eerily had very few shoppers. Normally a place like that would be crowded, but here our group made up maybe one-third of the customers. We were encouraged to buy things to show our support. Glenn and I wished we had more to spend.

As we walked from the bus to the shopping area, we gazed in reverence at the hole in the asphalt from a bomb that had killed a lady shopper a month or so earlier. We noted with dismay, the hundreds of shrapnel holes in the surrounding buildings.

We did not see any children outside at all, since they are kept hidden in safety, except for one girl about age 10 with her mother at the market.

They broke us up into small groups and took us to visit a few homes in an apartment complex. We walked through the neglected courtyard—tall, dry grass—clothes hanging permanently on the line. We knocked on doors until we found families who still lived there. All of the families told us, through an interpreter, of the constant fear they live under. At the first home they showed us the room that had been hit once. Oblivious to it all, their smiling baby was crawling around on the floor.

The next home looked amazingly fancy, considering what their courtyard looked like. They were an older couple that had raised nine children in that small apartment. Another home was an elderly Russian couple. Their timid, cute, 5-year-old granddaughter arrived home from school while we were there. They said she screams in terror every time a siren goes off and that she is scared to ride the bus. As I looked at the smiling, puppy-eyed wisp of a girl, my heart broke for her. We asked them why they don't leave. Her grandfather said he suffered a lot worse than this in Russia.

There is a very large Yeshiva (Jewish Torah school for young men) right in Sderot. Arutz 7 supports them. We ate our lunch in the round cafeteria building after the men poured out of it. The round walls were lined with shelves full of books. I guess they don't get a break from studying even to eat.

Their study room is set up sort of like a library, with row after row of short shelves with desks attached to them. The college-age students, all men, study at these desks in pairs. They read and discuss the material aloud together. There was a low hum of conversation going on in the room as we watched some of the young men having animated, almost debating discussions. They have to study the Old Testament, called the Tanakh (which includes the Torah—Moses' five books), and then they have to study the volumes and volumes of rabbi commentaries and commentaries on those commentaries. These are called the Talmud, the Mishna, etc., etc.

The head rabbi, a thin, black-bearded, family man, told us the schedule these students are on. They study from early morning until 11 pm with only a couple hours break in the evening for supper. Some of them are married, so they go home for supper. One student had his baby in a stroller beside him as he was studying. These men alternate their required three years of military with school, instead of finishing military service all at once.

The head rabbi showed us his office and told us that one day while he was sitting there preparing for a class, he heard the siren and decided not take cover this time, when suddenly, shockingly, the rocket fell right outside his window!! But, miraculously, it didn't explode. He showed us the picture on the cover of their magazine of the burning rocket with him crouched a ways behind it, watching it. Feeling rather shook up and wanting to know how the authorities were reporting this attack on his Yeshiva, he called them and asked what happened this time. They told him, "Nothing." Since the bomb didn't explode they called it nothing. He said to them, "What?! A guy enters your living room, shoots and misses, and you say nothing happened?!"

He says now he is the first one to the shelter every time!

Before eating lunch, the Arutz Orthodox director went into the kitchen to wash his hands, came out holding his hands upright, sat down at the table and said the "Baruch Ata melech ha olam…" blessing over his food before lowering his hands to eat. As an Orthodox, he didn't worry about the fact that none of the other Jews present, not even the Jews that work with him, who were co-leading this tour—stayed true to Jewish custom. He didn't act holier-than-thou, he just quietly, non-obtrusively carried out his traditions, continuing his friendly, joking manner toward all of us throughout the trip. Perhaps exemplifying Daniel and perhaps is why Daniel was so beloved by the kings he served under.

Damaged Synagogue

The most exciting part of our whole trip was when we visited the recently hit synagogue. We saw the caved-in roof, and looked in the window to see the trashed room. A roof across the alley was also damaged, and a house across the road stood abandoned due to damage. It just so happened that just as we arrived, the people who had experienced the attack were just returning from their time away to recover from the shock of it all. They were so excited to see the reporter again, who had come to see them shortly after the rocket fell. Two men, brothers, gave animated accounts, in Hebrew, of the whole event. It seemed very therapeutic to them to recount their story to listening, caring ears. They sent their children home to bring the newspaper featuring the attack on the front page. Then they sent for their sister to bring her baby whom they were all so thankful was not hurt from the explosion.

Their Story

In honor of their late father, these siblings bought a new Torah for the synagogue, for which they held a traditional Simcha Torah party where they march down the street playing music, carrying the Torah to the synagogue. It was a large crowd following the Torah and celebrating—all their brothers and sisters, spouses and children, etc.

While they continued the celebration in the synagogue courtyard, the red alert siren sounded. They rushed to take cover inside the synagogue, attempting to open the closest door—a classroom door, but found it locked. It was locked because the cleaning lady had just cleaned it and she wanted it to stay clean. Frustrated they all ran a few feet farther into the sanctuary for refuge. Just then the bomb came crashing with a loud boom into the very classroom they had just tried to enter!! Several of them certainly would have been killed if they had been in there. God protected them!! They were very shaken, but safe. We could see the shock still evident in their expressions, but their gratefulness was also very apparent.

They took us into both the demolished room and the sanctuary. They brought out the new Torah from its special "ark" cupboard (a tradition of every synagogue) to show us. Its case was a beautiful silver with intricately molded designs. Glenn got to hold it.

Giving Away a Blanket

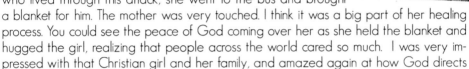

One young Christian girl from a large homeschooling family in California had come to Israel with several homemade, tied, flannel blankets to give away. Each one was embroidered with a Biblical message in Hebrew. She had wanted to give some away in Sderot, but, like us, had given up hope of getting to Sderot until this tour became available. As soon as she heard about this baby who lived through this attack, she went to the bus and brought a blanket for him. The mother was very touched. I think it was a big part of her healing process. You could see the peace of God coming over her as she held the blanket and hugged the girl, realizing that people across the world cared so much. I was very impressed with that Christian girl and her family, and amazed again at how God directs His people.

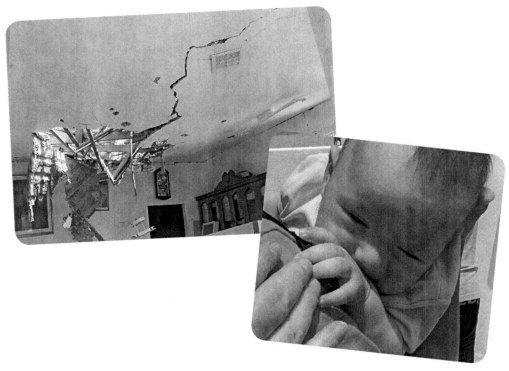

On Internet TV

June 11, 2007

I am very embarrassed to tell you this, and I don't want to tell you at all, but if it was one of you and you didn't tell me, I would be very upset. So here it is. We are on the internet TV news at israelnationalnews.com   We didn't get interviewed, but we are in the background of a couple shots. I'm the lady in a long green skirt and big white hat (which I have to wear to keep off the desert sun). I am very embarrassed. I had no idea we were being filmed. Please don't laugh at me. Well, I guess a little chuckle would be okay. ☺   (Tee hee!)

They chose two young Jewish people, a guy and a girl, for the TV interviews. Ten out of the twenty-five in the group were Christian, almost half, yet none were chosen. As Glenn and I discussed this later. We decided that the interviewing Walter did at the beginning of the trip, supposedly for his weekly radio show, was a decoy to sort us out so they could make sure they chose only Jews for the live program and for TV.

So, it's pretty definite that Glenn's interview will not be on that radio show next Sunday, especially since he was sort of witnessing. (You have to click on the radio tab and scroll way down to find Walter's show.)

Here's a link to a photo feature story of the trip:
http://www.israelnationalnews.com/News/News.aspx/122724

Go to sderotmedia.com for the latest news on Sderot.

Dad an Actor

Wed, Jun 13, 2007 at 2:35 PM

Right this very minute Dad is being an actor on a Canadian documentary film that will come out in September. He's being a disciple. Can you believe it?!! He is so tickled. You should see him! God has been blessing him so much lately!!! - Love, Mom

Sabrina's Reply

Ha! That's great! I can just see Dad acting as a disciple! Wow. You'll definitely have to get a copy after that film is out on video. Which disciple is he? I've been praying for Dad, so this is just great.

Mom, how is the end of your semester coming? Are the students turning in big papers or anything yet? What was the response of your Arab teenage boy student to your comments about Jesus in response to his paper ?

Yeah, maybe you could even be the ones to pick me up from the airport? Then I'd get to slurge all about China to you on the drive back. I know how you love that. ☺

So, there were rockets near you?? Goodness... I pray for a barrier and shield of protection around you. I'm reading the psalms right now. David declares God as his Strength and Shield a lot. And in Samuel, too,

"As for God, His way is perfect.
His is a shield for all who trust in him." (II Sam 22:31)

"The Lord God is a Sun and Shield,
He bestows favor and Honor,
No good thing does he withhold from him whose walk is blameless."
(Shoot, I forget that reference, Isaiah?)

I love you two, too!

he he

Reply

June 14, 2007

The rockets were near where we traveled. They aren't near here where we live.

I'm busy trying to make a decent final for my students and grading papers. They don't have to do a big paper, just several small assignments—like journals.

It wasn't a teenage student. It was the adult. His reaction was totally nonverbal, but it was interesting. At least it wasn't negative. I had a chance to give him the little book of John once, but didn't think fast enough. I hope I will get another chance. [I did later.]

Got to go. Sorry.

Love,
Mom

P.S. Pray for Dad. They want Dad back to do more acting today, but due to circumstances beyond his control, he can't go. It is very strange and it is really hard for Dad to handle. It's like the devil had to come and destroy Dad's new blessing. Pray for the Lord's will to be done

Journal June 16 War Readiness. What Education Can Do

Glenn just had a roller-coaster-that-crashed ride this week!!!! He got to go to another palace of Herod's just newly discovered. They are still doing archeological digging there and the public is not allowed in. Then he met some people there from Canada who asked him to be an actor in a documentary they are doing. He went the next day and got to play a disciple. There was an Orthodox Jewish guy with curls, tzit-tzit, suit and all watching them do the filming. While Glenn was waiting for his scene to come up he sat next to the Jewish guy and had a long conversation with him about the film, Scripture, and Yeshua!. It was amazing!

... But now Glenn can't go back. Because of this and a couple other things, Glenn says he has had to fight anger. He says he has been put into an emotional state of war-readiness. But last night (Friday) some of us volunteers had a small prayer meeting and now Glenn says he feels much better! ...

The Fatah and Hamas are fighting each other.... (See p. 289) So, I told Glenn that he has been put into the fighting mode because this is a time of spiritual war. He countered that the devil was trying to distract him from doing prayer warfare for Israel.

While Glenn and I were having our private Shabboth before that prayer meeting, I opened my Bible to this.

> Jeremiah 25:32-34
> Thus says the Lord of hosts:
> See, disaster is spreading
> from nation to nation,
> and a great tempest is stirring
> from the farthest parts of the earth!
>
> Those slain by the Lord on that day
> shall extend from one end of the earth to the other....
>
> Wail, you shepherds and cry out;
> roll in ashes, you lords of the flock.

This morning I read James because Derek's paper says it is a Jewish book that wouldn't have offended the Jewish believers in Jerusalem who were against Paul. It makes you see it in a different light.

When we went to Sderot, I saw the observant Jewish attitude toward the Torah. The Orthodox leader was telling about a debate between him and a secular Jewish leader about the Gaza situation. He said, `She used the Torah to prove her point, but I used the Torah to counter her.` It soon became clear that he actually meant the Mishna or some other part of the Talmud (made up of centuries of Rabbinical commentary on the Torah), not the Torah itself—the five books of Moses, because later he was talking about something else and he said, `We can see this just from the actual Torah, which only takes a kinder-garten education to read and understand.`

!!! Can you believe it? !!!!

So, it's the same in Judaism as it is in Christianity. Yeshiva study is very different from American seminaries in its whole approach to studying Scripture, but it is similar in this one thing—that it makes you feel much more `educated` than the layman. It makes you think you are `elite.` And, most importantly, it piles on so much education and knowledge on top of the actual Word of God that you can hardly see the Word anymore, and you lose your reverence and awe toward God's WORD—the Words given by God Himself!!!

Well, There is Unrest Here!!

Sat, Jun 16, 2007 at 1:02 PM

There is war going on around the area we live, but we wouldn't know it at all if it wasn't for the news. When there was actually some gun fighting in Bethlehem, we didn't notice any more gun sounds than normal!! More than a month ago while I was praying at the Wall, I heard a jet flying overhead. That really shocked me. A week and a half or so ago there were tons of jets flying over Jerusalem while I was teaching. I had to stop talking a minute because it seemed so alarming. But the students paid no heed, so I ignored it, too. (It might have had something to do with the military exercises being done to prepare for war with Syria.) This week nothing strange happened.

What we read on the news now is very disturbing. The Hamas have taken over Gaza, so the Fatah have fled to Egypt and the West Bank. The Korean government has told their citizens to get out of the West Bank. I am praying for my student who lives in Ramallah who took me to her little Baptist church. She wasn't in class on Thursday. There are killings happening there. The Fatah are arresting and killing Hamas guys there.

It is so amazing to me that just before this we were at both places. We were in Ramallah only a couple weeks ago, and last Sunday we stood on a hill and gazed over into Gaza. Can you believe it?!! I hardly can. Who knows when it will be safe to go back to those places again.

All this is the beginning of a fulfilling of the vision God gave Glenn of the boiling pot of strife. And yesterday as Glenn and I had our private Shabboth, I opened my Bible to Jeremiah 25. Verse 32 stood out:

Thus says the Lord of hosts: See, disaster is spreading from nation to nation, and a great tempest is stirring from the farthest parts of the earth!

I sat there stunned as I read it. Glenn was also astounded when I showed him. The verse seems so timely.

We are not afraid. I feel a wonderful sense of calm and expectancy. I have a deep sense that God called me to be in Israel during a war, to be here to pray. Glenn does, too. (If war broke out, we were hoping to sell our airline seats to people trying to leave.) I have such peace in my inner being. I feel very secure. It is partly because of Psalms 29:

Verses 3-5 *The voice of the Lord is over the waters;*
the God of Glory thunders....
The voice of the Lord is powerful; the voice of the Lord is full of majesty.
The voice of the Lord breaks cedars... the cedars of Lebanon....

Verses 7-9 *The voice of the Lord flashes forth flames of fire.*
The voice of the Lord shakes the wilderness; ....
The voice of the Lord causes the oaks to whirl, and strips the forest bare;
and in His temple all say, "GLORY!!!"

We are in God's Temple. We are part of His Temple and we are near the place of His first Temple. In all this whirling, shaking, and stripping, we see the majesty of God; and in awe and reverence we say, "Glory!"

Glory!!
Cheryl

At the Wall

Mon, Jun 18, 2007 at 11:09 PM

A couple times ago, at the Wall, I discovered that they have English-Hebrew prayer books on a bookshelf near the entrance (where the beggars sit) for visitors to use. So I took one and I found out why the ladies do certain dips and bows, and steps forward and back as they pray. The prayer book actually tells you to do that!! After a passage there are teensy tiny printed lines giving such instructions. It also said in one place that your prayers shouldn't be completely audible to others, but they should be earnest (something like that). So that explains why all the ladies are just whispering their prayers!

At the Wall on Sunday I was praying a little ways back from the actual Wall because it was too crowded to get to the Wall. I was near the divider between the men's and women's sections, and there were some men praying loudly just on the other side. I was enjoying it as the background of my praying. There is just something so comforting about hearing men pray in earnest. Then the thought suddenly hit me that the men often pray loudly. So now I'm wondering if there is a different prayer book for women than for men. Theirs must encourage them to speak up!

Anyway, I felt especially anointed as I prayed there Sunday. The Lord's presence was very tangible and glorious. I think part of it was because I was fasting, but the other part was because of those men praying! At first I was enjoying it subconsciously. But their prayers were so powerful that it was touching me and lifting me. All of a sudden I realized my hands were raised up high in the air in praise to God because of the awesomeness of it all. I didn't think anything about it at first because I often lift my hands in prayer, but I slowly became aware of the fact that I was in a place where no one raises their hands ever! I decided to keep my eyes closed because I didn't want to know if anyone was staring at me. Eventually I lowered my arms and began to focus more on the men praying. It sounded like anointed Holy Spirit tongues praying. I thought, "Wow, these Jewish men really have hearts after God. These prayers are full of power!"

After I left the women's section, before leaving the plaza, I walked to where I could peer through the lattice to see what those praying men looked like. I expected to see bearded men in black hats and Talliths (prayer shawls). But to my surprise I saw Ethiopian men dressed in normal clothes! They were leaning their arms on the wall above their heads as many normally-dressed men do. (The Tallith guys don't, usually.) Now I wonder if they were possibly Ethiopian Messianic believers!

Before I began praying at the Wall, while I was standing back, just enjoying the view, I watched a group of about ten girls age 7-8 doing their individual praying with their prayer books. They were so darling cute, sitting in the big white chairs, discussing things with each other and instructing each other. Most of them had fashionably looking skirts on, but a couple had pants. They all looked alike enough they could have been cousins or something. Each one had a small backpack. The lady in charge of them had a scarf on and was dressed a little more religious than the girls were.

In the plaza there were some huge dump trucks and cranes working. All of a sudden there was a loud bang from a truck being loaded. Surprisingly this alarmed those girls. They all jumped and one yelled out, "Ima!" (Mommy!) and looked frighteningly to the lady who began speaking soothing Hebrew words that soon calmed them all down. But the fact that they were so easily terrified made you think they have been through tragedy. My heart cried out for them. Fortunately there was nothing at all to be afraid of. Then I thought of the children who live in Sderot who hear terrifying sounds nearly every day and really do have something to fear! I realized how terribly painful it would be to have to be with them and witness their fear, and how helpless you would feel trying to comfort them and protect them.

And how about the poor children in Gaza right now?!! In Iraq and Afghanistan?!! It grips your heart to think about it. But thank the Lord we have the power of prayer and pray we must!!! We know the God of all comfort and the Good Shepherd who takes care of the sheep.

As the girls were leaving, they were whisper-yelling at each other in Hebrew, reminding each other to walk backwards and slowly!! Oh how cute! It made me wish I had little children again!

Lord, please have mercy on all these frightened children,
Cheryl

Please Pray Against the Gay Parade Tomorrow!!!!
Wed, Jun 20, 2007 at 8:27 PM

They are planning to have it tomorrow! The Ultra Orthodox have already had a protest march against it 10,000 strong!!! But now they are urging their people to pray rather than protest, because prayer is stronger!! Isn't that great?!!

Please pray! Please spend all day praying! God has used big events to prevent it in the past. It will be exciting and interesting to see how He intervenes this time!! One lady prayed that God would do it through nature so people would know it is God!!! Amen! I agree!!

We serve a BIG God! We prayed at Monday's prayer meeting against the gay bar on Ben Yehuda street that they told us is the root of all this in Jerusalem. (A gay bar in Jerusalem? I was shocked!) We prayed for their "house" to be divided so it will fall, and for all their evil to be exposed, including any possible illegal business or tax deals, etc.

May God bare His right arm and show Himself tomorrow,
Cheryl

Bar Mitzvah's!!!

Happened Thurs. June 28 (Written later from Memory)

The Thursday before we left, we went to the Wall and we were amazed at what we saw! The men's side was buzzing with activity, especially along the dividing fences at the side and back. The other sides of those fences were lined with women standing on chairs. Why? It was some kind of special Bar Mitzvah day!! There must've been twenty Bar Mitzvahs going on at once! We watched them all with great interest. The only thing missing in all the celebrating was the usual dancing because it was far too crowded!

First, a rabbi helps the boy learn to wrap his arm and forehead phylacteries.

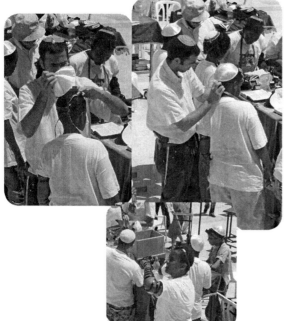

Some groups led the boy in with great honor and reverence under his Tallith (prayer shawl).

Then the boy goes to the corner room and brings out a huge Torah to much clapping and singing and blowing of shofars.

Then he reads from the Torah, in Hebrew, while everyone listens intently and quietly; then cheers loudly when he's finished.

Then the candy begins to fly from the women, and more singing and clapping erupts from the men.

Epilogue

Decision Time

Tues, July 10, 2007

About Us Staying in Israel

We are back in the States. The University is losing their volunteer housing. They've only been renting it and it is being sold out from under them. So, they want me back, but they told me I would have to raise all my own support. They will not be able to give me any compensation at all. We are praying and praying to see what the Lord wants.

We did find housing with this wonderful lady, Katalina. I met her the first week I was in Israel and we slowly became closer and closer friends. She is an older Jewish, Scandinavian lady who immigrated to Israel in the 1970s and eventually married an Israeli. She looks very Scandinavian with blue eyes. Her bright smile warms your heart.

She is an artist who was very famous in her country in the seventies and still is well-known there. She has published several books of her artwork and writing in her country. The latest one was in 2005. One of her earlier books was translated into English and published in America. Right now she is almost finished with a book to be published in Israel. It will be both in Hebrew and in English. She asked me to help her a little with the English text when I was there. Her writing is as beautiful as her art. Her book could have a great impact on Israel because she writes about the sorrows she has gone through and they are things many Israelis have experienced. Then she gives the Gospel message in such a gentle way. This is the first time she has to pay for the publishing of any of her books. There is no Messianic publisher in Israel. She has to do it on her own and it is costing her thousands of dollars. So pray for God to release all the funds for her.

Anyway, we stayed with her our last few days in Israel. We wanted to be near the Old City so we could walk to the Wall to pray and do other prayer-walking and seek God for what to do this fall. While we were there, she offered that we could live with her at a greatly reduced price, if Glenn would fix up some things around her home. She has a beautiful old home that is like walking into an ancient storybook. She welcomes anyone into her home and runs it like a bed and breakfast. She tells everyone about the Lord and many have received Him because of her.

Meeting Another Jewish Lady

The last night we were there she invited a friend—a Jewish lady she had met at the pool—to come to her small group. The friend is a British lady who has lived in Israel for thirty years. She teaches voice and theater. She was dressed in a very fashionable, black dress with an exquisitely shaped, matching hat. I loved her prim and proper British English and mannerisms!! At the meeting, Katalina showed us her book on her laptop, then asked us to pray for the book.

Two Swedish ladies present began immediately to pray in tongues so we joined in. Part of the time we were even singing in the Spirit together. Those ladies made it seem like a completely natural thing. Glenn's chair was near the Jewish British lady's. Afterward when she was saying good-by she took both Glenn's hands in hers and shocked us with the words, "Were you speaking in tongues?" (She had thought the Swedish ladies were just speaking in Swedish!!) Glenn told her yes. She said, "I loved it! I love things that flow so freely from deep inside like that. I want it. Can I have it?" Immediately Katalina and her friends gathered around the lady and began teaching her about baptism in the Holy Spirit. When she heard the word "baptism" she asked, "Will I have to go into the bathtub?" We all burst out laughing! Before the night was over she was receiving Jesus and speaking in tongues!! Afterwards Glenn and I kept saying to each other, "Can you believe what just happened?!!!"

God is still at work in Israel! Praise His Name!!

We would love to be around someone as evangelistic as Katalina because we could learn so much from her. (But we need an income to be able to pay the rent.)

The Boy Clerk

That last week while staying near the Old City at Katalina's we walked to the Wall almost every day. To get there, we always walked past one little Arabic tourist shop. The young, teenage clerk had not been around for a few months and the shop had been closed. But one day on our way out, there he was again, hounding us. We ignored him until he said, "You promised to shop here." I was so surprised that he remembered us! I said to Glenn, "He's right. You did promise." So we went in. He cajoled Glenn over and over about different items, whispering loudly to him, "I make special price just for you. No one else. Just for you." It amused us to hear the same line again that all the Arabic shop-keepers use. While we were in there, the Muslim loudspeakers came on. I had always assumed that they were chanting rote, traditional prayers that would be very boring to a young person. But as this teenage clerk was wrapping a necklace for me, he suddenly started chuckling. I asked him what the man said. He looked at me as if he was going to answer, then he shook his head. In a couple minutes he started laughing out loud. I asked again. "Please tell me what he's saying." No answer. So I decided to barter with him. "I'll buy more things from you if you tell me." I thought this would be an irresistible offer since he seldom has any customers in this out-of-the-way little store. But it didn't work. He wouldn't tell me. Either he thought I wouldn't like what was being said, or he didn't know English well enough to explain it.

On one of the days at the Wall, we had time enough for me to do my final prayer-walk around the Temple. Glenn stayed at the Wall and prayed until I got back. (I don't think he realized at all that I would be walking through that Muslim cemetery. I think he envisioned it being by the way of the road which is a very long walk, which is probably why he didn't want to go.) This last time was totally uneventful. I was able to pray earnestly the whole way.

About a Hassidim Boy's Wedding

We also did some more prayer-walking and shopping in the Mea Sharim neighborhood where the Ultra Orthodox (also called Hassadim or Haredim) live. Glenn let me taste the delicious sweets one last time. We also bought some Hebrew books and other things to take back as gifts. The shopkeepers were very kind and friendly to us. We looked and looked for something special to buy for the young, Orthodox couple as a thank you gift for letting us eat in their home. I wanted to buy something for their Shabboth table, such as a Challah (Sabbath loaf) cover or a tablecloth. In one of those kinds of shops, we heard a young, late teens boy talking, in perfect English, about his future wedding, of all things, He was telling the clerk, a middle-aged man, all the details of what he wanted his wedding to be like, what he wanted to wear, etc. I found this very odd. Glenn apparently did, too, because he piped up in his teasing/joking voice, "Do you have the woman yet!?" The guy answered, "No," in that tone of voice we use when we wish with all our heart that something was true. Afterwards we chuckled about that for awhile. It's funny because for us non-Jews, the wedding is the bride's affair. It's the girls who have it all planned with the only missing piece being the groom, not the other way around!

Also, that last week we finally met a missionary whom I had been trying to arrange a meeting with for a couple months. (He's from Glenn's denomination.) To our delight we discovered that he is very evangelistic. We were surprised, because most people of that denomination aren't. Too many of the modern, liberal ones we've known have been focused more on peace than on the Lord Jesus. This man is so evangelistic that right while we were talking to him some ladies walked by and looked curiously through the gate at the name of the college where he teaches. Immediately he began to tell them in Hebrew that the college teaches about Yeshua, the Messiah, and that they can prove from the Tanakh (Old Testament) that He is the Messiah. One lady was very interested and said she would come back later to talk to him.

I asked about volunteering for him and he said he would be happy for me to help him. I was very glad because I would love to work with someone that has such a heart for evangelism. His Bible college is training Messianic Israelis (in Hebrew) to be leaders for the Lord in the Land of Israel which is wonderful to us.

So we have a place to live and we have work we could be doing, but no income! So, we need the Lord to supply more funds, which we know He will do if it is HIS will.

Please pray for us in our listening for the Lord's will.

Blessings on all the decisions you are also making,
Cheryl

Jewish People Mourn the Destruction of the Temple

On July 23, the Jews spent the day and night mourning the destruction of the Temple back in 70 AD. They mourn every year on this day. Here are captions and the link from a photo essay.

Photo Essay: 100,000 Jews At Western Wall for Tisha B'Av 5767
by Nissan Ratzlav-Katz
http://www.israelnationalnews.com/News/News.aspx/123174

Over one hundred thousand Jews flooded the Kotel (Western Wall) Plaza on Monday night and Tuesday to say traditional Tisha B'Av lamentations for the loss of the First and Second Jerusalem Temples. Thousands encircled the walls of the Old City of Jerusalem, as well, to mark the day of mourning.

Masses gather in the Kotel Plaza seated on the floor and low stools to mourn the destruction of the Jerusalem Temples

Many sleep the night on the stone floor on the Kotel Plaza as an expression of mourning for the destroyed Temples....

A Palestinian Martyr for Jesus

Sun, Oct 28, 2007

Hi Friends,

Here is a letter from a professor in Israel about the man who was killed about three weeks ago in Gaza.:

Some of you may have heard last week that the Palestinian Bible Society announced that its Bible Society Bookshop manager, Rami Ayyad, was murdered near the bookshop in Gaza.

Remember that earlier this summer, radical Islamic jihadists blew up the Bible book store in Gaza, run by the Palestinian Bible Society. ... A friend who works closely with our brothers and sisters in Gaza attended our congregation yesterday. He noted: "Rami was one of the most gifted of the young leaders at the Bible Society. Rami was targeted because of his heart for lost Muslims and his wish to provide them the opportunity to buy Bibles. He was told that he was being 'watched.' But he kept serving the Lord."

One young woman from Gaza put it this way: 'He locked the doors and headed home. His earthly home was about 15 minutes away, but instead he was taken to his Heavenly home. Rami was kidnapped, tortured and finally killed. The Islamic terrorists threw his body from a car. One thing is clear, this dear brother would not be intimidated by threats, harassment, persecution, and even death. He stayed strong until the end and will be given a martyrs crown in Heaven. He is with Jesus right now."

... The Christian community in Gaza has been laying low because of continual threats. Now the eight Bible Society workers and their families are hoping to escape from Gaza. They are requesting entry to Israel for the sake of the safety of their families. Rami, 26, leaves behind two young children, and a pregnant wife, Pauline. Please pray for Pauline. Obviously, she is devastated....

... "Be faithful, even to the point of death, and I will give you the crown of life." *Revelation 2:10.* Rami has now received his eternal crown.

God's richest blessings,

Report From My Replacement in Jerusalem

Sun, Oct 28, 2007

My replacement is a Christian Jew married to a Korean who is immigrating to Israel. We got to know him just a little before we left. He and his wife took part in a special oriental medicine outreach in Galilee last summer as they plan to do every summer. (Jewish people love all the Eastern alternative medical methods.)

I just received a report from him that all is going well with my students. I am extremely impressed with his plans for Israel! He hopes to set up an oriental medicine clinic in Jerusalem with an evangelistic focus, and to offer English classes there! May God richly bless him and bring his plans to pass.

Oh, I Forgot to Tell You, We are Studying Hebrew

Sun, Oct 28, 2007

The Lord is so good. After being refused permission by one Reform Jewish congregation to take their Hebrew classes, He made sure we found out about classes at a different Reform congregation that doesn't mind if Christians attend their classes. I'm taking the conversation class. Glenn is taking the learn-to-read class. Glenn has a wonderful teacher. She gave him a wonderful website where he can practice what he is learning. You can go there and begin to learn Hebrew, too!!

http://behrmanhouse.com/

Try it!!

Cheryl

Gilo Shooting

Mar 5, 2008

There has been shooting again from Bethlehem by the Palestinians into the Gilo neighborhood where we lived when we were in Israel!! Can you believe it?!! It never happened when we were there, but now it is happening again!

Our friends who live in Gilo e-mailed us that they are safe. They said to remember that the Palestinians are firing from quite a distance away. But they don't live near as close to Bethlehem as the building we lived in was. Its big glass sliding door faces Bethlehem!! I wonder if it was hit! (It was sold so we don't know the people who live there now.)

Yeshiva Shooting

Sun, Mar 9, 2008

Hello, All My Prayer Warrior Friends and Relatives,

I'm sure you heard about the shooting at a religious school in Jerusalem. The western news media didn't emphasize that it was young unarmed boys that were shot. These boys were attending what is called a Yeshiva. All religious families send their boys to a Yeshiva when they reach a certain age. The boys study the Bible and religious books there. The boys who were shot were only 15 and 16 years old. They were not old enough to be soldiers yet.

If the Israeli army would have killed eight Palestinian 15 and 16-year-old boys, the news would have said they killed "innocent children." But when Palestinians kill young Jewish teens, the news calls them "people" not "children" or "innocent" people, nor even "unarmed" people. If the Israeli's kill children accidentally the world is outraged. But when Palestinians kill children on purpose, not much is made of it.

Very telling, isn't it? The news media's slip is showing.

Here is how our friends who are prayer missionaries in Jerusalem are praying for this situation. Let's join them in their leader's specific prayer:

Though the Lord may give you the bread of adversity and the water of affliction, yet your Teachers shall not be hidden anymore, but your eyes shall see your Teacher. ... And your ears shall hear a word behind you, saying, "This is the way, walk in it." (Is. 30:20, 21)

They [the Jewish people] have certainly had adversity and affliction in the past and are still having it, but I believe the time is come for them to truly hear that voice behind them saying "this is the way", It's time for them to see and hear their Teacher. Let's cry out to Him earnestly until it is fulfilled fully. That is the only way to real and lasting peace in this city or in the world.

Attack on a Messianic Family in Israel

Mar. 27, 2008

Dear Friends and Family,

Have you heard what has happened in Israel?! It's terrible news, yet God is using it to do awesome things. Our prayers for Israel are being answered.

The Jewish Purim holiday that celebrates the story of Esther over-lapped with Good Friday and the Easter weekend this year. It is cus-tomary for Jewish people to send each other Purim baskets of candy, etc. One such basket arrived at the door of a Messianic pastor family in the town of Ariel. This gated town is deep in the West Bank. Jewish people and Israeli-citizen-Arabs live there. This pastor has been reach-ing out with humanitarian aid to the Muslims and Jews alike. Their older sons have served in the Israeli army and have been honored soldiers. They are Jews who believe in Jesus. They have received persecution from Ultra Orthodox Jews many times. However, when their 15-year-old son, Ami (which means "my people"), was open-ing the basket, persecution was not on his mind. He had no idea it was a deadly bomb in disguise. The bomb damaged the family's whole apartment, blew a hole in the dining room table where he opened it, and shattered car windows three stories below. Ami was found on the floor in the kitchen, his back against the frig, saying, "Yeshua, I need you."

Ami has collapsed lungs from seven bolts used as shrapnel lodged there. He is unconscious, one eye is seriously damaged, and he has broken bones, but he is alive. That is the amazing thing. Logically speaking, he should be dead. People all around the world are praying for him. The administrator at our Messianic Synagogue knows him and his family personally.

How God is using this tragedy is so exciting. All of Israel is now hearing, through special news stories, all about Messianic Jews and what they believe in. Not only is the whole Israeli nation hearing Jesus' correct Hebrew Name, Yeshua, over and over, but they are hearing that a growing number of Israeli Jews (around 15,000!) believe He is the Jewish Messiah!!! They are also hearing about the healing miracles Yeshua is doing in answer to prayers for Ami.

Isn't it awesome?!!!!

Please keep praying!

(Update: The Lord is miraculously healing Ami Ortiz. He is back in school! You can find out much about him on the internet, including You-Tube and lionofgod.org)

Israeli's Calling on God about the Yeshiva Shooting

They are praying in sackcloth and ashes even!! Amazing!! I only know about it because of this e-mail from a prayer warrior in Jerusalem:

Sat, May 3, 2008

Dear friends,

Several weeks ago I had a unique experience. Because of the recent shooting in a Jerusalem yeshiva (religious school) and other threats to the nation, there was designated a special day of prayer in which groups of Israelis would meet in 40 cities and towns throughout Israel to call on God for help. Several of us went to the Western Wall area at the designated time. There in front of the wall was a tightly bunched group of religious Jewish men, most of whom were wearing sackcloth draped over their black coats, praying and at times calling out loudly to God. I entered the prayer area, donning one of the stiff paper yarmulkes that are provided for people like me who come without one. I tentatively approached the group, expecting that at any moment one of them would notice how out of place I looked, and throw me out—especially if they knew I was coming to pray in the Name of Jesus. But nobody did. I became bold enough to put on a spare sackcloth cloak, avail myself of the large saltshaker of ashes that was being passed around, and mingle my quiet prayers with theirs for while. After a few minutes I turned in my sackcloth and left, but they faithfully carried on.

Previous to this I had noticed the passage in Isaiah 30:18-19, where God says that He will "*wait that He may be gracious to them.*" Later, He promises the people of Jerusalem that they won't weep anymore, but He will be "*gracious to them at the voice of* [their] *cry.*" It reminded me of a father with an angry, rebellious child. He has done everything that he knows to do to bring reconciliation, but nothing works. So he lets the child go, and just waits—hoping that eventually the child will come to his senses so he, the father, can work with him again. God has been waiting for His people in Jerusalem for thousands of years. I'm trusting that He'll hear the cry they raised all over Israel that day, and be gracious to them. Sooner or later, it will happen—and they will join me in praying in our Messiah's Name!

In joyous faith

Final Note

October 2008

We didn't get to go back to Israel in the Fall of 2007 as we had hoped. That summer of 2007 was very scary for us. We had no place to live, no jobs, and no more support coming in, plus we were in debt for the land. We stayed in a hunting cabin, mice and all, for awhile. We thank our parents, children, and friends who let us stay in their homes, and especially, we thank Glenn's sister and husband who let us live in their camper for the last part of the summer.

The Lord provided as He always does, I repeated the words "The Lord will provide" over and over, in faith—but most of the time it was in naked, scared faith. We ended up back at the Bible college. I worked as a community nurse so Glenn could study full-time, and he FINISHED HIS DEGREE!!!! Praise the Lord!! He is now a pastor at a small church in a tiny village near some mountains.

The Lord inspires Glenn with great sermons Sunday after Sunday. Praise His Name! And the people are wonderful. Some of them have such a deep heart for Israel, so we are waiting expectantly to see what exciting things God has planned for us all.

As for the land, we are waiting to see what God has planned for that, too, and how He will provide for that plan.

In the meantime, God has been giving Glenn plenty of side work, so I have had the extensive time needed to get this and other books ready to be published. Also I'm having plenty of time alone with God, so I can breathe spiritually again!!

This whole year I have been haunted with the question, "Did we miss God? Is that why we aren't back in Jerusalem?" But just the other day God revealed to me while I was working on this book that my dream in 2006, of the flood of beautiful water that carried us to the upstairs of our house, was the prediction of this last year. (See journal 10/31/06) The year *was* like a scary flood and we *have* ended up in an upstairs parsonage apartment in the old church building!! So God is comforting me that He had this in the plans all along.

It is fascinating, though sometimes too sad, to watch what God is doing in the world and for Israel. On September 17 in the news, I read that President Bush and Condoleezza Rice have been working hard on the two-state solution, trying to get an agreement between Israel and Hamas, giving all of the West Bank and most of East Jerusalem (both the Old City and the modern part) to the Palestinians They are trying to get all this settled on paper and have Bush sign a binding agreement——so binding that the next president would have to adhere to it This had been going on all of August, and then Ahmadinejad was allowed to speak on our soil, and look at the storms that hit America!! Hurricane Hannah and then Ike!!

After reading that news, I immediately sent an e-mail out for people to pray that such an agreement does not get signed!! The next day is when the stock markets all around the world began to collapse after the Lehman Brothers' bankruptcy, etc. Bush has been so busy since then that he hopefully has had no time to sign any Israeli agreements!! Also the Israeli government is being shaken up and Ohmert is out, so hopefully that will also further thwart the two-state plans.

Last May, with much envy, we watched on the news all the celebrations of the 60th anniversary of Israel's independence. We had wanted so badly to be there to join the crowd of Messianic Jews planning to carry huge banners giving honor to Yeshua, the Messiah, in the Independence Day parade. Our rabbi and people in his congregation were even going. We had gotten our return-to-Israel tickets moved to May, but sadly, we couldn't afford the fares to come home. My extreme disappointment was soothed a little when I found out that the parade never happened due to heightened security!

[Nov. 2008: I just found out that in July 2008 Israel expelled all volunteers of two years or more. So we would have been expelled this year anyway. God has His plan! He must be about to do something big in Israel because this is causing quite a shake up in all the Christian volunteer organizations, being suddenly shorthanded and all. Please pray for them and for all the expelled Christians wondering what they are supposed to do now!]

In May 2008 I witnessed a new, exciting, further answer to my prayers that Jesus be honored on loudspeakers in Jerusalem instead of Islam. The leaders of *God TV* broadcast a series of outdoor services they held in Jerusalem to celebrate Israel's 60 years. And you'll never guess the location—(I talked to Charity who still lives in Jerusalem, to verify this.)—on the south side of the Temple, in the Archeological Garden area!!

Right in the place that I was bemoaning its neglect and its not receiving the reverence it deserves (p. 94). Can you believe it?!! They had loudspeakers and everything for the huge gathering of tourist Christians! So the Jewish people praying at the Wall would've heard them singing, praying, and preaching; and the Muslims praying on the Temple Mount would've also heard them!! I hope their music, (which was so beautiful!!) drowned out the Muslim loudspeakers!!

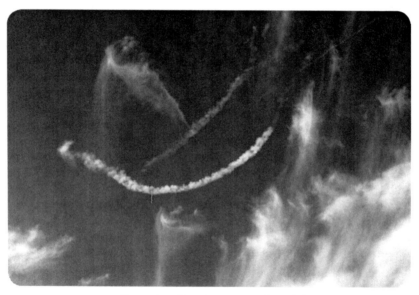

The smiling, blue sky over the Sea of Galilea in Dec. 2005

I tell you, there is just no end to the excitement and adventure of serving God!!
He is sooooooo MAJESTICALLY AWESOME!!!!
PRAISE BE TO HIS NAME FOREVER!

Contents in Detail

Printed in the United States
219546BV00002B/2/P